D1370945

IMPLEMENTING PRODUCTION-QUALITY CLIENT/SERVER SYSTEMS

Barbara Bochenski

John Wiley & Sons, Inc.

New York • Chichester • Brisbane • Toronto • Singapore

Associate Publisher: Katherine Schowalter
Senior Acquisitions Editor: Diane Cerra
Associate Managing Editor: Jacqueline A. Martin
Editorial Production: Pageworks

This text is printed on acid-free paper.

Designations used by companies to distinguish their products are often claimed as trademarks. In all instances where John Wiley & Sons, Inc. is aware of a claim, the product names appear in Initial Capital or ALL CAPITAL Letters. Readers, however, should contact the appropriate companies for more complete information regarding trademarks and registration.

Copyright © 1994 by John Wiley & Sons, Inc.

All rights reserved. Published simultaneously in Canada.

Reproduction or translation of any part of this work beyond that permitted by Section 107 or 108 of the 1976 United States Copyright Act without the permission of the copyright owner is unlawful. Requests for permission or further information should be addressed to the Permissions Department, John Wiley & Sons, Inc.

This publication is designed to provide accurate and authoritative information in regard to the subject matter covered. It is sold with the understanding that the publisher is not engaged in rendering professional services. If legal, accounting, medical, psychological, or any other expert assistance is required, the services of a competent professional person should be sought. ADAPTED FROM A DECLARATION OF PRINCIPLES OF A JOINT COMMITTEE OF THE AMERICAN BAR ASSOCIATION AND PUBLISHERS.

Library of Congress Cataloging-in-Publication Data:

Bochenski, Barbara
    Implementing production-quality client/server systems / Barbara Bochenski.
       p. cm.
    Includes bibliographical references.
    ISBN 0-471-58532-7. — ISBN 0-471-58531-9 (pbk.)
    1. Client/server computing.   I. Title.
QA76.9.C55B63 1993
004' .36—dc20   93-5684
                                                        CIP

Printed in the United States of America

10 9 8 7 6 5 4 3 2 1

To my mother,
Lillian S. Bochenski,
and
to the loving memory of my father,
Stanley J. Bochenski

ABOUT THE AUTHOR

Barbara Bochenski is President of The Bolden Group which specializes in client/server technology. She has over thirty years experience in information systems as a developer, analyst, manager, and consultant. Her consulting accounts have included many Fortune 500 firms and government agencies including the Executive Office of the President of the United States. Seeing the importance of client/server computing in its infancy, she has been writing about this technology since the mid-to-late-1980s. Known for her ability to take complex subjects and make them easy to understand, her feature articles have appeared in *Client/Server Computing*, *Software Magazine*, *Computerworld*, *Data Management Review*, and other IS journals.

PREFACE

Client/server computing is the most important change that has ever occurred in computing technology. While the very early client/server applications fell only into only certain categories—such as data access and decision support—as the related technologies improve, the variety of applications that are now being implemented as client/server systems continues to expand. Now, nearly all computing systems are being affected.

What we are witnessing is a complete restructuring of our industry. We are transferring from a monolithic architecture where all the work is done on a mainframe to one where many computers—smaller and more economical—are cooperating via a network to achieve the same goals previously accomplished by far more expensive hardware and software. It is no longer a matter of *whether* we should get involved with client/server and networked computing, but rather a matter of *when and how*.

WHO THE BOOK IS FOR

It is important for information systems (IS) professionals and end users to understand what is happening today, and why. This book was written to help readers gain that understanding.

The book provides an overall introduction to the subject of client/server systems. Managers and developers must understand all the basic concepts that are involved with this technology to gain maximum benefit from it. It is still a relatively new approach to computing—especially for those sites that are accustomed to mainframe computing as opposed to distributed computing approaches. However, this technology is also ready for mission-critical production systems. The hardware and the software exists to build excellent client/server systems. Thousands and thousands

of successful client/server production systems are in use today. In the increasing competitiveness of today's marketplace, it is vital that an enterprise be in a position to benefit from this technology.

This book emphasizes the fact that high-quality, industrial-strength client/server systems have been installed, continue to be installed every day, and will dramatically increase in numbers in the future. This book will explain both basic and advanced client/server computing.

CONTENTS OF BOOK

Chapter 1 provides an overall introduction to client/server computing. It explains why this approach is gaining in appeal right now, and why different people define terms in different ways. It offers ten characteristics that are widely accepted as representing a client/server architecture and compares client/server computing with cooperative processing, distributed computing, and peer-to-peer processing. Chapter 2 describes each of the components that are part of client/server systems. It discusses clients, servers, graphical user interfaces, networks, and interconnectivity techniques.

Chapter 3 describes how various companies are getting started with client/server computing. It discusses the learning curve involved with this new combination of technologies and how enterprises are overcoming it. This chapter also describes which systems are the best candidates for client/server systems and ways of migrating to this new architecture. Chapter 4 explains the affinity between open systems and client/server systems. The client/server architecture is modular with different software components working together. It is to vendors' benefit to have their software products work with complementary products from other vendors. This is an incentive to make products with high interoperability capabilities, a major component of open systems.

Chapter 5, on downsizing, discusses the similarities between client/server systems and downsizing and points out issues related to downsizing such as its hidden costs and what applications are candidates for downsizing. This chapter also describes an installation's experience with downsizing that resulted in a $2,000,000 a year savings.

Several of the chapters that follow provide detailed descriptions of the major components of the client/server architecture. Client tools are discussed in Chapter 6, graphical user interfaces are covered in Chapter 7, database servers are described in Chapter 8, and networking concepts are introduced in Chapter 9. Examples of products in each category are provided and major issues are explained. The role of object-oriented

techniques and how they are related to client tools, graphical user interfaces, and databases is covered in each relevant chapter.

Communication techniques and intercommunication among modules are vital ingredients in client/server systems. Chapter 9 describes basic networking concepts and standards related to networking, and Chapter 10 contains information about network operating systems and server operating systems. The major server operating systems such as LAN Server, LAN manager, Novell's NetWare, Banyan Vines, OSF/1, and Microsoft's NT, are described, as are peer-to-peer systems. Chapter 11 provides direction for interconnecting different networks with bridges, routers, and gateways. The subject of Chapter 12 is intercommunication among the client and server modules. The two most commonly-used techniques are SQL and remote procedure calls, which are explained and compared in this chapter.

An important issue is the difference between distributed databases, distributed processing, and client/server systems. A distributed client/server system does not necessarily imply a distributed database system, as explained in Chapter 13. Another important issue when building client/server systems is the area of systems management which is explored in Chapter 14. The primary management areas such as change management, configuration management, storage management, and network management are discussed. Security, a critical part of client/server systems, is saved for later in the book; Chapter 21 is devoted to the subject.

Chapter 15 explains the background, technical features, and growing importance of UNIX, while Chapter 16 describes UNIX networking. Many enterprises that have long been IBM shops are installing UNIX client/server systems. Many client/server systems include a combination of UNIX and Windows, UNIX and NT, and other combinations. The Internet, the world's largest network of networks, is also described.

Networking is impacting the computing industry in many ways. We will continue to find new ways to take advantage of networking while re-engineering businesses. Chapter 17 describes the basics of electronic mail and how E-mail and client/server systems relate to each other. Chapter 18 describes the importance of standards when building E-mail systems, especially if the E-mail systems are to stand the test of time. Standards like X.400 and X.500 are described and put in context. Chapters 19 and 20 describe new approaches to working together that are now available through networking and the client/server architecture. The more familiar groupware and workgroup computing concepts and products are described in Chapter 19, while the newer workflow, smart E-

mail, and mail enabled applications are put into a client/server context. The growing importance of electronic data interchange among businesses and how EDI relates to client/server systems is also covered.

Chapter 21 is dedicated to security in client/server systems. Since many mainframe systems developers have not had to provide security themselves—it was already provided by others in the enterprise—a review of some basic security concepts is given with an explanation of how they fit into a client/server architecture.

Examples of existing production client/server systems are provided in the final chapter. Chapter 22 describes various client/server implementations according to some of their main features. For example, mission-critical systems are described along with systems that provide improved customer service and those that emphasize connectivity as a critical success factor for an enterprise. Open client/server systems and prepackaged client/server software implementations are also discussed.

ACKNOWLEDGMENTS

I would like to thank my friend, Bill Saxon, for his patience and understanding while I was writing the book. I would also like to thank him for all his help, especially his assistance with the acronyms and the figures. He is a very special person. Thank you for your patience, help, moral support, and for your encouragement, Bill.

I would also like to thank my mother for her constant encouragement. She is a remarkable woman who, at 79, fought her way back to health after breaking seven ribs in nine places, puncturing her lung, and having a heart attack all at once. She is an inspiration to all of us. I also appreciate the encouragement of the rest of my family: Lennie and Dan Smith for their "can-do" attitude and phone calls; Stan and Jean Bochenski for keeping in touch throughout the time that I was writing; Cathy and Jim Dennis for always helping in so many ways, and Laura and Mark Condon for their enthusiasm and encouragement. My sister, Cathy Dennis, is one of the best information systems professionals that I know. And, for being such wonderful inspirations to me, I would also like to thank Sarah Condon with her excellent writing skills and remarkable, tender insight; Katie Condon with her ever-growing talents and sparkling impishness; and Christina Dennis with her many blossoming talents and bubbling personality. Sarah, Katie, and Christina, I love each of you and I look forward to reading *your* books in the future! I also want to thank my two friends, Robert Kerr and Jack Inman, who constantly help and encourage me.

The staff of *Software Magazine* also helped me in a number of ways. John Desmond, formerly the Editor of *Software Magazine and now Editor of CASE Trends*, and Damian Rinaldi, Editor of *Client/Server Computing*, a supplement to Software Magazine, both helped in a number of ways while the book was being written. Judy Boudrot, *Software Magazine*'s Design Director, has always been there to encourage me and brighten my day. Colleen Frye, Articles Editor for *Software Magazine*, deserves a special note of thanks for helping me with the glossary on very short notice. Thanks for a nice job, Colleen. John Desmond also deserves a special thanks for helping me find resource material and for always having faith in me. And John, I can't think of anyone nicer and more talented to work with.

I am also grateful to Jack Hymer for reviewing portions of the networking material and David Eagle for reviewing multiple sections of the book. And thanks to you, Lola Eagle, for always being a friend and believing in me, and to Barbara and John Del Colliano for your loyal friendship though none of you may hear from me for long periods when I'm involved in a writing project like this. And more than they know, Jack Schmitt, former U.S. Senator and the last man to walk on the moon, and his wonderful loving wife Teresa Schmitt, a successful writer, have both been a constant source of inspiration to me.

I would also like to thank Karen Watterson for her many suggestions about the book from the time of the book's origin to its final preparation. I owe thanks to Chris Grisonich, my copy editor and to the entire staff of Pageworks, but especially to Maggie Dana and Jamie Temple for their hard work and friendly attitude. Thanks especially for your patience through all of my changes to the manuscript. In addition, I'd like to thank Jackie Martin, Tammy Boyd, and the entire production staff at John Wiley & Sons for their work on the book.

And also very important, I would like to thank Diane Cerra, my editor at John Wiley and Sons. I liked Diane from the first time I spoke to her on the phone. We met in June, 1992, on the exquisite Italian Riviera, where Diane and Frank—her sweetheart of a husband—took me to a colorful Italian street bazaar, for a ride through some of the most scenic countryside I have ever seen, and to the charmingly picturesque seaside resort of Portofino. I particularly remember them treating me to a delicious dinner at a charming little trattoria on the Mediterranean coast. The food was only excelled by the company. The trattoria owner's entire family greeted Diane and Frank with great affection which included hugs, kisses, and a happy torrent of Italian words. I could not understand the meaning of the words, but I could feel the love behind them. They were not relatives. The owner's family just remembered Diane and Frank from previous visits and loved them. That's the kind of people Diane and Frank Cerra are. Wonderful.

CONTENTS

1

CLIENT/SERVER
INTRODUCTION

1.1   A NEW APPROACH TAKES HOLD

The computer industry is going through one of the most dramatic changes in its history. For over thirty years, the traditional computing architecture in large enterprises featured a mainframe or minicomputer where most of the processing took place. We communicated with the mainframe using terminal devices that had little or no built-in intelligence. That model is being replaced by a new and much more exciting model.

The new computing model features networking and extremely powerful microprocessors. By connecting powerful microcomputers together with networks, we are now able to rival the power of mainframes and minicomputers at a fraction of the cost. Why did we use large mainframe computers in the first place? Because we needed the power they provided to perform our processing needs. Microprocessor technology is advancing so rapidly, however, that smaller and smaller hardware devices are capable of incredible processing speeds. For a number of years, existing microprocessors have rivaled the power of minicomputers. Now, they rival the power of mainframes. But these microprocessors yield their greatest power when they are combined together with the use of networks.

The keys to client/server computing, distributed computing, cooperative processing, and the other labels used to describe the new computing architecture are simply the following:

- powerful microcomputers
- networking

Tools like graphical user interfaces and the software that we use on microcomputers are, of course, making significant contributions to these new architectures. We could not use the underlying technologies if we did not have software for them. Client software, server databases, network operating systems, network management software and many, many other software tools are helping to make this change in computing possible. But the most important things to remember is that the dramatic change that is occurring in data processing is a direct result of the advances in networking technology and the incredibly powerful microcomputers that are now available. And there will be even more powerful microcomputers that will become available in the future. It is important to completely understand this because *once we thoroughly grasp this, we can clearly see how important this new computing approach is*.

1.1.1   The Traditional Computing Model

The focus of the computing model we have used for many years was a mainframe which had various input and output devices attached to it. In the early days of computing, input was initially provided by punched cards. Once data was fed into a computer via punched cards, it was often copied to magnetic tape. That tape output could then be used as input to other systems. While output from early computer programs was stored on magnetic tapes and disks, the output that end users saw consisted of computer reports which usually consisted of more paper than was reasonable to work with.

Eventually terminals were connected to mainframe computers. The most popular terminal for IBM mainframes was the 3270 terminal. Many "look-alikes" were marketed, creating the term "3270-type" terminal since the functionality was similar, if not identical. Data entry operators could enter input data into these terminals rather than into punched cards. Programmers were able to write instructions on these terminals rather than on coding sheets which would then be punched into cards. In addition, end users could access mainframe systems using these terminals. They could enter a transaction using a terminal, and they could use the terminal to ask the mainframe computer to give them information related to their application. However, these terminals did not do any of the processing related to these requests. Any processing related to a transaction or a query entered on a 3270-type terminal was performed by the mainframe computer. A 3270-type terminal did not have a processor built into it, therefore it was not capable of performing any extensive computing. It was often referred to as a "dumb terminal." Within a few short years after 3270 terminals were introduced, the typical IBM computer configuration was one that consisted of a mainframe computer with dozens or hundreds of 3270-type terminals connected to it. (See Figure 1.1.)

1.1.2 A New Architecture

Now, a different architecture is available. With a client/server architecture, separate processes reside on different platforms and interact by means of networking to accomplish computing objectives.

In a client/server system, a client process makes requests of the server process, and the server process services those requests. Client and server processes generally reside on separate platforms, permitting them to share resources while taking the best advantage of different platforms and devices. These platforms can be either a personal computer (PC), workstation, minicomputer, or mainframe. While a mainframe can be the server in this architecture, the most cost-effective client/server systems often consist only of PCs, which are connected with networks. (See Figure 1.2.) The exponential increase in the power of PCs is one of the

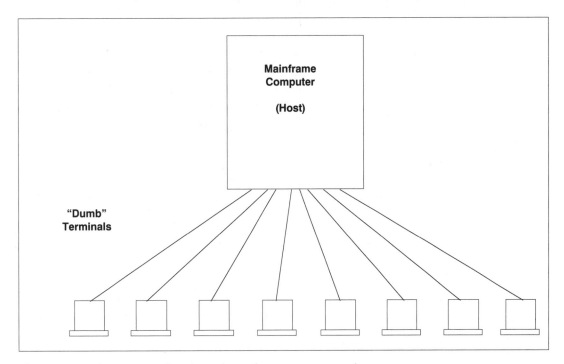

Figure 1.1 The essence of traditional mainframe computer architectures.

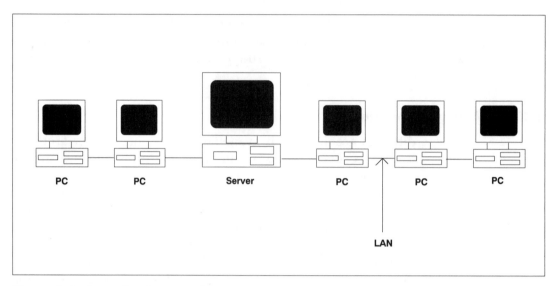

Figure 1.2 Basic client/server architecture.

factors that is making this new architecture so attractive. Special types of microcomputers like Compaq's SystemPro—designed specifically to be a server—are often used in client/server architectures.

Companies that have traditionally developed corporate computer systems on large mainframes are rethinking their strategy. Many large firms are either implementing client/server systems or studying when and how to begin. Certainly, we will not see all old systems replaced by new client/server or distributed computing ones within a short time frame. Many companies will have to wrestle with how to mix the old with the new for many years. But there will be a change in how new systems are developed and deployed.

A simple way to appreciate the capabilities of client/server computing is to think about the traditional 3270-type of architecture we described earlier. First, picture the desktop 3270-type terminal being replaced by an intelligent PC—a high-speed 286- or 386-based machine. This configuration would permit us to place a great deal of the processing on the desktop PC rather than requiring that the mainframe perform every bit of processing. That alone is a huge advantage. However, when we begin to expand our mental picture further so that instead of being connected to a mainframe, we are networked to extremely powerful PCs—maybe several 486-based PCs and/or Pentiums (586s) which are capable of processing our application, we begin to see more of the value of this new architecture.

Many companies that are adopting a client/server architecture will have their mainframe around for many years. That is because there are so many important systems running on the mainframe. In some companies, the bulk of production systems running on the mainframe is so large, that even if they wanted to move all systems to a client/server architecture, it would take them five to ten years to do so. As a result, many companies will continue to have the mainframe as a part of their client/server architecture. The most common ways of including a mainframe in a client/server architecture is to either use the mainframe as the server for some systems, or more frequently, to access data from it and move that data to a server so end users can access—but not update—it as much as they please. The data on the server is often referred to as "staged" data. (See Figure 1.3.)

1.1.3   The Synergism of New Capabilities

Client/server computing is not just one new development; it is an overall approach to computing that takes advantage of the synergism of several new developments. The convergence of graphical user interfaces, power-

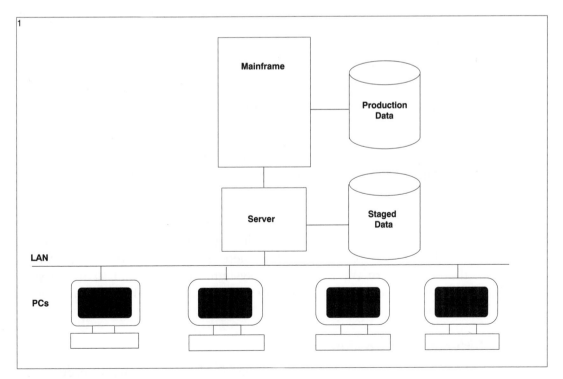

Figure 1.3 Mainframe in a client/server architecture.

ful personal computers, and increasingly reliable networks together form a new architecture which is flexible, versatile, and cost-effective.

Having experienced dramatic increases in power, desktop computers can now take on more responsibility within an overall computing environment. User-friendly interfaces on PCs make computer systems more understandable to users. Networking equipment is able to tie many individual PC users together so they can share data easily. New software is letting PCs access data in many different systems on large computers, minicomputers, personal computers acting as servers, or other individual PCs. All of these technologies, working together, constitute what is called client/server computing.

One of the most important aspects of client/server computing is that it takes maximum advantage of all of these new computing capabilities. It provides a way for different computing devices to work together, each doing the job for which it is best suited. By moving processing to new platforms, the client/server architecture offers significant advantages over traditional approaches. We all know that personal computers are as powerful as the mainframes of a former day, but up until recently, we did not know how to fully benefit from all that power. Client/server computing taps that power, maximizes it, and passes the benefits on to the corporation.

1.2   WHAT IS CLIENT/SERVER COMPUTING?

There are so many different definitions of the term "client/server" computing that it reminds one of an explanation of terminology offered by one of fiction's more colorful characters.

> "Whenever I use a word, it means just what I choose it to mean..." said Humpty Dumpty to Alice in Lewis Carroll's *Through the Looking Glass*.

Unfortunately, the attitude demonstrated by Mr. Dumpty is not restricted to just fictional characters. We are witnessing a somewhat similar situation in the real world, with everyone having his own definition of "client/server" computing. But then, maybe this is not the first time that veterans of the information systems field felt that their everyday work-world had some similarities to an *Alice in Wonderland* type of environment.

1.2.1   Differences of Opinion

What exactly does "client/server" mean? There are many different interpretations of the term "client/server" computing. And many people will assure you that *they* have the *true meaning* of the term. When the term first started to be used in articles and advertisements in trade journals, it seemed as if some vendors were defining the term in a way that was most beneficial for their own products.

It is very important to remember that there is no *one true* definition of client/server computing. If a term belongs to a company or standards group or is associated with the work of a specific individual, then that "owner" can definitively establish what the term means. Dr. E. F. Codd, as the father of the relational model, was able to settle the relational database disputes in the early 1980s with his twelve rules for a relational database. Unfortunately there is no one Codd-like figure in client/server to provide a tablet with the "ten commandments" of client/server.

Basically, a client/server architecture is an approach to computing that has separate processes on separate platforms interacting with each other permitting the sharing of resources while taking the best advantage of different devices. It is basically a form of distributed computing or networked computing.

1.2.2   Definition of Client/Server Terms

In 1990, Computerworld asked this author to write an article that would define what the term, "client/server computing," meant. Since everyone seemed to have a somewhat different idea, how could this be approached? No matter whose definition I used, there would be individuals who would disagree with it. I decided to find out what the major agreements and disagreements were. As part of this effort, I took an informal telephone poll of major industry analysts to create what could be thought of as a consensus definition of client/server computing.

That consensus definition still works today. At the time of the poll, the goal was to identify a set of characteristics to definitively establish what a client/server architecture is. In other words, if these features are not present, you have something—but you do not have "client/server." The emphasis of the poll was on client/server systems that perform database-related activities using DOS—usually with Windows—and OS/2 operating systems. (Unique characteristics of UNIX-based client/server systems will be covered in later chapters.) Of the ten characteristics that were identified, five had widespread agreement and five more had varying degrees of agreement.

After their appearance in Computerworld in December, 1990, these ten characteristics gained widespread acceptance. The fact that they now appear often in articles, other books, and presentations at client/server conferences shows that they are still considered as the key features of a client/server system. The first five characteristics can be considered as mandatory for a system to be regarded as a client/server system, while the second five are presented as optional—though highly desirable—characteristics.

The ten characteristics are listed below. The terms used in this list will be defined in the chapters that follow.

1. A client/server architecture consists of a client process and a server process that can be distinguished from each other, yet that can interact seamlessly.

2. The client portion and the server portions can operate on separate computer platforms—and they generally do—but they do not have to.

3. Either the client platform or the server platform can be upgraded without having to upgrade the other platform.

4. The server is able to service multiple clients concurrently; in some client/server systems, clients can access multiple servers.

5. The client/server system includes some sort of networking capability.

6. A significant portion (in some cases all) of the application* logic resides at the client end.

7. Action is usually initiated at the client end, not the server end. However, database servers can "take action" based on triggers, as well as business rules and stored procedures.

8. A user-friendly graphical user interface (GUI) generally resides at the client end.

9. A structured query language (SQL) capability is characteristic of the majority of client/server systems.

10. The database server should provide data protection and security.

While most of the analysts who were polled agreed with the first five characteristics, there was some discussion of some of these features. One example is with the second one, "The client portion and the server portions can operate on separate computer platforms, but they do not have to." The client portion of a client/server system usually operates on a personal computer, and the server portion generally resides

---

*See discussion of the word "application" later in this chapter.

on a powerful workstation, dedicated server hardware, minicomputer, or even a mainframe. However, it is possible for a client module and server module to function on the same hardware platform. While this capability might be used for testing a system, or as a temporary measure under certain circumstances, there are not many situations when this configuration would be used for a production system. Therefore some analysts would like the second characteristic to simply say, "The client portion and the server portions operate on separate computer platforms." However, other analysts felt it was important that this capability—that they can coexist on one machine—be included in the list of characteristics.

The same kind of qualification applies to the networking capability as well: a networking capability must exist, and while networking is usually involved, it does not have to be. Like the example above, if the client module and server module are for some reason located on the same physical device, then the networking capability, of course, would not be used. In addition, there was some discussion over what was meant by a "networking capability." For most, it simply meant that the architectural components of a client/server system communicate over a local area network. Others pointed out that internetworking capabilities should exist for true enterprise-wide client/server systems.

There are some characteristics like a graphical user interface and SQL capability that are highly desirable and are generally found in client/server systems. However, they are not absolutely mandatory for a system to qualify as a client/server system. In fact, there have been some excellent client/server systems that did not have these characteristics. For example, before Information Builders, Inc. (IBI) added their Enterprise Data Access (EDA)/SQL capability, IBI clients used the Focus 4GL as a front end for accessing server data. These were very useful client/server systems, but they did not have SQL. There were other early client/server systems that used character-based DOS software as the front-end module. However, as time goes on, both SQL and graphical interfaces are becoming common ingredients in client/server systems. Still, it should be remembered that the most important features of the overall client/server architecture are the presence of a client module requesting services of a server module with each of these components performing different functions and operating on the most appropriate physical platform.

Note that there is a difference between the phrases "client/server *architecture*" and "client/server *platform*." The latter refers to such things as the physical hardware or operating system used while the former is more concerned with the way an application is structured. Thus, a well thought out client/server architecture is needed to take best advantage of the various capabilities offered by a client/server platform.

This is the beginning of a new era in how to use computer systems. We are starting to use new platforms, like powerful microcomputers and workstations and networked servers, for implementing important computer systems. As a result, end users are experiencing new levels of user friendliness and corporations are able to provide better levels of customer service. In some cases, management is witnessing dramatic cost savings as well.

And this is *only* the beginning of this new era. The move toward this architecture did not happen overnight; it has been evolving for many years. It will continue to evolve. We will witness many more changes.

1.2.3   Different Uses of the Term "Application"

It is important to point out that different people use the term "application" differently. Or maybe it is just a matter of the term having slightly different connotations depending upon its context. Many mainframe developers spend their careers regarding an "application" as a system that performs a specific function for an end-user department. As a result, payroll, accounts receivable (A/R), accounts payable (A/P), inventory, and other similar systems are considered "applications" to mainframers. That is why many vendors who sell mainframe personnel, human resource, and manufacturing software are often regarded as application software vendors by people who are accustomed to mainframe parlance.

Software like operating systems and sorts were regarded as "systems software" by mainframe personnel. Database software fell into a class of its own. Most mainframe programmers just referred to it as "database software" or a DBMS. Actually, the specific categorization of database software by mainframe programmers is not the important point here.

The important point is that there is a new class of software that is being referred to as "application software." Today, word processing packages and spreadsheets are called "applications" that are used on a personal computer. Likewise, electronic mail and file transfers are applications that run over a network. While it is often easy to tell which way the word "application" is being used, there are times when confusion can occur. For example, PC-oriented database software can also be considered an application along with word processing and spreadsheet software.

One way to clarify use of the term application might be to refer to software like word processing and spreadsheets as "tool applications," while using the term "business function applications" for payroll, A/R, A/P, etc. However, it is always wise to be alert to how the term "application" is being used. In this book we will make every effort to indicate by context which way we are using the term.

1.3   BACKGROUND

1.3.1   The Evolution of Today's New Architectures

Network and distributed computing capabilities have been evolving for decades. Early forms of networking and computing go back to the late 1950s and early 1960s in terms of wide area networks as used by airline reservation and military systems. Local area networks (LANs) and distributed computing had their origin two decades ago with much credit going to the development of workstation technology and Ethernet at Xerox Corporation's Palo Alto Research Center (PARC) in the early 1970s.

By the mid 1980s, there were a significant number of distributed computing systems in use, primarily involving the multi-user UNIX operating system and powerful workstations from vendors like Apollo and Sun. Sun's Network File System (NFS) software helped advance the use of servers in distributed systems. NFS software facilitated the use of one workstation—within a network of connected workstations—as a file server.

With NFS, other workstations—called clients—could use the files located on that server. The file server, however, was not capable of going through the records in the file to locate a particular record. The software on the workstation had to do that. This would often result in a lot of messages and/or records being sent back and forth. Sometimes the file server would send the entire file to the workstation, whether it needed it all or not. Database server software came along and overcame that problem as well as others. The capabilities of this new breed of software—database server software—resulted in many new applications which utilized it.

In fact, the popularity of database *server* software may have been what made the term "client/server computing" more popular than other terms like distributed computing and networked computing. The appearance of many GUI-based front-end *client* tools that could access data in a database *server* seemed to have solidified acceptance of the term "client/server" over other terms.

1.3.2   The Concept of a Server Catches On

There are many different types of servers including file servers, print servers, database servers, applications servers, electronic mail servers, communications servers, and fax servers. This book will focus on database-oriented client/server systems. In such systems, the application on the client end generally controls the display management, data selection, and most of the application logic while the server end handles data-oriented concerns like physical data access and data integrity.

A distinction must be made between server hardware and server software. There are different types of software for each of the kinds of servers mentioned above. Since this book will focus primarily on database servers, that is the kind of server software we will emphasize. A discussion of prominent database server software is contained in Chapter 8. We will cover software for electronic mail servers in Chapter 17.

A variety of computer processors can provide the functionality of server hardware. Server hardware includes such platforms as personal computers, minicomputers, database machines and mainframes. Some sites are installing client/server systems using their existing mainframe as the server. This is often done to preserve their existing investment and because most of their existing data is located on the mainframe. These installations are often replacing 3270-type terminals with personal computers which have software that uses modern graphical user interfaces, making legacy systems easier to use. This is a legitimate tactic if replacing the 3270 with a GUI does indeed result in increased productivity. However, if there is no "intelligence" in the front end module, that is, if it performs no processing, most observers would not refer to it as a true client/server system. As we will see in Chapter 7, adding a GUI to a mainframe system is often referred to as "front-ending" a system.

One of the most important things to point out about a system that uses a mainframe as the server is that such a system is not benefitting from the potential cost-savings of the client/server architecture. One of the main reasons for the popularity of client/server systems is that microprocessors have become powerful enough to perform the work that mainframes and minicomputers have been performing. With modern networking techniques, we can connect many PC clients to a powerful microprocessor which functions as a server, responding to the clients' requests. Systems that were operating on mainframe computers have been moved to a client/server architecture with a 486 as the server, resulting in tremendous savings. Chapter 2 will discuss some of the hardware options that are popular as servers in client/server architectures today.

1.4   SIMILAR ARCHITECTURES

1.4.1   Cooperative Processing and Distributed Computing

The term "cooperative processing," taken at face value, implies individual computing components that are cooperating to accomplish an objective. The term has a little more history, however. IBM latched on to this term and used it extensively in promotions to mean a PC, or other device, *cooperating with a mainframe.* When IBM first used the term "cooperative processing," the architecture always involved a mainframe. Many observers interpreted that as IBM's way to make the mainframe as prominent as possible in a client/server architecture. In fact, for a while, a few market analysts who were aware of the term's origin considered "cooperative processing" as an IBM marketing term rather than a technical term. Since IBM made a distinction between client/server computing and cooperative processing, however, various pundits started to add their explanations of what the difference was between these two terms. As a result, many individuals argue endlessly about what the *real* meanings of these two terms are. It is an unworthy, if not futile, exercise. Rather than debate their meanings, the most important thing about these terms is the creative ideas they are providing for new, productive, and cost-effective architectures.

Many consider the terms "distributed computing" and "networked computing" synonyms for what the information systems community now refers to as "client/server computing." In the late 1980s, some trade journals were referring to the movement toward a client/server architecture as "networked computing." However, the term "networked computing" sounded a little intimidating to some readers.

In part, the fact that the term "client/server architecture" became the accepted term to describe the phenomenon of two modules on remote systems interacting can probably be attributed to the comfort level associated with the term. It sounds less daunting to many developers than "networked computing." A few years ago Software Magazine, a major information systems magazine, had a section devoted to "networked computing" which described systems that consisted of a client module and a server module that was connected by networks. The section was not read very much by many of its mainframe application development readers. These readers considered themselves generalists, but not necessarily network-knowledgeable. After the magazine changed the name of that section to "client/server computing," these generalists started reading that section—even though the subject matter remained the same. As far as those readers were concerned, "networked computing" sounded like something only the data communications people should read, not the all-around systems developer. "Client/server computing," however, sounded like something that was more in line with their interests.

Each company implementing these new technologies, in effect, needs to define client/server in a way that works for it. Each organization needs a custom definition that permits it to pursue and reap the benefits of today's new technologies. If "terminology" debates start to take up too much time, members of the organization can be reminded that there are specific meanings that the enterprise has agreed upon for its purposes.

It should be pointed out, however, that client/server computing is actually a form of networked computing. In fact, if instead of "client/ server computing" the term networked computing had won out, other approaches such as peer-to-peer systems—which are explained below— could easily have been classified under the term "networked computing."

1.4.2   The Role of Peer-to-Peer Processing

There are many similarities between peer-to-peer processing and client/ server computing. The big difference is that in peer-to-peer processing, the processing components are considered as equals and can switch roles: either can make a request of the other. One end can be the client module or client process for some applications and the server module or server process for other applications. (See Figure 1.4.) In a client/server approach, one module (the client) always makes requests of the server and another module (the server) provides a service to the client. Peer-to-peer applications are gaining in popularity.

Workgroup software is also becoming increasingly popular. This software permits a group of workers to work together in a cooperative

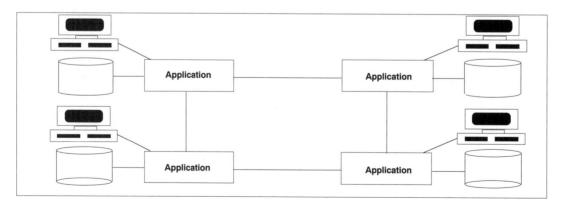

Figure 1.4   Peer-to-peer processing.

manner. For example, they can easily share a document, each making changes that the others can then review. The peer-to-peer architecture is particularly well suited for workgroup software.

While peer-to-peer systems will increase, they will more likely complement rather than replace client/server systems. Like cooperative processing and other current terms, peer-to-peer systems basically represent another way to utilize new computing technologies.

1.4.2.1   A Comparison of Client/Server and Peer-to-PeerProcessing

As previously mentioned, in the client/server model one or more servers provide services to the personal computers and workstations connected to it via networking, while in the peer-to-peer model all devices are equally able to be clients and servers.

The essence of the client/server model means that one or more centralized servers are responsible for all the shared resources on the network. Devices not controlled by the server cannot be shared. If there is an attractive device (such as a laser printer) that is connected to only one specific PC or workstation, then the other PCs and workstations on the network cannot have access to it. However, if the laser printer is attached to a server, all the other PCs and workstations can benefit from it.

In most installations today, desirable devices like laser printers are associated with a server for the specific purpose of permitting others to share it. However, there have been instances where one particular individual does have a strong need for his or her own laser printer and therefore has one connected to his or her own desktop machine. Generally, in this instance, no one else can have access to it. However, if the network configuration were a peer-to-peer one, it would be easy for that individual to let others use it when he or she did not need it.

While a major benefit of the peer-to-peer model is that it facilitates the sharing of resources, it can also make it easier to share data. In general, there is usually more flexibility in a peer-to-peer architecture. However, many developers believe there are drawbacks to the flexibility of the peer-to-peer model. They say its flexibility can make it more difficult to manage, more difficult to secure, and can reduce the system's performance. They argue that with the client/server model, security and network resource management can be somewhat centralized. As a result, resources can be more easily controlled and can be optimized to more quickly meet the needs of the attached PCs and workstations.

Software products are generally built for one model or the other. At the present time, there are far more products in the distributed, networked computing category that are for the client/server model than there are for the peer-to-peer model. In the future, we may begin to see products that can take advantage of either model. Such a product might be more oriented to the client/server architecture—where it would access data, for example—yet, provide the ability to use a resource that is attached to a specific workstation on the local area network.

1.5 VENDOR ADAPTATIONS TO CLIENT/SERVER

1.5.1 New Vendors Appear, Old Vendors Adapt

While vendors who have been around for many years are offering client/server products, this new approach has also given birth to many new vendors. Cooperative Solutions is an example of a firm that was created specifically to meet a need within client/server software environments. Cooperative Solution's Ellipse provides software that facilitates building transaction processing applications in a client/server environment. Some vendors who now have many client/server products used to be known primarily as PC-software vendors. The biggest example here, of course, is Microsoft. They made their start with DOS, the operating system for IBM personal computers. They now are a major player in the client/server market.

Many vendors who were traditionally mainframe players exclusively now offer client/server products. Mainframe database vendors like Cincom have client/server versions of their products, while Computer Associates offers client/server versions of many of their software products including their database lines. Application package software vendors, like Dun & Bradstreet, are very active in the client/server market. Some application package software vendors are saying they plan to provide a complete line of client/server applications to match their mainframe application package offerings over a period of time. Some say they will help their customers migrate to the client/server versions.

Client/server systems have been a boon for many young, new, entrepreneurial software firms. However, client/server systems have been a serious problem for some of the older firms who made their living selling very expensive mainframe hardware and software. The high expense of mainframe hardware was always accompanied by correspondingly expensive software that ran on mainframes.

The client/server movement has not been easy for Digital Equipment, but it has been far harder on IBM. IBM always earned the bulk of its income from selling hardware—particularly large mainframe computers. For thirty years, IBM sales personnel could count on receiving upgrade orders from their traditional customers. Clients would run out of space on their existing mainframe and either order a second one or replace their current one with a larger model. However, orders for mainframes have diminished significantly in recent years. While the slow economy has contributed to this decline, the move to client/server systems is having a big impact on IBM. Instead of ordering larger mainframes for new work, sites are putting the new systems on client/server architectures. In each of the last two years, IBM suffered losses in the billions of dollars. During the same period, IBM's stock lost more than half its value.

1.5.2   Examples of IBM's Client/Server Products

After a period of little emphasis on the technology, IBM is now making a serious effort to compete in the client/server area. IBM's PC-based products are described in various places in this book They include such products as OS/2, Database Manager, the LAN Server (originally built by Microsoft), and SystemView for OS/2. In recent years, when describing such tools, IBM typically called them PC-based or LAN-based products, rather than client/server products. In late 1992, however, IBM representatives were beginning to use the term client/server in reference to their PC-based products.

Not surprisingly, several of IBM's client/server products are related to accessing data from a mainframe. Most of them are related to IBM's Information Warehouse strategy which is described in Chapters 12 and 13. These client/server products provide a way for users to access mainframe data, store it on a server, and then analyze it on their PC. For a while, IBM's client/server strategy seemed to focus on providing data access tools to mainframe data, however, their product line is getting broader now.

The DXT product line represents IBM's long-standing data extract approach. Using DXT can be a cumbersome procedure, often requiring that the entire production database be saved instead of permitting the user just to post changes to the existing copy. To improve this procedure, IBM announced a database management utility to automatically create database extracts for client/server applications. The utility, basically a copy manager, will be able to extract data from other vendors' databases as well as DB2.

Also related to IBM's Information Warehouse strategy is the new Business Information Locator. This product will help client/server applications find the mainframe data they need. The product will permit the use of customized database labels for client/server applications residing on LANs. The Business Information Locator will come with a tool kit to help database administrators collect information on data categories contained in distributed databases, including those from other vendors, such as Oracle.

Another area of client/server products from IBM is related to application development. For example, IBM is expanding the role of AD/Cycle, an application development blueprint, to more rapidly incorporate application development at the workgroup level. IBM said it will bring together the best functionality from its AD/Cycle and AIX CASE products. To accomplish this, it will move into AD/Cycle many features of the AIX Software Development Environment Workbench/6000. This will provide a consistent development platform for OS/2 and AIX.

IBM's RISC System/6000 workstation hardware and software products may represent some of IBM's most serious client/server activity. However, there is fierce competition for the same set of customers between IBM's RS/6000 unit and its AS/400 unit. It is interesting to note that the AS/400 (a minicomputer) and RS/6000 (a workstation used in client/ server systems) were among the few divisions in IBM making a profit in 1993.

We can expect to see some additional changes in IBM's attitude toward client/server systems. In recent years, we witnessed IBM beginning to adopt more of an open systems approach which was a change from its former "all-proprietary" approach. IBM's customers demanded open systems, and when Big Blue saw that open systems were the direction systems were taking, IBM responded. Likewise, we will see IBM adopt a much more aggressive approach to participating in the client/server market. That is where market demand now lies.

2
COMPONENTS OF A CLIENT/SERVER ARCHITECTURE

2.1 CLIENT/SERVER ARCHITECTURE AND MODULARITY

The basic components of client/server systems are a client portion, a server portion, and a networking portion. The client portion makes a request and the server portion provides a service which responds to the client request. Networking hardware and software connect the client and the server portions. In addition to the client, server, and networking portions, client/server systems usually have a graphical user interface (GUI) to facilitate the use of the client portion. There is additional software needed in client/server systems for such things as helping to manage, administrate, and secure the system.

Client/server systems, by their very nature, are modular in structure. They consist of multiple modules or components working together. One of the most note-worthy aspects of a client/server architecture is that you can mix and match different client software products with different server software products. This modularity is an important aspect of the client/server architecture because it makes many vendors eager for their products to work with products from other vendors. Client/server products have only limited interoperability at the present time. However, since it is to vendors' advantage to interoperate with as many other complementary products as possible, vendors are increasingly interested in interoperability. Client/server modularity offers information system (IS) users much more choice of products than ever before.

2.2   THE MAJOR COMPONENTS

The basic components of client/server systems consist of a client portion, a server portion and a networking portion. Software located at the client end of a client/server system is often referred to as front-end software; similarly, software located at the server end is often referred to as back-end software. Back-end database servers are database management systems (DBMSs) that have been designed specifically to operate on servers or that have been adapted to work on servers. Networking hardware and software connect the client and server portions over a local area network. Each of these components will be discussed briefly in this chapter and then examined in more detail in subsequent chapters. When trying to combine these three components, it is important to determine which vendors' products work with each other. You will also need to determine which products work with your workstation's operating system, GUI, and local area network.

2.2.1   Client Front Ends

Client/server front-end application software can be built in a variety of ways. Programmers may code the entire client application themselves with languages such as C or Cobol. Vendors like Micro Focus and Computer Associates provide Cobol compilers for personal computers and workstations. Early client/server systems—particularly UNIX-based ones— were written in C. Today there is a wide variety of application software tools that can be used to build client/server systems.

Front-end software tools can vary from simple query tools for casual end users to fully-equipped, industrial-strength application development environments used by developers to build mission-critical client/server applications. In some cases distinguishing between these two extremes of front-end tools is very easy; however, at times it can be quite difficult. In addition, many vendors are constantly adding capabilities to end-user tools, making them more sophisticated, and thereby making it harder to put the tools into specific categories.

Some of the software tools like spreadsheets, which have been popular with end users since the early days of personal computers, can now be used as front ends in client/server systems. Many spreadsheet vendors have added the ability for their products to access data from database servers as well as from a variety of other software packages. While Lotus Corporation's Lotus 1–2–3 with Data Lens is a primary example of this, nearly all the major spreadsheet packages can now be used as client/ server front-ends.

Like there are different levels of end user tools, there are different levels of application development tools also. An example of a simple front-end development tool might be one that helps a developer build a specialized query system for end users. Using the development tool, the application developer might build a system so that the end user could use custom-built icons and menus that are specifically related to the nature of the application. The end user could then use these custom-built provisions to quickly create queries to obtain data from a database server.

Many vendors who have had Fourth-Generation Languages (4GL) in the marketplace for many years have modified their 4GL products to be front-end tools for client/server systems. In many of these cases, the original 4GL product included a query language and database management system. Many of these 4GL query languages now have Structured Query Language (SQL) capabilities and can access data from other relational databases. SQL is the industry-standard data language for relational databases.

Other software vendors who have been around for many years are also adding client/server capabilities to their products. The SAS System, from SAS Institute Inc., based in Cary, N.C., started out as a statistical package many years ago. The SAS System, which now consists of a database query module and other new modules, has features like SAS/Connect which can reside on a PC and query data on a server equipped with SAS components.

There are also many new vendors appearing on the scene featuring products with excellent GUI capabilities. Many of these new front-end products are able to access data from a wide variety of back-end database servers. Some of these front ends access the databases directly, and some use popular database gateways like Micro Decisionware's Database Gateway. Many of the database server vendors are also providing front-end tools to support their database server.

We are increasingly seeing more sophisticated application development environment tools. Two examples are PowerBuilder from PowerSoft located in Burlington, MA and Ellipse from Cooperative Solutions in San Jose, CA. Tools like these help developers build industrial-strength applications. PowerBuilder has been selected by software houses like Dun & Bradstreet as the tool they will use to convert their existing mainframe applications software to a client/server architecture. Ellipse provides transaction processing capabilities which will be covered in more detail in a later chapter.

2.2.2　Server Back Ends

A server is a device that provides a service. Chapter 1 indicates that there are many types of servers such as file, application, mail, and network servers among others. (See Figure 2.1.) The focus of this book will be database servers. A broad range of computing devices can be used as the hardware for database servers, and a multitude of database server packages exists from which to select. Many of the major hardware and software options are described in Chapter 8.

2.2.2.1   Database Servers

What is a database server? As the name implies, it is a database product that resides on a server. In the early days of distributed computing, workstation users frequently used file servers. A file was kept on a server where several people on the network could access it. The benefit of this was that many people were able to share the same data. However, one of the problems with a file server was that the server software was not able to search for and access a particular record. The software on the client end had to be smart enough to do that by sending instructions and messages to the file server software. Sometimes the file server would send the entire file to the requesting client module. In these cases, even if the person accessing the file needed only one record, they would have to deal with the entire file. With a database server, that changes.

Server databases are multi-user databases that provide most, if not all, the capabilities that a traditional mainframe or minicomputer database

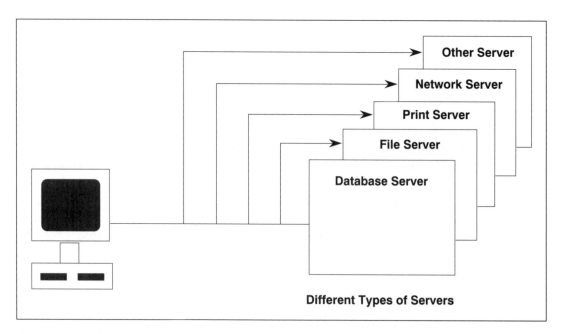

Figure 2.1 Different types of servers.

provides. And they are growing in power and capabilities every day. Server databases should not be confused with microcomputer databases like dBase. In fact, microcomputer databases like dBase are sometimes used as front ends for server databases. Server databases were built specifically to be used on a server by many users. Some technicians point out that some server databases were originally designed for mainframes or minicomputers and were subsequently adapted to be server databases. However, if you ask the vendors most will insist that their databases were always modular and, therefore, were always client/server in nature. This is reminiscent of the time when all of a sudden all databases—including hierarchical and network-model databases—became "relational databases." Some observers called them "born-again relational databases."

Most server databases have stored procedures, event alerters, and triggers. Business rules often reside in the server database as stored procedures. That way the business rule just has to be in one place instead of being repeated in each separate client application. Most server databases also provide features like field-level locking, concurrency management, data protection, security for data access, logging, and recovery. And, of course, they have capabilities for database creation and definition.

Many server databases are being used in mission critical applications by large corporations. Hyatt Hotels is using the Informix database to run a reservation system for its worldwide network of 160 hotels. Hyatt downsized from an IBM 4381 mainframe to AT&T's System 7000 reduced instruction set computing (RISC) based symmetric multi-processor computers which act as servers. They achieved a cost savings of over 25% as a result of this downsizing.

Client/server database system architectures are often used to provide a way for end users to access data from many databases. Many companies are using server databases as staging or holding areas for mainframe production data. Software downloads data from diverse, corporate-wide, mainframe-based, production databases into the server database where the end user can query the data. This provides a way for the end user to query important data without holding up production schedules.

The most widely used database servers are Microsoft/Sybase's SQLServer, Gupta Technologies' SQLBase Server, Informix's Informix database, Oracle Corporation's Oracle/Server, ASK/Ingres' Ingres, Borland's Interbase, IBM's OS/2 Extended Edition Database Manager, and DEC's RDB. These products are regarded as industrial-strength database servers. Sybase and Gupta are credited as being two of the earliest vendors with a database product specifically written to be a database server.

2.2.3   GUIs

GUIs contribute to client/server systems because they make them easier to use and increase productivity. GUI capabilities such as multi-tasking, task-switching, and data interchange among applications also add appeal. A GUI does not *have* to be present for a system to qualify as a client/server system—where a client module networked to a server module constitute the essential components. However, GUIs are widely used in client/server systems due to their benefits.

Expenses associated with GUIs include end-user training and the cost of building a GUI. If a site wants a GUI tailored for an in-house application, developers must build that GUI. For example, if end users want different icons (pictorial representations) to depict different types of purchase orders, the in-house developers must create those unique icons and write the code to be associated with them—thus creating an *application-specific* GUI.

GUI development consists of event-driven programming where code responds to an end user's actions. This is different from traditional, sequential program code. There are different approaches to developing in-house graphical interfaces. If you use a low-level tool like Microsoft's Software Development Kit (SDK), you may get a GUI that runs faster (one reason why software vendors use SDK-type tools); however, this approach is very time-consuming. There are many hundreds of functions with numerous parameters that are available at an SDK level. Estimates say that up to 80% of overall application development time is spent on the GUI alone.

GUI-building tools speed up the process of creating GUIs. Using a GUI-building tool vs. writing to an SDK can be compared to creating a report using a 4GL vs. creating it by writing assembly language code. With a GUI-building tool the developer "paints" icons and creates actions by selecting tool-provided options instead of using complex functions with many parameters and arguments.

A style guide gives each GUI its "look and feel." The style guide for IBM's Presentation Manager and Microsoft Windows is IBM's Common User Access (CUA)—despite any similarity Windows may have to the Macintosh interface. Microsoft has made some minor changes to the style guide, but for now, they still adhere for the most part to the CUA style guide.

Using a specific style guide is important when working with the UNIX-based X Window system. Using just the basic tools that come with the X Window system, resulting GUIs could look quite different from each other if the work is not coordinated by a common style guide. Popular style guides for the X Window system are the Open Software Foundation's Motif and Sun Microsystems's Open Look. Motif is more popular, partly because its style guide is very close to that of the CUA. For example, in most systems, mouse button one pulls down a menu. However, in Open Look, mouse button *three* pulls down a menu. If end users need to use diverse GUIs, differences like this can very frustrating.

Installations generally try to adopt one style guide. However, since there are multiple options within a style guide, a site may need to establish and enforce standards related to its chosen style to ensure consistency. An enterprise can also create its own unique style guide. Aetna Life & Casualty, for example, has established their own stylized Aetna User Interface—modeled on CUA interface guidelines—as their corporate-wide standard.

"Front-ending" systems with a GUI consists of adding a GUI to existing mainframe systems. Some criticize this as merely adding dumb, "pretty faces" to systems, but if they help users work more quickly, then they are justified. However, front-ending a system with a GUI does *not* automatically turn old systems into client/server systems.

In the UNIX-oriented X Window system, a server provides GUI display management, whereas in a DOS/Windows environment all GUI-related software resides in the client module. In X Windows, the GUI server provides graphical display capabilities to client applications located anywhere on the network. While a little different, the essence of having a client request a service from a server is still the same.

Tools are available to generate a GUI that will work with a variety of platforms. For example, a developer could use Neuron Data's Open Interface to generate a GUI and then port it to either DOS/Windows or the X Window system. This saves training developers in the details of both systems. Also, there are tools like PC-Xview from Network Computing Devices, Inc. in Beaverton, OR, which permit users to have both Microsoft Windows and X Window GUIs operating on their PCs at the same time. In such an environment, it is easy to see why consistency between GUIs is important to the user.

GUIs provide many benefits and are contributing to the increasing popularity of client/server systems. GUIs are also an important part of the dramatic changes now occurring in computing.

2.2.4 Networks

One of the interesting challenges about the client/server architecture is that it brings application developers a lot closer to networking concepts.

Ten Important GUI Considerations

1. GUIs can increase productivity by making systems easier to use and providing capabilities like multi-tasking and data interchange among applications.

2. Ease-of-use is not automatic; some degree of training for users will be necessary.

3. GUIs can be time-consuming to build—using GUI-building tools speeds up the process.

4. Lack of GUI consistency can confuse, irritate, and frustrate end users.

5. A style guide is what gives a GUI its "look and feel."

6. In-house standards must be enforced to ensure that a chosen style guide or enterprise-developed style is adhered to.

7. "Front-ending" an existing system with a GUI—while a controversial technique—is useful for some hard-to-use systems.

8. GUI software for Microsoft Windows and IBM's Presentation Manager resides on a client platform; however, in the UNIX-oriented X Window system, a server provides GUI display management.

9. Tools are available to build "generic" interfaces that are "portable" to a variety of GUI frameworks.

10. End users can have different GUIs such as X Window and Microsoft Windows operating on their PCs at the same time.

Formerly, data communications concerns were usually relegated to the "networking experts." These experts took care of everything related to communications or networking almost magically. Most application developers did not have to worry about communication problems very much.

That changes somewhat with client/server computing. Now application developers need to be more aware of the capabilities of the local area network since it is an integral part of the overall client/server system (see Figure 2.2). They do not have to become networking experts, but they should at least be knowledgeable about some networking basics and what they will need to know, have, and do in order to connect the various components of their system.

The system planners or developers need to perform a requirements analysis to determine what kind of networking capabilities the planned system will require. They will need to know what networking software is

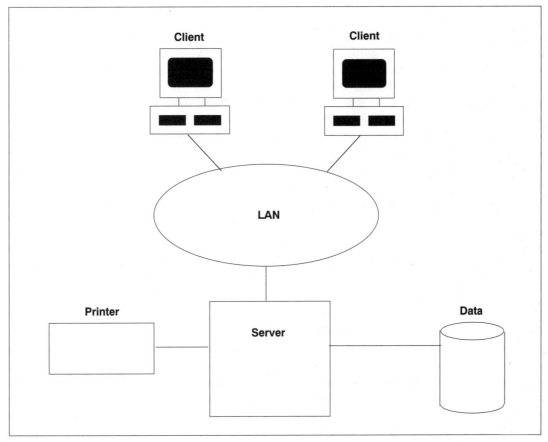

Figure 2.2 Networking is an integral part of client/server systems.

currently available, and what they will need to have installed. They will also need to determine if the software they plan to install on the front end and on the back end will work with the kind of network software they have in mind.

It is important to determine if the planned system is feasible given the state of the art. There were some early client/server image systems that were installed with a network that did not have enough bandwidth (capacity) to support them. As a result, those systems did not work as planned until the network was upgraded. CAD/CAM, image systems, and multimedia systems can require a tremendous amount of bandwidth. It is important to make sure that a network can handle the requirements of the planned system.

The developers also have to be able to determine how they can get to the required data from the client locations. Sometimes this involves connecting several local area networks together. This is called internetworking. Internetworking requires some knowledge of bridges, routers, and gateways (which will be discussed in Chapter 11).

Another area that needs to be examined is how the client operating system will work with the operating system on the servers and the LAN software. For example, the client/server architecture might consist of Microsoft DOS and Windows on the PCs (remember DOS rather than Windows is actually the operating system), IBM's OS/2 on the database server, and Microsoft LAN Manager as the networking software.

To distinguish between the various operating-system type services, the operating system on the client platform is often referred to as the "native operating system." IBM's OS/2 could be the native operating system (residing on the client platform), but not many companies have chosen this configuration because OS/2 requires a very powerful personal computer—far more powerful than the ones they already owned. Since there were already so many copies of DOS installed on personal computers, DOS (with Windows for ease of use) became the operating system of choice on the client platform—the native operating system—in most early client/server systems.

Networking specialists say that when using a client/server architecture, the network operating system is installed "on top of" the native operating system. Basically this means that the underlying native operating system has primary control and the network operating system provides additional services over and above those of the native operating system. The networking specialists indicate that the network operating system is actually a misnomer because it is not a true operating system of a specific device, but rather a set of services that run over a network. Any new operating systems that come into the marketplace from now on will be expected to have networking capabilities built into them—as Microsoft's New Technology (NT) has—if they are to compete in the client/server arena.

2.2.5 "Middleware" or Interconnecting Software

"Middleware" is a term that is used differently by different people. In fact, the term may have created more confusion than contribution. Some writers use "middleware" to refer to data access software while other writers use it to refer to software that connects two modules, letting them communicate with each other. For example, a client module needs to communicate with a server module. Some people use the term "middleware" to refer to software that performs this function. In some situations, a developer does not need to be aware of middleware; in other cases, this software is critically important to the developer.

A client/server system that can rely completely on SQL calls from a client module to a relational database on a server may not require that the developer be concerned about middleware. In this situation, SQL performs the function of letting the client and server modules communicate with each other. Remote procedure calls (RPCs) are an example of middleware that developers must be concerned about. Chapter 12 contains a discussion of systems that use SQL as compared to RPCs. For example, it explains that SQL is far easier to use than RPCs, but a system that uses RPCs offers the developer more control over the functioning of the system. For example, different software packages behave differently if a distributed update fails at one location. Using RPCs, the developer would be able to code specific routines to respond to various types of error conditions.

Part of the reason why the term "middleware" has many meanings is that there are many different ways of being in the middle of two other pieces of software. For example, a wire or cable has to lie between two pieces of software in order for them to communicate. Shall we, therefore, call the wire or cable "middleware"? Probably, someone somewhere does. However, there are a number of "layers" of software above the physical wire that lie between any two pieces of software. For example, there is a layer that deals with converting ASCII code to EBCDIC if needed. Shall we call that "middleware"? There is also a separate "layer" of software that is related to the communication procedures involved and a "layer" of software that tells one piece of software how to access data (for example, with an SQL statement). It is in these two layers of software that different people use the term "middleware" differently. That is why some people will say that "middleware" is a communication mechanism, others will equate it with a type of data access software like EDA/SQL, and others will say it is an interprocess communication call.

This book does not use the term "middleware" very much because of how differently the term is used by different people. When there is little agreement on what a term means, it can be more of a hindrance than a help. Therefore, instead of using the term "middleware" and having people wonder which meaning is intended, other terms will be used to describe particular subjects.

2.3 OTHER IMPORTANT CONSIDERATIONS

2.3.1 Distributed Databases are a Different Issue

The relationship between client/server systems, distributed processing, and distributed database systems is sometimes confusing. Technical literature from universities and research centers refers to client/server systems as a form of distributed processing. There is fairly wide agreement on that point from a number of industry analysts as well. In the academic definition of distributed processing, various components that are in separate locations interact with each other.

Some believe it is more accurate to say that client/server is remote processing rather than distributed processing. We can understand their point of view when we realize that most client/server systems consist of a number of clients interacting with only one remote server. Their point is that there should be more components that are distributed to qualify as distributed processing. They say that when we reach the point where many clients are interacting with many different servers in separate locations, that is when client/server systems can be considered true distributed processing systems.

While client/server database systems may be a form of distributed *processing*, they are *not* the same as distributed database systems. The term "distributed database systems" has come down to us from universities and other research efforts. As a result, distributed database systems have very clear and stringent requirements such as location transparency, replication transparency, fragmentation transparency, and other transparencies—which will be described in detail in Chapter 13. The great majority of client/server database systems do not come close to meeting these requirements. Application developers must realize that they will not necessarily have the features they need for distributed databases in most current client/server architectures.

A few vendors do have client/server database systems which contain distributed database features. However, in most of those cases, the vendors have been working on the distributed database features for many years. After developing DBMSs with distributed database capabilities, the vendors then added features that would permit the database to operate on a server. The most important thing is that application developers should not assume that a client/server system will also have distributed database features.

2.3.2   System Management and Other Issues

A major concern in the client/server arena is related to systems administration—which has also been a concern in mainframe installations for some time. In large mainframe environments, many companies are moving into systems managed storage to handle the complexities of managing data storage for the thousands of datasets they have. Things will only get more complicated as many of these datasets find homes on network servers.

Another area of system administration concern is how to distribute, install, update, and provide version control for client software sitting on numerous personal computers and workstations and for server software located on dozens, hundreds, or thousands of local area networks within an enterprise. Unified approaches like IBM's System View strategy address some of the many client/server system administration issues, but the need for support products is expected to outpace the availability of such products.

Security in a client/server environment is another issue that must be faced. While client/server systems should be protected with the same security as any other type of computer system, there will be some special needs in specific types of networked, client/server systems. Overall system administration issues are discussed in Chapter 14, while security issues are covered in Chapter 21.

Despite such concerns, many companies are moving quickly in the direction of client/server architectures.

2.4   NEW POSSIBILITIES OFFERED BY NEW ARCHITECTURES

Distributed, networked architectures are offering capabilities that were either not available before or not available on the scale on which they are now available. Even more exciting, various technologies are being combined that will result in completely new capabilities.

2.4.1   Groupware

Groupware is an example of the type of software enabled by the same technologies used in client/server systems. Groupware is software that facilitates the work performed by a group of people. It is also known as workgroup computing. Research groups in universities refer to groupware as Computer-Supported Cooperative Work (CSCW).

The term "groupware" has been used to refer to software ranging from electronic mail (E-mail) to workflow automation. E-mail is the capability of sending messages to other computer users through networking facilities. Workflow automation provides features that permit a group to automate a repetitive office procedure such as filling out expense reports. Both of these technologies are discussed in more detail later in this book.

Some observers say that whether there should be a separate category of software products called "groupware" is really debatable. They say this because a primary characteristic of groupware is the ability for individuals to share information and to work on it cooperatively. Since so many PC applications are becoming linked to E-mail capabilities, these observers say that soon nearly every PC package will permit at least some degree of work sharing capabilities.

2.4.2   E-Mail Enabled Software

The growing availability of E-mail is one of the many advantages resulting from the new architectures. An intriguing development is how E-mail is being combined with other technologies to create brand new opportunities. Chapter 17 will describe E-mail in detail, and Chapter 20 will describe some of the new combinations that are evolving. We will just provide some of the highlights of these developments in this chapter to make the reader more aware of how dramatic the changes we are now witnessing really are.

The architecture of E-mail software consists basically of two components: a front-end user interface and a back-end which provides the E-mail service. In between, of course, is the communication mechanism that connects these two components.

E-mail is a network application just like database or file server software can be considered network applications. And just as there are file servers and database servers, there are E-mail servers. Of course, one physical device can function as the server for all three of these applications.

The use of standards will be important as E-mail usage becomes worldwide. Two standards that directly impact electronic mail are X.400, which deals with the format of messages, and X.500, which deals with directory services. These standards were developed by the International Telephone & Telegraph Consultative Committee and are covered in Chapter 18.

The Message Handling Service (MHS) is a de facto standard for transporting E-mail messages and is widely used at the current time within LAN-based E-mail systems. Part of its popularity is due to its connection with Novell which has a large presence in the LAN market today. Two application programming interfaces (API), Microsoft's Messaging API (MAPI) and the Vendor-Independent Messaging (VIM) API, are also gaining in importance. However, for E-mail systems to achieve their full potential in heterogeneous, worldwide environments, standards like X.400 and X.500 will probably play an important role. All of these de jure and de facto standards will be discussed in Chapter 18.

E-Mail is being combined by many corporations with their EDI functions. This is discussed in more detail in Chapter 20.

Other software that can benefit by being "mail-enabled" includes groupware, workflow software, workgroup computing, and collaborative computing. In general, these terms refer to network-accessible productivity software packages. They consist of tools that facilitate people working together to accomplish a common business objective even if they are separated by time and distance. Such packages might involve the integration of a database, multimedia electronic mail, a calendar or scheduler, document-management capabilities, routing abilities, and the ability to connect to a variety of other software packages.

2.4.3   Lotus' Notes and Other Products

Lotus' Notes is another example of the useful types of software that can result from the technologies used in a client/server architecture. Notes is a software package that permits co-workers to organize, manipulate, and share various types of information. When Lotus 1–2–3 introduced Notes in 1989, sales did not take off quickly. It took a while for companies to realize how the product could be used. Accounting consulting firms such as Coopers and Lybrand and Anderson Consulting are some of the large firms that have had Notes installed for a number of years and are now extremely enthusiastic about it. Over the course of several years, the product has become widespread within these firms and employees have become trained in how to benefit from it. Now, many say they could not do without it. Managers in these firms say that big changes have occurred in the way they handle business and respond to customers.

Notes permits Anderson Consulting analysts to share a wide variety of financial information. It also permits workers to share advice and analysis from outside specialists. This boosts productivity since the firm can leverage the talents of a small group of highly-skilled specialists with rare knowledge. Groups of workers can contribute to complete audits much more quickly with the use of Notes.

Users of Notes report that they continually find new ways to use the product. For example, at Coopers and Lybrand users started utilizing Notes to keep their business clients informed of tax law changes. Users also report that Notes sells itself to co-workers. When employees from another division or plant visit a site that has Notes installed, they start asking for access to the product. Ethyl Corporation, a chemical company, bought Notes in 1991 for 100 employees. They used Notes to more efficiently distribute research reports to field offices. After seeing the product in use, employees from the sales department requested Notes so they could use it to track customer contracts and distribute product information.

After Notes achieved a measure of success, Lotus came out with version 3.0 which further fueled enthusiasm for the product. One of the most important features of the new version was that Notes clients could operate on Macintosh and UNIX platforms as well as the earlier OS/2 and Windows platforms. Other features made it much easier to customize Notes and to write new programs for the product.

Lotus has been pushing its Notes product as a type of software "platform." The company wants other vendors to incorporate Notes into their applications permitting users to share information—for example, a Notes word processor would permit several users to work on the same document. Lotus is aggressively pursuing this strategy, saying Notes could become an "infrastructure for creating new classes of applications."

Other vendors are actively pursuing similar paths, however. WordPerfect Corporation, for example, is adding information-sharing features to its word processing software. Other software vendors are adding mail-enabling capabilities to their application packages. It is not easy to predict how much of the market Lotus will have for this new kind of software in five years time, but it is easy to predict that there will be a lot more of this kind of software available in that time frame.

2.5   BENEFITS AND ISSUES OF CLIENT/SERVER SYSTEMS

2.5.1   Benefits

The benefits of a client/server system include such items as easier to use systems, better developer and end user productivity, lower costs, and increased access to corporate data. Dun & Bradstreet Software in Framingham, MA reports that their customers express two primary motivations for moving to client/server systems: reduced data technology costs and enhanced productivity.

2.5.1.1   Hardware Cost Savings

For many large mainframe shops, one of the primary benefits of client/server computing is the ability to downsize computer systems by moving applications from mainframes to LAN servers. This can result in a considerable reduction in operating cost. The far less expensive MIPs (millions of instructions per second) of workstations—long underutilized—can now be put to good use.

This does not mean that a lot of shops are getting rid of their mainframes and moving all of their applications to client/server environments, but many companies that were planning to get a larger mainframe have been able to avoid doing so because of their client/server strategy. This is one of the primary ways that client/server systems are saving corporations money. First, they were able to shift some existing mainframe applications to client/server systems. Second, they found that some of the new systems they had planned to develop for the mainframe could be developed and deployed on a client/server architecture. Quite a few installations have been able to downsize from an IBM 4300-series mainframe computer to an IBM AS/400 minicomputer. In numerous cases minicomputers were completely replaced by multiple client/server systems. The cost savings in all of these situations have been substantial. There have also been cases where a mainframe computer has been replaced by client/server systems.

The issue of cost savings can be a thorny one. Some enterprises that expected big cost savings did not realize them because of other, unexpected costs with the new architecture. Often, companies do not realize how expensive and time-consuming the learning curve and requisite training will be. To try to avoid training will just wind up causing other expenses, like having employees make unfortunate hardware and software choices, or winding up with systems that do not work properly.

2.5.1.2   Other Benefits

With client/server systems, companies have been able to install systems that served their customers better and/or improved the productivity of their own in-house end users. For example, a transportation system in San Francisco was moved from a mainframe computer to a client/server architecture so it could provide better service to customers. The new system made good use of the graphical capabilities that are now widely available in software for client platforms. The new system responded to customer questions by illustrating maps of sections of San Francisco and appropriate transportation routes so customers could see how to get from one place to another.

Another benefit is that end users now have better access to data. This is partly due to the basic architecture of client/server systems and partly due to the ease-of-use of the systems. The modularity of the client/server architecture has resulted in many data access packages being made available by vendors. There are numerous packages that offer access to data in a variety of databases. Many packages offer access to any relational database, but there are also packages that offer access to data in flat files as well as hierarchical (e.g., IMS) and network-model (e.g., IDMS) database systems.

The ease-of-use of client/server systems is attributed to graphical user interfaces which can make a computer system not only easier to use, but also much pleasanter to use. This ease-of-use is not automatic, however. Developers must be aware of users' needs to make sure that graphical interfaces are built to satisfy those needs.

2.5.2 Issues

Issues related to client/server systems range from a lack of understanding what the systems are and why they are desirable, to a lack of sufficient infrastructure software such as system management tools. Sometimes in-house developers and programmers are required to provide some missing software pieces for a production client/server system. Hopefully, the developers will realize the need for such additional software before a production problem occurs to point out the need.

In some installations, one of the most serious issues is that some developers and managers feel threatened by the many changes that are taking place in technology, changes that are embodied in the relatively new client/server systems.

2.5.2.1 Lack of Expertise

Lack of infrastructure software and lack of expertise with this architecture are the two biggest problems faced by client/server developers at the present time. Lack of expertise in new, emerging technologies is a problem that has been faced many times by people who have been in the information systems industry for a long time. The field is constantly changing. Many professionals take it upon themselves to keep up-to-date with new technologies. This is not always possible, however, especially if the IS professional is putting in long hours keeping the existing systems functioning for the enterprise. Books, trade journals, seminars, conferences, and vendor information can help provide information about this new technology. Eventually IS will develop expertise in all facets of client/server technology just as expertise in other new developments in the industry has been developed. The next chapter has additional recommendations regarding overcoming the learning curve that enterprises face.

2.5.2.2 Lack of Infrastructure Software

Infrastructure software is software that surrounds and supports application and operating system software. It includes software for such things as security, systems management, change management, configuration management, and network management. IBM mainframes have an excellent selection of infrastructure software. This infrastructure software has had over twenty years to be developed and refined. Of course, infrastructure software for client/server systems does not match that available for mainframes. There has not been enough time for it to reach the level of maturity that exists for the mainframe. However, this is an area that software developers are working on diligently at the present time. Whenever there is an urgent demand for a particular type of software, many vendors try to fill that need.

More supporting software for client/server systems is being developed all the time. One of the biggest problems that will be faced for many years is trying to get it all to work together. Will an excellent configuration management package work well with the packages selected for security and network management? Of course, vendors are working on these issues as well. The problem is that there will be a lot of competitive offerings. It will be necessary to examine the capabilities of each and determine which best meets the specific needs.

2.5.2.3 Represents a Perceived Threat to Some

Part of human nature seems to be to avoid change—or at least to avoid change that is threatening. Thirty years ago when computers were brand new, many office and clerical workers perceived the computer as a serious threat. They were afraid they would lose their jobs because the work would be performed by a computer program. This danger was so threatening that some computer systems were sabotaged to prevent or delay their success. Workers sometimes purposely entered incorrect information or otherwise tried to reduce the effectiveness of the system.

Today, office and clerical workers are not the ones who perceive changes in the computing industry as a threat. These workers generally see the new capabilities as a tool that will let them perform their jobs more efficiently. Unfortunately, today, it is often IS professionals who see the changes as a threat. Many individuals who have years of highly-skilled knowledge with IBM mainframe computers feel threatened by the potential changes. Managers often feel this threat more than programmers and developers. However, the individuals who are knowledgeable about an enterprise's legacy systems (older systems) and data repositories can be the most valuable people to help migrate to newer client/server and distributed computing architectures. This topic is covered in more detail in the next chapter.

3

GETTING STARTED WITH CLIENT/ SERVER COMPUTING

3.1   ISSUES RELATED TO GETTING STARTED

This chapter will describe various ways that an enterprise can get started with implementing client/server computing. It will describe how various companies are making the transition from mainframe computing to a client/server architecture. A diversity of basic transition approaches will be discussed.

Companies are using different ways to get started with client/server computing according to their own specific circumstances. The various approaches range from a slow, gradual introduction of change to the implementation of entire client/server systems by buying application software packages such as human resource or accounting systems from vendors. There are also tools to help convert a system which is currently running in production on a mainframe to one that will run in production in a client/server environment. Computer Associates offers such tools to convert mainframe IDMS systems to a client/server architecture without recoding the system. However, most companies seem to be taking a gradual approach to client/server computing.

Many companies have a specific, urgent problem that provides the immediate motivation to examine a client/server solution. For example, a firm may have reached the operational limit on its current mainframe computer. It is now faced with trading the mainframe for a larger, more expensive model. A number of years ago, that would have been the only option. Now, however, firms have a new option: spread the processing requirements out over less expensive platforms like personal computers, workstations, and servers connected by networks. This approach, used correctly, has resulted in savings for some companies and better interfaces for end users in many companies.

The heavy pressure to reduce costs in general, felt by many companies, has provided additional motivation to turn to client/server systems. Some companies have been able to move all of their applications from a mainframe—often a 4300 series—to a mid-range machine like IBM's AS/400. Other companies have downsized from a minicomputer to a network of client/server systems. Many companies chose to put new applications on a client/server architecture instead of buying a larger mainframe to fit in the new applications. While these smaller platforms are less expensive, the real benefit companies gain is improved service for internal end users and external customers.

Some of the cost savings from transitioning from a mainframe to client/server computing have been very significant. A military installation was able to save $2,000,000 a year as described in Chapter 5, Section 5.3.1. While most cost savings are not that dramatic, such savings are possible. It is very likely that there are additional enterprises that could realize such dramatic savings as well. Today's competitiveness requires that all potential cost savings be carefully studied.

3.1.1   Overcoming Resistance

Many factors must be taken into consideration in getting started: hardware, software, the company's requirements, the firm's long-term strategy, existing production systems, the learning curve, and office politics. The human factor is sometimes a major stumbling block in transitioning to client/server systems.

Helping employees learn new technologies is one of the best ways to overcome resistance. Communicating the information that efforts will be made to re-educate people and find new jobs for positions made obsolete will overcome resistance as well. If funds are too limited to offer training to everyone, employees can be encouraged to learn new technologies on their own when possible. For example, some programmers are taking evening courses in networking in local universities to broaden their knowledge.

In fact, many application developers learned about networking on their own time and transitioned into networking responsibilities as the need for communication specialists grew. Some of these individuals made the transition over time as they assumed new jobs with different firms. Others did this by gradually assuming more networking responsibilities while staying within the same company. Most of them earned much more money in networking than they did in application development programming. This kind of opportunity may not only overcome resistance, but could be a very positive motivating force.

Some firms have established a clear transition path with retraining for employees who are replaced by new systems. For example, when Foxboro Company in Foxborough, MA downsized from three IBM 4381 mainframes to one 4381 and networked servers, the work performed by a number of data entry clerks was no longer needed. The director of corporate information services for Foxboro said that some data entry people grew into operations and others went into network analysis positions. One former data entry clerk became a telecommunications support analyst, helping to maintain the X.25 wide area network. That was quite an opportunity for that individual. Or was it that that individual created the opportunity? After all, some individuals chose to leave the company to find work they were used to doing.

Some people rush to learn new things, while others resent learning something new. In the computer industry, many people have invested years in developing an expertise in a particular programming skill and take great pride in that skill. There have been cases of programmers with a particular skill who have chosen to leave the computer industry completely rather than abandon their years of knowledge and do what they perceive as starting from scratch with a completely new type of technology.

One of the most important things to guard against is accepting the analysis of individuals who say a new technology will not work when they are really masking their own personal reluctance to change. Fortunately, for each one of those who are unwilling to change, there are many more who know the computing industry is constantly changing and are willing to learn new things.

Economic realities have a way of getting attention. The slow economy of the early 1990s made many people aware that they are in a world that is changing dramatically. For better or for worse, things are different. It will be necessary to be more productive and cost-effective merely to survive. People will need to be flexible enough to constantly learn new technologies and improve the way they work. When some managers have refused to try new technologies, higher level management has brought in new management to implement the new technologies or have outsourced all information system services.

Another major area of resistance that may have to be dealt with is related to the location of data. Some centralized information systems (IS) departments are reluctant to permit departmental data to reside just on a server in the originating department. Some IS managers are reluctant to let a department have full responsibility for the data—even if it is their own data. Some sites, therefore, are backing up this departmental server data to mainframe DASD devices every night. If central IS is going to bear the ultimate responsibility for all data, naturally it will want to have full control over it. Situations like this can be eased when adequate procedures and areas of responsibility are clearly established.

Unfortunately, sometimes the most resistance comes from IS management. Various observers have different theories for this. Some believe that Cobol programmers feel relatively secure because there are millions of Cobol programs that will be around for a long time—all needing constant maintenance. Others say that many managers do not have time to keep up with the details of technology. When technology changed more slowly, managers often knew which of their employees they could rely on for good advice. However, when all the technology is so new, how do managers know who they can rely on for the best advice? Worse yet, they are the ones who will ultimately be responsible for any disasters. Under these circumstances, who can blame them for being somewhat conservative?

Still, a lot of the resistance just comes down to a basic distaste for change. End users seem to be the ones who want change the most just now. They have seen what they can do with personal computers in recent years and they are eager for more.

3.1.2   The Learning Curve

There are many new concepts and tools to learn with client/server computing. Frequently, a company will have some programmers who know C, have worked with UNIX, and/or know something about networking. Such individuals are often chosen to work on the first client/server projects. However, as we have seen, a knowledge of C or UNIX is not considered a necessity for constructing client/server systems. These systems can be constructed using a tool like PowerBuilder or Cobol with an OS/2 operating system. No knowledge of C or UNIX is needed for such client/server systems.

Some managers are taking advantage of the interest shown in new technologies by those who are most eager to learn. Jesse Rodriguez, director of information technologies in the Tucson Unified School District, in Tucson, AZ, set up a new position called an emerging technology specialist. Individuals in this position are dedicated to learning new technologies as they become available. Some sites are using such dedicated individuals to perform technology transfer by also teaching other staff members the new technologies.

It is helpful to remember that individuals in the computing industry have been through many challenging learning curves. When hierarchical databases like IMS first came out, it was not easy for some programmers to learn this database structure and how to maneuver within it. In fact, there were some IS professionals who could not or did not care to make the effort to learn this new technology. One employee of a large bank took the IMS programming class for the third time before deciding not to pursue the technology any further. Most IS developers, however, made the transition putting in whatever effort was required on their part.

3.1.2.1   Seminars, Conferences, Classes

Various approaches are being taken toward training employees in client/server computing. Many companies are beginning to send employees to conferences and seminars about client/server computing, downsizing strategies, and distributed computing. 1992 was the year when such seminars started to become widely available. Numerous two- and three-day seminars and conferences are now offered in large cities throughout the country. A seminar is usually in the format of a course given by one teacher, while a conference often has many different speakers offering attendees a choice of topics. Many conferences invite vendors who demonstrate and explain their client/server products, sometimes offering hands-on experience.

Two of the largest companies sponsoring seminars and conferences are Digital Consulting, Inc., Andover, MA, and the Technology Transfer Institute, Santa Monica, CA. Others include American Expositions, Inc., in New York City; American Research Group, Inc., Cary, NC; Corporate Education Center at Boston University, Data-Tech Institute, Clifton, NJ; Information Technology Association of America, Arlington, VA; Microsoft University, Redmond, WA, and Network Career Advancement Institute, Tustin, CA. These firms would be happy to provide detailed information about their services.

Some companies are sponsoring in-house training. Sometimes an outside firm like Anderson Consulting is invited to teach the courses. Other companies train their own personnel to teach the in-house courses. This approach permits them to tailor the courses to their own specific needs.

3.1.2.2   Trade Journals

Technology is changing so fast that constant attention is required to keep up with it. Reading trade journals is the way most practitioners keep abreast of developments. There are a wide variety of trade magazines to select from. Many of them are free to those who qualify for a subscription. With a qualified list of readers, a magazine can guarantee vendors that the appropriate audience will be reading their advertisements. As a result, the magazine is not sold on newsstands to the general public (who may not buy server software, for example), but sent to readers in industry who "qualify" for a subscription by being in a position to buy the vendors' products or to influence their company to purchase them.

The following is a list of trade journals that often carry stories about client/server issues. Some of them have qualified subscriptions and some are paid subscriptions.

Weekly:

Communications Week, CMP Publications, Manhasset, NY

Computerworld, CW Publishing, Inc., Framingham, MA

Digital News, Digital News Publishing, Inc., Boston, MA

InfoWorld, InfoWorld Publishing, San Mateo, CA

InformationWeek, CMP Publications, Inc., Manhasset, NY

Network World, Network World, Inc., Framingham, MA

PC Week, Ziff Communications Company, New York, NY

Monthly, semi-monthly, and monthly with special issues:

Byte, McGraw-Hill, Inc., New York, NY

CASE Trends, Software Productivity Group, Shrewsbury, MA

Client/Server Computing, Sentry Publishing, Westborough, MA

Corporate Computing, Ziff-Davis Publishing, New York, NY

Data Communications, McGraw-Hill, Inc., New York, NY

Data Base Management, Technical Enterprises, Inc., Milwaukee, WI

Database Programming & Design, Miller Freeman Publications, San Francisco, CA

Datamation (semi-monthly), Cahners-Ziff Publishing Associates, Newton, MA

DBMS Client/Server Computing, M&T Publishing, Inc., San Mateo, CA

Dr. Dobb's Journal, M&T Publishing, San Mateo, CA

LAN Magazine, Miller Freeman, Inc., San Francisco, CA

LAN Times, (semi-monthly) McGraw-Hill, Inc., New York, NY

Macworld, Macworld Communications, Inc., Boulder, CO

Microsoft Systems Journal, Miller Freeman Inc., San Mateo, CA

Network Computing, CMP Publications, Inc., Manhasset, NY

Open Systems Today, CMP Publications, Inc., Manhasset, NY

PC/Computing, Ziff-Davis Publishing Company, New York, NY

PC Magazine, (bi-weekly), Ziff-Davis Publishing Company, New York, NY

Software Magazine, Sentry Publishing, Westborough, MA

Some of the most widely read magazines include *Software Magazine*, *PC Week*, *InfoWorld*, *Computerworld*, and *Datamation*. Individuals who are interested in getting their first networking publication might be interested in starting with *Lan Magazine*, *LAN Technology*, or *Network Computing*. While these magazines are not just for beginners, they often take time to explain concepts to those who are still learning.

The above list is by no means exhaustive. There are additional trade journals, some of which are sold on newsstands and in bookstores. Now and then a trade journal does not survive. Do not be surprised if some trade journals disappear, and be assured that new ones will constantly appear.

People who work for large companies with an in-house library, should visit it and see which of these magazines it carries. Browse through the magazines to develop an idea of their coverage. Those who do not work for a large company can visit a library in a large city or university nearby. Many large universities have several libraries where computer trade journals are kept. A phone call in advance can determine the best location for browsing. Many of the trade journals listed above would be happy to send a sample issue to those who call and request one. One of the best ways to learn about client/server computing—and the only way to *keep up* with the technology—is to read, read, and read some more.

Thousands of articles have been read by the author of this book. Some contributed in minor ways and others contributed in more significant ways. Some of the more significant ones are listed in the Bibliography at the end of the book.

However, the author also found that some articles were misleading because they did not define a topic accurately or clearly. Readers should be wary of articles written about new technologies if the background of the author is unknown.

3.1.2.3   Who Writes Articles?

Some of the best articles about client/server systems have been written by individuals who have implemented them. In addition, some of the best articles have been written by writers who were journalism majors, and who are learning about client/server, and carefully interviewing individuals who are implementing the technology. Unfortunately, some writers will place journalistic "attention-getting" qualities to their writing above accuracy. These are the writers of whom readers should most beware.

My hat goes off to journalism majors who have never implemented systems, yet who are doing an absolutely excellent job of reporting about this technology. Grasping some of these technologies is difficult enough for those of us who work with them daily. Maybe the quality that serious journalists bring to writing about client/server technology is their training in investigating, examining, and confirming the accuracy of the facts they learn. Of course, another critical quality they bring is clarity of writing style, making their work understandable to their readers.

3.2   CANDIDATE SYSTEMS FOR CLIENT/SERVER PLATFORMS

3.2.1   Types of Systems

What systems are the best candidates for migrating to client/server platforms? While opinions vary somewhat, many people agree that departmental applications can be better candidates for early migration than worldwide enterprise applications. The least likely candidate application might be a time-sensitive enterprise-wide system with thousands or tens of thousands of users needing split-second response times while accessing and updating millions of records in multiple databases.

The fact that an application is corporate-wide does not rule it out for migration to client/server platforms. Frequently, good migration candidates are departmental portions of a corporate-wide personnel, payroll, or other human resources type of system. One example might be having a personnel department track applicants for a job application on a local server database. Then, when the applicant is hired, the information could be shifted to the mainframe. This permits a gradual introduction to client/server systems. A lot of similar systems basically "feed" larger mainframe systems. They are often good candidates for initial client/server systems. Basic information gathering systems are also good candidates for client/server systems. This includes simple data query systems as well as more advanced decision support executive information systems as discussed in the next section.

3.3 DIFFERENT APPROACHES TO GETTING STARTED

There are many different ways of categorizing the diverse ways that various companies are getting started with client/server computing. One way of categorizing these approaches is as follows:

- New Systems
- Add-on Systems
- Phased Approach
- Redevelopment
- Rapid Downsizing
- Application Packages

Each one of these will be discussed in the following sections. The advantages and disadvantages of the various approaches and their similarities and differences will also be discussed.

3.3.1 New Systems, Add-On Systems, Phased Approaches, and Redevelopment

The category "new systems" refers to systems which have not been on a computer before. These are newly automated systems. Such systems are often developed to meet new business needs. They may reflect a new business opportunity for the enterprise, or they might reflect the need for additional information like decision support systems or executive information systems.

Many companies are examining all new systems development projects to see whether any of them could be installed as a client/server system. If so, they examine what additional hardware, software, and procedures they would need to acquire and develop in order to implement the new system with a client/server architecture. They perform an alternatives analysis and make their decision based on an examination of the alternatives.

Add-on systems, like new systems, also reflect a need for additional information. An add-on system is simply a subsystem which is added to an existing system. Sometimes this can be a data query subsystem that provides new information from data already in an existing database. There are many excellent and easy to use data query tools that can access information from existing databases. If the existing database is a relational system, the job is much simpler. But there are data query tools that access data from IMS, IDMS, and VSAM as well as flat file structures. Information Builder's EDA/SQL, described in Chapter 12, can access information from a great many databases and file structures.

Add-on client/server systems that provide new information have many advantages. They are easy to design, easy to implement, have very little risk involved, and can result in a fast payback and good visibility. Often these systems access data that has been downloaded from a mainframe to a server. Figure 3.1 depicts downloading data.

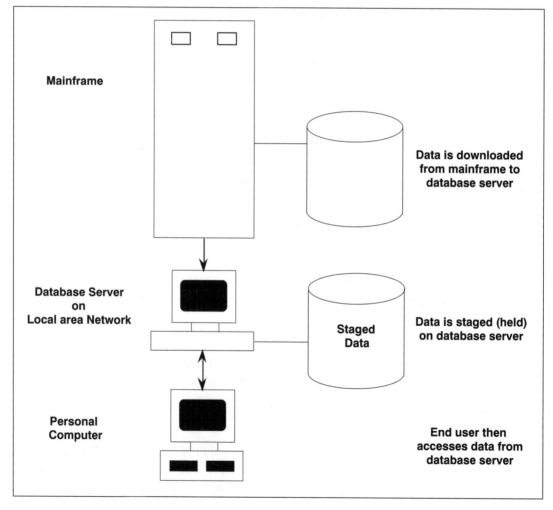

Figure 3.1 Downloading data.

Frequently, the downloaded data is *a copy* of the production data. This downloaded data is not updated by end users; it is used to satisfy information requests and to provide data for data analysis and decision support systems. Of course, each specific situation will need to be analyzed to determine whether up-to-the-second data is needed for the application. If the need for updated data is important enough, it can be accessed directly from the production files. The benefit of a client/server architecture is that it provides an easy way to let users access data as much as they want from servers that stage (hold) mainframe data.

A phased-approach is one where front ends and back ends are added separately to an existing system. Add-on systems could also be classified as a phased approach. However, there are times when a phased approach is used and no new functions will be added to the system. For example, sometimes a new front end is added just to make the system easier to use. In such instances, a GUI replaces what used to be a complicated 3270 screen.

This technique is occasionally called "front-ending" and has been severely criticized by some people. They say that front-ending an existing application—replacing a character-based screen with a graphical user interface—is nothing more than putting a pretty, but dumb, face on an old system. However, some of these newly front-ended systems save a company a substantial amount of money because the system becomes much easier to use. Everyone involved must understand that replacing a 3270-type character screen with a GUI does not automatically convert the system into a full-fledged client/server system; it merely simplifies the use of the existing system.

Redevelopment consists of building a new version of an existing system. Computer systems, like other things, do not last forever. Eventually the needs of the enterprise change, or the procedure used in the old system becomes obsolete. A major system redevelopment effort represents an excellent time for an enterprise to examine the possibility of moving the entire system to a client/server environment. Several years ago, when client/server technology was newer, there were some limitations on database sizes and speed requirements. However, server storage is available in many gigabytes, speed is constantly increasing, and fault tolerance is available now so that mission critical systems can be accommodated in a client/server environment.

3.3.2 Rapid Downsizing

Rapid downsizing refers to a unique situation available for specific software products. This approach allows an installation to take an application that is running on a mainframe and downsize it quickly so that it runs in a client/server environment. One vendor providing full support for this approach is Computer Associates (CA) in Islandia, NY with its IDMS system.

A company that used this approach to downsizing is Computer Programming and Systems, Inc. (CPS) in Stamford, CT. CPS is a consulting and software development firm specializing in life insurance and reinsurance. By 1988, CPS's various mainframe-based insurance software application packages were used by over 150 customers nationwide. At that time, the demand for PC-based systems among its customers was great enough that CPS realized it had to respond in order to maintain its competitive position. An analysis revealed that it was faced with three to five years of coding to create new PC versions of their mainframe-based applications.

At the time, CPS was using software called The Application Builder (TAB) from On-Line Database Software which is now a part of Computer Associates. A tool for building IDMS applications, TAB was originally intended to off-load development work from a mainframe to a PC, and the completed application was intended to execute on a mainframe. CPS not only wanted to develop the application on the PC, it also wanted to deliver the application on the PC. That is, CPS wanted the application to operate on the PC. The software had never been used that way before.

Analysis performed by CPS and the vendor indicated that it might work, although CPS had no guarantee that the attempt would work. It did know what had to be done if the attempt failed. The only alternative was to start from scratch and entirely recode all of the PC applications over a four to five year period.

Peter O'Karma, a manager with CPS, says that prior to starting this experiment, his experience had been entirely with mainframes. He was not at all sure of this procedure. He says it was a "Let's see if we can do it" type of experience. In fact, he said it was more of an "OK. Let's prove it can't be done" situation. That proof that this approach did not work would have justified the recoding that would have been necessary for the next four or five years.

When using new technologies for applications, the advice is often "start small." That is, to select a small enough project to ensure success. That was not good enough for CPS. It started with its *largest* system to make sure that what it was doing would work for its largest systems—and therefore for *all* of its systems—or it would not use this approach at all.

As the test case, CPS selected its Life Reinsurance Processing System, a data processing tool for administering life reinsurance, used by professional reinsurers as well as life insurance companies. The large, mainframe-based IDMS system consisted of a mix of batch Cobol programs, command level CICS, and ADS/O, the Application Development System/On-Line 4GL for IDMS. CPS used the Cobol compiler and CICS preprocessor from Realia Cobol based in Chicago, IL.

The results were very successful and even surprising to some. O'Karma said that some end users could not believe that the new systems—running on PCs—were really the original systems that had been executing on 3090s under MVS. CSP's software customers were able to save a significant amount of money on processing costs since PC MIPs are far less expensive than mainframe MIPs. A few customers—those who were able to migrate all their applications to PCs—reportedly even got rid of their mainframes.

Despite this particular success story, rapid downsizing may not be the ideal way to convert to client/server systems. Since systems are not recoded, they will not take best advantage of the modularity of client/server architectures. That is, processing may not be divided efficiently across different platforms. However, CPS's experience demonstrates that such rapid downsizing can be an extremely quick and cost-effective strategy.

3.3.3   Application Packages

Another approach is to buy client/server or network-based software application packages, install them, and therefore be able to install client/server systems rather quickly. Sometimes these client/server packages replace existing mainframe applications—whether homegrown or purchased. At other times, they are installations of new software applications for the enterprise.

Many large software vendors are actively migrating their mainframe software packages to client/server architectures, while new software companies are being formed to take advantage of this new opportunity. Each type of firm has its own unique advantages and disadvantages. The new software vendors have no existing packages on mainframes and they are completely free to use new object-oriented techniques and other approaches without worrying about how those approaches will tie in with their installed base of packages.

On the other hand, vendors who already have an installed base of mainframe packages have a track record they can point to. A brand new software vendor has to start from scratch, while existing vendors already have customers who are (hopefully) happy with their products. Such customers would be concerned with having a carefully thought out migration plan to transition their mainframe systems to client/server systems. After all, installing client/server systems is a complete, on-going change in direction in the way computing is performed. The wisest of enterprises want assurances that there will not by any disastrous surprises after they start down this road. Having the weight of experience of an established mainframe software vendor can be like having an ally in an unfamiliar, new situation.

Dun & Bradstreet Software, in Framingham, MA (D&B), is an example of a vendor who has a large, installed base of existing mainframe software. D&B Software was formed in 1989 by the merger of McCormick & Dodge—a unit of Dun & Bradstreet Corporation—with Management Science of America (MSA). As a result of this merger, D&B has an installed base that amounts to over 15,000 corporate customers, including over 75 percent of the Fortune 500 companies. The overall approach that D&B is taking is one of incremental adoption of the client/server architecture. The goal is to help its clients to migrate gradually to client/server systems.

D&B plans to provide a gradual release of client/server modules for what are now mainframe-based systems to initiate this migration. (The mainframe versions will continue to be available.) Roe Henson, business area manager for the services and human resources product line for D&B, says the human resources area provides a good example of this incremental approach. A personnel application, for example, often can be divided into separate, individual user systems. Some personnel employees may specialize in compensation, while others specialize in benefits, or recruiting, or safety and health management. These specialists might go to work in the morning and analyze what happened in their area of concentration over the last day. D&B's incremental approach could provide a client with individual client/server modules for different specialties while the rest of the personnel application is still on the mainframe.

D&B is completely rewriting its applications to take maximum advantage of the client/server and networked computing architectures. When asked if D&B's clients are interested in a client/server version of its software, a D&B manager said "If you ask our clients if they are interested in less expensive and more productive systems, all of them would say 'Yes.'" D&B expects the client/server versions of its software to be less expensive and more productive.

One of D&B's first releases of client/server software was its SmartStream line of products. This package is intended to give existing D&B customers streamlined client/server access to information in a variety of databases, whether they are located within the company or in external sources such as Compuserve, MCI News, and the Dow Jones News Service. These databases and information sources all have different data formats, of course, and SmartStream simplifies access to them with what D&B calls intelligent "agents." These agents are automated task handlers that make decisions on the user's behalf based upon pre-set choices. SmartStream resides on a personal computer or workstation, and it analyzes and distributes information across a LAN network.

PeopleSoft, headquartered in Walnut Creek, CA, is an example of a relatively new vendor. PeopleSoft was founded in 1987 for the explicit purpose of developing client/server application package software. It has received favorable reviews in the press, and customers seem to be very happy with the vendor's high-quality software products.

Some of PeopleSoft's first and most widely purchased offerings included human resources, benefits, and payroll packages. The PeopleSoft Human Resources package, PS/HR, offers provisions intended to permit it to easily be integrated with other PeopleSoft packages. PS/HR provides date-sensitive functions and features that include personnel administration, recruitment, position management, salary administration, training and development, health and safety, skills inventory, career planning, EEO/Affirmative Action planning, and basic benefits record keeping. Also available are a basic Benefits Administration component and a more extensive Flexible Benefits component.

Many firms buy "ready-made" client/server application packages as a quick way to implement this architecture. This strategy can spread the learning curve over a longer period of time. Developers can undergo training in the new technologies while end users are already utilizing their new client/server systems.

4

OPEN SYSTEMS AND CLIENT/ SERVER COMPUTING

4.1 THE INTERACTION AND BENEFITS

4.1.1 How the Client/Server Architecture Encourages Open Systems

The fact that the client/server architecture requires cooperation among multiple systems may accelerate the move to open systems. Two of the primary characteristics of open systems are interoperability and portability. These are also primary characteristics of client/server systems. Interoperability between the client and the server software is necessary in order to have a client/server system. By definition, a client/server system is one where a client portion and a server portion cooperate with each other to accomplish objectives. They must be able to interoperate to form this kind of cooperation. The modular architecture of a client/server system actively encourages a mix and match approach.

It is definitely in a vendor's interest if its products can interoperate with a wide range of products from other vendors. For example, if a front-end database query can operate with many back-end database servers, more sales of the query tool are likely. The same goes for database vendors; to be able to interact with as many front-end query tools and application development platforms is to their advantage.

Regarding portability, there is such a broad range of hardware and software platforms used in client/server environments, that it is also in a vendor's interest to be able to have its software run in as many environments as possible. If a front-end tool can only operate under OS/2 on a client station, its sales could be severely limited. If it can operate under OS/2 and Microsoft Windows, sales could increase significantly.

This need for interoperability and portability extends to networking software as well. It is not sufficient for a major database server package to work with just one network operating system and network configuration. For example, if a product works only with LAN Server, the database vendor would miss potential sales that could be made from the many sites that have only Novell networks.

In order to achieve client/server portability and interoperability, vendors often have to write completely different versions of their software for the diverse platforms. This, of course, is not the ideal situation. A preferred approach would be to have standard interfaces. Then all vendors could write to the standard interface. They would only have to have one version of their software: the one written to the standard interface, not half a dozen copies written to other vendors' proprietary specifications.

The move to client/server systems cannot help but fuel the demand for open systems. Not only is it in the interest of end users to have open systems in terms of interoperability, portability, and scalability, it is in vendors' interests as well. A desirable long-range goal would be the interoperability among all portions of a client/server system so that users at any node could benefit from the services of any server.

4.1.2 Definition and Benefits of Open Systems

The Institute of Electrical and Electronic Engineers' (IEEE) Technical Committee on Open Systems defines open systems as follows:

> a comprehensive and consistent set of international information technology standards and functional standards profiles that specify interfaces, services, and supporting formats to accomplish interoperability and portability of applications, data, and people.

Open systems are composed of parts that have a publicly specified interface. When an interface is publicly specified, then any vendor can write software for it. In such a situation, end users are able to buy components from various vendors and benefit from a competitive marketplace. This reduces costs while improving performance and function.

Open systems are in direct contrast with proprietary systems. A proprietary system is one that is privately manufactured and sold. Usually, proprietary systems are made and marketed by one company with the exclusive rights to manufacture and sell the product. An example of a proprietary system is IBM's IMS database or MVS operating system. If a company wants IMS, it goes to IBM for it. It is not available from any other vendor. IBM designed it, architected it, sells it, and maintains it.

Proprietary systems are generally more profitable for vendors. A proprietary system can "lock-in" a customer to that product or line of products. That way, a vendor builds up a following, or customer base, that it can rely on for repeat sales. Open systems do not have that advantage for vendors. So, why would vendors have the motivation to build open systems? The motivation exists only if enough customers demand open systems or if it develops into an advantage for the vendor.

Sometimes vendors will "open up" an interface to their line of software or provide an API for developers because it is to their advantage to have other vendors write to that interface. Vendors who have a large market share are in a position to do this. That large market share can make it worthwhile for other vendors to write to that interface. Companies like IBM and Microsoft are in such a position.

In late 1991, Microsoft announced its Open Database Connectivity (ODBC) API which facilitates interoperability between Microsoft Windows and many different databases. With ODBC, Windows vendors can write applications without having a specific end database in mind. When the time comes to connect to a database, users add database-specific modules. Since the product has an open interface, many vendors can create products to work with it. This will result in increased sales of ODBC—a distinct advantage for Microsoft.

4.2   THE ROLE OF STANDARDS AND STANDARDS ORGANIZATIONS

Standards include things like establishing a universal calendar that every country uses. For computers, some standards are the ASCII character set and standards for programming languages like C, Cobol, and Fortran established by the American National Standards Institute (ANSI). Standards facilitate the functioning of systems, organizations, and infrastructures.

Standards are a key factor in open systems. Open systems adhere to standards in order to achieve interoperability and portability. While some critics argue that standards limit innovation, standards advocates counter that there is still plenty of room for innovation and added-value that can be provided for and built around formal standards.

4.2.1   Different Types of Standards and Standards Organizations

We know that open systems are related to standards, but who is to establish what the standards will be? There are many different standards groups. Some individuals say that only national or international standards groups can establish standards, while others say that the popularity of a product in the marketplace establishes it as a standard. Standards are established both ways, but they are very different kinds of standards.

There are de facto standards and de jure standards. De jure standards are established by formal national groups or internationally recognized standards bodies. Examples of such organizations are the International Organization for Standardization* (ISO), the International Telegraph and Telephone Consultative Committee (CCITT), the IEEE, the American National Standards Institute (ANSI) and the National Institute of Standards and Technology (NIST). De facto standards are established by the market place. A product becomes a de facto standard out of wide spread acceptance. Once a product has established a certain market share, it has become a de facto standard.

An example of a de facto standard is Microsoft DOS for the personal computer. No standards body was involved in establishing Microsoft DOS as the standard for PCs. DOS is implemented on over a hundred million PCs worldwide. That clearly establishes it as the standard for these machines. An example of de jure standards are the OSI protocols. The overall realm of de jure standards includes not only protocols, but specifications and interfaces as well.

The Portable Operating System Interfaces for Computer Systems (POSIX) is an example of a standard interface. POSIX was developed by the Technical Committee on Operating Systems of the IEEE Computer Society. POSIX is closely related to UNIX, but POSIX is an interface, not an operating system or an implementation of one. It was derived from a combination of UNIX kernel system calls and a number of facilities that are often found as user library routines in implementations of UNIX.

POSIX is very important when developing systems for the U.S. and European governments. The European Commission (EC)—the coordinating body for Unified Europe—and the U.S. National Institute of Standards and Technology have both indicated that computer-based procurements will need to be compliant with POSIX. NIST, formerly called the National Bureau of Standards, is a government agency which creates Federal Information Processing Standards (FIPS) among other things. FIPS specify the standards to be used in the procurement of information system components by the federal government.

Many standards groups have been formed within the information

---

*While the International Organization for Standardization is the formal name of the body, ISO is often referred to in the United States as the International Standards Organization.

systems arena in recent years. They include X/Open, the Open Software Foundation (OSF), the SQL Access Group (SAG), the Object Management Group (OMG), the Standards Promotion and Application Group (SPAG), the MAP/TOP Users Group, and the Corporation for Open Systems (COS), among many others. Each contributes to the move toward open systems.

X/Open and OSF are both consortiums—voluntary groups of vendors and users—which are having quite an important impact on the client/server movement. Their influence is expected to grow. Both of these groups will be discussed in more detail in later sections of this chapter.

OMG is a consortium of software vendors dedicated to creating standards related to objects in object-oriented systems. For example, the purpose of OMG's Object Request Broker is to provide mechanisms by which objects can transparently make requests and receive responses from applications on different machines in a heterogeneous, distributed environment. Their work will first have an impact on network management and later will begin to pervade more aspects of distributed computing.

SPAG is a European group formed to promote OSI standards. The Manufacturing Automation Protocol and Technical and Office Protocol (MAP/TOP) Users Group supports the use of a suite of networking protocols. The Corporation for Open Systems performs conformance testing and certification for products that are related to OSI. Both SPAG and MAP/TOP are involved in de jure standards. SAG is involved with de facto standards for SQL.

4.2.2　X/Open

X/Open is a consortium of software and hardware vendors that focuses on end user requirements. As a result, it is growing in importance every day. X/Open does not create any new standards. The group selects existing standards which have come into wide usage in the market place.

X/Open is very active in getting user input through its X/tra Program, a worldwide user requirements research program. X/Open performs its requirements analysis through a mail survey. The survey is international in scope with requirements gathered from 17 different countries. The completed survey forms the foundation for the following World Congress on Open Systems. The congress serves as a forum where members further identify and prioritize their requirements for open systems technology.

After the congress, X/Open publishes the requirements in a document called the Open Systems Directive, which is available to users, vendors, and standards organizations. The results are also used to prioritize X/Open's technical work programs which create vendor-independent specifications.

The published specifications form the X/Open Portability Guide (XPG). The XPG is a portfolio of practical interface specifications for interoperability and portability at the source code level. The XPG is updated periodically, typically annually. Thus, the term "XPG4" refers to the fourth official release of the X/Open Portability Guide.

The specifications offer a guide to the necessary interfaces and considerations involved in the implementation of open systems. As a group, the specifications contribute to forming what X/Open calls an open, multivendor Common Applications Environment (CAE). X/Open's goal is to gain widespread acceptance of CAE from the computer industry, including both software vendors and users. X/Open also opens its CAE to other groups like the SQL Access Group.

The basic architecture for the CAE is shown in Figure 4.1. Examples of tools for the middle layer are Windows, programming languages, and data management tools.

The CAE uses the POSIX interface.

X/Open has a branding process to ensure that products conform to X/Open specifications and will interoperate. Software suppliers who want the X/Open brand on their products must first pass the test suite and then sign a license agreement. The test suite is very thorough with over 5,000 test cases. The license agreement requires them to maintain conformance with new releases and requires them to publish any waivers—whether customers ask for them or not. Branding can be done by third-

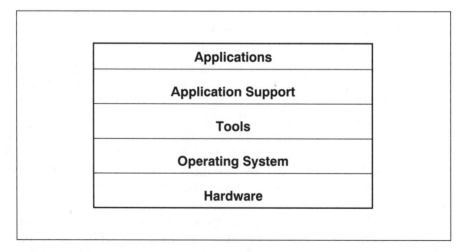

Figure 4.1 Common application environment architecture.

party laboratories, by a software supplier or even by development organizations that bring the test suite in-house. That is exactly what an increasing number of large companies are doing.

Bellcore, which provides research and technology support to the divested Bell operating companies, is an example of a company that is adamant about buying X/Open-compliant products. As a result, the Livingston, NJ-based Bellcore bought the X/Open verification test suite to perform its own testing.

Other companies say that while they would like to have them, they do not demand X/Open-branded products because they are afraid that with the limited number of such products, they would be reducing their software choices. Kyle Barringer, director of development support for DHL Systems, Inc., in San Mateo, CA, says they are not demanding X/Open branding, but they are asking for it. DHL Systems provides software support for DHL Worldwide Express, the Brussels-based international air express company. Dean Fitzbag, division vice president of Electronic Data Systems (EDS), an information technology services company and systems integrator in Dallas, says EDS asks software vendors for X/Open-compliant systems. These two large firms are just a few of the growing number of companies establishing a strategic direction that includes the interoperability of open systems.

X/Open addresses transaction processing in a distributed environment with its Distributed Transaction Processing (DTP) model. The DTP model provides for interaction among an application program which defines transaction boundaries, resource managers such as databases or file access systems that provide access to shared resources, and a transaction manager which takes overall responsibility for transaction completion and/or recovery. X/Open's XA interface—a system level interface between DTP software components—is bi-directional between a transaction monitor and a resource manager. Another interface, the Application Transaction Manager Interface (ATMI) provides various communications services. Many vendors are beginning to adhere to these standard interfaces, offering the hope of more open systems in the future.

4.2.3　The Open Software Foundation (OSF)

OSF had its start with establishing a platform environment for UNIX and has now grown to be an extremely important part of the distributed computing movement. OSF's Distributed Computing Environment (DCE) and Distributed Management Environment (DME) software and specifications are expected to have an important impact on client/server systems and other distributed computing systems. DCE allows information to flow across a heterogeneous, distributed hardware and software environment while hiding a great deal of the underlying complexity.

In the late 1980s, there were several popular versions of UNIX, with the two most widely used versions being from AT&T, as specified in the AT&T System V Interface Definition (SVID), and the other from the University of California at Berkeley. The latter version is often referred to as BSD which stands for Berkeley Standard Distribution. In 1987, Sun Workstations, a major user of UNIX, and AT&T made an announcement of their intent to define a standard implementation of UNIX.

OSF was founded in response to the 1987 announcement by AT&T and Sun. The original members of OSF were Apollo Computer Inc., Digital Equipment Corporation, Groupe Bull, Hewlett-Packard, IBM, Nixdorf Computer AG, Philips and Siemens AG. Hitachi Ltd. subsequently joined the sponsor group. Among the original members, Hewlett-Packard acquired Apollo, and Siemens and Nixdorf merged. The first two products from OSF were the OSF/1 operating system and the Motif GUI. The next product, OSF's Distributed Computing Environment, is an integrated set of products that permits sites to combine computers from multiple vendors into a single system for developing and executing applications. OSF's DCE has been widely accepted and has a chance at becoming the de facto standard for open distributed computing environments. OSF also offers DME, which is discussed in Chapter 14.

OSF now consists of over 350 organizations, including educational institutions, research organizations, businesses, and government organizations. A company or group does not have to be a member of OSF to license any of their technologies. The value of membership is the ability to contribute to decision-making and early access to technologies.

OSF does not build its products and platforms from scratch. It selects its technologies through an open request for technology (RFT) process. With many vendors responding, OSF has a wide variety of relevant and promising technologies from which to make its selections.

4.2.3.1 OSF's Distributed Computing Environment (DCE)

DCE is an integrated set of services that supports the development, use, and maintenance of distributed applications. The architecture of the DCE is shown in Figure 4.2.

Notice that this architecture uses a layered model. The bottom layers represent the most basic services—the operating system and transport services—and the top layers represent application services. Security and system management capabilities are shown on the sides because they pervade all levels of the architecture. To applications and end users, the

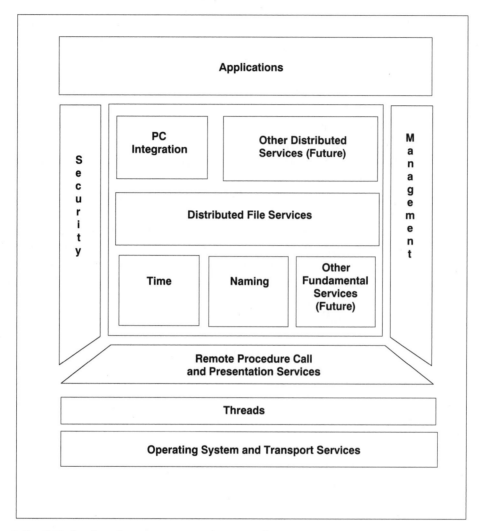

Figure 4.2 OSF distributed computing environment architecture.

overall setting appears as a unified, full-service environment instead of a milieu consisting of separate, diverse functions. One of the main benefits of the DCE is that it masks the physical complexity of the networked environment, simplifying things for end users, application developers, and system administrators.

The same set of DCE services needs to be present on every platform in a system to achieve the full benefits of DCE. In this manner a single-system image is created. The various components are called into service when an application requests data or services. No matter who makes the request or where they are located, they have access to the same uniform set of services that is available elsewhere in the network. This contributes to overall integration and effective use of the computing resources on the network.

OSF says that the concept of a cable-ready television is similar to a DCE-ready environment. When a user buys a cable-ready TV, he or she expects to plug it in to be able to benefit from cable services. A site needs to have the same set of DCE services—RPC, the threads package, directory, and security services—on every platform to have a DCE-ready environment offering plug and play capabilities with various applications.

DCE is intended to be both network-independent and operating system-independent. OSF says DCE can be used with any network hardware and transport software, including TCP/IP, OSI, and X.25, as well as other similar products. It makes use of standard interfaces for operating system services such as POSIX and X/Open guidelines. It can be ported easily to OSF/1, AIX, DOMAIN OS, ULTRIX, HP-UX, SINIX, SunOS, and UNIX System V operating systems. Also, since delivered in source form, DCE can be tailored to system environments that offer similar services but different interfaces, such as IBM's OS/2, Digital Equipment's VMS, and other operating systems like Microsoft's NT.

The services provided by DCE fall into two main categories as shown below.

1. Fundamental Distributed Services
   - Remote Procedure Call
   - Directory Service
   - Time Service
   - Security Service
   - Threads Service
2. Data-Sharing Services
   - Distributed File System
   - Diskless Support

The Fundamental Distributed Services provide the tools that software developers use to create the end-user services needed in a distributed computing environment. The Data-Sharing Services are built on top of the Fundamental Distributed Services and provide additional capabilities without the need for additional programming.

OSF's remote procedure call technology (RPC) is discussed in some detail in Chapter 9. The RPC technology is closely integrated with the other features of the Fundamental Distributed Services. For example, the RPC mechanism uses the directory service to access network resources, provides security services using remote procedure calls, and integrates threads services with the RPC mechanism.

One of the most important things about DCE's Directory Service is that it supports the internationally recognized 1988 standard, the ISO Directory Service (CCITT X.500). This is a global directory service which allows clients to share and access directory information with organizations anywhere in the world that support implementations of this standard. The DCE implementation, based on Siemens' DIR-X product, is an extension of the CCITT X.500 standard. The extensions provide directory replication, performance enhancement through caching techniques, and security for data stored in the directory. The global portion of DCE's Directory Service provides its X.500 support through the X/Open directory Service API and a management interface.

DCE's Directory Service also helps integrate systems that support only a local naming service. As a result, programmers can move from an environment that supports full OSI X.500 functionality to one providing only the local name component. Either way, users can identify resources like servers, disks, files, or print queues by name without knowing where they are located on a network. The system is scalable, permitting additional servers and directory levels to be added readily.

The Time Service provides a uniform time throughout the network. Various applications need timing services for such things as scheduling activities, determining event sequencing and duration, and time stamping transactions. In a large network with many individual devices, it would be easy for some devices to have slight differences in time. This service regulates each computer's clock according to a widely-recognized time standard, providing accurate, synchronized times throughout the network.

DCE's Threads Service facilitates concurrent programming through the use of multiple threads of execution within an application, permitting the application to perform many actions simultaneously. This service is available to application developers and is used by the other DCE components as well.

Security is a special problem in a distributed environment that could span many servers, multiple networks, and several host systems, each with their own security systems. The Security Service is incorporated into DCE's basic Fundamental Distributed Services and the Data-Sharing Services to provide integrated security. The Security Service provides three basic services: authentication, authorization, and user account management. The authentication service is based on the Kerberos system from MIT's Project Athena which validates the identity of a user or service. After a user is authenticated, the system uses the authorization services to determine which resources the user may access. User account management is facilitated with the User Registry, a single repository of user account information. This eliminates the chance of conflicts in logins and passwords. Security concerns are covered in more detail in Chapter 21.

Within the Data-Sharing Services, the Distributed File System gives users a uniform name space and file location transparency. Its log-based physical file system permits quick recovery after server failures. The Data-Sharing Services' Diskless Support provides general-purpose protocols which facilitate the use of servers' disks by low-cost diskless workstations.

DCE's attention to international standards also includes support for X.400 and the File Transfer Access and Management (FTAM). X.400, an e-mail standard, is a service specification and protocol for the encapsulation and delivery of mail messages. (It is described in Chapter 18.) FTAM is a protocol for transferring files from one computer to another. Both of these standards are at the application layer, layer seven, of the ISO model as described in Chapter 9.

DCE supports all existing, relevant POSIX standards and OSF has promised continued compatibility as POSIX evolves in the future. DCE also supports X/Open application programming interfaces.

OSF's Distributed Management Environment (DME) is a vendor-neutral platform for managing distributed systems and distributed networks. This topic will be covered in Chapter 11.

4.2.3.2 OSF's Architecture Neutral Distribution Format (ANDF)

One of the most interesting projects within OSF is its Architecture-Neutral Distribution Format (ANDF). Its goal is impressive: the availability of portable, shrink-wrapped software that would work on a wide variety of computer systems. ANDF is a set of tools with the goal of permitting developers to create a single version of an application which could be installed on computers with different hardware architectures and operating systems. Today, even if vendors write their software in C—which is quite portable—there are still problems. As a result, vendors wind up writing different versions of their software for different computer architectures. Not all vendors can afford that.

Such software portability would, of course, offer many benefits. Hardware innovations could take place without disrupting existing production applications. Portability could also significantly increase a software package's installed base since it could be used in more environments.

Applications are usually distributed in compiled, object code form to protect source code confidentiality. However, every computer requires its own compiler, and different compilers can introduce unexpected and undesirable changes in an application's behavior. Even the most "portable code" can experience difficulties.

To overcome such difficulties, ANDF provides a compiler intermediate language which protects source code yet allows for hardware differences. The source code compilation is divided into two procedures. First, the source code is processed with the ANDF *producer* which vendors would use to create the ANDF code for distribution to customers. Then, the end user processes this ANDF code with the ANDF *installer* which is unique for the specific machine at the end user's site. The ANDF installer creates the executable code for that system.

The UNIX Systems Laboratory has taken a significant interest in the ANDF project. OSF and USL have pledged to work together to achieve synergy and rapid delivery of ANDF technology to the open systems marketplace. The two groups have specifically said that they will deliver a single ANDF specification to the marketplace.

4.3   OTHER FACTORS

4.3.1   Open Transaction Monitors

Transaction requirements for two-phase commit are described in Chapter 13. Two-phase commit is a protocol for ensuring that a transaction successfully updates all appropriate files in a distributed database architecture. RPC mechanisms by themselves do not have a notion of two-phase commit. If a two-phase commit procedure is required when a developer is using RPCs, that functionality will need to be added.

4.3.1.1   Encina

Encina, from Transarc Corporation in Pittsburgh, Pa. is an example of a a transaction monitor that extends the DCE RPC with transaction semantics. Encina was built specifically to work with OSF's DCE. Figure 4.3 shows the Encina architecture. The base services of Encina are layered on top of DCE and include the Encina Toolkit Executive and the Toolkit Server Core.

The Encina Toolkit Executive consists of a number of core APIs for defining transactional clients and servers. It includes:

- Transactional-C, (TRAN-C) a high-level API that provides transaction demarcation, concurrency control, and exception handling.
- Transactional RPC (TRPC) extends the DCE RPC with transaction properties.
- The Distributed Transaction Service (TRAN), based on the two-phase commit protocol, is the means by which a consensus is reached among the transaction participants as to whether to commit or to abort. A transaction coordinator polls all participants to determine the success or failure of its action.
- The Base Development Environment (BDE) isolates operating system dependencies of Encina. As Encina is ported to different operating system, the BDE calls (e.g., file I/O, memory allocation, POSIX threading) are reimplemented.

The Toolkit Server Core provides services to support the storage and maintenance of recoverable data and includes an X/Open XA interface to permit interoperability with compliant databases.

The upper tier of services shown in Figure 4.3 are called the Extended TP Services. The Structured File Server (SFS) is a record-oriented file system with full transactional capabilities. The Recoverable Queuing Service (RQS) provides for transactional queuing and dequeuing of data. The full-feature TP Monitor provides a development, execution, and administrative environment. The Peer-to-Peer Communication (PPC) Services include the PPC Executive which lets Encina platforms carry on transactional peer-to-peer conversations over TCP/IP and the PPC Gateway/SNA which permits communication to mainframe systems that support LU6.2 (e.g., CICS.)

4.3.1.2 Tuxedo

Tuxedo, originally from UNIX System Laboratory, is another example of a transaction monitor. Tuxedo's Enterprise Transaction Processing (ETP) environment is shown in Figure 4.4. Tuxedo expects that the typical ETP system configuration will consist of personal workstations on tier 1, UNIX transaction processing servers on tier 2, and proprietary transaction processing systems like CICS on a tier 3 mainframe host. This configuration reflects a situation where firms are gradually downsizing on-line transaction processing (OLTP) systems installed on mainframes. Applications are integrated across the tiers by a common TP application programming interface (TP-API) within Tuxedo.

Tuxedo provides two-phase commit as well as capabilities like trans-

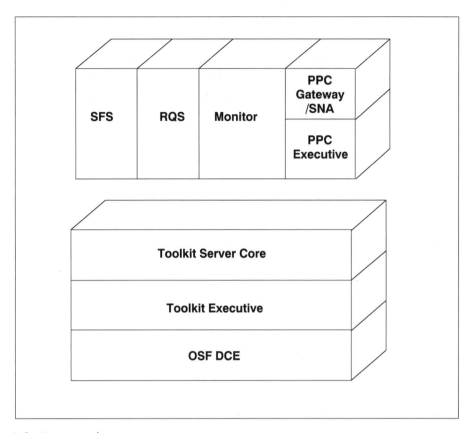

Figure 4.3 Encina architecture.

action name and queuing services. It supports publicly available standard interfaces like the ATMI and XA, both from X/Open.

4.3.1.3   Top End

Top End is the DTP software from NCR Corporation. It was built specifically for OLTP open system environments and for client/server environments. Like the Tuxedo system, Top End ensures global transaction integrity by supporting the X/Open-compliant two-phase commit protocol. It does so in a way that makes the two-phase commit protocol transparent to applications.

Top End consists of the following components:

- Application Server instances
- Transaction Manager

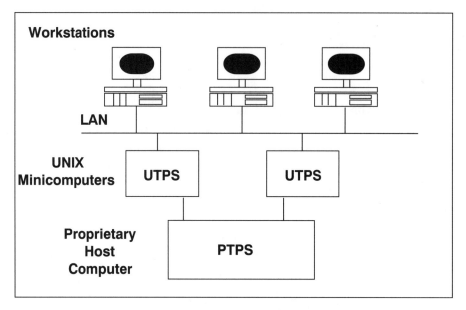

Figure 4.4 Tuxedo's enterprise transaction processing environment.

- Resource Manager
- Communications Resource Manager
- Network Interface

These components are designed for a distributed message-passing environment. The Application Server instance executes application programs. The Transaction Manager performs transaction routing, commit and rollback, security and timer functions, and regulates execution within a processing node. The Resource Manager manages resources, while the Communications Resource Manager provides the ability for application programs to communicate. The Network Interface permits separate Top End Transaction Managers to communicate with other transaction managers on the network.

Top End components are distributed across the network to support applications in a distributed environment. Top End keeps track of the components that are distributed across the network and uses this information for dynamic workload balancing.

4.3.2 The Battle Over Open Systems

An interesting thing about open systems advocates is how often they are at open warfare with each other. Individuals who easily accept de facto standards may say, "The Open Software Foundation sponsors open systems," while others who support only de jure standards might say, "No, OSF is just a consortium—a *gang* of proprietary vendors."

There are also disagreements among people who actively promote de jure standards. Some are flexible while others adamantly say that only formal standards bodies like ISO, IEEE, and ANSI can establish standards. Supporters of de facto standards sometimes refers to adamant de jure standards promoters as "standards bigots." One of the few things warring open systems advocates usually seem to agree on is how close-minded the others are. Some large companies have large in-house staffs of people working on opposite sides of this war. The political ramifications make for interesting fireworks.

Basically this argument is a disagreement over whether de facto standards or de jure standards should be the basis for open systems. Proponents of each side actually have a lot of merit in what they say. As mentioned earlier, de jure standards are those that are established by formal standards bodies and de facto standards are determined by popularity and wide usage in the marketplace. The advocates of de jure standards say that these international standards have been carefully worked out in a forum that is fair to all parties concerned. The advocates of de facto standards say that de facto standards have been selected by the most important forum—the paying customers.

Of the various open systems groups discussed in this chapter, advocates of de jure standards generally seem to support X/Open more than they support OSF. X/Open seems to bring warring parties together. Observers remember that when OSF and UNIX International were fighting, X/Open was one thing they both agreed on.

OSF is working to be more in compliance with X/Open specifications which may win it additional support. As a result, some large companies that have both de jure and de facto advocates see OSF as at least a temporary middle-ground until more products conform to international standards.

An interesting development in open systems in recent years has been the change in IBM's attitude. For many years, IBM had a reputation for promoting its own proprietary products; it was in IBM's business interest to do so. Now—due to the pressure of the marketplace—it is in IBM's business interest to help its customers in their quest for open systems. IBM has made some very important strides in this direction—one of the most significant is its support for OSI.

IBM says that its customers are making it very clear that they are interested in open systems. In the fall of 1992, IBM opened the IBM Open Systems Center a few miles from the Dallas/Fort Worth airport. Texas was chosen due to its fairly central location within the country, hopefully making it accessible to more people. IBM says the Open Systems Center is where its customers can come to find out how open systems solutions from IBM can solve their business problems through the effective use of information technology.

4.3.3 Specific Standards of Wide Interest

Standards are discussed in many places in this book. The Open Systems Interconnection Communications Reference Model of the International Standards Organization is described in Chapter 9. Local area networking standards such as 802.3, 802.4, and 802.5, which were established by the CCITT, are also described in that chapter.

Two other international standards that are of wide interest are X.400 and X.500, which are also established by the CCITT.

The X.400 standard deals with handling messaging requirements across multivendor computer platforms and diverse protocols. X.400 establishes interchange specifications for E-mail, voice, graphics, facsimile, and video text. However, most implementations of X.400 are related to E-mail. X.500 is a directory standard. It is capable of finding people, computers, networks, and other devices across diverse networks on a worldwide basis. The X.400 and X.500 standards are discussed in Chapter 18 along with de facto standards that apply to E-mail.

5
DOWNSIZING

5.1 WHAT IS DOWNSIZING?

The term downsizing in information processing refers to the process of taking an application system that is running on a larger machine and moving it to a smaller, less expensive machine. Often this means taking a system that is running on a mainframe and moving it to a minicomputer (mid-range computer) or to a LAN-based client/server system. It can also mean moving a system from a minicomputer to a LAN-based client/server system.

Downsized systems are not necessarily smaller *systems*. The term "downsizing" generally does not refer to items like the size of the application itself, the number of transactions processed, or the number of records in a database. Very often, all that remains the same, but it is processed on hardware and software that is far less expensive. This less expensive equipment is usually smaller, resulting in the term "downsizing." Usually, there are additional motivations for downsizing. A major one is the increased productivity that results from letting end users work with GUIs and have direct access to data from their desktop PCs.

5.1.1 Similarities Between Client/Server and Downsizing

There is a clear relationship between downsizing and client/server computing. The growing abundance of, and the increasing quality of, client/server software is making downsizing possible. The market for client/server software dramatically increased in size in the early 1990s. This increased usage resulted in a growing number of new vendors who were willing to raise venture capital to create sturdier client/server software and existing vendors who were willing to invest in creating client/server versions of their mainframe application packages.

Each year, the number of high-powered client/server tools increases. As even more sophisticated client/server tools become available, the trend toward downsizing is bound to increase. In the early 1990s some mainframe-based installations hesitated to investigate client/server computing because it did not have the systems infrastructure that has been built up around the mainframe for over thirty years. This systems infrastructure includes software like change and configuration management, sorts and merges, network management, and similar systems administrative tools. However, the quality of system management tools for a client/server environment is constantly improving. These issues are covered in more detail in Chapter 14.

Since downsizing and client/server systems are so closely entwined, the issues raised throughout this book for client/server systems also apply to downsized systems.

5.1.2   Other Types of Resizing

The term "downsizing" is used in fields other than just information processing. In general, the word means "to make smaller," and during the early 1990s that became a common direction for many firms. Worldwide competition and slow economies resulted in firms wanting to be "lean and mean." They wanted to earn more money with fewer people, raising their overall efficiency. Frequently, that meant layoffs with many people losing their jobs.

As a result of this use the term, many people in information systems do not like the term "downsizing." They are afraid it could mean that *they* are downsized out of a job.

Some people suggest the term "rightsizing " instead. They say this is more appropriate anyway, since what is being done is putting the right portion of the system on the right platform. This was a particularly effective argument in some early downsizing/rightsizing systems which kept data on the mainframe, but moved simple data reads (e.g., query functions) to a personal computer. Unfortunately, the term "rightsizing" had a problem. Many people felt that it implied that the system was "wrong" prior to the "rightsizing." So a good bet is that the term "downsizing" will be around for a while.

The term "upsizing" has its place in the client/server distributed computing arena. When PCs first came out, many individuals in separate departments bought them out of their departmental budgets. They also bought software like the spreadsheet Lotus 1–2–3, and single-user PC-based databases like dBase which was originally brought out by Ashton-Tate, a firm in Torrance, CA, but is now owned by Borland International in Scotts Valley, CA. As time went on, some of the systems, originally built for just one end user, assumed more and more importance in the enterprise. People in other departments bought the same packages and started doing similar things. Groups of end users shared data across the systems. Some of these systems are important enough to move up from a single-user environment to a server-based environment where it is much simpler for people in different departments to share the software and data files. Moving an application from an individual PC to a LAN-based server is called upsizing.

5.1.3 Primary Reasons to Downsize

A major reason for downsizing is cost savings. However, as a section below will explain, there are "hidden" costs in downsizing. Cost savings are not always the primary factor; some sites downsize for anticipated productivity from GUIs for end users and easy-to-use application development tools for developers.

There have been many instances where companies have saved a great deal of money as a result of downsizing. We will provide examples of this later in this chapter. One downsizing experience described in a later chapter explains how a site was saved in the neighborhood of $2,000,000 a year when they were able to cancel a timesharing contract on a mainframe. Downsizing is an area where case histories are welcome reading, because these instances *prove* that it can be done. However, there are precautions that one must take if a client/server downsizing effort is to be successful. The entire configuration—hardware and software—must be analyzed to make sure it is adequate. The reader of case histories should also keep in mind that successful implementors are willing to describe their experiences, while unsuccessful ones are not eager to advertise their failures.

5.2 ISSUES RELATED TO DOWNSIZING

A frequent question heard at downsizing conferences and seminars is "Are some applications more appropriate for downsizing?" At one time only a limited number of systems were appropriate for downsizing. Now, many of the limitations of early client/server systems have improved so much that many mission-critical systems are being downsized.

5.2.1 The Hidden Costs of Downsizing

When calculating the savings that can be gained by downsizing, one must not rely solely on hardware and software costs. Intel-based microcomputers and RISC machines are becoming faster than minicomputers and are aiming to reach the speeds of mainframes, yet they are far less expensive. These cost differences are easy to see. They are dramatic and widely-publicized. However, they are not the only costs a downsizing site will incur. Many other costs go along with changing *any* computer environment, and there are some unique costs that accompany a downsized environment.

The reason why we refer to the "hidden costs" of downsizing is because there are costs that many sites do not think of or even know of during the time they are making their analysis. They may be aware that with any conversion there will be training costs. However, the training costs associated with moving from a mainframe to a client/server environment cannot be compared to the cost of changing from one mainframe database to another—even though those costs are high enough. Developers and programmers will have to be trained; end users and data entry personnel will have to be trained; new categories of personnel will have to be hired or trained (system integrators, LAN administrators, etc.); and information systems managers will have to learn to manage in new ways.

The cost of retraining everyone involved has been cited as the biggest area of cost overruns. Many sites are surprised with the extent of training that is involved. Event programming (covered in the GUI section of Chapter 2) is a completely new way of thinking for some programmers with many years of experience. People who are resistant to new approaches will take much longer to learn new systems. It is often to an installation's benefit to retain these individuals because they know the existing systems so well. An interesting side benefit of client/server systems is that installations will not be as dependent on specific programmers' knowledge of existing production systems. Client/server systems will be easier for a newcomer to learn than the old mainframe systems were. The individuals in demand in the new environment will be those who are most flexible and can adapt to a constantly changing environment.

IS managers may now be *sharing responsibility* for overall development and operation of systems with people from whom they previously received services or for whom provided services. For example, mainframe shops were often set up so that the data communications section provided services for the developers and programmers while end users received services from the information systems department. With the new components and architectures that exist in downsized systems, these separate groups of people will be working much more closely together. While teaming and cooperation among different departments has been encouraged in many enterprises, it is a necessity in the downsizing environment.

Another hidden cost could be the last minute need for faster equipment because the planned configuration cannot meet performance requirements. Hardware and software speeds that are quoted by vendors are only achieved under optimum conditions. The configuration the vendor uses to achieve that speed may not match the user's configuration at all. Even if the composition of the system is a little different, that difference could be enough to impact the overall speed of the system. As a chain is as weak as its weakest link, one slow component in a system could create a bottleneck and make the difference between success and failure. Other sections of this book address this problem. For example, the internetworking section explains that the way subnetworks are interconnected can impact a network's speed.

Systems administration and software distribution are two of the biggest hidden costs in downsizing. Systems administration issues are covered in some detail in a later chapter. It is critically important to be aware of these issues before a serious downsizing effort is started. Software distribution, which is a part of what we are calling overall systems administration, is much more complicated in a distributed environment where many individual PC or workstations all need software updates and revisions. Progress is being made with electronic software distribution. This is the only reasonable solution for the long range. The high expense of local area network administration is another cost that often surprises new users of downsized operations. Progress in the development of network administration tools is being made daily. Good tools—especially those allowing centralized control of remote servers and integrated tools—will substantially reduce the burden of network administration.

5.2.2 Candidate Applications for Downsizing

Some of the early client/server systems were data access systems. When the concept of downsizing was first being formulated, a data access system was considered to be the safest type of system as a candidate for downsizing. In the chapter on getting started with client/server systems, new systems and add-on systems that are frequently used to access data were discussed. Downsizing in many installations was first tried because of the need to access new or additional data. In many cases, mainframe data was downloaded to a server where end users could only read it. In these early systems, users were not allowed to update the data. This was controlled initially through in-house programming and was later controlled by features built into database server software. Data access systems were seen at the time as appropriate for downsizing because they were not critical to the immediate survival of the enterprise. If the system went down, the company would continue in existence.

In those early years, companies were not willing to bet the company on client/server computing. For one thing, both software and hardware were not as reliable as they are today. A lot of safety features had not yet been built in, and the capabilities for controlling data integrity were limited. Backup and recovery procedures were primitive. Many of the early problems in client/server computing are covered elsewhere in this book, so this chapter will not go into further detail. The point is that when client/server hardware and software first came out, it was true that only limited types of systems were appropriate for this environment.

This has changed dramatically in recent years. Hardware and software are more reliable, safety features are built-in, data integrity provisions exist, and backup and recovery—as well as other system management tools—have improved substantially. This completely changes the types of systems that can now be considered candidates for client/server systems.

Another limitation of client/server systems in the late 1980s was the size of the database and the number of transactions. However, servers are now available in many gigabytes and technologies like Redundant Arrays of Inexpensive Drives (RAID) are available. Transaction speeds are increasing significantly. By the early 1990s, many observers said that the only systems that were not candidates for a client/server architecture were the largest, high-volume, high-speed transaction processing systems, like credit card verification and airline reservation systems, which require the processing of hundreds of transactions per second. By early 1993, most client/server systems were running at 10-20 Transactions per second (TPS), but a few systems were being clocked at 50 TPS. These tests abided by the Transaction Processing Council's standards. Tests reaching the higher speeds were run on 486-based machines and used databases like Oracle, Gupta's SQLBase and Sybase's SQLServer on NetWare. Parallel computing and some high-powered RISC machines were being clocked at 100 TPS in the early 1990s. Transaction speeds will continue to increase. In fact, software capabilities could have a hard time keeping up with hardware speeds.

5.2.3 Downsizing Impacts Mainframe Software Pricing

Vendors with a vested interest in encouraging their customers to continue running applications on mainframes have started to alter their mainframe software pricing structure. IBM is an example of this. While a large extent of IBM income has traditionally been from mainframe hardware, the company also profited from high-priced software for mainframes. Therefore it is to IBM's advantage if customers continue to use its mainframe software packages. The same is true for any vendor that predominantly sells mainframe software.

In 1992, vendors introduced what they called partitioned pricing. The purpose of this plan was to give customers who were most likely to downsize a reason to stay on the mainframe—or at least to reduce their incentive to take on the cost burden of moving their software to another platform. Under this plan, vendors charged customers based on the amount of the processor resource that the software package consumed. If the software used less than fifty percent of the mainframe's resources, the customer received a lower price for the software. Since customers would incur an additional cost burden if they converted their software to another machine, the reduced price of the mainframe software lessened the cost reward of downsizing.

IBM devised a plan whereby software that used less than half of the computer's capacity would be discounted up to 30%. Additional discounts were available for customers who had multiple machines running the same software.

There are a number of issues related to pricing software using such schemes. For example, one problem is finding a good way to automate tracking what software is running on a particular processor and how much of that processor the software is consuming. Other issues relate to the fact that software usage peaks at certain times during the day as well as during key periods such as month- or year-end processing. Many users feel that new pricing formulas do not adequately take into consideration these peak processing periods.

Other pricing models that have been studied include user-based pricing and a lending library approach. Under the former a variety of user characteristics enter into the pricing picture, and under the latter customers would be charged for the amount of time they had the software checked out of—that is, downloaded from—the vendor's software library.

Vendors will continue to explore new options and ideas related to software pricing. They say they are listening to feedback from customers regarding what is fair and will continue to refine their approach over time.

5.3   DOWNSIZING EXPERIENCES

At first it was hard for information systems departments to believe that mainframe-based systems could run on a LAN-based server system. As actual experiences became publicized, there was initial skepticism, with the suspicion that vendor-hype was really behind it all. However, as more and more experiences became documented, more sites started to trust what they were hearing and reading.

5.3.1 Timesharing Demise Saves Close to $2,000,000 a Year

One of the most dramatic cost savings from a downsizing project was realized by the Navy's Pacific Missile Test Center in Point Mugu, CA. This site had been renting time on a 3090 mainframe from Litton Industries. They were paying over $2,000,000 a year to keep the system running on the 3090 and to receive related telecommunications and report generation services. When they downsized to a client/server environment, they were able to immediately point to the fact that the annual bill for $2,000,000 no longer existed. Of course the cost of the new system needs to be subtracted from that figure, but still Point Mugu realized a very dramatic savings. Most sites will not realize anywhere near that kind of savings from downsizing, especially in the early years of the new system. However, this example indicates that timesharing situations are good candidates for downsizing.

This particular downsizing project took place relatively early in the evolution of client/server systems. Before the end of 1990, the Point Mugu site had ported their 3090-based weapons system to an 80486. This was so early in the game that after the system was operational, Judith Farrar, the program manager, said they were not working with leading edge technology but with "bleeding edge technology." They had a lot of challenges to overcome because so little experience with downsized, client/server systems existed at that time. Farrar said that when they decided to downsize in 1989, everyone told them they were crazy. She adds that after the system was operational and successful, those skeptics became believers.

The downsized application was the Navy's Configuration and Data Management Support System, (CADMSS) which had more than 3 gigabytes of data related to the status of weapons systems. A number of other Navy sites provide data to Point Mugu including the Naval Weapons Center in China Lake, CA, and the Naval Warfare Assessment Center in Corona, CA.

The decision to change platforms came at a time when Point Mugu's contract to rent time on Litton's 3090 was coming to an end. CADMSS was built using a combination of software, (Cincom's Total and a lesser known package called Envirol), for which there was not much expertise. Point Mugu could not find a contractor or resources within the Navy to maintain the software, and their budget did not allow for buying or building new software for a mainframe-based system. They examined various alternatives, but each one took more money than they had available. There was extremely valuable data in the CADMSS data base, but the dilemma was where to house it and how to access it. That is when they started examining what they called "PC-based" alternatives.

The CADMSS data base is one of three data bases with status, logistics, and maintenance data on airborne weapons systems under the authority of the Airborne Weapons Information System (AWIS). Technicians from AWIS performed a lot of the research that indicated that the CADMSS system could operate with adequate performance on a 486. The software configuration involved Oracle Corporation's Oracle database along with other Oracle software. The original hardware configuration included a Tandem 486 25 MHz computer with a small computer system interface (SCSI) driver to connect up to seven 766Mb hard drives and digital audio tape (DAT) storage devices. The original DAT equipment was able to store 1.2G of data on a single tape.

The new system cost approximately $120,000 to build. In addition, Navy personnel at Point Mugu are now less dependent on contractors to keep their systems running. They operate the system themselves, securing additional savings.

The system was not without its problems. The most severe problem was a system crash after they were operational for several months. Eight employees worked in shifts around the clock for over a week to get the system up and running again. The crash was attributed to incompatibilities between the SCSI drivers and network drivers. They had two network drivers installed: an Excelan Ethernet driver and an Interlan Ethernet driver. That experience was part of the reason for the reference to "bleeding edge" technology.

After all the difficulties were solved, AWIS was so happy with the system that they immediately started work on converting the other two systems to a client/server architecture.

5.3.2   From IMS to SQL Server

Chevron Canada chose to downsize as much for improved productivity and efficiency as for cost savings. The combination of their manual and computerized procedures were no longer adequate—especially since the Canadian deregulation of crude oil in 1985. In a market where world oil prices can change dramatically from one day to the next, they needed a system that would help all their end users—purchasing, marketing, and billing, among others.

In mid-1989, when Chevron decided to look at alternatives, field agents hand–wrote delivery notes and then forwarded the customer invoice to Vancouver, B.C. In Vancouver, actuaries manually priced products using a desk calculator and a price-listings book. Their calculations were entered by data entry clerks and sent in nightly batches to an IMS system on an IBM 3090 in San Francisco. The computer sent an invoice to the customer. That could be two weeks later. An additional disadvantage of the system was that the field agents could not immediately determine how current their customers were with their payments.

One of the most important requirements of the new system was to permit field offices to access data they needed. Chevron Canada wanted to let field agents in 35 different remote sites be able to easily access current data about their customer accounts and to download relevant data to their PCs where they could use the data in spreadsheets and other PC-based software tools. Some of the additional requirements of the system included: on-line transaction processing capabilities for order-entry and billing; a relational database system that would permit users to build their own views and perform ad-hoc queries; the ability to support some distributed database features like partitioned data; and referential integrity to prevent end users from deleting something inappropriately.

With the new system users can select front-end PC-based tools from a list of 100 approved products for spreadsheets, additional analysis, word processing, and other needs they may have. SQL Server is the database server. Another tool from Sybase, the prototyping APT Workbench, was used to develop the application for deployment. LAN Manager connects the 225 clients who are either using OS/2 or Windows on their PCs. Most of the client PCs at the start of the project were 286-based, AT-compatible systems, but Chevron planned a constant and consistent upgrade to new 386- and 486-based Compaq DeskPros.

5.4 MAINFRAME DOWNSIZING CONVERSION TOOLS

Some vendors have tools that will assist clients in downsizing applications that use that vendor's software. An example of this is IDMS/PC and related tools from Computer Associates in Islandia, NY. Clients who have CA-IDMS database systems running on mainframes can use IDMS/PC and other tools to convert the system to operate in a client/server environment. Computer Associates offers similar downsizing tools for other software packages in addition to IDMS. While it took a while for other mainframe vendors to adopt this strategy, some of them are now offering such tools or are planning to do so.

Users should speak to the vendor of the mainframe software products they are currently using to see what their vendor's plans are to help their customers to downsize. While vendors would prefer to sell mainframe versions of software to clients—due to the higher price tags—they realize it is better to keep a customer than to lose the customer to another software vendor who does offer client/server software.

Sometimes the software that a vendor offers for the client/server environment is so similar to the mainframe version that the transition is simple, fast, relatively headache-free, and quite inexpensive. When the software offered can make such a transition quickly, the process is referred to as "rapid downsizing," which was described in Chapter 3.

6

CLIENT TOOLS

6.1   CLIENT SOFTWARE

Client software represents the "front-end" portion of a client/server application in a DOS/Windows, OS/2/Presentation Manager, or Macintosh environment. Client software lets the end user interact with the computer system and contains at least some application logic. While it does not *have to* have a user-friendly GUI, the great majority of client modules do provide this popular feature. Technically speaking, the most important characteristic of a client end of a client/server system is that it requests a service from the server end.

6.1.1   Characteristics of Client Software

A client front end can consist of a wide range of software. The client software can be an existing end-user tool like Lotus 1–2–3, a complex C or C++ program, or an application that has been custom-built using heavy-duty, sophisticated client/server application development tools. Many of the traditional 4GL vendors are updating their products to work as front ends in a client/server environment.

The client software can have all, most, or very little of the application logic in the overall client/server system. Some client/server systems are so simple that the application logic merely consists of SQL statements which access data from a server database. In this case, the client software might be a graphical version of the SQL statements available to the end user. The end user might, for example, make menu selections and the application would convert those selections into SQL commands.

While a GUI will make the client/server system easier to use, the client software should facilitate use of the system in other ways, too. For example, client software should make the separation of the client and server portions transparent to the end user. It should also insulate the user from the complexities of networking by simplifying access to network resources. In addition, it might simplify sharing data with other applications by taking advantage of various data exchange technologies provided by client/server software vendors.

Most client software has a GUI to facilitate user interaction, but this is not necessary. For example, DataEase International offers tools that run under Windows and other tools that run in character mode under DOS alone. The tools that run under DOS alone can also be used as client software. The primary feature that characterizes client software is not the GUI, but that it makes a request of the server.

Many front-end tools work with a wide variety of back-end tools. However, not all front-end tools work with all back-end tools. It is to each front-end vendor's advantage that its tools interoperate with as many tools from back-end vendors as possible. The reverse is true, too, of course.

Some vendors offer both front-end and back-end tools. Many database server companies are now marketing tools to be used as front ends for their server database software. Gupta Technologies, Inc., which is primarily known for its SQLBase server database, provides Quest, an excellent query and report writing tool. However, Gupta, along with other server database vendors, still welcome other client software vendors that offer front ends for their database.

As mentioned above, client software is the software that lets the end user interact with the computer. However—technically—the primary characteristic of client software is that it *makes a request* of the server software. In the DOS/Windows and OS/2/PM world, the client software provides for interaction with the end user *and* makes a request of the server software.*

6.1.2 The Evolution of Client Software

Many early client/server systems were written in C. While a good number of systems continue to be written in C, many companies are also using application development tools to create part or all of their client/server applications. There are a wide range of front-end tools available for

---

*As will be pointed out in the next chapter, in the X Window system, a *server* provides window presentations and handles input from keyboard and mouse devices. The X Window server software usually sits on a PC or workstation and is accessed by applications via the networking facilities. Applications—which may reside anywhere on the network—using the capabilities of the X Window server system are known as the *clients*. If this seems confusing, go back to the basic meaning of the terms "client" and "server." A client requests that a service and a server provides a service.

client/server applications. They range from very easy-to-use data query tools for end users to sophisticated application development environments for building mission-critical, corporate-wide applications. More sophistication is being built into tools all the time. This trend will certainly continue.

The market for sophisticated, high-powered tools is expected to grow dramatically. Forrester Research, Inc., Cambridge, MA, predicts that the market for such tools will expand from approximately $475 million in 1992 to $2.6 billion by 1995.

Front-end tools will also continue to incorporate more object-oriented capabilities. While some of the early front-end tools had GUIs with icons, few, if any, had real object-oriented capabilities. Soon, however, object-oriented tools started to appear. Then it was a matter of catch up for the earlier vendors to update their initial products, incorporating object-oriented features. For some forward-looking companies that are installing client/server systems, having object-oriented capabilities is an important requirement. In fact, large installations like Citicorp are busy building object-oriented libraries (class libraries) that will be reused by many individual client/server applications.

6.2   ROLES OF CLIENT SOFTWARE

6.2.1   The Difficulty of Classifying Client Software

Categorizing tools is difficult because there is so much overlap of features among them. In addition, vendors are constantly adding new capabilities to their software products. While industry analysts have tried to divide front-end application development tools into different categories, their results seem to vary widely. The following list indicates some of the categories that are being used to classify client/server development tools. Different analysts generally have differing subsets of these categories, and some analysts may use other categories.

- Data query (data access) tools
- Decision Support Systems (DSSs) and Executive Information Systems (EISs)
- Report writers
- Third-generation languages (3GLs)
- Fourth-generation languages (4GLs)
- Fifth-generation languages (5GLs)
- Object-oriented tools
- Transaction processing tools

• Application development environment tools

• CASE products

Many decision support tools also have report writer features, so this raises the question of into which category such tools should go. The difference between 3GLs and 4GLs is the traditional one: Cobol is a 3GL, while a product like Information Builders' Focus is a 4GL. 5GLs are sometimes defined as 4GLs with some object-oriented capabilities. This, then, raises the question of whether to categorize a tool with object-oriented capabilities as a 5GL or as an object-oriented tool. The best answer is "By the degree of object-orientedness," but most people would agree that in many cases, that could be a tough call. An example of a transaction processing tool is Cooperative Solutions' Ellipse—though Ellipse does more than just provide transaction processing capabilities; an example of an application development environment tool is Powersoft's PowerBuilder; an example of a CASE product is Anderson Consulting's Foundation. Each of these products are described in more detail elsewhere in this book.

Trying to separate products into the very broad categories of "end user tools" vs. "application development environment tools" can be difficult. For example, Gupta's Quest is an end user tool, however, it also has some fairly sophisticated capabilities. In addition to Query, Report, and Table activities, it has a Catalog activity. The Catalog activity lets one see how each table, view, column, and index is defined. Using the Catalog capabilities, the user can find out about existing tables or create new ones. The user can even create databases and database objects for personal use in addition to accessing corporate data residing on database servers, minicomputers, or mainframes. Perhaps this kind of tool should be categorized as an *end-user application development* tool. These additional features do not necessarily make the tool harder to use. Quest has an excellent reputation as a powerful, yet easy-to-use tool.

Likewise, tools that are primarily aimed at application developers often offer features for end users, too. While Advanced Revelation is oriented more for application developers, the vendor, Revelation Technologies, based in New York City, provides capabilities so that end users can easily modify their applications by themselves. PowerBuilder also has easy-to-use features that can be used by end users.

6.2.2 Software that Accesses Databases

One of the popular uses of client/server systems is to let end users access and analyze mainframe-based production data. Many data query tools are available specifically for this purpose. Sometimes the query is done directly against the actual production database on the mainframe, but more commonly the mainframe data is brought down to a server—referred to as staging the data—and accessed by the client software there. The downloaded mainframe data is often inserted into a relational server database where it can be accessed easily by end users with SQL or SQL-generating tools. By using a server as a staging or holding area for the corporate data, end users are able to query this data without impacting production schedules. Often data is downloaded just once a day, but it can be downloaded more frequently—depending on the end user's needs.

While some database query tools are dedicated to accessing data from just one database, others access a number of databases. There are many database query tools that are designed to access data from any relational database management system (RDBMS). SQL made a significant contribution to making this possible. The great majority of tools provide access to databases through SQL. The widespread implementation of SQL by RDBMS vendors offers a common vehicle through which third-party vendors can access data across multiple relational systems.

An increasing number of PC-based database query tools are also providing access to non-relational systems. Some of these tools allow users to express data requests in terms of SQL, and then the software converts the request into a format that the target database will understand. PC-based database query tools can be used to access data from any number of sources: LAN servers, minicomputers, database machines, or mainframes.

Some vendors are providing products that serve as gateways to mainframe databases for front-end tools. This allows front-end vendors to concentrate on front-end capabilities and not worry about back-end concerns. One popular product is the Database Gateway from Micro Decisionware based in Boulder, CO, which provides access to IBM's mainframe DB2 database. Other widely used products are EDA/SQL from Information Builders and Q+E from Pioneer.

Many relatively small firms started using computers just a few years ago. They found that databases like dBase or FoxPro were adequate for their needs. However, many of these firms have experienced significant growth and now have many critically important systems on different microcomputer database systems. For these companies, another category of tools which permit end users to combine data stored in multiple microcomputer databases has been developed. Such tools may let a user use data from IBM OS/2 Database Manager, dBase, FoxPro, and other PC databases.

An interesting advantage that many of these database query tools offer is that end users can load mainframe data into familiar software like spreadsheets. The users can then play "what if" games with the data or put the data in graphs. Many early client/server tools supported Microsoft's Dynamic Data Exchange (DDE), a mechanism for exchanging data with other Microsoft Windows-based applications. Now products are incorporating Microsoft's Object Linking and Embedding (OLE) which offers similar, but more advanced functionality.

6.2.3   Software for Developing Entire Applications

6.2.3.1   Software from New Vendors

Some of the first vendors to have front-end application development tools were relative newcomers to the software market. In fact, some of the earliest tools came from software firms which had been created specifically for the purpose of building tools for a client/server environment. Cooperative Solutions, Inc., based in San Jose, CA is an example of such a company. Its primary product, Ellipse, is an application development tool for building transaction processing systems in a client/server environment.

Cooperative Solutions was formed by Dennis McEvoy, Kim Worsencroft (now CEO and executive vice president, respectively), and others who had been with Tandem Computers, Inc., which is known for its fault-tolerant transaction processing technology. The founders of Cooperative Solutions had been the primary architects and developers of that technology for Tandem. From that experience, they were experts on intricate problems associated with transaction processing—such as two-phase commit and error recovery. They knew these problems were compounded in a distributed environment. They also knew that such capabilities would be critical in a client/server environment in order for people to be able to build mission-critical, distributed transaction processing applications in the client/server world. Their goal became providing these capabilities for client/server systems.

Cooperative Solutions is credited with coining the phrase "client/server transaction processing" (CSTP), which is basically on-line transaction processing in a client/server environment. James Martin, a well known writer, speaker, and consultant in information technology (IT) for nearly thirty years, provided financial backing for the firm after studying its software development plans.

Another powerful tool is PowerBuilder from Powersoft in Burlington, MA. PowerBuilder came about in an interesting way. Powersoft's original product, GrowthPower, was an integrated set of manufacturing and financial applications. When the firm searched for a development tool to create a client/server version of GrowthPower, it could not find one so it developed its own. However, PowerBuilder was created not solely for the in-house redevelopment of GrowthPower, but also as a tool to be marketed. After PowerBuilder was built, and Powersoft realized how much such a tool was in demand, it sold its manufacturing software division and concentrated on selling and further developing PowerBuilder.

Dun & Bradstreet, the large application software vendor, gave the product an important boost when it selected PowerBuilder to convert its mainframe-based application software packages to a client/server architecture.

PowerBuilder was built with object-based technology, but it retains characteristics that are familiar and comfortable to the professional developer of the 80s. As a result, developers can create systems for a graphical, client/server environment without going through a traumatic learning curve.

Part of the uniqueness of PowerBuilder is that although development takes place in an easy-to-use graphical environment, the tool meets the needs of large scale mainframe-type projects. It also supports teams of developers as well as providing a built-in repository and a shared library management system.

PowerBuilder has an "open systems" design permitting applications to be migrated to different database server environments. It initially supported Microsoft's SQL Server, Gupta's SQLBase, and Oracle Corporation's Oracle Server with support for additional databases being added over time. An example of its openness and portability is that if the developer stays close to the ANSI standard portion of Powersoft's SQL, the application that is painted will run on Oracle, SQL Server, or SQLBase.

4GL programmers are familiar with "painting" such components as data entry screens. Now they can "paint" an entire system. With PowerBuilder, developers create an application using a series of mouse-driven graphical painters: Database Painter, Application Painter, Window Painter, Menu Painter, DataWindow Painter, Script Painter, and Library Painter. Probably the most popular painter tool is the SQL-smart DataWindow which lets developers access a database without writing SQL code. DataWindow is a major innovation of PowerBuilder, acting as a window into a database. Instead of writing SQL code to format and display fields, developers paint it all instead. A developer joins two tables by clicking on a picture of the tables. In other words, PowerBuilder provides pictures for the data functions a developer needs to perform.

The painter tools let the developer select various objects (e.g., RadioButton, CommandButton, DropDownListBox, SingleLineEdit), and specify events (such as "CLICKED" or "MODIFIED") to which the objects can respond. Objects respond to events by executing scripts written in the high-level PowerScript programming language.

PowerBuilder's PowerScript is an interesting combination of object-based and procedural programming concepts. It is object-based because the scripts created by it are used to determine the behavior of objects. It is procedure-oriented because it includes a set of statements for value assignment, conditional execution, looping, and branching similar to those found in the Basic programming language.

PowerBuilder provides a highly productive, cost-effective means to migrate from the old world of procedural, terminal-based applications to the modern, graphical, object-based applications running on client PCs. It serves as a "bridge" from the old way to the new.

PowerBuilder also provides a windows-supported debugging process. The developer can have several windows open simultaneously during the debugging process. As a result it provides good tracking for what is happening. This is important because of the special requirements for debugging in an event-driven environment. PowerBuilder's debugging capabilities facilitate the entire debugging process.

6.2.3.2   Software from Traditional CASE Vendors

Many of the traditional CASE vendors (those who existed before the "client/server explosion") are revamping their products to make them suitable for generating client/server systems. Providing a LAN-based repository is one of the features they have added or are working on. A number of vendors have CASE tools that can assist with portions—but not all—of client/server system development. One of the major problems vendors experience when migrating their mainframe-oriented software application products to a client/server architecture is that traditional CASE tools were not designed to split applications between platforms.

The fact that client/server software resides on multiple platforms presents several problems for a CASE tool. What portion of the system should go on the client platform, and what should go on the server platform? The modularity of client/server systems presents another problem. With mainframe-based applications, the components that comprise the system being developed are fairly predictable and restricted. The components that could go into a client/server application, on the other hand, are far more variable. A client/server system could involve several server databases, multiple GUIs, and more than one operating system. This diversity makes the job of the client/server CASE tool far more complex.

One of the earliest vendors to provide CASE tools to help build client/

server applications was CGI Systems based in Pearl River, NY. Several years ago, CGI ported their mainframe-based PACBASE CASE tool to a PC LAN environment. The resulting PACLAN set of tools has a LAN-based repository and front-end design tools which can design applications for a wide variety of platforms. PACLAN's lower CASE tool components can generate some of the code for the client/server application.

Some of the other vendors that are actively involved in providing client/server CASE tools are Anderson Consulting, Intersolv Inc., KnowledgeWare, Seer Technologies, Sybase, and Texas Instruments.

6.2.4   Application Software Packages

Many of the large application software package vendors are providing client/server versions of their mainframe or minicomputer-based products. Many of them are using application development tools to create their client/server products.

D&B announced that it will develop client/server versions of its mainframe-based application software using the PowerBuilder toolset as previously mentioned. D&B said it will provide the new modules in a time-phased manner, allowing customers to incrementally adopt the new technology while maintaining current systems investments. D&B said it will also distribute the PowerBuilder toolset with its applications, letting customers tailor those applications to their own specific requirements.

D&B is the world's largest provider of financial information, human resources, material management, manufacturing, and higher education software products. The firm serves more than 10,000 customers worldwide, including most of the **Fortune 500** companies. The introduction of client/server products from such a large vendor will have an important impact on the movement toward client/server systems. It will lend credibility to the client/server architecture in the eyes of IS managers who have hesitated to adopt it for more than simple data query applications.

6.3   SELECTING CLIENT SOFTWARE

6.3.1   Selection Issues

The choice of front-end client software depends on many things. First, of course, it depends on what the particular application is supposed to do. The objectives of the application will determine what software components are purchased or built to accomplish that objective. Just as with any other tool selection process, a prioritized list of all the requirements of the planned application is necessary. The products available are then compared to the list of requirements, and the original list is narrowed to a subset of products that meet the major requirements. These products are then examined in detail until a final selection is made.

When a company first explores the use of client/server systems, the early systems that are implemented are often limited by the hardware and software capabilities that already exist in the company. If the site is already a heavy DOS and Windows user, client products that rely on the UNIX-based X Window system are probably not good candidates to consider initially. However, after a while, a company's long-range client/ server strategy can determine what new software, hardware, and networking equipment will be purchased. For example, some companies that place a high value on open systems are switching to open-based UNIX systems even though they already have a substantial investment in DOS and Microsoft Windows-based systems. In many of these companies, the long-range strategic direction is to make new purchases that will aid in their eventual migration to open UNIX-based systems.

However, in initial client/server implementations, a practical consideration is the various capabilities that already exist. Items that should be considered are the existing client platforms (PC or workstation), the operating system (DOS with Microsoft Windows, OS/2, UNIX, etc.), the software on the server end, and the networking capabilities. The various components that are assembled for a client/server system must be able to work together. Therefore a piece of client software cannot be selected in isolation.

For example, if the primary goal of the application is to access data, a major consideration is what database—or databases—the client software needs to access. If a PC must access data from DB2, then clearly the client software that is to be considered must offer this capability. Another important consideration is which operating systems and networking software must be supported. In a strictly UNIX shop, products that run only on DOS can be eliminated. But before too many products are eliminated, it is wise to check with the vendor. Vendors are porting their software products to additional platforms all the time. However, if a vendor promises future support for a particular platform potential customers should make sure the delivery data is firm and will meet their scheduling needs before committing to it.

Similar considerations should be applied to networking software. Users who have only Microsoft's LAN Manager and want to keep it that way will not be interested in a product that runs exclusively on Novell networks. Most database query products operate with several network products, and many vendors are adding to these capabilities constantly. But again, anyone who is interested in something a vendor plans to deliver in the future should see how firm the vendor's delivery date is and what its past record in meeting target dates has been.

Good portability and interoperability capabilities are additional criteria that many companies are including when they evaluate client/server software. These capabilities add to a product's openness. Open systems are more and more desirable as computer systems spread throughout an enterprise. Large enterprises have a diversity of hardware platforms, operating systems, and networking products. A tool that can function in many of these environments is more valuable than a more limited tool.

Interoperability is also increased by a tool's ability to share data and procedures with other applications. As mentioned earlier, many tools support Microsoft's DDE. The ability of DDE to share data among various Windows-based tools offers increased flexibility for applications. DDE permits automatic information exchange between applications. Figures in a spreadsheet are often used to create graphics which will appear in a word processing document. DDE can link the applications so that a change in the spreadsheet will create a corresponding change in the related word processing document.

Many tools also support Microsoft's Dynamic Link Library (DLL). DLL facilitates sharing common software routines. Custom functions written in languages such as C can be incorporated into applications through dynamic link libraries. By supporting a capability like DLL, products not only have added flexibility, they also have increased power.

Microsoft's Object Linking and Embedding (OLE) is another technique that adds power to vendor products and user applications. OLE goes further than DDE because it can launch a different application from within the currently operating application. The simplest example of this is provided by a word processing document that has a graphic within it. Suppose a user is currently working in the word processing software when he or she sees the graphic and wants to make a change to it. The user just clicks on the graphic; this action launches the graphics application software so the user can make the change. Without OLE, the user would have to make the word processing software inactive, activate the graphics software, make the change, and then replace the existing graphic in their document with the modified one.

There are several other features that are available in various front-end tools. For example, tools vary in their ability to shield the developer from details of the system calls necessary to produce the GUI. If high-level function calls to produce items like radio buttons, push buttons, list boxes, and pull-down menus, are well integrated with the development environment, GUI development work can be facilitated.

A variety of miscellaneous items must also be considered. For example, the tool should be examined to determine how it integrates with server tools. If reports are needed, the available report formats should be reviewed. If SQL is being used, does the vendor support current SQL standards? The list could go on and on. Each company will need to develop a list of its most important requirements.

In addition, the vendor's licensing arrangement should be analyzed to see if it fits the needs of the user. Some vendors provide a standard development package which allows a number of developers to use the tool. However, many products require that a separate license be purchased for each developer. If a runtime environment is required to execute the completed application, the runtime licensing requirements will need to be determined.

Vendors are constantly modifying and improving their software products. It is always a good idea to keep in touch with vendors to check on the latest developments in their products.

6.3.2 A Wish List of Features

Many features are desirable in an ideal client/server application development suite of tools. Of course, most of the desirable features of a traditional development environment tool would also apply to a client/server tool set. The following characteristics represent some of the most desirable features for client/server application development tools. This list might provide food for thought for things to look for in such a tool set.

- Functions with widely-used operating systems
- Provides complete support for team development
- Provides a LAN-based repository that can be shared concurrently by all developers
- Supports popular GUIs
- Supports standard SQL specifications
- Supports all of the popular LAN software
- Provides a graphically-oriented code generator
- Provides a windows-supported debugging process
- Has good object-oriented capabilities
- Comes with easy-to-understand documentation
- Provides a good infrastructure of object-oriented class libraries
- Has an industrial-strength programming language or can generate the code for most or all of the client/server application

- Assists with transparent integration of diverse client/server components
- Supports portability and interoperability
- Has a vendor-supported, highly responsive hot-line
- Is committed to supporting evolving standards over time
- Is provided by a financially strong vendor that will endure competitive shake outs

6.4 EXAMPLES OF CLIENT TOOLS

The remainder of this chapter provides an overview of some of the many client/server tools that are available. This list represents a sampling of the large number of products that are on the market at the present time. Current tools range from products like Interactive Image's Easel, originally built to add graphical interfaces to 3270-type screens, to offerings like Powersoft's PowerBuilder, built for industrial-strength application development with the most advanced object-oriented techniques. A wide variety of tools for many different purposes are available, with new ones appearing every day.

The following product overviews describe the features each tool had during its early years. As time passes, vendors continually add features to their products. Prospective users should call the vendors for updates on products in which they are interested.

6.4.1 Asymetrix's Toolbook

Toolbook is an object-oriented toolkit that allows developers and end users to produce custom applications without using traditional programming languages. Toolbook, introduced in May, 1990 by Asymetrix in Bellevue, WA, was popular from its introduction, receiving awards from various trade journals in the U.S. and Europe. In fact, a French magazine referred to the product and its diverse capabilities as the Swiss Army knife of application development.

Toolbook is used as a front end for database access and is known for its flexibility and ease of use. dBase capabilities are built into Toolbook, and connectivity is possible not only to dBase files, but also to dbVista, Microsoft's SQL Server, Paradox, Novell SQL, and Btrieve files.

Asymetrix offers a Toolbook Multimedia Resource Kit which permits even first-time developers to cut-and-paste full multimedia functionality into applications. It also offers capabilities like a prebuilt VCR-like control panel. This control panel can be pasted directly into an application providing features like play, pause, stop, fast-forward, and rewind. In addition, there are other objects for sound and animation which can also be added to an application without programming—just with cutting and pasting. It features more than 85 fully functional prescribed multimedia objects, called widgets, that can be pasted into an application by the user.

6.4.2   Borland's Paradox SQL Link

Paradox SQL Link from Borland, located in Scotts Valley, CA, provides access to a number of data sources. Originally, support was provided for IBM's OS/2 Database Management System, Microsoft's SQL Server, and Oracle Server. Subsequently, additional support was provided for data access to DB2 through Micro Decisionware's Database Gateway and other servers. Borland also offers a Paradox connection to Digital Equipment Corporation's Rdb/VMS as a separate product, Paradox SQL Link for Rdb.

Borland offers products to help both end users and program developers. End users can use query-by-example (QBE) for ad hoc query, while programmers can use the Paradox Application Language (PAL), a programming language, for application development. PAL is part of an application development environment which comes with a built-in script editor and interactive debugger.

Paradox SQL Link, according to Borland, has been designed to work as simply and intuitively as possible. End users do not have to learn SQL. Instead, end users can use the QBE format which is then translated by Paradox SQL Link into SQL format. Borland says it provided the first PC-based implementation of QBE—which was first developed by IBM for 3270-terminal and mainframe use.

Data in relational databases residing in a server on the network is queried as though the data were contained in local Paradox tables. Paradox users select a table and then enter the query criteria in a QBE form. Paradox translates the query into the proper SQL dialect, communicates with the server, and places the answer records into a Paradox-format table. At this point, the table may be further queried, reported on, graphed or otherwise manipulated. Paradox SQL Link automatically handles everything related to communications between the workstation and SQL server whenever data is accessed.

6.4.3   DataEase International's DataEase SQL

DataEase SQL from DataEase International, Inc., Trumbull, CT, is used both by end users who need a query tool and by application developers who need a full-strength development package. End users generally use the menu-driven features of DataEase to create queries and then build a simple application around the queries, adding sophistication over time. Users can also create reports by selecting from a list of choices, filling in blanks, "painting" screens, and/or using QBE techniques.

Meanwhile, programmers have a strong set of application development tools for building production-oriented systems. Programmers can use the DataEase Query Language (DQL) which is DataEase's 4GL. Data can be accessed from the DataEase relational database or from a variety of other databases.

Microsoft's SQL Server was the first database DataEase supported. Then, over time, DataEase provided support for Oracle Server, IBM OS/2 Database Manager, Micro Decisionware's Database Gateway for DB2, and Teradata DBC/1012. One of DataEase's goals was to permit end users and developers to transparently combine information from many sources for queries, transaction processing, and decision support.

DataEase Prism, which is part of the DataEase SQL product, helps overcome difficulties with integrating multiple vendor-supplied server and front-end tools. Prism consists of the following four components:

1. client API
2. server API
3. repository
4. client/server processor

The client API of Prism is designed to permit easy connection to any client tool, including analytical tools, decision support, application development, or CASE tools. It also allows multiple tools to access data simultaneously.

6.4.4 Easel Corporation's Easel

Easel from Easel Corporation in Burlington, MA, was originally built to help enhance existing host applications by adding a GUI to them. In May 1989, Easel Corporation entered into a product development and marketing agreement with IBM. Big Blue wanted Easel to offer IBM's huge customer base the ability to add GUIs to its mainframe applications. Many observers credit this relationship with Easel's initial rapid growth. As a result, many developers think only of "front ending" when they think of Easel, however; it is also evolving into an application development environment.

The Easel development system consists of a high-level, event-driven programming language that is non-procedural. Visual programming tools automatically prompt the developer for optional conformance to IBM's SAA/CUA standards. Easel Corporation has added some object-oriented capabilities and supports IBM's Audio Capture Playback Adapter, allowing programmers to incorporate digitized sound as part of an application.

Two business modules are part of Easel Corporation's overall product offering called the Managers Portfolio. These modules consist of: Easelview, which helps create applications that access data and graphically display data in PC-based reports; and Stockwatch, which is an interface to the Dow Jones News/Retrieval service. Another module is Easeloffice, a GUI for IBM's Professional Office System (PROFS).

6.4.5   Gupta Corporation's Quest and SQLWindows

Gupta Technologies, Inc., Menlo Park, CA, offers both Quest and SQLWindows as tools for accessing data using a PC. Quest is intended for end users and SQLWindows is for programmers. Gupta regards SQLWindows as its 4GL application development system for creating Windows applications. SQLWindows provides pre-defined objects like forms, fields, menus, list boxes, and push buttons, which are associated with event-driven logic. To assist programmers who have difficulty getting used to event-driven programming, Gupta provides a step-by-step guide to walk them through the event-driven development process.

SQLWindows has an good reputation for being able to help programmers create industrial-strength transaction processing front ends that are quite robust. Since SQLWindows development can be somewhat complex, Gupta offers tools to make the product easier to use. For example, ReportWindows is a tool to help users create reports quickly, while Express Windows allows a user to develop a master-detail form quickly without writing program code.

Quest is designed to meet the needs of the end user who wants to perform the functions of data access, report generation, query, and analysis without doing any programming. It is geared to the business professional who needs point-and-click access to corporate databases. Quest can also be used by the SQLWindows user who wants to develop ad hoc reports and queries from SQL-accessible data.

Using Quest, users can create, edit, and browse SQL tables; issue simple to complex queries; and build reports using corporate databases without any programming or knowledge of SQL. Quest also supports simultaneous access of data from a number of SQL databases including

DB2, Oracle, OS/2 Database Manager, Gupta's SQLBase, Microsoft's SQL Server, and Novell's NetWare SQL.

Quest also offers extensive data transfer and exchange capabilities. It provides the ability to transfer data between Quest and other Windows applications like Excel, Microsoft Word, and Pagemaker. The user can also import and export data tables between SQL, ASCII, and dBase file formats.

6.4.6 Information Builder's EDA/SQL

Information Builder's Enterprise Data Access (EDA/SQL) is a tool that can be used to access data from a wide variety of databases. It is described in detail in Chapter 12.

6.4.7 Microsoft's Visual Basic

Visual Basic from Microsoft in Redmond, WA, is a graphical application development system for Microsoft Windows. It is a derivative of Microsoft Quick Basic, modified for the graphical and event-driven environment. Virtual Basic combines visual design tools with Basic, one of the most widely used general purpose programming languages. The product is targeted at a range of users, including professional developers, part-time programmers like engineers, scientists, analysts, and educators, and general PC "power users" who want to create their own Windows applications. Microsoft says Visual Basic does not require programming experience, but user familiarity with general programming concepts is helpful.

The Visual Basic programming system can be used to develop many different types of Windows-based applications, including front ends for database access to mainframes, server, or local databases. The Visual Basic Library is built on Microsoft's standard SQL Server API called DB-Library. The Visual Basic Library and SDK can be used to build applications that access Microsoft SQL Server and tap into DB2 and other mainframe data sources through the Database Gateway from Micro Decisionware. With support for DDE, Visual Basic can also be used to integrate multiple Windows-based applications such as Microsoft Word for Windows and Microsoft Excel.

An icon library of approximately 400 designs and an icon editor written in the Visual Basic language are also included with the Visual Basic package. The online help system provides context-sensitive reference information. Sample code that can be copied and pasted into the user's Visual Basic program is also provided. An additional fact that many PC BASIC users will be glad to know is that there is almost no learning curve for users who are already familiar with the Basic language.

6.4.8   PowerSoft's PowerBuilder

PowerBuilder from PowerSoft in Burlington, MA, is a graphically-oriented PC product targeted at programmers and application developers. It is described in detail in Section 6.2.3.1 of this chapter.

6.4.9   Revelation Technology's Advanced Revelation

Advanced Revelation from Revelation Technologies, Inc., New York, NY, is primarily intended for application developers. The vendor says its strategy focuses on Enterprise Processing, the concept of corporate-wide information systems utilizing disparate data from existing databases through cooperative processing. In addition to helping firms downsize, the vendor says it wants to help customers improve their utilization of existing database investments.

In Spring, 1991, Revelation Technologies added QBE to Advanced Revelation so that end users could easily utilize the product. The QBE capability was added to provide an intuitive front end for interactive relational queries. Using the QBE format, users type an example of the information they seek, rather than writing a line-by-line program describing how to search for the desired information and manipulate it. The QBE features can be used in conjunction with Revelation Technologies' Environmental Bonding. This is a proprietary method of accessing data in a variety of data formats. QBE and Environmental Bonding can be used to build relational queries against both relational and non-relational databases.

Revelation provides standardized access to a variety of systems through its Environmental Bonding technology. For example, Revelation's SQL Server Bond provides a link between Advanced Revelation and Microsoft's SQL Server, while its DB2 Bond provides access to DB2 through Micro Decisionware's Database Gateway. Revelation Technologies also provides bonds to ASCII, dBase, Oracle, Lotus 1–2–3, AutoCAD, and Btrieve data.

6.5   OTHER CLIENT PLATFORMS

Most client modules in client/server systems are based on either Microsoft Windows, IBM's OS/2, or UNIX. Most of the tools mentioned earlier in this chapter reside on an OS/2, plain DOS, or Windows-equipped client platform.

6.5.1   Macintosh Tools

Enterprises that are interested in having Macintosh computers serve as the platform for client modules in a client/server architecture can get information about Macintosh tools from a number of sources. Several trade journals are dedicated to Macintosh software. Also, sites that have had a Macintosh installed for a period of time are sure to be on mailing lists that are used by Macintosh client/server software vendors. In addition, Apple Computer would be happy to provide customers with information about client/server tools and products that they and other vendors provide. *Macworld*, from Macworld Communications, Inc. in Boulder, CO, is an example of a trade journal covering Macintosh products.

6.5.2   UNIX Tools

An introduction to the UNIX environment is provided in Chapter 15, and UNIX networking is covered in detail in Chapter 16. Those chapters contain information about client/server tools that are available for a UNIX environment. The UNIX world has had a long and distinguished history connected to distributed computing. In fact, many of today's client/server approaches owe a debt of gratitude to concepts that originated in the UNIX environment.

The UNIX environment is a distinctly different environment from a DOS/Windows or OS/2-based environment. While it has not always been a simple matter to interconnect UNIX and DOS or UNIX and OS/2 environments, a lot of progress has been made in that area.

6.6   OBJECT-ORIENTED TECHNIQUES AND TOOLS

While object-oriented techniques have made contributions to the client/server explosion in a number of ways, the most dramatic initial contribution was in the area of GUIs. Objects are the essence of the icons that are found in today's most popular GUIs. How object-oriented techniques have impacted GUIs will be covered in Chapter 7. Chapter 8 will discuss how object-oriented databases are being used in client/server systems. This chapter will discuss how object-oriented techniques are impacting client/server development tools. This section will also explain some of the basic object-oriented concepts.

Object-oriented techniques are having a significant effect on client/server front ends and application development tools and will make client/server systems much easier to build in the future. The ease of building front-end client modules or entire applications using object-oriented tools will undoubtedly increase the number of client/server systems because these systems will be built much more quickly.

6.6.1 An Overview of Object-Oriented Concepts

Objects are entities or "things" in a program's domain consisting of structure, value, and behavior. Objects contain both data and code. The code permits the object to act upon itself.

Objects belong to—and are grouped by—class or "type," with classes organized into a hierarchy. A class is a general category of similar objects. An object in one class can inherit attributes and procedures—called methods—from a higher class. Every object is a member of a class. An object's class membership determines its structure and defines the operations that can be performed on it.

An example of classes is provided in Figure 6.1 provided by Servio Corporation.

The Collection class hierarchy in Figure 6.1 moves objects from general definitions to increasingly specialized structures and methods. Class "Collection," at the top of the figure, is designed as the method needed for collections and aggregations of objects.

Each class contains procedures (methods) for performing operations on its members. For example, in the figure, class Bag contains methods for adding and removing elements of an unordered collection and for taking the union, intersection, or difference of two unordered collections.

Objects inherit both data attributes and methods from objects in higher levels of the class hierarchy. An object's component part can only be read or updated by executing the methods defined by the object's class. To invoke one of an object's methods, a message is sent to the object. (A message is a request for an object to perform an operation). The message might just consist of the object's name and the name of the method to be invoked.

While an object inherits methods from a higher level class, it also contains its own methods. Once defined within a programming environment, objects may be used by other programs. The objects may be used as they are, or a new class may be developed to create an object that is slightly different. The important point is that objects are easily changed and easily shared within an environment. This capability allows for tremendous reusability of code and is a powerful feature of object-

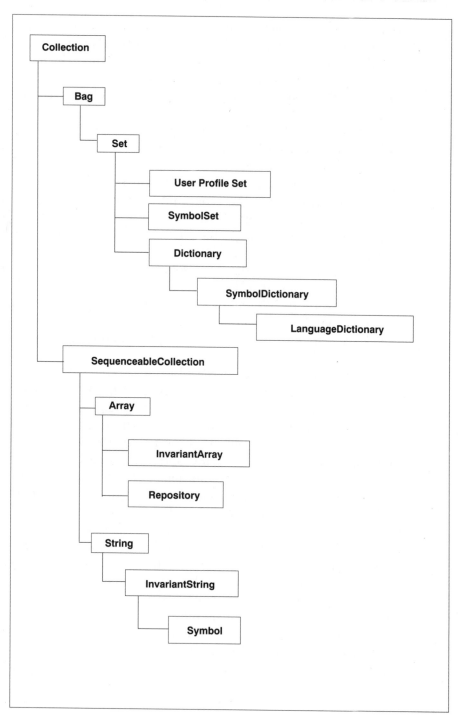

Figure 6.1 Class hierarchies. *Source:* Servio Corporation.

oriented systems. However, skeptics point out that while code reusability was anticipated from structured programming, not much reusability was actually realized. Another factor will be the complexities of making a large staff of programmers aware of all the objects that exist as they grow in number. Some sites already have hundreds of objects and are creating more.

If object-oriented systems really do come through with the extensive amount of code reusability that is projected, this feature alone will be a tremendous asset. One needs only think of the tremendous productivity that reusable parts made to the manufacturing industry to realize what an asset this could be in the programming industry. If code reusability could offer an equally dramatic change in the software industry, it would offer a tremendous strategic benefit to enterprises. This kind of code reusability is already used in GUIs. It could also be used beneficially in building client modules, database server routines, and intervening portions of modular client/server systems.

The extensibility offered by object-oriented systems is expected to make modifying systems after they are in production much easier. This could have a major impact in reducing the high cost of software maintenance.

Bertrand Meyer, active in the object-oriented movement, offers an interesting comment on the difference that object-oriented languages could make in the software development cycle. He says that object-oriented languages would significantly facilitate changes after systems have been developed and put into production. Meyer explains that traditional approaches emphasize the software cycle only up to the first delivery of a working version and neglect the whole afterlife of change and revision that follows. He points out that this is as remote from real life ". . . as those novels which stop when the hero marries the heroine—in reality, the time when the really interesting part begins."*

Overall, the most important features of the object-oriented approach are encapsulation, inheritance, reusability, and extensibility. Encapsulation refers to packaging data and procedures together in a single structure called an object. Inheritance permits objects of a lower class to automatically benefit from capabilities of a higher class. Reusability is possible because objects are self-contained and can serve as standard software modules in various applications. Extensibility is achieved as a result of the ease with which objects (or software modules) can be

---

*Meyer, B., *Object-Oriented Software Construction*, New York, Prentice Hall, 1993.

modified or specialized. All in all, object-oriented techniques make it easy to build new systems from off-the-shelf modules.

6.6.1.1 Why is the Object-Oriented Approach Different?

Many of the techniques of the object-oriented approach sound somewhat similar to traditional programming goals. After all, extensibility and reusability have been programming goals for a long time. Why and how does the object-oriented approach come closer to delivering on these objectives?

The answer lies in the fact that an object is much more than a traditional entity in a hierarchical, relational, or flat file system because an object contains code as well as data. An object not only specifies the structure of the data, it also specifies a collection of procedures—known as methods—which can access that data (the object's own data) directly. An object has the capability of acting upon itself or sending messages to other objects.

The most unique aspect of the object-oriented approach is the fact that code, or behavior, is attached to objects. Objects "encapsulate" both state and behavior as well as value. This represents a major divergence from conventional programming approaches.

Traditionally data has been passive. It was created, and then it sat in a file or in a database until it was accessed and manipulated or deleted. All action was done to data by an application program. The data never did anything by itself. It just hung around until something happened to it. It was always an application program that made something happen to data. The procedural steps contained in a program—a separate entity from the data—caused action to be taken using that data.

Data takes a much more active role in an object-oriented system. Data now has procedures stored along with it. Data now knows how to do some things for itself. For example, a large group of data in the form of a file may know how to open or close itself. Another example is that a data field may know to insert slashes into its six digits before it allows itself to be printed.

The behavior of data that is associated with an object falls into two separate categories—a private part and a public part. The private part is available only to other internal members of that class. An example of a private part of an object is the knowledge of how to store itself. For example, the object might contain the instructions to store itself as a bit map.

The public part is available to any function inside or outside that class. This structure is important for reusing the software. An application can be changed by modifying the functions that act on the public part of a class, rather than by rewriting the application itself.

6.6.1.2 Examples of Object-Oriented Techniques

The banking industry provides a convenient example of the concept and benefits of a class structure that has inheritance. Suppose we have an object named Bank_account. The Bank_account object would define data storage for the account balance of its instances and implement operations such as "deposit" and "withdraw." All these definitions would be inherited by the Bank_account's subtypes, Checking_account and Savings_account. On the other hand, Savings_account might contain additional methods of its own, like "calc_interest."

In conventional systems, though data and procedures interact, the two concepts are kept quite separate—data is stored in file structure or DBMSs while instructions are stored in application programs. Objects, however, are discrete entities containing both data and procedures.

The National Oceanic and Atmospheric Administration (NOAA) in Rockville, MD is using object-oriented techniques for making navigational charts for ships and airplanes. These charts are made of many data types. Chart features include objects like buoys, submerged shipwrecks, rocks, overhead obstructions and many other things. In fact there are between 200 and 300 different chart features. Charts get built from a wide variety of these objects.

Since these chart features are stored as objects, they know how they are supposed to go on the final chart. As a result, the chart is built more easily because these objects know what to do and where to go on the chart. This is important for several reasons: The physical chart that is created is much smaller than reality. At any one particular spot, there might be several different chart features which occur. For example, two large shipwrecks might be right next to a large rock. One shipwreck might have nitroglycerin stored in it and the other might have a mast sticking up to a dangerous height. At this same spot, there might also be a buoy. Since there is limited space on the physical chart, depicting all of these features in this one place is challenging.

Since the features are stored as objects, they have—built into them— the intelligence to perform the necessary conflict resolution. As a result, they can figure out the biggest threats to a boat and portray those threats on the chart in the best manner. One way to resolve such conflicts is to rotate the direction of the symbols on the chart so that more than one symbol can be depicted at the same approximate spot.

6.6.2   The OOP Learning Curve

Many developers who have used traditional programming techniques admit that they had a struggle switching to object-oriented programming. In fact, object-oriented techniques can be an extremely difficult transition for programmers to make. Object-oriented programming (OOP) requires developers to change their basic approach to developing a system.

Many of the programmers who have successfully made this switch have become OOP's biggest advocates. It seems that once developers get the hang of it, start developing a little proficiency, and start seeing the benefits of this approach, they become enthusiastic converts. However, it is wise to expect some initial resistance. Creatures of habit tend to favor what they know best—even the most advanced of technical personnel!

The learning curve will not be mastered in a few days. In fact, it might not be mastered in a matter of weeks. When one is evaluating whether learning OOP is worthwhile or not, one might look at the advantages object-oriented approaches have contributed to the area of GUIs. A company might try to keep abreast of the successes that other enterprises are experiencing with this technology—particularly their competitors—and take that into consideration when determining whether having some of their developers go through the learning curve is worthwhile.

6.6.3   OOP Language Implementations

Several object-oriented programming languages have evolved directly from the original SmallTalk language developed at PARC. The two most well-known are SmallTalk-80 from ParcPlace Systems, Mountain View, CA, and the SmallTalk/V series from Digitalk, Inc., Los Angeles, CA. Smalltalk enthusiasts say that the language gives developers a more powerful ability to describe the entities in the world and to deal with them in a very natural way.

Digitalk's Smalltalk series provides a family of products. They consist of powerful windows-oriented graphics programming tools based on the Smalltalk language. The series includes Smalltalk/V for IBM PCs and compatibles, Smalltalk Mac for the Macintosh, and Smalltalk V 286, which has 32-bit architecture permitting access to 16Mb of memory.

While Smalltalk/V is being used for expert system development prototyping, database-related activities, and many other applications, its most powerful use is in advanced user interfaces. A spokesman for

Digitalk, Dan Goldman, vice president and general manager, says that Smalltalk/V was specifically designed for user interface programming. He says that programming for interfaces like IBM's Presentation Manager has created new challenges and that the old programming tools are not meeting these challenges. He adds that if a developer is writing an application just to internally grind numbers, that developer might as well use procedural code since it would be faster. Smalltalk/V, however, is strongest at user interface-oriented applications, says Goldman.

Goldman suggests that applications could be built using combinations of languages. For example, Smalltalk/V could be used for the parts of the application that interface with a human and then Smalltalk/V could call the other, procedural portions. Such a combination would offer maximum performance and productivity.

Smalltalk is also gaining a reputation among end users for its ease-of-use. After developers build up a library of classes—with object containing "intelligence"—end users can easily build complex applications for themselves. Since the objects are able to perform many activities without assistance, in many cases, the end users merely have to develop a scenario for the objects to follow. As a result, they are able to build complex applications without the assistance of MIS managers and developers. Most important, they no longer have to add their requests for applications to an ever-expanding backlog of requests.

Both Smalltalk-80 and Smalltalk/V, as well as languages such as Actor from the Whitewater Group, Evanston, IL, are known as "pure" object-oriented languages because they adhere strictly to the object-oriented model. "Hybrid" object oriented languages, on the other hand, try to bridge the gap between traditional procedural language and the object-oriented paradigm. C++, originally developed by Bjarne Stroustrup at AT&T's Bell Laboratories, Murray Hill NJ, is an extension of C and permits a programming style that is a combination of procedural and object-oriented approaches. Objective C, from Stepstone, Sandy Hook, CT, which was incorporated in the original NeXt Computer, is another example of a hybrid object-oriented language.

Many observers consider C++ as the defacto standard in the object-oriented programming realm. However, some critics say that the hybrid combination of techniques in C++ dilutes the strength of the object-oriented approach and results in a severe loss of benefits. Proponents of C++ counter saying the hybrid approach offers a way to bridge the gap between procedural and object-oriented approaches, and C++ will permit developers to make the transition to object-oriented programming more easily.

7

GRAPHICAL USER INTERFACES (GUIs)

7.1   GUI OVERVIEW

GUIs may increase end-user productivity, but they can still yield a poor return on investment. Depending on the type of tools used, development time for the GUI portion of an application can significantly offset the time saved by end users. For example, writing directly to a Microsoft Windows API using the vendor's Software Development Kit (SDK) can be complex and time-consuming. While there are times when writing directly to a GUI API is warranted, many developers are turning to GUI building tools which make creating a GUI for an application much easier.

7.1.1   Benefits of GUIs

GUIs have made a significant contribution to the popularity of client/server computing, and they will continue to do so. They offer a welcome relief to end users of IBM mainframe systems who were never very comfortable with the difficult-to-read displays typically shown on 3270 type of screen. And for PC DOS users, selecting an icon that looks like a file folder is much easier than remembering the cryptic format of a DOS command. Not only are GUIs easier to use, they are quite pleasant to use.

GUIs offer benefits in other ways as well. Having GUIs that are consistent across many applications shortens the amount of time that it takes for a user to learn how to use applications. The fact that the graphical appearance of the application is already familiar to the user from another application is a major asset; the fact that many GUIs resemble each other facilitates learning. For example, opening a file folder using Windows is very similar to opening a file folder on a Macintosh. This can be particularly important for individuals who may have to use different computers at different times.

An additional benefit of a GUI is that it enables multitasking, task switching, and data interchange. Using a GUI, an end user can easily run multiple tasks at the same time (multitasking). Tasks or programs active in a multitasking environment are allotted slices of processing time. Using task switching, the end user can move from one task to another without closing or exiting the first task. Combining multitasking and task switching, the end user can easily exit one task and go to another while the first one continues to process. With data interchange, moving data from one application to another is a simple task. All of these capabilities make the end user more productive.

7.1.2   Object-Oriented Concepts Contribute to GUIs

Many of today's GUIs are similar to the Macintosh interface from Apple Computer, Inc., in Cupertino, CA. The Macintosh interface was one of the earliest implementations of object-oriented programming. By understanding the Macintosh approach, one can begin to grasp the basic concepts of this new paradigm or programming model. Using object-oriented programming for user interfaces is only one of many powerful ways to use this new approach, however.

The ideas used in the Macintosh screens were born at Xerox PARC. Earlier object-oriented programming work can be traced back to the mid-1960s and a simulation language called Simula. But OOP was given real substance at PARC where icons, pull-down menus, and windows were born. The researchers invented a special language, SmallTalk, to incorporate their new ideas. The SmallTalk language incorporated the essence of object-oriented programming.

The user must realize that the icon itself is not the object. The icon is simply a visual, graphical representation of the object. For example, the folder icon on the Macintosh is not the object within the object-oriented systems; it is only a symbol of the actual folder object. The object, stored internally, contains data about the folder's structure, its current status, and procedures that it can perform, as well as activities that can be performed on it.

To provide another example, a file is an object in the Macintosh user interface. The file object consists of data representing the structure of the file and it also consists of procedures (or methods) commonly associated with a file. Some typical procedures that might be part of a file object include how to open itself, how to close itself, and how to print itself.

Many proponents say that object-oriented techniques more closely mirror our real thought processes. They say that traditional systems design and programming techniques force us to take real world problems and dissect them into a format that is acceptable to a computer. While these dissected formats may be comprehensible to a computer, they no longer reflect the real world. The object-oriented approach permits developers to represents problems more realistically.

7.1.3   GUI/Operating System Boundaries

One area that is a little fuzzy to some people relates to the exact boundaries of the GUI and the operating system. Where does the operating system end and the GUI software start? Most people can see clearly that IBM's OS/2 is an operating system and IBM's Presentation Manager is a GUI. With Windows, the boundaries are less clear. DOS is the operating system that supports Windows. Windows is the GUI though Windows also provides some of its own operating system-type functions as extensions to DOS. Many people think of Windows as an operating system, but in reality DOS is the operating system in a DOS/Windows environment.

Different people express the relationship between Window and DOS a little differently from one another. Some people say that "Windows runs on top of DOS," while others say that "Windows runs under DOS." Regardless of such terminology, DOS is still the operating system and Windows is the GUI.

Normally an operating system provides input and output services as well as other system services. However, since DOS is a very limited operating system, it does not provide some of the input/output and system functions that Windows needs. Therefore, Windows must provide these services itself. For example, Windows provides multitasking operations, and it also provides Windows applications with queued input messages which permit event-driven interaction. Additionally, Windows also provides actions such as moving objects, scrolling, and moving windows, and provides capabilities such as resource management, memory management, and the ability for two applications to communicate through DDE or OLE.

In the UNIX environment, UNIX is the operating system and X Window belongs to the GUI realm. X Window is described later in this chapter.

7.1.4   The GUI Gamble

A major question for many companies is which GUI to use. GUI APIs are not what you would call open. Certainly, there is no automatic interoperability among applications built for different GUIs. Each has its own steep learning curve as well. This can create problems for large corporations that have some departments using PCs and other groups using UNIX workstations. Such sites need to have some employees that can build Microsoft Windows-style GUIs and other employees that can build X Window GUIs using such tools as Motif from OSF.

This is also a problem for large application vendors who would like their software products to be used by a large cross-section of users. Many vendors report that the problem of multiple GUIs is one of the most difficult problems they face. For example, Computer Associates—one of the world's largest software vendors—says it is easier to have its applications be portable across operating systems than be portable across GUIs.

Many large software vendors feel that determining which GUI to support is a gamble. A few years ago, many software vendors bet on Presentation Manager and lost—big. After writing their applications for PM, those vendors saw Microsoft Windows far outstrip sales of OS/2. Many of these vendors then scrambled to build a Windows version of their product. However, vendors who had built software for Windows from the start were in a much more competitive position.

Some observers believe that the GUI war is not over yet. They say that the OS/2/PM combination may have lost the first battle, but not the war. OS/2 advocates say that building applications for Presentation Manager is similar to building applications for Windows except that the Presentation Manager API is much more robust. They point out that with Windows, developers must contend with memory management. With Presentation Manager they do not have to worry about memory management. With Windows, developers must do *all* the memory management. Another factor in OS/2's favor is the ability to run multiple DOS sessions. While OS/2's hardware requirements are so heavy that many PCs have to be upgraded to run it, some companies express a willingness to do that to get the benefits of OS/2.

New operating system/GUI combinations will be coming out in the future that are predicted to have significant advantages over existing ones. However, there is the argument that by the time they come out, enterprises will already have made a very large investment in applications for existing GUIs and that investment will make switching to something new difficult for most sites. As a result, Windows NT—the forthcoming operating system/GUI combination from Microsoft—could automatically benefit from the momentum of the existing Microsoft Windows product since they will be compatible.

7.2   DEVELOPMENT CONCERNS

7.2.1   Building GUIs for Your Applications

Many application products, like Word for Windows and Microsoft's Excel spreadsheet, operate under Windows. Such products have their own graphical interface *that is tailored for that product* and takes care of all the interactions between itself and the underlying Windows systems software. For example, Word for Windows has separate menus for categories like FILE, EDIT, VIEW, FORMAT, and so on. As the user selects menu options, the Word for Windows software takes care of all the required interactions with the complex Windows API. The user is unaware of all the complex programming that makes using the Word menus easy.

In the same way, if a company wants to allow its end users to have a GUI that is tailored for a specific application, its in-house application developers must build it. For example, the application might present different icons that can be selected depending on whether the end user wants to issue a purchase order or create an invoice. The application developer must create those icons *and* write code for the actions that will be associated with the various icons.

The application developer must also take care of all the interaction that takes place between the application that is being built and the Windows software. As a result, many new programming considerations are necessary to get application programs to run properly with the windowing software.

Fortunately, application developers do not have to create all of the windowing activity from scratch. If they did, it would take an unreasonable amount of time to create these user friendly applications. Instead, the vendor provides software to help. For Windows and NT, Microsoft provides an SDK which helps develop applications with a graphical front end. Unfortunately, developing GUIs this way is very time consuming. That is why many GUI building tools are now appearing. This chapter will first explain what is involved with building a GUI using an SDK, and then it will explore the use of GUI building tools.

Tools like Microsoft's SDK provide detailed instructions for how the development programmer links up with the Window's system software. While C is the recommended Windows programming language by Microsoft, assembly language can also be used with Microsoft's SDK. The interaction between the developer's program and the Windows system software is accomplished through APIs provided by the vendor.

When writing directly to a GUI's native API—which developers do using Microsoft's SDK—the job of creating the end user interface is complex and time-consuming. A programmer must become familiar with hundreds of functions, widgets, and other intricacies when working with the APIs for popular windowing environments. Estimates of the amount of time that is devoted to creating the interface portion of an application range from 60 to 80%. This is true no matter which of the popular products one is working with: Microsoft's Windows, Presentation Manager from IBM, X Windows-based Motif* from the Open Software Foundation (OSF), or Open Look from Sun Microsystems, Inc.

7.2.2   Building GUIs

7.2.2.1   A GUI API

What exactly is a GUI's API? One interesting way of looking at it is that the GUI API is the interface with which the developer's work, while the GUI is the interface with which the end user's work.

The API is the method by which a developer references the services that are available in the environment. It is a set of functions (programming routines) and function calls that the programmer uses to access those services. Examples of Windows' function calls are AccessResource, AdjustWindowRectEx, CreateWindow, and WriteProfileString. The API consists of many function calls as well as numerous arguments that can be used with them.

Interestingly, APIs in general are becoming more important. An API is essentially a type of "go-between;" it basically helps to link one type of software with another. In the increasingly heterogeneous information systems world, all kinds of APIs are available. Outside the GUI world, for example, two important APIs are those for networking and for database servers. Each of these will be discussed later.

Writing to a native windowing API (as when using Microsoft's SKD) vs. using a GUI building tool can be compared to developing screens for CICS using Basic Mapping Support macros vs. using a 4GL screen painter. Another analogy is that it is like creating a report by writing an assembly language program compared to using RPG, Mark IV, or a simple 4GL. However, the time savings when using a GUI building tool is probably even more dramatic. On the other hand, with the SDK the

---

*Some people regard Motif as a style guide for the X-Windowing system (as described later). Others refer to Motif simply as an implementation of the X-Windowing system. Note that the two concepts are not mutually exclusive. This book regards Motif as both.

resulting application may run faster and more smoothly due to better integration between the GUI and the resulting application.

A programmer can use over 600 functions for Microsoft Windows. In addition, there are several hundred Windows messages which are separated into many different categories. Window-management messages are sent by Windows to an application at each input event, such as when a user presses a key or moves the mouse. An application processes messages using one of the hundreds of functions available.

7.2.2.2 Event-Driven Programming

Programming for a windows environment is quite different from traditional programming. Most traditional program code written by developers is sequential. Throughout the program, one instruction follows the next. Even when branches are taken, the overall logic still follows a sequential flow. Windows programming, however, is event-driven. That is, the program must respond to an event. An event can be initiated, for example, by the end user making a menu selection.

When the end user takes any action—like pressing a key or clicking the mouse—the user interface code must respond appropriately to that action. Since an end user may take any particular action at any time, the code cannot be sequential; it must be ready to respond to whatever action the user takes. Since the code must respond to an unpredictable series of events, it is called "event-driven."

An event is basically a notification that some condition has changed. Windows generates a message at each input event. Windows places messages that belong to a particular application in that application's queue. (Keep in mind that several applications can be running at once using multitasking capabilities.) Application queues are first-in/first-out queues. The application basically reads the messages by using the **GetMessage** function. Specifically, what happens is that the application checks the message queue using the **GetMessage** function to see if there are any messages. If there are no messages, the **GetMessage** function waits for a message to be placed in the application's queue. While waiting, **GetMessage** relinquishes control to Windows so other applications can take control and process their messages.

If there are messages, the **GetMessage** function returns the message at the top of the queue to the application. The application can then send the message to the appropriate window function for action using the **DispatchMessage** function. The **DispatchMessage** function tells Windows to call the window function of the window associated with the message. That function also passes all the contents of the message as function arguments. The window function then processes the message and makes any requested changes to the window.

Any windowing API contains several different categories of functions. For example, the Windows API contains functions that can be used by an application for window management, device-independent graphic operations, and system's services (string translation, memory management, sound creation, etc.). In addition to functions, the API consists of messages, data structures, data types, statements, and files that application developers can use to create programs that run with Windows.

Two books written by Microsoft and sold in bookstores give a good idea of what writing programs that link directly to Windows is like. These books can give potential users an understanding of what is involved before they commit to building interfaces using Microsoft's Software Developer's Kit. The *Microsoft Windows Guide to Programming* is over 500 pages while the accompanying *Windows Programmer's Reference* is well over 1000 pages.

Some companies are building their own GUI development tools for in-house use by their own programmers. These GUI development tools generally contain a subset of the many options that the SDK offers. When a company does this, it also builds a special API for their programmers to use in accessing the capabilities of their in-house GUI builder. Some of the companies doing this are software vendors who are building commercial software, but companies that are building software for their own in-house use are also doing this.

For example, American Management Systems (AMS), an application software developer and management consulting firm headquartered in Arlington, VA now provides some APIs for their own programmers. AMS has been writing GUIs for their own software and for customers since Presentation Manager first came out several years ago. At that time it wrote directly to the Presentation Manager API. It was so early in the game that there were not many—if any—GUI building tools back then. So AMS created GUI building tools to make it easier for their developers. Now, AMS also uses several of the commercially available GUI building tools.

7.2.2.3 Style Guides

Another issue that creates some confusion relates to style guides for a GUI. A style guide provides the "look and feel" of a particular user interface. Many—but not all—GUIs have pre-established style guides. The style guide for both IBM's Presentation Manager and Microsoft Windows is IBM's Common User Access (CUA). That was established back in the late 1980s when IBM and Microsoft were working together on many software projects.

The UNIX-based X Window system has no pre-established style guide. Some observers feel this is due to the political nature of trying to satisfy all the people who were involved in establishing the X Windowing system. Having its origin at MIT, the X Window system had input from many vendors. Observers say that the X Window system—subsequently supported by a group called the X Consortium—was established at a low enough level so that all the vendors involved could agree on it and then be able to provide their own added value.

Since there are so many benefits to a standard look and feel, many in the industry want a standard look and feel for the X Window system. OSF's Motif is reportedly the most widely used, but Sun Workstation's Open Look has its supporters, too.

A big factor in favor of Motif is that its style guide is very close to the style of CUA, while Open Look has far more differences. That alone has brought Motif a lot of support. Large corporations that already have Windows and Presentation Manager applications prefer the consistency that Motif offers so end users will not become confused.

As mentioned earlier, most systems use mouse button one to pull down a menu. However, in Open Look mouse button one activates the default action, while mouse button three is used for menu pulldown. A difference like this can be aggravating to users. They will automatically use mouse button one thinking they will consistently get what they want and wind up being disappointed and annoyed.

The style guide is what gives a GUI its real power. One of the primary benefits of GUIs is that since they make all applications look the same to end users, they make applications easier to use. The style guide basically "writes down the rules" for how the GUI should look.

Even with style guides clearly established, having everything look the same will not happen automatically, however. Programmers have to pay attention to the rules of the style guide to make everything look the same from application to application. Sometimes even following the style guide is not enough. For example, because Motif offers many options, it does not guarantee a consistent look and feel from one program or application to the next. Therefore, it is important to establish enterprise standards to ensure that all applications will have the desired consistent appearance.

7.2.3   GUI-Building Tools

A whole range of different tools can be considered GUI building tools. Some are basically a C shell and only build a resource file. Resources are items like icons, cursors, and strings. Resource files—or resource-definition files—contain statements that describe a module's dynamically loadable resources. Some of the tools may have capabilities that are far more limited than their advertisements imply. As always, buyer beware. Certainly, the wide variety of tools available adds to the confusion of trying to pick a GUI building tool.

Overall client/server application development environments like the one provided by Burlington, MA-based PowerSoft's PowerBuilder contain powerful GUI development capabilities. Sophisticated CASE tools like Anderson Consulting's Foundation contain GUI building components. Foundation has many different components to aid in GUI development. Among them is the Presentation Services component which includes Window Editing Services, Window Controls, and Window Level Services.

Examples of tools that assist developers in building GUIs for the X Window environment are UIM/X 2.0 from Visual Edge Software Ltd. in Montreal and the Builder Xcessory 2.0 from Integrated Computer Solutions in Cambridge, MA.

The Builder Xcessory is an interactive, graphical tool for building, prototyping, and testing Motif-based user interfaces for the X Window system. It is like a paint program, letting the application developer paint menus. Visual Edge's UIM/X also lets developers interactively build user interfaces. Instead of writing code to create a button, the software lets the developer click on a button and then write the code that is to be associated with that button. Another feature is that the GUI code can be tested right away. The developer does not have to link and compile to test.

UIM/X features a core GUI Builder Engine surrounded by configurable editors, thus enabling custom configuration of various interface development tools. The developer can permit end users to modify the interface—but only within carefully controlled bounds.

These are just a few of the GUI-building tools that are available. Other products include BlueSky, WindowsMAKER, ProtoView, KaseWorks, and JYACC, XVT, and Open Interface. XVT and Open Interface are discussed later in this chapter.

7.3   THE X WINDOW SYSTEM

The X Window system is set of display-handling routines, developed at MIT for UNIX workstations, that permit the creation of hardware-independent GUIs.

7.3.1 X Window's Use of Terminology

A major area of confusion relates to how the X Window system uses the terms "client" and "server." In an X Window system, the GUI systems software resides on a server. As a result, X Window terminology seems to be the opposite of how the terms are used in the DOS/Microsoft Windows world. The part that is consistent is that the component referred to as the server does indeed provide a service. So, while some may say that the X Window system is "backward" in its use of client and server terms, that is not true—though it certainly seems that way at first. In the DOS/Windows environment, clients provide their own GUI activities; in an X Window environment, clients request services from a GUI server.

In the X Window system, a *server* provides window presentations and handles input from keyboard and mouse devices. The X Window server software usually sits on a PC or workstation and is accessed by applications via the networking facilities. Applications that use the capabilities of the X Window server system are known as the *clients*. If this seems confusing, remember to go back to the basic meaning of the terms "client" and "server." A client is something that requests a service and a server is something that provides a service.

7.3.2 Mixing Microsoft Windows and the X Window System

Generally an end user either has a PC or a workstation on his or her desk. PC users usually have Microsoft Windows installed and UNIX workstation users usually have X Window with Motif or Open Look. But products are now available that will let a user have both.

For installations that already have a lot of applications written for both Microsoft Windows and the X Window system, PC-Xview from The Beaverton, OR-based GSS Personal Graphics Division of Spectragraphics might be very helpful. PC-Xview permits X Window applications to appear on personal computers which normally run Microsoft Windows applications. With a tool like PC-Xview, end users can have both Windows applications and X-based applications appear on one screen at the same time.

7.4 OTHER GUI CONCERNS

7.4.1 GUIs for Existing Production Systems

Existing production systems are often referred to as "legacy systems." The term "legacy system" refers to an existing production system that is showing its age. Usually applications are referred to as legacy systems when they have been inherited by developers who would prefer to use newer technology than can be applied to these older, sometimes archaic, systems. In many cases, the great majority of a company's systems are considered legacy systems; however, it would be extremely expensive to replace them all at once. Often, the plan is to replace them little by little over time.

Many companies are adding front-end GUIs to their legacy systems. This is a sound approach for some systems. Systems that have a particularly difficult to use set of input screens are prime candidates for having GUI front-ends. As discussed earlier, the approach has been criticized by some people who refer to it as "front-ending" a system. They point out that the system has not been changed at all, that it just has a "pretty face" now. They are absolutely right about that, but as long as this is something everyone understands, there should not be a problem. After all, some extremely happy end users who no longer have to deal with confusing 3270-type screens could not care less if that amounts to "front-ending."

Also discussed earlier, a legacy system cannot be converted to a client/ server system simply by replacing a 3270-type screen with a GUI front end. This approach can make an end users' work easier, however, and sometimes data validation can be added to the PC front-end module, giving additional value to the front-ending technique.

KnowledgeWare provides Flashpoint which permits developers to add a GUI front end to existing mainframe applications. Many of Flashpoint's customers are independent software vendors (ISVs) who are using the product to revamp their mainframe-based application package software products. (Flashpoint also helps build new applications which connect to popular server databases.)

7.4.2   Creating Portable GUIs

For installations that must develop applications for different GUIs, tools are appearing to help developers build GUIs that will work on multiple platforms. With these tools, a developer creates the GUI once and then can port it to a variety of environments. Two examples of such tools are XVT from XVT Software Inc. in Boulder, CO and Open Interface from Neuron Data in Palo Alto, CA.

Neuron Data says that Open Interface originally came about as a result of its efforts to port its popular expert system, Nexpert Object, to many different platforms. Open Interface is a toolkit for building GUIs that are portable and can support the look and feel of any of the following: Macintosh, Microsoft Windows, Presentation Manager, Motif, and Open

Look. It provides a common API which means there is a single learning curve as opposed to multiple learning curves—each of which can be very steep.

Open Interface consists of an Open Editor module and a set of libraries for each windowing environment. The Open Editor generates portable C code and resource files for the execution and description of the interface. The developer then customizes the C code to link in application functionality. When developers want to use the GUI in a different environment, they recompile using a different library.

XVT (eXtensible Virtual Toolkit) provides an interesting approach to the problem of porting a single application across multiple GUIs. XVT provides a thin insulating layer between application programs and windowing systems. It does not actually provide window and graphics support. Instead, it provides a common interface that applications can use to access the features of the underlying window and graphics system.

The application program that the developer is writing makes calls to XVT. Then, XVT calls the underlying window system to invoke the functions that are needed. Thus, XVT can be considered as a mapping between the application and a window system.

The XVT toolkit is supplied in the form of a library. A developer writes in C or C++ using the XVT API calls to access GUI services. The application is then compiled and linked with the appropriate library. There are six library products.

Thus, XVT is not considered a GUI builder, but rather a library of functions. For example, with Microsoft Windows, XVT acts as a layer between the application and the Windows SDK. When developers need to write a function, instead of specifying the Microsoft function name, they specify the XVT function name. By using the XVT function name, the resulting code will work not only on Windows, but on other platforms like the Macintosh as well. In order for it to work on a particular platform, the resulting code is compiled and linked with the appropriate library.

XVT's approach was liked well enough by the NIST to be included as part of its Application Portability Profile (APP). APP is the U.S. Government's Open System Environment (OSE) profile. The OSE aims for interoperability, portability, and scalability of computerized applications across heterogeneous platforms.

Standards experts say that ISO and other recognized standards bodies are likely to pay careful attention to NIST's activities in the area of GUI API standardization. When the IEEE took steps to formally start defining a standard API for GUIs in 1991, one if its working groups selected XVT as the base document from which to draft the standard.

8
BACK-END DATABASE SERVERS

8.1   THE CONCEPT OF A SERVER

A server is a device that provides a service. Server software consists of a logical process that provides services to requesting processes. Server hardware is where the server software resides. The many types of servers include file servers, print servers, database servers, communication servers, application servers, and fax servers. As local area networking facilities became more and more available, the concept of a server became popular because it permitted people to share things easily. For example, print servers were an efficient way for users to share the cost of expensive printers. In general, servers filled the need of letting many people share the capabilities of a device which provided a valuable service. As a result, the use of servers started growing in the 1980s, and continues to grow—even more rapidly—today.

File servers were widely used in the early days of local area networking, particularly in UNIX installations. With a file server, important files could be kept in a location where everyone who needed them could access them. As mentioned earlier in this book, a file server architecture offered significant advantages, but caused major problems as well. The software on the file server was not able to go through the records in the file and select the particular one that the client module or end user wanted to work with. If one specific record was desired, the client module had to have the logic to go through the entire file and select it. That meant that a lot of commands and instructions would have to go over the network between the client and server. Sometimes, the server simply sent the entire file to the client.

> While the various types of servers are very important,
> this book will primarily focus on database servers.

When the server sent the entire file to the client module, the client configuration had to have enough space to be able to hold the entire file. Another problem with sending entire files from a server to a client computer was the significant increase in network traffic. Much of this network usage was basically wasted because the client application did not need the entire file in most situations.

Eventually database servers became available and provided tremendous benefits over file servers. The client did not have to contain record access logic and the server did not have to send entire files to the client. With a database server, the client application specifies which records or tables it needs. The database server software locates the desired information and sends only the requested data to the client module. Database servers are coming into wide use because they provide many advantages, including an economic way for end users to access corporate data for their daily work. In a survey by Forrester Research, Inc., of Cambridge, MA, 68% of respondents indicated they will use a server database by 1995. While the various types of servers are very important, this book will primarily focus on database servers.

There are two main areas to think about when considering servers. One is hardware and the other is software. The choice of these components depends upon many considerations and selection should be done with care. Many of the factors discussed in the section entitled Selecting Client Software in Chapter 3 also apply to selecting server software. Such factors include defining and prioritizing system requirements and identifying what hardware and software platforms are already available.

8.2   SERVER HARDWARE

Hardware used as a server should have sufficient disk space and processing power to meet the needs of the applications being run. The hardware being used as a server can range from being a powerful PC to a minicomputer, a database machine, or a mainframe. In the early days of networking, one of the regular office PCs—one that was no more powerful than the other workstations on the LAN—was selected and assigned the role of being the server. In this configuration, the data rates of the LAN technology were often faster than the access rate of the hard disk drives on the server PC. In addition, the personal computers being used as servers were designed to be single-user devices; however, since they were being used as a server, they were forced to provide a multi-user service. As time went on, more powerful devices were used as servers. At the minimum, a PC that was more powerful than the end user PCs was designated to be the server. Eventually, hardware that was specifically built to be a server—like Compaq's SystemPro—became available and widely used in client/server architectures.

Many sites are using a minicomputer as a server. With this configuration, they have the advantage of being able to use the infrastructure that already exists for most minicomputers. This is especially true with the AS/400. Its excellent infrastructure of supporting software adds to its appeal as a server in a client/server system. Many sites are downsizing from IBM mainframes to move to an IBM AS/400 minicomputer—a mixed blessing for Big Blue.

Mainframe computers are being used as servers, too. In fact, IBM has started referring to its mainframes as servers. As with using a minicomputer as a server, having the mainframe infrastructure of supporting software is an advantage here, too. In addition, the information systems department is still able to exert all of its traditional control over the data. The disadvantage is that this architecture does not offer the cost benefits of using a high-powered PC as a server. One of the reasons many people are turning to client/server architectures is to realize the cost benefits of microcomputers. Using a mainframe as a server is sometimes done when there is a significant advantage to having a PC-based GUI as a front end for a system that needs to access mainframe data.

8.2.1   A Diversity of Hardware is Available

Server hardware consists of a number of components including the CPU, disk drives, disk controller's, buses and superbuses. The CPU is the central engine of the server. The most widely used CPUs in client/server systems are those manufactured by the Intel Corporation. Many vendors use the Intel chip in their dedicated servers such as Compaq's SystemPro server. The Intel 386 CPU chip was popular in early client/server systems; later, it was the Intel 486 CPU chip that was predominant. The Pentium (sometimes referred to as the 586 since it follows Intel's 486 chip) became available in 1993. While its clock speed is approximately twice the speed of the 486, actual speeds realized will depend on having fast peripherals and software that optimizes the power of the Pentium. Analysts estimate that once everything is in place, the Pentium will be able to process applications three times as fast as the 486. Sequent Computer Systems offers a 30-Pentium multiprocessing computer that will be able to run applications faster than low-end mainframes.

Reduced Instruction Set Computers (RISC)—pronounced "risk"—are quite popular in client/server architectures. As the name implies, this is a computer architecture that reduces the complexity of the computer chip by using simpler instructions. For example, the RISC architecture bans the indirect addressing mode, keeps instruction size constant, and keeps only those instructions that can be overlapped and that can execute in one machine cycle or less. As a result, the RISC chip is speedier than many Complex Instruction Set Computers (CISC)—pronounced "sisk"—which use microcode to execute very comprehensive instructions. However, many CISC computer manufacturers have responded to this by finding ways to speed up their computers. It can no longer be taken for granted that all RISC machines are faster than all CISC machines.

The major manufacturers of RISC CPU chips and their products include IBM's RS/6000, Sun Microsystem's SPARC, Digital Equipment Corporation's Alpha, Hewlett-Packard's PA-RISC and Silicon Graphics' Mips R4000. A new entry is the PowerPC 601 from IBM, Motorola, and Apple Computer. An advantage that RISC manufacturers have is that they can use new instruction architectures, while Intel must maintain backward compatibility with older 80x86 processors. Advantages for Intel and other CISC manufacturers is that their machines are far less expensive than RISC boxes. Also, CISC computers run software that is in high demand. The new PowerPC 601 (also known as the MPC 601) is much less expensive than other RISC machines and can compete with CISC machines in pricing.

Having a fast CPU chip is not enough if the rest of the system cannot keep up with it. As a result, faster buses, disk drives, and disk controllers are now being used. Earlier CPU chips were teamed with the standard ISA bus which moves data at 16 Mbps. Newer CPU chips are teamed with Micro Channel Architecture and EISA bus architectures which move data at 33 Mbps.

Disk controllers have become faster, too. Some of them can keep a large amount of data in their cache memories so they can provide additional data to the application at memory speeds. Superserver manufacturers like NetFrame Systems, Parallan Computer, and Tricord Systems have designed high-speed buses specifically to take advantage of the fast new disk controllers.

8.2.2 Disk Mirroring and Disk Duplexing

Mission-critical client/server systems are usually protected against data corruption with the use of disk duplexing and disk mirroring. Disk mirroring is sometimes referred to as disk shadowing. These approaches use the technique of redundancy to protect data.

Disk mirroring generally involves the use of two disk drives at the same time. The second drive has an exact copy of the data on the first drive. If either or both disks have unreadable portions, they will be in different places. If the first drive fails, the second drive takes over. Some sites provide multiple redundancy. They may have two or more extra backup disk drives. When this is done, it usually involves extremely important transaction processing systems.

Depending upon the method used to determine whether a server is working, software overhead can be a cost to consider in disk mirroring systems. Disk mirroring systems cannot merely write data to multiple disks; they also need to determine when one of the disk drives has failed. This involves additional software.

Disk duplexing is similar to disk mirroring: one or more additional disks contain back up copies of production data. The difference between the two terms is often debated. One agreed upon difference is that disk duplexing uses channel duplexing. This can involve the use of a second (redundant) disk coprocessor board. More often it involves redundant disk controllers. Controller failure is less likely than disk failure. However, controller redundancy adds another protective measure to the overall system.

An interesting side benefit of disk duplexing is that it can improve network performance. Since two separate disks are involved, offering split-seek capability, the system can let users read two identical files simultaneously. The system can then determine which of the two disks is able to service each read request more quickly.

8.2.3   Server Fault Tolerance

Fault tolerance is the ability of a system to continue operating after a major problem has occurred. With adequate fault tolerance, the system can keep operating with no damage to data and little, if any, change in operation. Frequently, server fault tolerance involves having redundant hardware devices. However, different sites have a variety of opinions regarding what adequate server fault tolerance includes.

For some sites, adequate fault tolerance is having duplicate file allocation tables and directory entries on separate areas of a disk, or providing read-after-write verification, which ensure that data is never written to a bad sector on a disk. Other sites have duplicates—and even triplicates—of hardware to ensure that under no circumstances will an operation ever terminate unexpectedly. This degree of fault tolerance will have its cost, of course. Adequate fault tolerance is often determined by calculating the costs that would be incurred if operation did terminate compared to what it will cost to ensure that operation will continue.

Having duplicate file and database server hard disks is the most common form of redundancy. This is because hard disks on file servers and database servers are said to constitute nine-tenths of client/server system failures. The reason why hard disks are so much at risk is that they are one of the few mechanical elements in an otherwise all electronic system. Hard disks have many moving parts which can malfunction, break down, or wear out. In addition, sectors of hard disk surfaces often go bad after extensive usage. Fault tolerance systems should be able to detect such bad sectors and prevent data from being written on them. If data is written on bad sectors, it will be corrupt and unusable.

8.2.4   RAID Systems

With Redundant Arrays of Inexpensive Drives (RAID) systems, fully duplexed systems are available. Many installations that have mission-critical client/server systems with vital data on servers use RAID technology to provide them with the security of fully redundant systems. When we remember that hard disks are complex *mechanical* devices, we realize that it is not a matter of *if* a hard disk will go down, it is more a matter of *when* a hard disk will go down. When a hard disk fails, it usually takes data with it. As a result, with an unprotected disk failure, not only does the hard disk have to be replaced, the data also has to be replaced or restored. If there is no way to do that, it may cost the company business and valuable customers.

A disk array involves multiple ordinary disks that are used in parallel. In disk arrays, data is often distributed evenly across the disks using a technique called "striping." Striping involves breaking every file into small data blocks (stripes). These small blocks are then written to different disk drives.

The different levels of RAID technology were originally proposed in some research work done at the University of California in Berkeley. Some of the individuals who were involved in this RAID research include Ann L. Chervenak, Garth Alan Gibson, Randy H. Katz, and Edward K. Lee.

The following descriptions of the different RAID levels are paraphrased from the white paper, *Fault-Tolerant Storage for Nonstop Networks* from Storage Dimensions, Malpitas, CA. The figures are a modification of ones shown in the white paper. RAID technology is complex, and the following description of the different levels of RAID systems will only give you a general idea of how it works. If a site is seriously considering using RAID technology, its personnel will need to gain a more extensive knowledge of the technology.

- •RAID Level 1 – This level combines disk mirroring and data striping. Each mirrored disk has an exact copy of the data. Read performance is high in level 1, but writes must be performed for each of the two disks. The main drawback to level 1 is the cost of the redundant storage.
- •RAID Level 2 – This level is used primarily in supercomputers, not in personal computers. This level performs data striping at the bit level. The fist bit in a data block is written to disk one, the second bit in a data block is written to disk two, etc. Multiple disks are needed to store error recovery data.
- •RAID Level 3 – This level uses a dedicated parity drive as shown in Figure 8.1. Level 3 uses an even number of drives for storing data and then uses a separate drive for parity. On the drives where the data is stored, the data is striped either a sector at a time or a byte at a time. (The byte level is the most common choice.) This level is most suitable when large, sequential read requests are frequent, rather than random access reads, especially with small blocks of data.
- •RAID Level 4 – Level 4 is similar to level 3 in that a dedicated parity drive is used. However, in level 4, data is striped at the block level. This technique is more efficient to some degree than level 3.
- •RAID Level 5 – Level 5, like level 4, performs data striping at the block level. The most important difference is that level 5 distributes parity information evenly across all of the drives in the array. This means that level 5 can perform multiple writes in parallel, and thereby is able to outperform levels 3 and 4. Since each disk in RAID 5 arrays can function independently to satisfy multiple, simultaneous read requests, this approach performs quite well with systems that involve random reads.

Figure 8.2 illustrates how parity works to protect data in levels 3, 4, and 5. Figure 8.3 illustrates how RAID Level 5 works. It indicates how parity is striped across all drives.

8.3   DATABASE SERVER SOFTWARE

8.3.1   Characteristics of Database Server Software

The software used as a database server is sometimes referred to as a "back-end database engine." While it may sound a little odd, the phrase

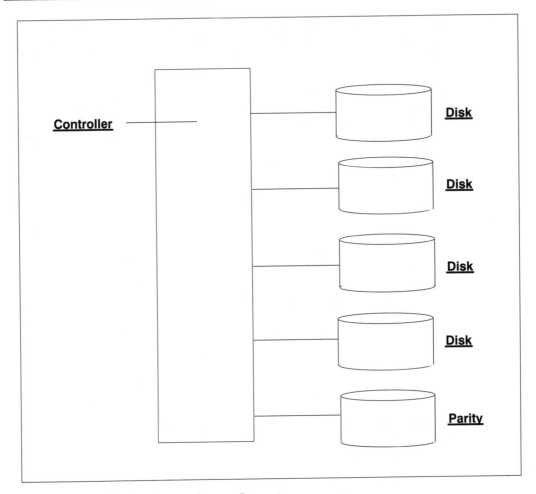

Figure 8.1   RAID level 3. *Source:* Storage Dimensions.

"back-end database engine" is actually a fairly accurate description. Just as the client application is at the client—or front end, the database is at the server—or back end. The "database engine" part of the phrase refers to the fact that the software is specifically dedicated to database functions. It is concerned only with activities directly related to the data it contains.

There are some general database characteristics that are found in most database servers. These include such things as data retrieval and update, locking mechanisms, multi-user access control, security, query optimization, caching, as well as data definition capabilities. These are pretty much the same characteristics that are found in traditional production-system databases. Additional characteristics that are desirable, but which may not be present, are referential integrity and two-phase commit.

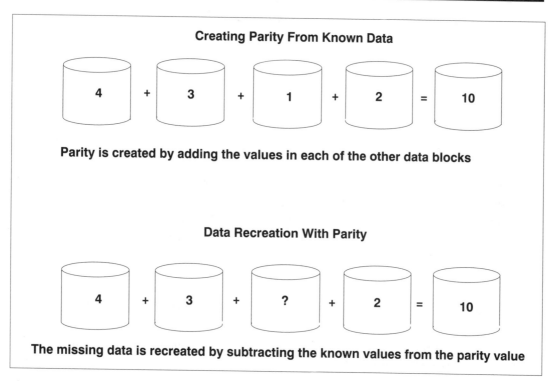

Figure 8.2 Parity in RAID levels 3, 4, and 5. *Source:* Storage Dimensions.

Two-phase commit guarantees the validity of distributed updates in times of hardware or software failure. Referential integrity is a mechanism in databases which ensures that every foreign key matches a primary key. For example, suppose the customer number in a customer file is the primary key and the order number in the order file is the foreign key. If a customer record containing an order were permitted to be deleted, the corresponding order record's foreign key would not be able to match a primary key in the customer file.

Two-phase commit is one of the most challenging features for software vendors to provide. It is a very complex procedure, particularly in a distributed processing environment. In addition, not all two-phase commits are the same. That is, vendor B's two-phase commit may be less robust than vendor A's two-phase commit. Therefore, even though vendor B has a two-phase commit, a programmer might have to write a lot of coding to supplement it.

Comparing server databases with traditional mainframe and minicomputer databases is interesting. Many mainframe and minicomputer databases have the characteristics listed above, but they also have addi-

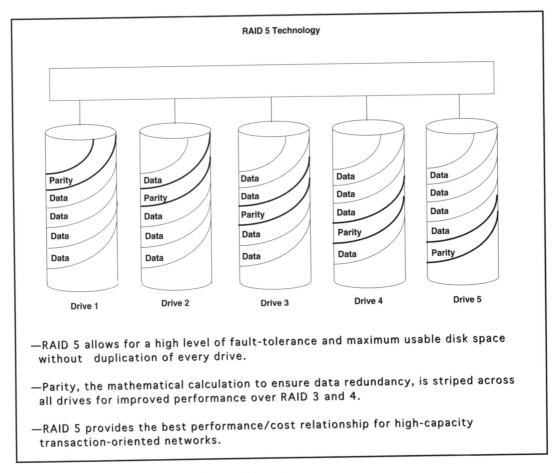

RAID 5 Technology

Drive 1   Drive 2   Drive 3   Drive 4   Drive 5

—RAID 5 allows for a high level of fault-tolerance and maximum usable disk space without duplication of every drive.

—Parity, the mathematical calculation to ensure data redundancy, is striped across all drives for improved performance over RAID 3 and 4.

—RAID 5 provides the best performance/cost relationship for high-capacity transaction-oriented networks.

Figure 8.3 Raid level 5. *Source:* Storage Dimensions.

tional characteristics that users need. Many mainframe and minicomputer databases come with a 4GL that allows fast application development and report writers that facilitate report creation. Server databases do not generally come with 4GLs or report writers *built into them*. In a client/server system, 4GL-type capabilities are found *on the client side*, not the database server side. Most database vendors do provide tools— 4GLs, data query and decision support tools, etc.; however, they provide them as client, front-end software rather than as part of the server, back-end database software. This, of course, is in keeping with the division of labor that occurs in a client/server architecture.

Triggers and stored procedures are very useful features found in a number of server databases. A trigger is something that is activated automatically by the database when certain conditions occur within the database. Accordingly, triggers generally consist of a condition component and an action component. Either a particular state of the database or the execution of a database operation can activate the trigger. The action component is a database program or routine.

Stored procedures are collections of SQL statements that are executed by end users or application software and which can be reused easily. Flow-control directives like IF, THEN, ELSE are usually part of a stored procedure, too. The SQL statements are parsed, checked for syntax and semantic accuracy, compiled and stored in the server's data dictionary. Stored procedures can be executed by application code or by other stored procedures. Stored procedures are useful in a variety of ways. They save time in the development process because new applications can use existing stored procedures. Stored procedures also reduce network traffic and do not have to be compiled each time they are used. Both the Microsoft and Sybase versions of SQL Server have stored procedures and triggers.

Sybase and Gupta are credited with being the earliest vendors with a database that was specifically designed to be a database server. Now there are many database server products. The most commonly used ones are:

- Microsoft/Sybase SQL Server
- Gupta Technologies Inc.'s SQLBase
- Oracle Corporation's Oracle Server
- Digital's Rdb/VMS
- Informix Software's Informix
- Novell's NetWare SQL database
- IBM's OS/2 Database Manager
- Ingres/Ask's Ingres database
- Progress' Progress database

8.3.2 The Role of RDBMSs and SQL in Client/Server Computing

All of the server databases listed above are relational databases. In addition, each of them can be accessed by client software using SQL. SQL is a non-procedural, English-like language that is used for data definition, queries, access control, and data manipulation. It processes sets of records rather than the one-record-at-a-time processing of most procedural languages.

The relational model and the use of SQL are common to the great majority of server databases. In Chapter One, we pointed out that SQL is not *mandatory* for a system to qualify as a client/server system. It was important to point that out because the most important feature of a client/server architecture is the presence of a simplified requester/server model. If someone wants to put a hierarchical database on a network server and access it from a client platform using a particular vendor's proprietary language, he or she still would have met the basics of a simple requester/server model. However, this would certainly not be a typical client/server system.

Some analysts feels strongly that if a database server does not support SQL it should not be recognized as a client/server database. As a result, in the 1980s Information Builder's Focus was not considered by these analysts as qualifying as a client/server database since it did not have SQL at that time. Information Builder's subsequently took a giant step into the official world of client/server with their Enterprise Data Access (EDA)/ SQL. EDA/SQL is covered in more detail in Chapter 12.

The relational model and the use of SQL offer tremendous advantages. Since SQL is a declarative language rather than a procedural one, the client module does not have to be concerned about how the server accesses the data. The client software passes the declarative SQL statement and lets the server take care of everything related to fulfilling the request. The client needs only to be concerned with "what" data it wants, not with the "how" of obtaining it. If a procedural language were used, the language would need to describe each step related to accessing the data. An additional advantage is that the client application does not have to be concerned about changes in the database which occur over time.

Some server database software packages permit SQL queries that contain no reference to the location of the data, thus offering location transparency. In these instances, the server database locates the data for the client module. This means that data can be moved to different physical locations without requiring that changes be made to the client application.

The combination of relational databases and SQL also has the potential of providing portability and interoperability. There are standards for both relational databases and for SQL. ANSI adopted SQL as the standard language for relational databases in 1986. ISO also supports the SQL standard. Most RDBMS vendors and many other tool vendors support the ANSI SQL standard. The SQL Access Group is involved with establishing de facto standards for SQL.

If both client software and server software adheres strictly to SQL standards, interoperability of components is possible. End users have more flexibility if they use SQL rather than get locked into a vendor's proprietary data manipulation language. A developer should be able to take a client module that adheres to SQL standards, change server databases, and still have the client application function, as long as the server databases also adhere to SQL standards. That does not always happen at the present time because there are so many vendor extensions made to SQL standards.

SQL has come to be very important in client/server systems. SQL goes well with some of the primary characteristics of client/server systems which are modularity and ease-of-use. For users who are building client/server systems from scratch, and who have a choice of software, there are many significant advantages to selecting SQL.

8.3.3   Distributed Processing vs. Distributed Databases

Client/server systems are a type of distributed processing, but that does not necessarily mean they are distributed database systems. Distributed processing spreads processing across a set of computing resources. In a client/server system, most of the application processing is on a client workstation, and the database processing takes place on a server machine which is located somewhere else in the network. This situation fits the description of distributed processing: distributed database takes a database and spreads the *data* across a set of computing resources.

Having data in separate locations does not necessarily indicate a true distributed database system. Many mainframe systems involve several heterogeneous databases which are located in different places, but they do not qualify as a true distributed database system in the academic sense of the term. The difference is that the location of specific data in a distributed database is carefully planned in advance. The location of data in heterogeneous databases that have evolved over time often seems to be a bit haphazard. In fact, most of the data in existing mainframe heterogeneous databases could more appropriately be called "scattered data" rather than distributed data.

There are very formal definitions for distributed database systems. As pointed out in Chapter 2, the term "distributed database systems" has come down to us from research laboratories and universities and involves very clear and stringent requirements. One such requirement is complete data location transparency. Other transparencies that must be present are replication transparency, and fragmentation transparency. Chapter 7 contains more information on the similarities and differences between client/server systems and distributed database systems.

8.3.4   Multiple Server Transaction Processing

The big difference between a client/server system that is doing database transaction processing (TP) on one database server from one vendor and one that is using several databases on multiple servers from different vendors is the more complex the configuration, the more sophisticated the transaction processing software that is needed. Transaction processing software now provided by database vendors can usually handle most of the simpler TP situations. However, as data becomes spread out over additional database servers, transaction processing becomes increasingly complex. With distributed database processing, many devices could interact. Sophisticated software is needed to manage complex, distributed transaction processing, especially if database software from more than one vendor is used.

At this stage of client/server technology evolution, an enterprise would need to perform a lot of analysis and research to implement distributed client/server systems that involve transaction processing on multiple servers using databases from multiple vendors. Some large installations are pursuing this kind of complex configuration, but they have done their homework—and are continuing to do it. Since they are using databases from multiple vendors, these sites are not relying on the two-phase commits provided by individual database vendors. In fact, they are not even relying on SQL because they feel SQL will not give them the kind of interoperability they need. Most of these shops are looking at UNIX and examining transaction monitors like Tuxedo, Encina, and Top End. These transaction monitors were discussed in Chapter 4, Open Systems and Client/Server Computing.

8.3.5   Database Servers and Operating Systems

Database servers operate under an operating system (or network operating system) that resides on a server. Different database servers work with different operating systems. For example, Sybase's SQL Server originally ran under UNIX while Microsoft's SQL Server originally ran only under OS/2. Sybase has introduced a SQL Server version for the Novell NetWare platform, and Microsoft has introduced a SQL Server version to run under NT. The NT operating system runs on more platforms than just the Intel-based PC.

Note that the operating system under which a database server operates is different from the operating system under which client software is running. For example, a common configuration is to have front-end software running under DOS/Windows on the client platform and accessing data from SQL Server, which is running under OS/2 on the server platform. There is no multi-user database server software that runs under DOS since DOS is not a multi-user operating system. That is why DOS is rarely used as the operating system on a server. Occasionally DOS is the server operating system when combined with additional software that extends it. While some database products operate under DOS, they are not multi-user databases intended for use on servers. One of the important criteria in selecting a database server is the operating system it operates under and whether that operating system is—or will be—part of your installation's configuration.

When a database server runs under Novell's NetWare—a *network* operating system—the database server software is usually designed and implemented as what Novell calls a NetWare Loadable Module (NLM). NLMs are dynamically linked to the operating system and they actually become *a part of* the operating system. When a database server operates with OS/2, the operating system services requests for resources, sitting between the hardware and the server application to service these requests. With an NLM, since the database server has become part of the operating system, no additional layer of operating system software between the hardware and the server applications is necessary. The advantage of the NLM structure is enhanced speed; the disadvantage is that a misbehaving NLM can crash the entire system.

Another difference between a database server operating under OS/2 and NetWare has to do with the fact that OS/2 is preemptive and NetWare is non-preemptive. With a non-preemptive operating system, each process runs to completion without being interrupted. NetWare will not interrupt a process, but the NLM is responsible for releasing control of system resources at convenient times so that other resources can have access to those resources. With a preemptive operating system, the operating system may interrupt a process at any time in its management of system resources. If this interruption occurs at an inconvenient time, the completion of the process could be significantly slowed down. So the advantage of this characteristic of the NLM structure is advanced speed and the offsetting factor is the increased risk of the entire system crashing.

8.3.6 Similarities and Differences in Database Servers

While there are many differences among database servers, many of them have certain characteristics in common. As mentioned earlier, most are relational databases that offer SQL, and most of the widely used ones also offer capabilities like data retrieval and update, locking mechanisms, multi-user access control, security, query optimization, and caching.

Another difference among database servers is the way a vendor supports SQL. In 1986 and 1989, ANSI published standards documents to standardize SQL. The ANSI standard specifies two levels of compatibility: Level 1 and Level 2. Level 1 establishes a base core of standards and Level 2 adds to these making Level 2 a superset of Level 1. Level 2 also has a separate Integrity Enhancement addendum. The highest level of ANSI compatibility that a database server can have is ANSI SQL Level 2 with the Integrity Enhancement addendum. A number of vendors provide enhancements to ANSI standard SQL. The Microsoft/Sybase SQL Server's stored procedures and triggers are enhancements to ANSI SQL; however, these features will be part of the next ANSI SQL specification.

Database servers also differ in whether and how they implement referential integrity: with declarative referential integrity or procedural referential integrity. Declarative referential integrity adheres to the ideal of the referential model for data storage which says that all information about tables should be stored within the tables themselves. With declarative referential integrity, referential integrity is implemented through keys stored within the database tables following the ANSI Level 2 Integrity Enhancement addendum. Procedural referential integrity is implemented with triggers which are automatically executed when an UPDATE, DELETE, or INSERT command is executed. If a "parent" record is deleted, for example, all the "children" (dependent records) are also deleted in a cascading delete or else the delete is not allowed.

Gupta's SQLBase is an example of a database server that uses declarative referential integrity, while Microsoft/Sybase SQL Server implements procedural referential integrity. Although some database servers did not have referential integrity built into them at first, nearly all of them either have it, are adding it, or plan to add it. Users should make sure to have the current information from vendors when assessing different packages. For example, Oracle's and Ingres' database servers did not originally have built-in support for referential integrity. However, they both now have some form of referential integrity. Again, the vendor should be contacted for up-to-date information in this constantly changing environment. If a vendor does not provide referential integrity then it is the responsibility of the front-end application programmer to ensure referential integrity for the database.

Multi-user capabilities are implemented a little differently by different vendors. In some database servers, a process is created for each user; in other database servers, a thread is created for each new user. A process is often defined as a program in execution. A thread could be considered as an execution path within a program. A central processing unit (CPU) executes steps in sequence. The passage of the CPU through an instruction sequence is called a thread of execution. Multiple threads of execution can be supported within a single process. In effect, the program is executing in two or more spots in its code "at the same time."* Multi-threaded servers create a thread for each new user instead of creating a new, separate user process for each new user. Threads are more efficient than processes. Multi-threaded servers use less memory and CPU resources than a server that creates a new process for each user. Sybase's SQL Server and Gupta's SQLBase are two examples of database servers that implement a multi-threaded single-server architecture.

8.4   PRODUCT DESCRIPTIONS

8.4.1   Sybase/Microsoft SQL Server

Microsoft/Sybase SQL Server, supported by more third-party vendors than any other SQL database, is regarded as a market leader. We pointed out earlier that Sybase's SQL Server originally ran under UNIX and later under Novell's NetWare, while Microsoft's SQL Server originally ran under OS/2. Microsoft licensed SQL Server code from Sybase and then optimized it to run under OS/2 on a server. Both Microsoft and Sybase SQL Server have stored procedures and triggers which were discussed earlier in this chapter. With the release of Version 4.2 of Microsoft SQL Server in March 1992, the product had all of the features of Sybase SQL Server, meaning that the two products were finally "in synch." These database servers are expected to run under additional operating systems in the future. Microsoft SQL Server is expected to be a popular choice to run with Microsoft NT.

Some of the differences between the two products are that they operate on different platforms and that their speed, price, and packaging are different. Sybase SQL Server for NetWare is an extremely fast product and therefore comes with a high price. Prices for software change all the time, but at one time Microsoft SQL Server was $7,995 for an unlimited-user license, while Sybase SQL Server for NetWare was $29,995 for an unlimited-user license. In addition Sybase charged $290 for each client workstation (minus a 25% discount for multiple purchases). Microsoft had no additional per-client charges, and it bundled in a number of

---

*Since most computers have only one CPU, at any one instant in time only one program or thread can actually be executing. However, with preemptive scheduling, execution can shift among programs and threads many times a second causing people to view the system as if programs or threads execute simultaneously.

extras at no additional charge.* Sybase's product is often used in large, high-volume applications which require its high speed processing.

8.4.2   Gupta Technologies' SQLBase

Gupta's SQLBase is considered a leading database server in the client/ server market. It had early support for DOS, OS/2, NetWare, and UNIX. Gupta's SQLBase did not have the stored procedures and triggers of SQL Server when this was written; however, the SQLBase Server NLM has some features that SQL Server did not have, like declarative referential integrity and true forward- and backward-scrollable cursors. Other advanced features include data compression between client and server, cost-based optimization, online backup, and declarative referential integrity—which was described above.

SQLBase offers several options with its declarative referential integrity, permitting a developer to specify how a DELETE should be handled. The developer has the choice of the CASCADE option: automatic deletion of dependent rows when the parent is deleted; the RESTRICT option: prevention of the deletion of a parent row when dependent rows exist; and of the NULL option: setting the values of the foreign key column in the dependent row to NULL when the parent row is deleted.

SQLBase lacks the widespread support from third-party front-end vendors enjoyed by SQL Server, but Gupta provides a number of its own highly-regarded front-end products for SQLBase. Quest is a well-liked end user tool, and SQL Windows is Gupta's application development package for SQLBase.

While SQLBase does not have stored procedures, Gupta offers something similar called chained SQL. With this capability, frequently executed SQL statements can be stored on the server and accessed by any application. As a result, a chained set of multiple SQL statements can be executed with a one-statement call to the database server.

8.4.3   Informix Corporation's Informix OnLine

The Informix OnLine database is considered another top performer and is often used with mission-critical transaction processing systems. An example of a mission critical OLTP system using Informix is Hyatt Hotel's reservation system. This system is described in Chapter 22.

The Informix OnLine database operates under the UNIX operating

---

*While these software prices may change, it is likely that Sybase SQL Server will continue to be more expensive than Microsoft SQL Server.

system. The vendor, Informix, has been dedicated to open systems since the company was formed in 1989. In addition to wanting an open system platform—which UNIX is regarded as—Informix says that performance was another important issue, and UNIX could deliver that as well. Informix OnLine provides high performance and high data availability. It uses a cost-based optimizer, shared memory, and direct I/O. Additional features include on-line archiving, disk mirroring, and fast recovery mechanisms.

In on-line transaction processing systems, Informix OnLine is used with Informix-Star, the vendor's network product. Informix-Star, with its distributed database architecture, can transparently route data to individual database sites. Additional information about the Informix database architecture and related tools can be found in Hyatt Hotel's implementation description in Chapter 22.

8.4.4   IBM's Database Manager

Some history is needed to follow the course of IBM's database server. IBM's OS/2 Standard Edition was announced in December 1987. OS/2 Extended Edition (EE) was announced in July 1988 and had two additional subsystems: the Communications Manager and the Database Manager. In October 1991, IBM combined those two components into a separate package called Extended Services, allowing customers to buy the Database Manager and the Communications Manager either together or separately.

Database Manager has a capability called Database Application Remote Interface (DARI) which it calls a stored procedure, although using this term could cause some confusion. The similarity between DARI and Sybase's stored procedures is that DARI permits code to be stored at the database server; the big difference is that with Sybase's stored procedures, SQL code is stored, while with the DARI capability, C, Fortran, Cobol, or Rexx code is stored. DARI basically lets programmers store large pieces of compiled client application code in the database server in the form of DLLs. Actually these DLLs are what IBM's Database Manager calls stored procedures.

DLLs enhance the speed of applications. Queries that involve multiple statements can be stored in the DLLs. Thus, as with stored procedures, the client application software has to send only one statement to the server to have multiple statements executed as a result.

For companies that want their client/server systems to also access DB2 data on the mainframe, Database Manager offers a number of advantages. For one thing, its SQL syntax closely matches that of DB2. Also, the declarative integrity features of the two databases are very similar. In addition, IBM can provide installations with transparent connectivity to DB2 databases on mainframes with its Distributed Database Connection Services/2.

As a result of its effort to be compatible with DB2, Database Manager does not offer triggers to enforce referential integrity. With IBM's support of declarative referential integrity, triggers are not needed to enforce referential integrity in Database Manager. However, triggers are also used for enforcing business rules unrelated to referential integrity, so their absence is a disadvantage.

8.4.5   Oracle Corporation's Oracle Server

A number of characteristics make Oracle a strong contender in the database server market. First, Oracle has always been known for its portability. This SQL database runs on more hardware, software, and network platforms than any other relational database. Second, Oracle Server is supported by more than 70 third-party front-end applications. In addition, Oracle is known for its strong customer support. We mentioned earlier that in a survey by Forrester Research, Inc. 68% of respondents indicated they will use a server database by 1995. Twenty percent of those respondents indicated they plan to use Oracle as their database server.

While Oracle has always had many strengths, for quite a long while its database server product did not have a lot of the features that an industrial-strength database server must have in today's market. However, Oracle7—as Version 7 of the Oracle database is known—provides support for Oracle's version of triggers and stored procedures. The stored procedures must be written in Oracle's own proprietary 4GL, PL/SQL. Version 7 also provides support for other important features like cost-based optimization and declarative referential integrity.

While Oracle7 provides compliance with ANSI SQL level 2, their PL/SQL 4GL extensions to ANSI SQL offer some very useful capabilities like syntax for error handling, looping, and branching. It also permits programmers to send blocks of statements from the client to the server at once. This can reduce the need for communication between the client and server, and it can speed up overall network performance. PL/SQL can be ported to another Oracle platform by recompiling the code on the new platform.

8.4.6   Ask Corporation's Ingres Server

Ingres is known for several primary features one of which is its technical excellence. Ingres first released a database server for the UNIX platform and then ported it to OS/2. With Version 6.4 of Ingres Server for OS/2, the UNIX version and the OS/2 version matched each other.

One of Ingres' major innovations is its cost-based optimization techniques. This involves a procedure where the database engine analyzes the various ways of resolving the database query and statistically estimates which approach would be the most efficient. The syntax that the programmer uses does not impact the quality of the optimization results. The optimization technique includes converting the query into syntax-independent relational algebra. As a result, no matter how the query is phrased, the optimizer will still deliver the same result. Ingres pioneered this technique which has since been adapted by other vendors.

The statistics-based optimizer also places limitations on resource consumption by user queries. Before executing a query, the optimizer determines the number of rows that will be returned and the amount of disk I/O that will be required to process the query. This capability prevents "runaway" user queries which can seriously impact system performance. When software cannot automatically prevent such runaway queries, system administrators are forced to limit user access to production data.

Ingres provides Level 1 ANSI SQL support and also supports its own Quel language. Quel was a competitor of SQL before SQL was made the standard language for relational databases. Since Quel is a fast language in operation, it still has a loyal base of users.

Ingres enforces business policies and provides referential integrity with "rules," Ingres' term for triggers. Rules are procedures which are activated when a specific criteria—defined by the user—is met. The procedures can be coded in SQL and in Ingres/4GL. Ingres supports an unlimited number of independent rules per table. In addition, changes that are made by the execution of a rule can activate other rules to an unlimited depth—called unlimited forward chaining.

An additional feature provided by Ingres is a database event alerter which is somewhat similar to a cross between a trigger and a stored procedure. It consists of SQL statements stored in the database and can cause actions to automatically take place as a result of a condition within the database. For example, if a payment from a credit customer is more than five days overdue, a late notice to be sent to the customer can automatically be generated.

8.5 OBJECT-ORIENTED DATABASES IN CLIENT/SERVER SYSTEMS

Object-oriented databases are often used in client/server systems. One benefit object orientation offers to databases is the ability to handle substantially different types of entities, including complex data types, within a database structure. CAD/CAM applications with their complex data requirements and engineering drawings are often considered as natural candidates for object-oriented database management system (OODBMS) technology. An OODBMS offers engineers capabilities that hierarchical and relational systems could not provide to handle parts and the large number of interrelationships that parts involve.

An example will show how important an OODBMS can be in a manufacturing environment. If an engineer changes the diameter of a bolt, the stress on the plate to which the bolt is attached will also change. If that happens to be on the bottom of an airplane and the plate changes shape, the fuselage of the plane also changes shape. If the fuselage changes shape, the wing changes shape.

The fact that the object-oriented environment is a message passing environment can make a significant difference in this situation. When the engineer changes the bolt, the bolt object can automatically trigger a message to the plate to change the size of the plate. The plate object, in turn, can automatically trigger a message for other elements to change their size as well. This cascading message effect saves a tremendous amount of time that would have been necessary for the engineer to ensure that all these changes were made.

An OODBMS combines the fundamental concepts of object orientation with such traditional database capabilities as persistency (retention) transaction support, concurrency sharing, and recoverability.

As mentioned earlier, object-oriented databases are able to store complex data types. These include Binary Large Objects (BLOBs). Items that can be stored as a BLOB in an OODBMS include entities such as spreadsheets, facsimile, digitized images, and word processing documents. This further enhances developers' ability to devise new combinations of technologies to increase productivity.

Many of the traditional database vendors are adding object-oriented capabilities to their databases. The addition of BLOBs is one of the most prominent steps that vendors like Informix are taking to expand the capabilities of their existing databases with object-oriented features.

8.5.1   Implementations of OODBMS Client/Server Systems

Innovative Systems Techniques (Instye), based in Waltham, MA, has an object-oriented database system, Vision, that is popular with financial customers. It is used for investment analysis and other situations where it is necessary to keep history and various versions of information.

T. Rowe Price is using Instye's Vision client/server OODBS to complement and supplement their IMS and DB2 databases where their production data resides. The firm does a nightly download of data from IMS to the Vision database. T. Rowe Price is using Vision's capabilities to add new functionality to the types of things their portfolio analysts are able to accomplish using the system's object-oriented capabilities. One of the most popular features of the new system is that due to its ease-of-use, end users are now able to build their own complex applications. When the firm had transferred some data from IMS to DB2, end users were able to start doing their own queries, although they still had to go to the MIS department for complex queries. With Vision, however, they have an easy-to-use Smalltalk type of environment. As a result, the end users are able to build very complex applications by themselves.

8.5.2   Other Object-Oriented–Client/Server Connections

There are many ways that the object-oriented approach and the client/ server approach are connected. Client modules and application development tools are two of the ways mentioned at the start of this section. A new vision of the connection between these two technologies is offered in a book entitled *Intelligent Offices, Object-Oriented Multi-Media Information Management in Client/Server Architectures*. Written by Setrag Khoshafian, A. Brad Baker, Razmik Abnous, and Kevin Shepherd, it was published by John Wiley & Sons in 1992. According to the authors, the goal of the book is to demonstrate how mature database management systems, office automation, and GUIs can be integrated with imaging/ multi-media hardware to create affordable document-imaging solutions for PCs.

The authors of the book maintain that the underlying conceptual model of a modern, intelligent office should be object-oriented. In such an environment, a user would interact with a collection of metaphors that represent office objects and office activities. For example, the user would interact with icons that represent such things as forms, folders, and cabinets. The objects represented by these icons would be stored in the database server. As a result, the user would be able to locate objects by accessing its icon, updating it, and returning it. The procedure is very similar to the physical procedures found in a traditionally manually-oriented office. The description of the modern, intelligent office closely resembles that portion of work that is currently being performed using icons in GUIs in client/server systems today. The book envisions a dramatic increase in the portion of office work performed with icons and objects in the future.

9
NETWORKING CONCEPTS

9.1   UNDERSTANDING THE BASICS

Networking is a complex and elusive subject. Communications designers often use the symbol of a cloud in their network drawings. (See Figure 9.1.) It seems like a fitting symbol for an area as elusive, abstract—even nebulous—as networking.

While client/server developers do not have to be experts in networking, it is important that they have some knowledge of the subject. Applications can experience serious difficulties when LANs are not planned right and set up appropriately. It will not always be obvious when a problem is network related rather than database or application related. As a result, a database administrator could spend a long time wondering why a database server is slow when it is actually a network problem.

Insufficient bandwidth (capacity) and bottlenecks (points of congestion) are two primary problems that slow down a network. While bottlenecks within a LAN are probably the biggest culprit, insufficient capability for bandwidth-hungry applications like imaging could mean the difference between success and failure for a client/server system. In some cases, developers have built imaging or other bandwidth-intensive applications and expected the network people to provide them with infinite bandwidth. When building systems that are dependent upon networking, developers need to be aware of what the networking capabilities and limitations are.

Since most client/server application developers will probably know

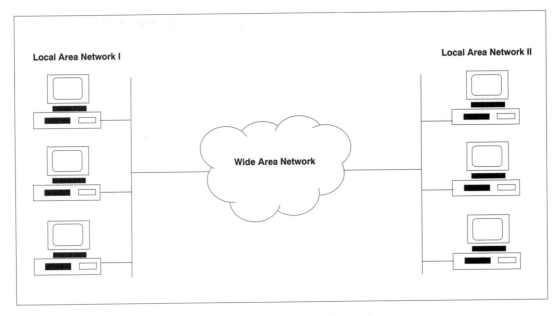

Figure 9.1 A "cloud" represents a wide area network in this configuration.

only a little about networking, it is advisable that they work closely with networking people. When possible, network people should be involved with the design of a new client/server application from the start. This is becoming more and more important with the increasing number of options and mixes of software and hardware related to networking.

This chapter is intended to cover the basics of networking. If a section within this chapter contains information in which you are not interested, like topology or transmission media, we recommend that you jump to the next section rather than jumping to the next chapter. Also, there may be a number of topics that are not essential for you right now, although you may find that an understanding of some of them will come in very handy in the future. For example, a basic understanding of the ISO's OSI seven-layer Reference Model is a useful framework for understanding various networking concepts even for those who have no interest in implementing an OSI network.

9.1.1 The Role of Networks

Networking is actually a prerequisite to developing a client/server system. In fact, one of the main reasons why client/server computing is becoming so popular is due to the growing availability of LANs which are now present in large and small companies alike.

While it is technically true that both the client and the server portions of a client/server system can be on the same machine, most systems are not built that way. Often, when both the client and the server portions are located on one machine, it is a temporary situation or due to some special circumstances. One example relates to application development. Consider a development situation where a PC will be the client and the mainframe will be the server. Developing systems on a personal computer is far less expensive than developing systems on a mainframe, so it would make sense to develop and test both the client portion and as much of the mainframe portion as possible on a PC platform. After the system is developed and tested, the server portion is moved to the mainframe. So, while there are times when the client and server portions are resident on one platform, that is the exception rather than the rule.

Networking is at the core of today's important client/server implementations because a local area network permits the exploitation of desktop computing in solving an enterprise's information needs.

9.1.2   Network Components

While many separate components make up a local area network, there are three primary categories of components that are essential to any LAN:

- Cabling system/s
- Network interface card/s (NIC), also called network adapters
- Network operating system/s (NOS)

9.1.2.1   Cabling Systems

A cabling system consists of the wire or cable that connects networking devices and the attachment unit that permits the device to be connected to the cable.* A network interface card is installed in each PC in order to connect that PC to the network. Different network interface cards are used for different types of networks, such as Ethernet, token-ring, Arcnet, or fiber optic cable. Network operating systems control the flow of messages and provide other important services. Network operating systems are covered in the next chapter.

_____

*Wireless networks are becoming more and more common. Any installation that has users who move around a lot (e.g., salespeople) should examine wireless network technology.

Each of the PCs on a network are interconnected with a cabling system. Communication takes place when the PCs send and receive messages over this cable. Cabling can consist of shielded or unshielded twisted-wire pairs, coaxial cable, or fiber-optic links. The selection of cabling is made in conjunction with the choice of other components within the network. Unshielded twisted-pair is normally used on smaller LANs, with the other choices used on larger LANs. Fiber optic is a high-performance choice.

9.1.2.2   Benefits of Fiber Optic Cabling

Fiber optic cabling has more bandwidth which leads to its high-performance. Once very expensive, its price is getting lower all the time. Even though it is still somewhat more expensive then other cabling, it may offer the best value due to its capacity and ability to carry signals over long distances. It is immune to electromagnetic interference. It is also more secure as discussed in Chapter 21, Security in Client/Server Systems. This security comes from the fact that with fiber, an intruder has to physically tap into the cable. The resulting dip in light levels can be detected with security measures. (With copper wiring, an intruder can listen in by simply placing a radio frequency receiver nearby. It is not necessary to physically tap into the cable.)

9.1.2.3   Network Interface Cards (NICs)

PCs are able to connect to networks with the addition of a network interface card (NIC), also known as a network adapter. It generally takes the form of a circuit board that is added into the system unit. Usually, PCs that do not have room for an internal NIC can have one added as an external device which is cabled to the computer. Some portable computers are connected to networks in this manner.

The NIC listens to all the messages being sent over the cable and determines which ones are meant for the PC in which it is installed. In turn, when the PC wants to send a message, the NIC determines when there is an appropriate time in the network traffic and then sends out the message. A variety of different NICs have been developed for different types of cables.

9.1.3   Early LANs

Many early LAN architectures were implemented so users could benefit from print servers and file servers. While those LANs were limited in their capabilities, they paved the way for today's client/server systems. This situation has its advantages and disadvantages. The advantages stem from the fact that these early LANs provided some degree of experience with networking. Also the proliferation of LANs provided a basic infrastructure for an architecture that mandates the presence of a LAN. The disadvantages stem from the fact that early LANs did not have the capabilities and robustness that are required for today's client/server systems. The early LANs actually did not need much robustness.

The early LANs that were established for print and file sharing were basically simple in set up and operation. They did not have requirements to support a constantly heavy flow of traffic. Their usage was more "bursty" in nature—activity came in bursts when a large file was sent over the wire. Since most of the early networks were used by small workgroups, security requirements were minimal and often met by simply securing the work area. Network management requirements in small workgroups were also minimal.

Early LANs had limited capabilities, but they satisfied the needs of their users who basically wanted to share resources. Problems began to occur when these LANs were used for applications that required more robust capabilities. Since it is often the presence—indeed proliferation—of these early LANs that stimulates interest in client/server applications, some caution is called for when users are considering using an existing LAN for new applications. The capabilities of a LAN that satisfied the needs of sharing a printer may not be adequate to satisfy the requirements of a client/server application. Upgrading the LAN may sometimes satisfy the additional requirements; installing a completely new LAN may be required.

Some of the earliest LANs were UNIX-based ones. In fact, many client/server concepts were originated in early UNIX-based local area networks.

9.1.4 Factors Affecting LAN Selection

Very basic, practical issues can impact LAN selection. In fact, the choice of a LAN may be even be pre-determined in some cases by existing circumstances. For example, a network may already be installed that meets the needs of the client/server application. When an existing LAN is available, a requirements analysis should be performed to see if it will meet the needs of the proposed system. If it will, using the existing LAN is the economical way to proceed. If no network is installed, then the wiring that already exists in a particular building—the premises wiring—may be an important consideration. Nearly all buildings are wired for telephone services. Usually this telephone wiring is twisted-wire-pair cable, consisting of two insulated strands of copper wire that have been braided. This wiring is capable of supporting networking. When installing their very first LANs, some companies make the cost-based decision to use this already-existing cabling.

Networking groups within most companies of any significant size have been installing LANs for a number of years now. In fact, many mid- to large-size companies have a wide variety of different cabling systems installed in various parts of the company. In many companies, where new cabling is being installed, it is fiber optic cabling, which is a wise choice for the future because of its superior capabilities and diversity.

As mentioned above, sometimes there may be no "selection" at all, because if there is a LAN already installed, that is the LAN that will be used for the initial client/server system. This is not a problem as long as the existing LAN will be able to meet the operating and performance requirements of the proposed client/server system.

9.1.4.1   Performance Considerations

Performance considerations are among the most important requirements in LAN selection, and the type of transmission media is an important aspect of a network's performance. Higher data rates usually require more sophisticated media. Fiber optic cable provides the best capacity. Fiber optic cable also offers long-run cabling support without requiring the use of repeaters. With other cabling, the strength of the transmission signal weakens over a certain distance and must be regenerated with a repeater. While fiber optic cabling used to be quite expensive, its cost has come down in recent years. Shielded twisted-pair wiring, CATV, and coaxial cable are other options for high data rates. Unshielded twisted-pair phone wiring is used for lower speed, short-range use. LAN operating systems and network server software can also impact LAN performance.

Two commonly used local area network architectures are Ethernet and IBM's Token Ring. Ethernet was originally available at a speed of 10 megabits per second (Mbps). Two transmission technique options were specified for Token Ring: twisted-wire pair cable was available at data rates of 1 Mbps or 4 Mbps, and transmission over coaxial cable was available at rates of 4 Mbps, 20 Mbps, or 40 Mbps. Fiber optic cable offers higher rates. The Fiber Distributed Data Interface (FDDI) standard specifies a data rate of 100 Mbps using multimode optical fiber transmission. A relatively new approach known as "Fast Ethernet" offers speeds of 100 Mbps over voice-grade unshielded, twisted-pair copper cabling. Another high speed alternative is cell relay or asynchronous transfer mode (ATM) technology (discussed in the next subsection.)

Potential users should keep in mind that LANs rarely achieve their highest rated speeds. In reality, they generally go much slower due to the combination of various kinds of equipment in the overall network. When estimating the actual operating speed of the production network, this must be taken into consideration.

The future requirements of the system are important, too. If the system will need to have increased speed in the future or will need to carry new information formats, there must be a plan for how those future needs will be met. If the next system to be installed will double the number of end users, a plan for how these additional users will be accommodated should be formulated in advance of that need.

The need for individual LANs to interoperate in the future should also be taken into consideration. There is a strong possibility that all of the LANs within an enterprise will eventually need to interoperate. This will be much easier if it is thought out in advance rather than left to chance. LAN interoperability is covered in Chapter 11.

Also, as with all other hardware and software selections, vendor reputation and vendor support are important considerations, too.

9.2 STANDARDS RELATED TO NETWORKING

Standards become increasingly important as systems need to become interconnected. When networks need to be connected to other networks, standards can ease the job. Large enterprises that plan to proceed with long-term development of client/server systems should be aware of the different networking standards that exist so they can develop a sound plan. Anyone who has wrestled with the increasing difficulty of trying to interconnect different subsystems, programs, and files in very large mainframe installations can appreciate that similar problems will occur when trying to interconnect completely diverse networks.

9.2.1 The ISO Seven-Layer OSI Reference Model

The seven-layer Open Systems Interconnection (OSI) Reference Model, established by the ISO, is a convenient tool for helping to understand networking concepts. It takes a divide-and-conquer type of approach to the overall problem, using a layered architecture to partition the functionality of a network. A basic understanding of the OSI model is helpful in understanding many different networking concepts.

The IEEE has developed an important set of standards regarding architectures for LANs. A *detailed* description of the OSI Reference model and the related IEEE LAN standards are beyond the scope of this book. There are many excellent books with details on the ISO and IEEE standards. These standards are described in enough detail later in this chapter so the reader may see how they relate to the overall context of networking in a client/server environment.

The seven layers of the Reference Model and their basic functionality are shown in Figure 9.2.

The highest layer of the reference model provides a means for application processes to access system interconnection facilities, while the

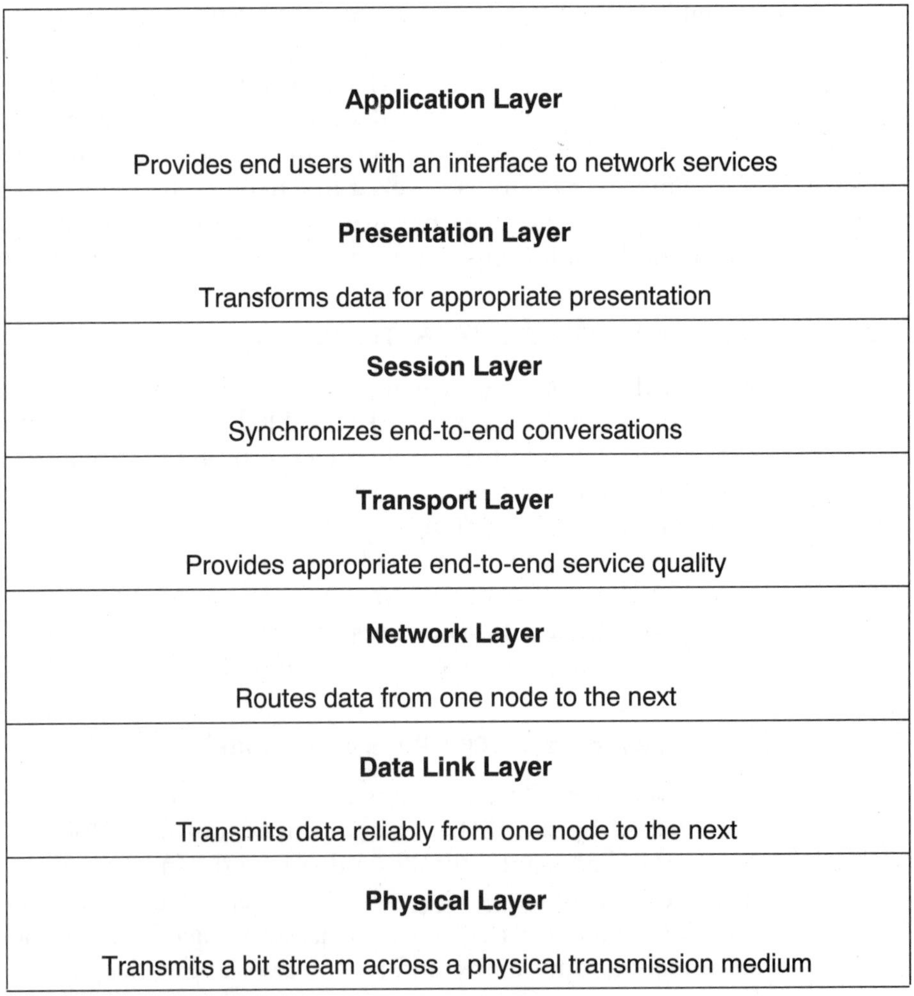

Application Layer Provides end users with an interface to network services
Presentation Layer Transforms data for appropriate presentation
Session Layer Synchronizes end-to-end conversations
Transport Layer Provides appropriate end-to-end service quality
Network Layer Routes data from one node to the next
Data Link Layer Transmits data reliably from one node to the next
Physical Layer Transmits a bit stream across a physical transmission medium

Figure 9.2 OSI reference model.

lower layers are responsible for the transmission of bit streams across a physical transmission medium. Proceeding from the bottom up, intermediate layers provide increasing levels of service, with each layer building on and adding to the services of the layer below it.

The OSI reference model is concerned with the interconnection between systems. It is involved with how systems exchange information. It provides a generalized view of networking as a layered architecture. Incidentally, reference models and layered architectures *in general* are becoming increasingly important concepts to describe the complexities of how many different aspects of information technology fit together.

The layered approach takes the many functions that must be performed by a network and organizes them into groups called layers. Each layer performs a specific set of functions and provides a specific set of services.

Imagine an instructor trying to explain to a PC novice how various pieces of software in a personal computer work together. One way to do this might be to draw two layers with the operating system on one layer and the application program (e.g., Lotus 1–2–3) on the other. The instructor would explain that different functions are performed by the different layers. That explanation is analogous to understanding the seven layers of the reference mode: different layers perform different functions.

The functions and services provided by each layer are defined in a protocol specification. Protocols, in general, describe any set of rules that allow entities (machines, pieces of software, people) to coordinate with each other without ambiguity. For example, to use an everyday example, a protocol that everyone uses on the telephone without even thinking about it is when the phone rings and a person picks it up, he or she is expected to say something, not just to hold the phone and listen. One might say "hello" or—if in an office—identify the company. The person who is calling waits until the speaker is done, and then identifies himself or herself. The two parties exchange information. When they are finished, each says good-bye before hanging up the telephone. All of this is a commonly accepted protocol for using the telephone. Communication protocols are similar. They define the rules that are followed in the processing performed as part of a service. In the OSI model, there are protocol specifications related to each of the seven layers.

The lower layers—layers one (physical) and two (data link)—of the OSI model are concerned with the delivery of information from one point to another. The physical layer delivers bits from one end of a wire to another. Actually, of course, it adapts the bits into a form suitable for transmission over the available media. This functionality is often implemented in hardware and takes care of things like bit serial transmission, synchronization, and clocking. The second layer—the data link layer—provides reliable data transmission from one node to another.

The primary function of the third layer, the network layer, is routing. There may be many possible routes by which two points can be connected. The network layer is responsible for establishing, maintaining, and terminating a network connection between two points.

The transport layer, the fourth, is a true end-to-end layer. It is responsible for providing data transfer between two machines at an agreed-upon level of quality. The lower level layers are concerned with interaction between a particular machine and its immediate neighbors which may be nothing more than a variety of hardware devices. The transport layer is concerned with the ultimate source machine and the ultimate destination machine. It selects the particular class of service to use and monitors the transmission to ensure that it is maintained.

Layer five, the session layer, as its name implies, establishes sessions between different machines. One example of a service provided at the session layer is dialogue control. With dialogue control, the session layer controls when users can send and receive data. If traffic can only go one way at a time like a train on a single track, the session layer manages whose turn it is.

The presentation layer, layer six, is concerned with the syntax and semantics of the information transmitted. Services provided by the presentation layer may include data conversion, character code translation, and data compression and expansion.

Application processes access the networking system through the seventh and final application layer in order to exchange information with other application processes. Services provided by the application layer are establishment and termination of connections between users and managing the systems being interconnected.

9.2.1.1 How the Layers Work Together

The way communication occurs is that messages are passed between entities in two adjoining layers. In each instance, the upper layer entity is called the user, and the lower layer entity is called the provider. That is, each layer makes use of the services of the layer below it, and provides services to the layer above it. Layered architectures must try to achieve as much independence among layers as possible in the hope that future changes can be limited to just one layer. In addition, designers aim for simple interlayer boundaries and the ability to add future options within individual layers. While absolute independence of layers is difficult, since parameters for one layer are generated in or passed from other layers, a reasonable degree of independence is achievable.

To understand how each layer uses the services of the layer below it, consider an example starting with end user A at the application level wishing to communicate and transfer information with end user B, located at a remote system. For this example, both end users are at a level just above the application layer (top-most level—layer 7) of the OSI Reference Model).

End user A requests a service of the application layer (on his or her system) to send the message. Essentially, what the application layer at end user A's system needs to do is to perform this requested service by the exchange of messages with its *peer application layer* on user B's system. To do this, the application layer requests a service from a presentation entity (layer 6). To respond to this request for service from layer 7, the presentation layer initiates the required function through an exchange of messages with *its peer presentation layer* on end user B's system. Again, to accomplish this, the presentation layer requests a service from a session layer entity (layer 5). This type of action happens all the way down the seven layers. It is sometimes referred to as a "cascading action."

As each lower layer provides the service requested by the higher layer, additional information is added to the original message. In fact, the original message is encapsulated by the new information that has been added to it by the lower layer. For example, different types of addressing data may be added to end user A's original message. Eventually, the message which has been "encapsulated" (or has had information added to it) several times reaches the physical wire and is sent to end user B's system. On "System B," the reverse process takes place. As the message travels up each layer, that layer accesses the information that its peer level sent, "reads" it, and then removes it from the message because the higher layers do not need that information. Each layer reads and removes the information that was meant for its own particular use. By the time the message gets up to the application layer on the receiving system, end user B gets the message as end user A sent it.

9.2.1.2 Comparison to Other Layered Protocols

As previously stated, a basic understanding of the seven OSI layers can be valuable to an understanding of other networking concepts and protocols. In reviewing other networking architectures, we will see that they generally are layered; however, it should noted that not all network architectures use all seven layers of the OSI model. In some protocols, two layers may be combined because the functions that those two layers provide in the OSI model are provided in a different or combined way. In other protocols, some functions are provided in a different layer than they are in the OSI layer.

Figure 9.3 shows a simplified comparison of the architectural layers of OSI and IBM's proprietary Systems Network Architecture (SNA).

While the overall services provided by SNA are quite similar to OSI, there are some differences so there is not an exact correlation between the layers. For example, the SNA Path Control Layer provides services that are similar to those in OSI's Transport and Session layers. The figure also shows that the four lower layers in SNA are considered the transport service provider.

9.2.1.3 The Special Role of the Transport Layer

The transport layer plays a significant role because it provides end-to-end communication. End-to-end communication means the same as host-to-host communication or sender-machine to remote-receiver-machine communication. Looking at the layers from the bottom up, the transport

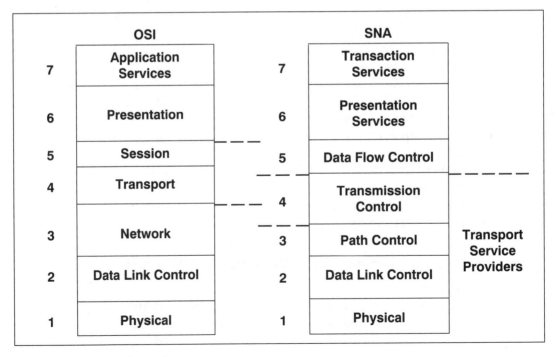

Figure 9.3 OSI and SNA layers.

layer is the first one that is able to provide reliable communication. From the perspective of the top layer looking down, the transport layer is the layer that involves taking into consideration the actions being taken at both ends of the connection. Some consider the transport layer as the heart of the entire protocol hierarchy because of the services it provides. In providing its end-to-end service, the transport layer provides reliable, cost-effective data transport from one machine to another independent of the physical network being used. The hardware and/or software that does the work within the transport layer is called the *transport entity*.

The term "Quality of Service" is often used in conjunction with the transport layer. A major role of the transport layer is to enhance the quality of service provided by the network layer. If the network layer provides an excellent service, the transport layer does not have to do much. However, if the network layer provides a poor service, the transport layer has to bring that service up to the quality that the transport users want.

Why would the quality of service provided by the network layer vary? It varies because actual implementations use different products from various vendors and the features that diverse vendors choose to implement in their products can vary widely. This can happen even when vendors adhere to OSI specifications because there are so many options available in OSI standards.

One of the most important things that the transport layer does is to isolate the upper layer protocols and services from the technology, design, and imperfections of the subnetwork. The transport layer performs error handling functions for subnetworks that are not designed for reliable data exchange. Therefore, whatever the underlying subnetwork, the transport layer will provide the session layer with a reliable data transmission service.

The term "subnetworks" is used differently by different people. In Figure 9.4, the area that is surrounded and entitled "Communication Subnetwork" is what we will refer to as a subnetwork in this section. The layers below the transport layer perform point-to-point communication instead of the end-to-end communication indicated by the dashed line which goes directly from Host A to Host B at the transport layer.

In most wide area networks (WANs), subnetworks consists of transmission lines and switching elements. Transmission lines transfer bits from one machine to another. Switching elements are specialized computers that connect two or more transmission lines. Data arrives at the switching element on an incoming line and determines on which outgoing line to forward the data. In WAN communication, there may be a number of subnetworks between Site A and Site B.

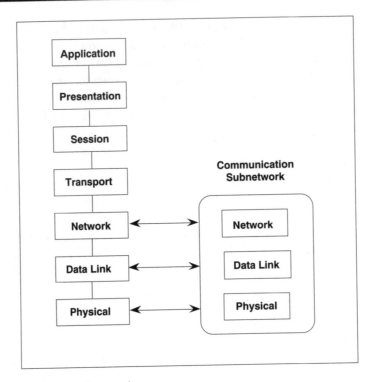

Figure 9.4 A communication subnetwork.

9.2.1.4 Connection-Oriented vs. Connectionless

Subnetworks can be connection-oriented or connectionless. These decisions generally take place at the network layer and the transport layer. Deciding between implementing connection-oriented and connectionless service may be an important decision in client/server LANs when these LANs will be connected to other LANs and WANs. Details related to connectionless and connect-oriented service can be found in many books that are available describing data communication technology and enterprise-wide networking. However, since they are important concepts, a brief overview of them is necessary, and readers should be aware that this is an area they may want to research further.

Quite simply, connection-oriented subnetworks operate by establishing a connection. A connection in networks or subnetworks can be understood by thinking about a telephone call. In order to talk to someone on the phone, we establish—or rather, the telephone company equipment establishes—a connection. The telephone company maintains that connection for as long as the two parties are conversing. When they are finished talking, they hang up. This terminates the connection.

An analogy to help explain connectionless service is to think about how the postal system handles letters. Each letter sent contains the address of its destination. Suppose someone wrote a letter, addressed the envelope, and sealed it and then remembered something else he or she wanted to say. Suppose for some reason that person did not want to open the first envelope and instead wrote another note, put it in another envelope, and addressed it to the same destination as the first letter. If the letters were mailed on different days, chances are that the one that was sent first would arrive first. However, there is no absolute guarantee of that. The first letter sent could be delayed somehow—mistakenly sent to the wrong state, for example—and arrive after the second one. This can happen with message delivery in connectionless service, but could not happen with connection-oriented service. However, when connectionless service is installed, software can be used at a higher level to re-establish the appropriate order of messages.

9.2.1.5 OSI Profiles

One of the problems related to the OSI Reference Model is the sheer volume of protocols that are included. There are too many for any one vendor—or user organization—to support all of them. In addition, the OSI standards contain many options—far more than would be practical to implement in their entirety. As a result, vendors implement only a subset of the multitude of options. Since different vendors may easily select a different set of options to implement, there is no guarantee that the resulting products will interoperate, though each is fully compliant with the OSI standards.

To overcome this problem various groups have defined a subset of the OSI protocols (a profile) for their needs. The Government OSI Profile is an example of such a subset. The United States adopted GOSIP in 1989. Other governments that have adopted some form of Government OSI Profile include Australia, Belgium, Canada, France, Japan, the Netherlands, Sweden, the United Kingdom, and West Germany. GOSIP is covered in more detail in Section 9.2.3 in this chapter. An example of an industry profile is the Utility Communications Architecture (UCA).

Another of the more well-known profiles are those of the Manufacturing Automation Protocol/Technical and Office Protocol (MAP/TOP).

9.2.2 MAP/TOP

MAP originated in General Motors (GM) in the early 1980s. GM had benefited, like other automotive firms, from the standardization among automobile parts, but suffered, like all other firms, from the lack of standards for communicating among different computers. This was particularly problematic in manufacturing where the proliferation of different communication devices often resulted in a mass of point-to-point wiring cluttering the factory floor. In 1984 Roger Smith, chairman of GM, pointed out that only 15 percent of the 40,000 programmable devices in GM could communicate outside their own processes.*

GM established a task force which eventually became the nucleus of the MAP effort. It specified a subset of networking protocols for the specific purpose of facilitating communications among computers and programmable devices in a factory environment. The first successful demonstration of MAP interoperability took place at the 1984 National Computer Conference (NCC). Seven vendors were involved, as was the NIST (then called the National Bureau of Standards) and the Industrial Technology Institute of Ann Arbor, MI.

The Boeing Company in Seattle, WA, being a large airplane manufacturer, saw the benefit of the MAP effort and actively participated in it. However, standards proponents in Boeing also saw the need for a standards profile that would meet the needs of operating units not directly related to the factory floor. As a result, the Technical and Office Protocol (TOP) effort was born to ensure effective communication among PC users in office and engineering environments.

NIST played an important role in the evolution of MAP/TOP by stepping up to the problem of ensuring the interoperability of vendors' products. In 1983, they organized and sponsored the Open Systems Interconnect Implementors' Workshop. The goal was to provide an environment where interoperability could be tested and demonstrated. Over the years, there have been more products available for MAP than TOP.

9.2.3 GOSIP

The Government OSI Profile (GOSIP) is important because the buying power of those who support it is substantial enough to induce vendors to create more OSI-compliant products. In the U.S., a Federal Information Processing Standard (FIPS)† specifying GOSIP was adopted on February 15, 1989 and enforced in August, 1990. The GOSIP FIPs mandated that U.S. procurement documents for new and major upgrades of networking products and services must specify the Government OSI Profile.

---

*Jones, Vince C., *MAP/TOP Networking, Achieving Computer-Integrated Manufacturing*, New York, McGraw-Hill Book Company, 1988.
†FIPS Publication 146.

The government issued the mandate anticipating, like commercial companies, that vendors would soon provide a healthy number of OSI-compliant products—something that did not happen. Meanwhile many installations have turned to Transmission Control Protocol/Internet Protocol (which will be described later in this chapter) to help solve their interoperability problems. This includes many government sites. As a matter of fact, TCP/IP has become a part of the GOSIP specification creating more uncertainty about the future of OSI-compliant products.

9.2.4 The IEEE LAN Standards

IEEE developed an important set of standards regarding architectures for LANs. The IEEE definition of a LAN is as follows:

> A data communication system allowing a number of independent devices to communicate directly with each other, within a moderately sized geographic area over a physical communications channel of moderate data rates.

The IEEE 802 Project defines a network architecture specifically oriented to the implementation of LANs. While the approach the IEEE used conformed with the OSI model, the IEEE Project 802 only addresses the lowest two layers—the physical layer and the data link layers. The functions performed by the higher layers are left up to the individual LAN implementors or the users of the network. Figure 9.5 shows the relationship between the OSI seven layers and the IEEE layers. In the IEEE 802 architecture, the data link layer is divided into two separate sublayers: logical link control and media access control.

The logical link control layer lets the ISO network layer (layer three) access the services of the LAN without regard for how the network is physically implemented. It shields the higher layers from concerns about the specific LAN implementation. It is responsible for data link functions that are independent of the medium used.

The media access control (MAC) layer defines the way that sharing of access to the physical transmission medium is managed. A LAN has multiple devices that contend for access to the single transmission medium. The MAC layer is concerned with the access control method that determines how use of the transmission medium is controlled.

The physical layer—as in the OSI model—is concerned with the physical transmission of signals across a transmission medium. It deals with the types of cabling as well as plugs and connectors.

The IEEE Project 802 participants knew they could not define one standard that would meet all the needs of various LAN systems. There-

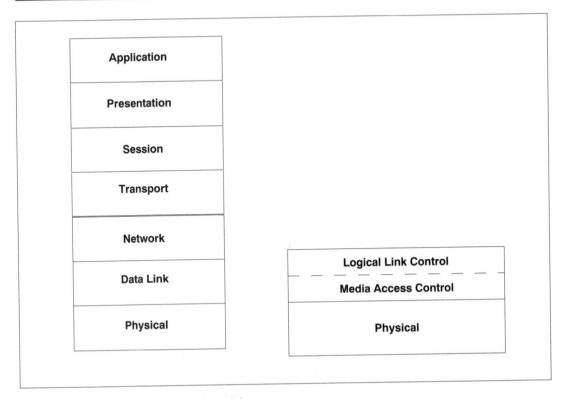

Figure 9.5 OSI and IEEE network models.

fore, they decided to develop sets or families of standards. For example, 802.3 is a standard which addresses Carrier Sense, Multiple Access with Collision Detection (CSMA/CD) access to physical transmission media. CSMA/CD plays something like a "stop, look, and listen" game. The term "carrier sense" means that a station listens before it transmits.

CSMA/CD is commonly used as the MAC method in Ethernet, a widely-used LAN architecture. With this approach, a transmitting station "listens" to see if another station is currently transmitting. If another station is transmitting, the first station waits. If no other station is transmitting, the first one starts to transmit. However, another station could have been "listening" at the same time to see if it could transmit. If two stations start transmitting at the same time, there will be a collision and both stations stop transmitting immediately. Each station then waits for a random period of time and then "listens" to see if it can now transmit.

IEEE's 802.4 describes a token bus architecture, and 802.5 describes a token ring architecture. With these architectures, a token (a small information packet) is transmitted from one station to the next. The station that has the token is allowed to transmit for a pre-determined period of time. When that time is up, the station must stop transmitting and pass the token to the next station. In a token ring architecture, the network is physically arranged as a ring; in a token bus architecture, the network is physically in the form of a bus, but it is logically arranged as a ring for the purpose of passing the token.

9.3   TCP/IP

The Transmission Control Protocol/Internet Protocol is another widely used protocol. TCP/IP was designed by the Department of Defense (DoD) for ARPANET, a network built to connect various sites of the DoD Advanced Research Projects Agency. Therefore, TCP/IP is a public, not a proprietary, protocol. As a result of a mandate from the DoD that TCP/IP be used for all federal civilian government and military contracts, TCP/IP use spread quickly within the government. However, it also gained popularity in universities and scientific installations.

TCP/IP is actually a set of protocols that provides functionality that is similar to that provided by layers three and four of the OSI model. TCP/IP is often portrayed as an architecture having four layers:

- A physical network access layer
- The internet protocol (IP)
- The transmission control protocol (TCP)
- The application layer

The Transmission Control Protocol is roughly equivalent to layer four, the transport layer, and the Internet Protocol is very roughly equivalent to the upper portions of layer three, the network layer. A variety of LANs can be used to provide the functionality of the rest of the lower layers of the OSI model. X.25, a packet-switching protocol, can also be used under TCP/IP to provide the functionality of the lower layers. Applications must provide their own equivalent of the session and presentation layers if they need them. TCP/IP generally comes with a set of utilities like the following: the FTP, a remote program execution capability (Telnet), and the SMTP which is an electronic mail utility. While the term "TCP/IP" actually refers just to the TCP and IP protocols, the term is often used to refer to the protocols *and* the utilities.

TCP/IP is now beginning to be widely used in commercial installations as well. It first started appearing as the solution to the problem of tying together existing heterogeneous LANs and now is being widely used in the planning process as the way to interconnect new LANs from different vendors. The Internet Protocol not only supports the network layer of OSI, it was built to route data through networks of networks, called internets. The fact that OSF chose TCP/IP instead of OSI or MAP/TOP is bound to further promote the use of TCP/IP.

Many companies that were waiting for vendor-supplied OSI-compliant products for all layers of the OSI model could wait no longer and have turned to TCP/IP. For a while the U.S. and the EC governments mandated that the GOSIP replace TCP/IP in all government contracts. Some observers predicted that by the late 1990s, OSI protocols would replace most of the TCP/IP implementations at government installations. Others are not so sure that will happen.

As mentioned earlier, the U.S. federal government put the GOSIP mandate into effect in August, 1990. Interestingly, overall TCP/IP installations have not slowed down since that mandate went into effect; rather they have increased dramatically. The expanding interest in TCP/IP has been attributed to the growing use of UNIX, the proliferating need for LAN-to-LAN communications, and a lack of high quality OSI-compliant products. Use of TCP/IP has become so widespread that by mid-1993, government users were demanding that TCP/IP become part of the GOSIP specification.

9.4 TRANSITIONING TO GOSIP OR OSI

This section will address strategies for transitioning to GOSIP; however, these strategies can either be used as they are, or with modifications to create a strategy for transitioning to OSI.

There is no specific migration strategy that will work for all enterprises. A migration plan should be developed after a careful analysis of existing networking systems and protocols as well as the enterprise's short-, mid-, and long-term goals. A major factor in such a migration is the need to protect the enterprise's investment in existing systems. Most migrations take an evolutionary rather than a revolutionary path. To replace all existing products with OSI- or GOSIP-compliant ones would be quite expensive.

9.4.1 Transition Approaches

Some approaches used in migration are dual protocol stacks, mixed protocol stacks, and multiple protocol routing and bridging. The term "protocol stack" simply refers to a stack—pictured as a vertical layering—of protocols that meet communication needs. (Figure 9.2 shows the OSI "stack.") In a dual stack approach, a single host computer generally contains two separate, full communication protocol stacks. For example protocol stack A might be TCP/IP-related, and protocol stack B might be OSI-related. When data is received on stack A, the data is processed up the TCP/IP stack. If the data is to be sent to an OSI application, the host will perform the necessary translation between the protocols and send the data down the OSI stack. Thus, a TCP/IP FTP user could send a file to an OSI FTAM user.

Operating above the application layer of the OSI model, dual stacks are also referred to as application gateways. In mixed protocol stacks, part of one protocol stack is combined with part of another protocol stack. Transitions using mixed protocol stacks generally can be implemented in a top-down approach or a bottom-up approach. A top-down approach implements GOSIP applications—such as FTAM or the X.400 Message Handling System—over an existing network such as SNA or TCP/IP.

9.5   WIDE AREA NETWORKS

Wide area networks are networks that cover a large geographical area. They may span a city, state, country or even the world. Wide area networks have been in use since the early days of computers. Global— and some national—wide area networks use technologies like T1, a 1.544 Mbps multichannel wide area transmission system; T2, the equivalent of four T1s; and T3, the equivalent of 28 T1s, as well as microwave and X.25 links (described below.)

9.5.1   The Role of Wide Area Networks in Client/Server Systems

Whether or not a client/server system will need a wide area network depends on the nature of the client/server system. If the individuals who use the client/server system are geographically dispersed over a wide area, then a wide area network will be necessary. Enterprises are also finding it beneficial to connect individual LANs with other LANs. Client/ server systems residing on any particular LAN can then contribute to the overall enterprise's information base.

Many large corporations have used wide area networks in connection with their mainframe or minicomputer systems for many years. Often it is to their benefit if they can connect the installed WAN to their LANs. An enterprise should study this situation carefully. While this approach may be appropriate as a way to start, the organization may find that its evolving long-range plans indicate that it should make changes to its wide area network architecture. If they have not already done so, enterprises should ensure that they carefully study their long-range client/server needs and enterprise-wide network needs and include them as an integral part of their overall strategic planning process.

Most early wide area networks were proprietary in nature. IBM's SNA and Digital Equipment's DECnet are prime examples. The OSI Reference Model of ISO gave a boost to open systems in networking, but open networking products did not become available as soon as predicted and hoped.

Some aspects of wide area networking are more important than others to developers of client/server systems. For example, a client/server planner should be aware of such things as packet-switching concepts, connection-oriented versus connectionless service, the speeds offered by various WANs, and interconnectivity capabilities, among other things.

This section will not try to provide answers to the many questions that will arise when client/server systems need to be connected to WANs. The variety of different combinations is very large, and the technical knowledge required to deal with them all is quite significant. Enterprises that are connecting a wide variety of LANs and WANs will need to develop in-house expertise to deal with these problems. Even if consultants are brought in initially to help with early implementations, there is no substitute for in-house experts that are familiar with the enterprise's unique situation. Reading a book about enterprise-wide networking would be a valuable aid to anyone who needs more information about wide area networks in relation to their client/server systems. The remainder of this section will provide an explanation of packet switching, frame relay, and ATM technology. These are three technologies that often come up when discussing connecting LANs to WANs.

9.5.2   Packet Switching

Packet switching is an important WAN technology because it is so widely used. It is important for client/server planners to be aware of how packet switching works because they will come across it so often in existing systems. Since developers will often be asked to use existing facilities they should be aware of the facilities' capabilities and limitations.

With packet switching, all messages are formed into discrete units called packets. Each packet contains a header which contains packet control functions and the packet network destination. Nodes within the wide area network read the information in the header and forward (switch) the packet to its destination. X.25 is the CCITT and OSI standard for packet-switching networks.

One of the limitations of packet switching is that it does not have the speed required by many of today's systems. The X.25 protocol was developed when transmission lines had a lower quality than those used today. Since the lines had low quality, error detection and correction capabilities had to be built into the protocol, requiring a relatively large amount of processing to be performed on each packet to ensure correct transmission. At individual nodes, incoming packets are stored and checked for errors; they are not forwarded until they are found to be error-free, or until the errors are corrected. The price for this error-related processing is slower speed and network delay. Packet switching networks are generally limited to 56 kilobit-per-second transmission speeds.

Packet switching is connection-oriented. (Connection-oriented versus connectionless communication was discussed briefly above, comparing the former to a telephone call and the latter to the post office mail system.) A packet network provides a virtual circuit—one that appears to be a point-to-point connection between end system, or data terminal equipment (DTE), devices. Most of today's packet switching is based on the international X.25 standard.

One of the advantages of X.25 packet switching is that it can be found universally. Nearly every country's telephone services group provides an X.25 network. Therefore, it can be a good choice for large enterprises that need to build a worldwide network.

9.5.3 Frame Relay

Frame relay is better suited to a LAN's traffic patterns than X.25 is. It is designed for interconnecting LANs to each other and to WANS. Frame relay offers high capacity with low delay, low overhead, and reliable data transfer over existing public networks. Speeds up to 2 Mbps are available.

Frame relay achieves its speed by eliminating some of the error detection that X.25 performs. The extensive error checking of X.25 is no longer necessary due to the high reliability of today's lines. Frame relay also expects the user's equipment to detect and correct errors. In today's networked computing environments, terminal equipment is nearly always intelligent equipment capable of this error detection and correction.

Some observers regard frame relay as a streamlined version of X.25 packet switching. Frame relay assumes that there is an error-correction protocol operating in the end devices. As a result, frame relay can operate at very high speeds such as 1.5 megabits per second, frequently referred to as DS1.

The disadvantage of frame relay is that it is not suitable for carrying both voice and data. This is because frame relay uses a variable length frame which can range from a few characters to thousands of characters. As a result, if a voice frame were transmitted immediately after several very long frames, an intolerable delay would be experienced. In addition, the delay on voice transmissions would be variable, depending on the makeup of other transmitted frames.

9.5.4 Asynchronous Transfer Mode (ATM)

Asynchronous transfer mode, or cell relay technology, is gaining in popularity as a networking medium. A common practice for many years has been to use different networks for voice, private-line services, and data. ATM simplifies the situation because it can seamlessly switch between voice, data, image, and video.

ATM also promises to deal with the current speed barriers between LAN and WAN environments. For many years, LANs have operated at lower speeds than WANs. The LANs typically used Ethernet at 10 Mbps or token-ring at 4 Mbps and 16 Mbps, while WANs used technologies that operated at speeds of 64 Kbps to 45 Mbps and higher. ATM promises the ability to provide service for both LANs and WANs, thereby unifying corporate networking.

ATM technology breaks information into uniform "cells," each of which is 53 eight-bit bytes long. While ATM is basically a packet-based network, it will also support circuit-mode operations (over a packet-based transport mechanism). A detailed explanation of how ATM technology works is available in recently written enterprise-wide networking books.

Predictions say that ATM will catch on much more quickly than ISDN (which has only come into its own quite recently) because of user fervor. A user group known as the Enterprise Network Roundtable had more than 1300 members very soon after ATM became available. There is also a vendor group called the ATM Forum, based in Mountain View, CA, which has over 250 companies as members. The ATM Forum is working toward ATM interoperability specifications. The Yankee Group, based in Boston, predicts that the ATM market—a $70 million one in 1993—will go to $840 million by 1996.

10

NETWORK AND SERVER OPERATING SYSTEMS

10.1 OVERVIEW

An operating system coordinates the inner workings of a computer. An operating system generally relies on an inner clock to make scheduling decisions like loading and executing user programs or sending data to a printer. The purpose of an operating system is to take care of routine, repetitive tasks and to make the system easier for developers and users to use. The work that a human's subconscious does has been compared to the work that an operating system does for a computer.* This is because both take care of important "background" necessities which are vital for functioning—scheduling breathing and heart beats in a human and scheduling input reads and output printing in a computer—but which would take up too much time if a human or a computer developer had to constantly take care of all of them.

10.1.1 Different Kinds of Operating Systems

An operating system provides a set of system services to application programs that are written for it. PC operating systems like MS-DOS were written for a single-user, non-networked environment. This operating system provides a way for applications to read and write to disk among

---

*The Waite Group's *UNIX Printer Plus* Second Edition, Mitchell Waite, Donald Martin, and Stephen Prata, SAMS, a Division of Pentice Hall Computer Publishing, Carmel, Indiana, 1990.

other services. In a LAN system, the PC operating system must be extended to support the sharing of data between applications running in different physical computers. A network operating system usually provides this extension. In order to more clearly distinguish between the two types of operating system software, an operating system like DOS is sometimes referred to as the "native" operating system. Thus, a *network* operating system can be thought of as an extension of the PC's *native* operating system.

While PC users still have their own operating system and all of its functions, they also have the additional capabilities of the network operating system. A portion of the network software—a redirector—resides within the PC. This redirector examines requests from the PC and determines whether the request is for the PC's operating system or the network operating system. If the request is for the PC's operating system, the redirector passes it on to DOS. If the request is for the network operating system, the redirector directs the request to the appropriate device on the network. (See Figure 10.1.)

In OS/2 LAN Server, the piece of code on the PC that performs this redirection is the called the LAN Requester. Using redirection, client modules access resources on the network as though they were locally attached. (As client/server systems become more widely used, new operating systems for PCs will have more networking capabilities.)

The UNIX operating system can be used in a networking environment, but it was not specifically written as a network operating system. It was written more as a time-sharing system where many dumb terminals could use time slices on a shared computer. UNIX, however, is a multitasking, multi-user operating system to which networking capabilities have been added, and it is often used in client/server environments. UNIX will be covered in Chapters 15 and 16.

10.1.2 Characteristics of Network Operating Systems

Different network operating systems offer different features. The following list provides some of the features that are of interest to network planners.

- Security and access control—the degree of network security provided through the control of users and resources.
- Hardware independence—the ability to operate in more than one vendor's network hardware environment.
- Multiple server support—the ability to support multiple servers and handle communications among them transparently.

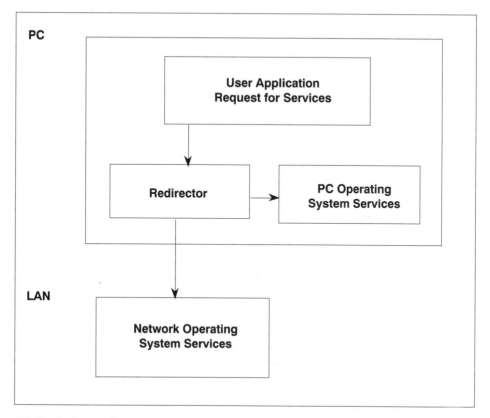

Figure 10.1 Redirector function.

- Multiuser support—the ability to provide protection for applications and their data in a multi-user environment.
- Network management—the ability to support management functions like system backup, performance monitoring, fault tolerance, etc.
- User interface—the quality of the user interface that is provided to assist with user control over network resources.

Vendors are constantly updating their products, adding new features. It is important to check with vendors to determine which features they offer at any particular time.

Some network operating systems are designed for very small workgroups—some consisting of only a few PCs. Artisoft's LANtastic and Novell's NetWare Lite are examples of products in this category. These networks operate on a peer-to-peer basis. That is, none of the devices acts as a central server; each device is on an equal footing with all the others. LANtastic has a large market share for these smaller networks and is well regarded by users and analysts. NetWare Lite has its advocates as well.

The most commonly used network operating systems for medium to large client/server applications are Novell NetWare, Microsoft LAN Manager, IBM LAN Server, and Banyan Vines. These network operating systems are intended for systems with many users who have sophisticated operating requirements. They provide access to server-based databases and other services as well as to wide area networks through internetworking devices.

Novell was one of the first companies to provide networking products. Novell's products were widely used when servers were predominantly used for printer and file sharing—before client/server systems were widespread. Novell quickly became the leader in networking sales and its NetWare is estimated by different sources as now having anywhere from 60% to 80% of the network operating system market. IBM and Digital Equipment also support Novell NetWare as well as their own network operating systems, indicating the clout that Novell carries. IBM is providing links between NetWare and IBM's LAN Server/Requester product to facilitate interoperation between the two. Many of IBM's large customers have both networking capabilities installed in their companies. A wide variety of network adapters work with NetWare, and reportedly more applications work on NetWare than on any other kind of network.

10.2   SERVER OPERATING SYSTEM DESCRIPTIONS

10.2.1   The LAN Server/LAN Manager Connection

Microsoft and IBM co-developed the OS/2 operating system in the mid-1980s, first shipping it in December 1987. In 1985, under their Joint Development Agreement, they developed plans for file server software to work with OS/2. That software became the basis for both LAN Manager (now marketed by Microsoft) and LAN Server (marketed by IBM). Both products share a common code base; in essence they are quite similar. Microsoft first marketed its network operating system, LAN Manager, using an OEM marketing strategy. Many different vendors licensed, packaged, enhanced, and marketed Microsoft's LAN Manager under their own labels and product names. Including IBM with LAN Server, there was Digital Equipment with Pathworks, as well as AT&T/NCR, Hewlett-Packard, and Ungermann-Bass, each with their own variations.

At one time, IBM and Microsoft said that they would converge the two products so that Microsoft's LAN Manager and IBM's LAN Server would be the same. They no longer have such plans.

10.2.2 Microsoft's LAN Manager

LAN Manager is used in many client/server installations that have OS/2 on the server. Since LAN Manager was originally built to work with OS/2 there are many ways they work together. OS/2 is a multi-tasking operating system, not a multi-user system. LAN Manager provides the multi-user capabilities. In turn, LAN Manager takes advantage of OS/2's pre-emptive multi-tasking. Since LAN Manager is based on the OS/2 network kernel, it is in a position to take advantage of other OS/2 features like its protected-mode memory. With the memory protection feature, LAN Manager can provide safe multi-tasking. Memory protection prevents other applications written to OS/2 APIs from crashing the entire system.

LAN Manager is a suitable LAN product for any size network. It was built for very large networks, but is priced so low that it can be considered for smaller networks, too. It also supports Novell NetWare connectivity. Clients can access data from both NetWare and LAN Manager servers at the same time. LAN Manager also supports NetBIOS and Named Pipes—which are protocols that can be used by programmers for communication between client applications and OS/2 servers. LAN Manager also supports TCP/IP transport, NetView, and network management agents for the Simple Network Management Protocol (SNMP)—all of which are discussed elsewhere in this book.

The fact that LAN Manager never took much market share away from Novell is attributed to many factors—the main one being the momentum that Novell already had. The fact that Microsoft originally chose to market the product through a large number of resellers—which resulted in different, incompatible versions of the product—may have contributed also. OS/2 itself never achieved the kind of sales that IBM and Microsoft had expected. The subsequent disarray with Microsoft's new emphasis on Windows, and the resulting uncertainty in the IBM/Microsoft relationship may have added to the picture as well.

However, it is still early in the evolution of client/server systems and other distributed computing. Novell attained the bulk of its market share when sites were primarily using networks for simple file and printer sharing. There will be new demands on networking as time goes on. Microsoft has incorporated LAN Manager into Windows NT, its newest operating system. Many applications can run under Microsoft Windows and will therefore run under Windows NT, giving NT an advantage.

While LAN Manager typically runs with OS/2, it can also run with UNIX, Digital's VMS or IBM's MVS. Microsoft also offers LAN Manager/X (LM/X) for systems that have the UNIX System V as the server operating system. LAN hardware for LAN Manager can be Ethernet, Token Ring, FDDI, or Arcnet.

10.2.3 IBM's LAN Server

LAN Server, just like LAN Manager, was built for very large networks, but is priced low enough to be considered as a candidate for small networks, too. Since they both originated from the same product, many of the things that apply to LAN Manager apply to LAN Server as well. However, there will be some differences in items like the transport protocols and other things supported by the two products.

It is interesting to note that IBM now sells Novell's NetWare with its LAN Server. IBM reportedly does not emphasize one product over the other. There are many large installations where both products are installed. According to the Gartner Group, IBM accounts for about five percent of NetWare sales.

There are a number of large LAN Server accounts. New York Life in New York City uses LAN Server in more than 25 LANs throughout the country. Their choice was based on the fact that LAN Server is a heavy duty product for a very reasonable price making it extremely cost-effective. Another large user is Fireman's Fund Insurance in San Rafael, CA, which runs LAN Server at approximately 60 different physical locations.

IBM has made a commitment to support LAN Server running natively under MVS. MVS is, of course, one of IBM's mainframe operating systems. A large installed base of applications running under MVS can take advantage of this kind of capability. IBM also has other offerings in the networking arena such as PC LAN and CICS for OS/2.

10.2.4 Novell's NetWare

NetWare is known as a fast, secure, high-performance network operating system that is used by over fifty percent of network installations. Started in a small office in Orem, UT in 1982, Novell began selling its first file server product in 1983. It captured market share by being one of the first network vendors and by having the right kind of products. Its initial distinction was its high-performance file system. The company has continued with a long string of "firsts:" Novell was the first to support multiple topologies, to support multiple, heterogeneous computers, and to support OS/2 and all versions of DOS. It introduced its System Fault Tolerance (SFT) and disk mirroring capabilities in 1986. It also provides connectivity to IBM computers as well as Digital, Apple, and UNIX systems.

IBM's LAN Manager and Microsoft's LAN Server require an operating system like OS/2 or UNIX on the server. NetWare is different from these network operating systems in that it does not require the support of another operating system. It provides all the functionality it needs. Lan Manager needs OS/2, for example, for the preemptive multi-tasking that OS/2 offers. NetWare does not require the additional overhead of another operating system because it is non-preemptive: each process runs to completion without being interrupted.

An operating system that is preemptive interrupts tasks to perform other tasks. Occasionally, this interruption can occur at an inconvenient time and significantly slow down the completion of a task. With NetWare, this does not happen, resulting in increased speed. Highest priority tasks run to completion. While NetWare does not interrupt tasks; tasks are required to release control of system resources at convenient times so that other devices can have access to those resources.

Another big difference between NetWare and other network operating systems is the existence of NetWare loadable modules (NLMs), server applications that offer extensibility by enhancing or expanding the functions offered by servers. Standard applications cannot run on the server processor with NetWare because NetWare does not offer the kinds of APIs that would accommodate this. Instead, applications run as NetWare loadable modules. The majority of database server vendors either already have NLMs or are working on them.

Novell has received a lot of criticism for the way NLMs fit into their overall architecture. NLMs run at what is called Ring 0 which is right at the heart of the operating system. This means they actually become part of the operating system. The advantage of this is that NLMs can run as fast as the operating system core. Other operating systems vendors criticize this saying that only the kernel of the operating system should exist at Ring 0. The problem is that an ill-behaved NLM could conceivably crash the entire system.

Novell takes precautions against this by having a stringent NLM certification program to which all third-party developers must submit their NLMs. Novell says it also monitors NLMs over time to ensure that they continue working properly. While the NLM certification program is expensive and time-consuming, many vendors have undergone the certification. Vendors want to have their products used by the large installed base of Novell users—plus they like how fast their products run as NLMs. There are many NLMs available and many more in the works.

The original version of NetWare was optimized as a file server. In 1989, Novell released NetWare 386 which provided true 32-bit processing and up to 16 terabytes of storage capacity. This permitted developers to take full advantage of the 80386 processor. As mentioned earlier, NetWare is constantly adding new capabilities to its product line. NetWare 4.0 offers directory service which simplifies overall management of complex systems. Specific resources are considered as resources of the overall network rather than of a particular server.

OS/2 and UNIX servers can now be installed on the same LAN as NetWare servers. As a result, products that require the support of OS/2 or UNIX can also be accommodated on a LAN that is running NetWare.

10.2.5 Banyan's Vines

Banyan System's Virtual Networking System (Vines), is popular for very large networking installations. Banyan says its system was designed from the enterprise down while most other network operating systems were designed from the PC up. Banyan states that its focus is fully-integrated enterprise networking solutions.

Vines has a number of capabilities that illustrate this focus, headed up by its StreetTalk distributed directory service. StreetTalk is a global naming service containing the names of all users and network resources on all the servers that are physically connected on the network. The names are contained in a distributed database and when there are changes, the updates are replicated across the network. The Directory Assistance feature permits users to substitute English sounding names when they do not know the actual physical network address. This would let someone use an address of Bldg101 Room210 instead of the actual network address—a long string of numbers which would not be as meaningful.

Vines is reportedly very easy to administrate. Network administrators can perform network management functions from anywhere on the network. It is not uncommon for only three or four people to provide network support for a Vines LAN consisting of over a thousand nodes.

Vines originally ran on top of UNIX, System V. It now includes support for the Santa Cruz Operation (SCO) UNIX and Novell NetWare, with support for additional NOS platforms and RISC-based UNIX implementations to follow.

10.2.6 OSF/1

OSF/1 is the Open Software Foundation's flagship operating system. The Open Software Foundation (OSF) was originally formed by a number of companies who were unhappy with the way AT&T was pursuing its own interests in the UNIX marketplace. However, OSF has now grown into a de facto standards-setting group for distributed computing consisting of over 74 companies. The group includes such companies as IBM, DEC, HP, Microsoft, Computer Associates, Groupe Bull, Nippon Telephone and Telegraph Corp., and even UNIX International Inc., the standards-setting group for AT&T's UNIX System V.

OSF/1 is based on a variant of UNIX from Carnegie-Mellon University called the Mach 2.5 kernel. It is very similar to most other versions of UNIX except that its structure can help applications run faster because of the way it supports threading. Threads are basically multiple paths through a program. They are similar to processes, but are less of a burden to a CPU. OSF/1 supports concurrent use of threads permitting applications which take advantage of this feature to run to completion more quickly. This feature also facilitates the implementation of symmetrical multiprocessing (SMP) since the kernel threads can execute on multiple processors simultaneously.

The newer OSF/1-MK release is based on the Mach 3.0 microkernel. In this release, the parts of the operating system that control CPU access and processes are in the kernel while other parts of the operating system have been "broken out" and run very similarly to applications. This permits multiple systems such as DOS, OSF/1, and other versions of UNIX to run separately and simultaneously on the same machine.

In addition to OSF/1, the Open Software Foundation is also known for its Motif, a GUI for the X Window system, as well as its DCE and DME, each of which is described elsewhere in this book.

10.2.7   NeXTstep

NeXTstep, the operating system from NeXT Computer, Inc., was based on the Mach kernel, too. However, NeXTstep was also built as an object-oriented system right from the beginning, and any UNIX complexity is hidden from view. For a while NeXTstep was the most advanced object-oriented operating system in the marketplace, combining a sharp GUI with a sophisticated application development environment. Originally the software was just available on NeXT's computers which contributed to its slow acceptance. The system software is now available on 486 computers as NeXTstep 486. In early 1993, NeXT Computer announced they would no longer manufacture their own line of hardware. NeXTstep was well received, but NeXT Computer's hardware did not sell well.

NeXTstep is noted for its easy-to-use development environment. A survey taken by Booz-Allen & Hamilton, Inc. in 1992 compared commercial development times on NeXTstep, Sun, Macintosh, and PC environments. Programmers surveyed had experience with NeXTstep and at least one other major platform's development environment. Developers surveyed said that NeXTstep applications took an average of half the time to develop, with some applications developed nine times as fast.

An early release of NeXTstep supported typical UNIX networking tools like TCP/IP, the Network File System from Sun, and Ethernet networking. The newer release 3.0 lets users share data with DOS, OS/2, Windows, Macintosh and UNIX computers as well as a number of different LANs and WANs. The vendor says that many existing UNIX applications can run with NeXTstep through use of the terminal emulator that ships with the system.

NeXT Computer, Inc. was founded by Steve Jobs with five others in October, 1985. Jobs also co-founded Apple Computer, Inc.

10.2.8 Digital's Pathworks

Pathworks, Digital Equipment Corporation's network operating system, is a version of Microsoft's LAN Manager. Pathworks allows a wide variety of client, server, wiring, platform, and application combinations. Recognized for creating a networking environment in which multivendor PCs, diverse communications protocols and networks, and different applications can coexist, Pathworks contains built-in WAN features and sophisticated PC network management and security features.

Pathworks is available on four platforms: DOS, Windows, OS/2, and the Macintosh. A PC client using DOS or OS/2 is able to access any combination of OS/2, Ultrix (Digital's UNIX), and VMS server systems. Through a VMS server, a Macintosh client can share information with DOS, OS/2, VMS, and Ultrix users.

Pathworks for OS/2 has an add-on feature that provides TCP/IP networking for OS/2 users. PC clients can be connected to OS/2, VMS, or Ultrix systems running the Pathworks server software and the TCP/IP network transport. The TCP/IP software permits a PC running as an OS/2 server to offer basic TCP/IP services to both DOS and OS/2 client systems. The DOS and OS/2 client systems involved must be equipped with Pathworks for DOS and Pathworks for OS/2, respectively.

10.2.9 Microsoft's NT

Microsoft Windows NT is a 32-bit scalable multitasking Windows operating system. While NT has been meeting with a good reaction, it will need to be out in the marketplace longer before a clear determination can be made about its success. However, it is a fairly safe prediction to say that NT *will* meet with success.

NT is aimed at 80386 and higher systems with 12 MB of RAM and 100 MB of hard disk space or similarly configured RISC-based systems. It features symmetric multi-processing and built-in networking. NT is portable across 386, 486, and Pentium machines to RISC environments, supporting the MIPs R4000 and Digital's Alpha RISC chips.

NT is compatible with Windows 3.x (Windows 3.0 and higher). Looking at the screen layout, users who are used to Microsoft Windows generally feel quite comfortable with NT. All of the source code that currently runs with Windows 3.x runs with NT. NT can run DOS, Windows, new 32-bit applications, OS/2 applications, and X Window applications within an NT window. As a result, NT has the advantage of the large number of available Windows applications—as well as Microsoft's clout.

The client version of NT is called Windows NT, and the server version is called Windows NT Advanced Server. NT is based on the Mach variation of the UNIX kernel. It supports multiprocessor systems and multiple threads of execution. All application threads, including the Windows NT kernel, are able to run on many different kinds of processors in a multiprocessor configuration. Multiple threads of execution can operate simultaneously to complete a task.

NT incorporates a number of features to provide stability. It comes with a new file system called NT File System (NTFS) which is a transaction-based system that keeps a log of every change to the disk and can reconstruct the disk in seconds if a failure occurs. It also includes other fault-tolerant features such as disk mirroring, duplexing, and data striping (explained later). Other features include the imposition of quotas on processes to protect system resources and the presence of exception handling routines to discern program anomalies.

10.3   NEXT GENERATION OPERATING SYSTEMS

10.3.1   Taligent

IBM and Apple Computer have formed a company by the name of Taligent Inc. to develop an object-oriented operating system from the ground up. In the late 1980s, IBM had a project called Patriot Partners which was beginning work on an object-oriented operating system. At the same time, Apple Computer was also working on an object-oriented operating system, but already had about a million lines of code. The two companies decided to pool their resources and work together. Taligent consists of both former Apple and former IBM employees. The evolving operating system was originally code named "Pink."

Both companies need an object-oriented operating system to keep up with the competition. They each bring different talents to the project which has a good chance of developing an extremely useful operating system. The problem is that it will not be out until the mid-90s. That gives Microsoft's Windows NT, IBM's OS/2, and UNIX a few years to establish market share and to establish a large base of software applications for their operating systems. A Taligent spokesman says its operating system will have adapters permitting existing software written for other operating systems to run on its operating system. Observers point out that if this works, Taligent's operating system could certainly achieve success at least on IBM and Apple machines. Also, due to the large number of IBM and Apple machines in use, Taligent should not have trouble convincing software vendors to develop applications for it.

10.4 PEER-TO-PEER NETWORKS

10.4.1 Description of Peer-to-Peer Networks

In a peer-to-peer network, every node is an equal. Each component can be the client or the server or both at the same time to different devices within the network. One of the benefits is that a specific computer does not have to be designated as a dedicated server. This reduces the cost of a peer-to-peer network, which is appropriate for small workgroups doing word processing or light record processing. If too many users are on the LAN or the volume of work is too high, performance will degrade.

10.4.2 Examples of Product Offerings

Some of the popular peer-to-peer networks include LANtastic from Artisoft, NetWare Lite from Novell, and PowerLAN software from Performance Technology. All three of these are good quality products. Most peer LAN products are DOS-based. LANtastic has been the market leader in peer-to-peer networks for a number of years. It is reasonably fast and very reliable. NetWare Lite is one of the more expensive packages. It is reportedly easy to install, manage, and use. PowerLAN is reportedly the fastest of these three. It also features a CUA-compliant user interface.

Microsoft's Windows for Workgroups can also be considered as a peer-to-peer LAN product. Windows for Workgroups, released in the fall of 1992, integrates networking capabilities with Windows 3.1. It comes with a Workgroups Starter Kit that has everything needed to connect two PCs. All the necessary hardware and software comes in the same box—including the cabling and the screwdriver to open the back of the PC! Microsoft includes a *Read Me First* card and a *Watch Me Second* videotape providing step-by-step instructions on how to proceed. Microsoft has set up an 800 number to help users make sure they have a network adapter card that is appropriate. After two PCs are hooked up with Windows for Workgroups, they can share files using the Windows File Manager. Printer sharing, E-mail, and group scheduling are popular features of the product.

11

INTERCONNECTING INDIVIDUAL LANs

11.1 NETWORK INTERCONNECTION

"Michael Isaac Steven Director's hand trembled as he reached for the doorknob of the study. He feared this mystery was so perplexing that even the great Sherlock Holmes could not solve it. He entered the study and peered at the man seated behind the desk and whispered, "Mr. Holmes? I'm M.I.S. Director; I need your help."*

Many networking vendors are searching for clues to find the best way to help puzzled laymen solve the mysteries of networking and internetworking. And some of them are breaking the monotony of what can be pretty dry technical reading with a little welcome light-heartedness as can be seen in the above extract from Proteon's booklet, *Taking the Mystery out of Internetworking*. Proteon is a router vendor located in Westborough, MA.

11.1.1 Why the Need to Interconnect Exists

A local area network, as its name implies, covers only a limited, local area. LANs generally have a limit on the physical size of each network segment as well. This is due to the fact that as signals travel along the network cable, they gradually lose strength. If the LAN needs to be enlarged—for example to add more users—an additional cable segment can be added with the help of a repeater. The repeater receives the

---

* *Taking the Mystery Out of Networking*, Proteon, Westborough, MA.

original signal and then retransmits it, regenerating the signal at its original strength.

If a client/server system will be used by just one department, the capabilities offered by a single LAN are generally sufficient. But many companies are finding that it does not take long before it becomes apparent that another department—which may use a different LAN—would benefit if it could share the data located on the first LAN.

The best way to achieve this is to connect the two LANs creating a LAN internetwork—often referred to as an internetwork, or internet for short. (This is not the same as "the" Internet, a widely used public network of networks which is described in Chapter 16.) Internetworks are created through the use of bridges, routers, and gateways.

The LAN internetworking market is one of the fastest growing segments of the computer and communications industries. Annual sales of internetworking products have been increasing at over 30% in recent years. Products are evolving constantly, with new capabilities being announced all the time.

The proliferation of capabilities among the constantly changing products presents a confusing array of choices. Networks which need to be connected to each other may be similar, a little different, or entirely different from each other. Different products are required for each of these different situations. Products to interconnect networks range from bridges, routers, and brouters to hubs, internodal processors, and gateways. The most common are bridges, routers, and gateways.

One of the simplest explanations of bridges, routers, and gateways is provided by Wellfleet in its booklet, *Simplifying LAN-WAN Integration, a Corporate Guide to Routers and Bridges.* It uses a mailroom where the workers' job responsibilities provide internetworking analogies. Dmitri's work resembles a bridge, Alexi a router, and Ivan a gateway. The analogy provides a quick and simple introductory overview. (See Box 11.1.)

11.1.2 Bridges, Routers, and Gateways

The basic difference between bridges, routers, and gateways is that each operates at a different *level* within the overall networking hierarchy. Using the OSI reference model to represent the different levels of networking functionality, we see that bridges, routers, and gateways operate at different *layers* of the OSI reference model. (See Figure 11.1.)

• A bridge operates at the data link layer; it connects networks that have different protocols at the physical layer.

In this analogy, Dmitri plays the role of a bridge, Alexi a router, and Ivan a gateway.

Dmitri is very fast, but he provides a limited function. Dmitri receives two pieces of correspondence: one is for an associate in the same building and one is for a customer in another state. Dmitri can very quickly process the correspondence by reading the addresses and throwing the first piece of correspondence into the "local" bin and the second into the "outgoing" bin.

Dmitri only deals with two pieces of information at a time: the source address and the destination address. First he reads the source address and consults a table of local addresses. If the source address is not present, he adds it, thereby eventually building a table that contains nearly—if not all—the local addresses.

Then Dmitri reads the destination address and looks in the same table to see if it is there. If it is, he knows the address is a local one and puts the correspondence in the local bin. The Wellfleet booklet points out that on a network this keeps "local" traffic local and thus avoids unnecessary message forwarding. If the address is not there, Dmitri puts the correspondence in the outgoing bin. He provides a simple—but very fast—service.

Routers provide more service. Alexi knows how to deal with source and destination addresses and makes decisions as to the "best" way to get to a destination. He accesses a variety of information sources to make his decision.

Let us suppose that Alexi receives two packages: first, a small parcel with a Post-it® note to Alexi saying the package is "urgent"; and second, a large box of books with a Post-it note requesting normal delivery. He consults his sources and considers a number of alternatives and tradeoffs. These can include the priority of the material being sent, the speed and cost of alternative services, and guarantees offered by various services such as a notification of receipt.

Alexi therefore routes the urgent parcel and the box of books quite differently. With the books, he may even decide to open the box and repackage it into smaller shipments.

The Wellfleet booklet says this points out several differences between bridges and routers. For one thing, routers are explicitly addressed, as indicated by the Post-it notes which were addressed to Alexi, the router. Bridges are not addressed. Second, routers access and use multiple sources of data. Bridges use only source and destination addresses. (Remember, the bridge's access table was just a compilation of source addresses.) Third, routers can open envelopes and manipulate (fragment or shorten) the contents of the envelope. This permits a router to provide service between LANs that have different message lengths. Bridges do not have that kind of access to the message envelope.

There are a few more differences. Routers provide for different types of service, while bridges treat all packets the same. Routers can provide feedback on network conditions to end users, while bridges cannot. Routers forward an envelope to a specific destination, while a bridge just puts it in an "outgoing bin."

A gateway is illustrated by a third mailroom worker, Ivan, who is bilingual. A worker could write a letter in English to a Russian-speaking associate and send it to the mail room where Ivan would translate it into Russian before providing for its delivery. In a network, a gateway will provide protocol translation between such protocols as TCP/IP and DECnet or SNA.

Box 11.1 Wellfleet's mailroom analogy.

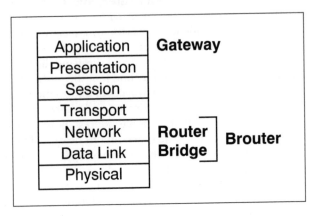

Figure 11.1   OSI and bridges, routers, and gateways.

- A router operates at the network layer; it can connect networks that have different protocols at the data link layer.
- Gateways operate at higher layers.

Figure 11.1 indicates where bridges and routers operate when viewed from the perspective of the OSI seven-layer Reference Model. However, as discussed in Chapter 9, in networking architectures for LANs, the data link layer is divided into two sublayers: the logical link control sublayer and the media access control sublayer. Figure 11.2 shows a more precise picture of where a bridge operates within a LAN architecture.

As also pointed out in Chapter 9, IEEE's Project 802 addresses the physical layer and the two data link sublayers. At the physical layer, (OSI layer 1) IEEE Project 802 standardized on three physical media: twisted-wire pairs, coaxial cable, and fiber-optic cable. Since bridges can connect networks consisting of completely different physical medium, one network could have twisted-wire-pair cable while the other network has coaxial cable.

At the logical link control layer, IEEE 802 defines a single standard that is a common element in all the IEEE 802 standards. It shields the higher-layer levels from details of the lower layers. At the MAC layer, IEEE Project 802 chose the following access control methods for standardization: CSMA/CD, token bus, and token ring. These access methods define the rules to be followed for stations to share the transmission medium.

In order to use a bridge, at least the protocol at the logical link control sublayer needs to be the same or compatible on both networks. So, for example, a bridge can be used to connect a token ring network with a CSMA/CD network if there is compatibility at the LLC sublayer. Both

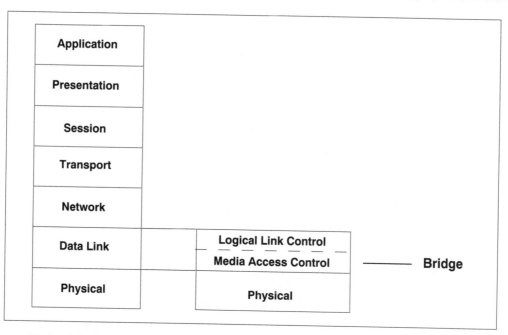

Figure 11.2 A bridge in a LAN architecture.

networks must use the same addressing format (16-bit or 48-bit); also, frame formats and sizes must be similar enough to be handled compatibly by the data link layer.

A bridge can be a separate device or it can be a network station like a PC that simultaneously belongs to two or more networks. Generally, a card with bridging software is inserted into the PC acting as the bridge. A bridge will usually receive all the messages on each network, thus earning itself the label "promiscuous" in networking parlance. It checks each destination address and if it determines that the message is intended for a different network, the bridge will transmit it to that network.

11.1.3 Other Internetworking Devices

Along with bridges and routers, other internetworking devices that are used are hubs, internodal processors and gateways. Hubs are intelligent wiring devices that let companies plug in LANs of all types in a central wiring closet. Internodal processors are basically highly intelligent boxes that can alleviate the problems of heterogeneity with multiprotocol packet-switching capabilities. Gateways operate at the higher layers of the OSI model and interconnect networks with completely different architectures. For example, gateways are often used to connect SNA networks to X.25 packet-switching networks.

Routers have been more widely used than bridges when connecting a LAN to a WAN. Since LANs are much faster than WANs, a LAN bridge would try to operate at the LAN speed, causing problems. A bridge would send packets out to the WAN too fast, and the analog LAN lines would have higher error rates. As WANs get faster, this will not be as much of a problem.

11.1.4 Repeaters vs. Bridges

Repeaters can be used to connect two different LANs. However, there are advantages to using a bridge to connect them.

Figure 11.3 illustrates three Ethernet LANs connected by two bridges. The bridge provides an extended network so users can access previously unavailable devices. Also, the two bridges segment the network, keeping local traffic from needlessly clogging up the extended network while forwarding appropriate traffic across the bridge to a remote device.

There have been sites where an engineering group and an accounting

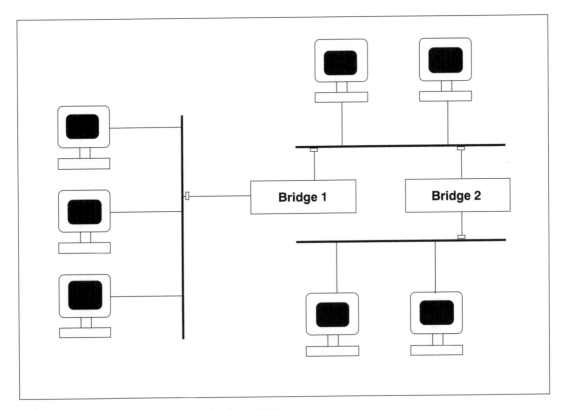

Figure 11.3 Two bridges connecting three LANs.

group connected their LANs in order to share devices. A repeater which does simple signal-regeneration could provide this connection service also, but it would indiscriminately and unnecessarily repeat all the bandwidth-intensive engineering messages onto the accounting LAN segment, significantly increasing the latter's traffic. A bridge knows how to connect the LANs without indiscriminately forwarding all messages to remote segments.

11.2   A COMPARISON OF BRIDGES AND ROUTERS

Despite the differences between bridges and routers, there are many instances where either one can be used and an installation will need to make a choice between them. For example, advocates of routers say that even if a bridge would do the job, the site would be better off if using a router. Bridges and routers both have their advantages and disadvantages and each one has its advocates and its critics. However, the biggest critics of bridges seem to be router vendors and the biggest critics of routers seem to be the bridge vendors.

Since many installations will face a choice between installing a bridge or a router, an overview of each one's advantages and disadvantages is helpful. With interconnection being so complex and changing so rapidly, the advocates on each side (bridges vs. routers) can offer counter arguments for many of the points highlighted below. Therefore, these advantages and disadvantages should just be used as a general guide.

11.2.1   Bridges: Advantages and Disadvantages

The advantages of bridges are as follows:

- Bridges are generally easy to install. Some advocates say that even advanced bridging features require only minimal configuration. Critics say, however, that the more defaults you accept, the easier the bridge is to install.

- Bridges are generally inexpensive and offer good price performance. Their low cost results from their underlying simplicity.

- Bridges are transparent to different high-level protocols. This means they can connect networks running different protocols without needing additional software.

- Bridges are flexible, adaptable, and transparent to users. Bridges add flexibility since computers in a bridged network can be moved without new network addresses being configured for them.

The disadvantages of bridges are as follows:

- Bridges cannot handle certain network problems and delays. If a bridge sends out a packet with an unknown address, this can significantly increase network traffic. Also, bridges cannot prevent "broadcast storms" which occur when certain broadcast protocols cause packets to be flooded to every port.
- Bridges offer little support for fault isolation. Since bridges form a single logical network, networks become hard to manage and maintain as their size increases.
- Most bridges are limited and cannot perform load-splitting. Bridges cannot take advantage of alternate or redundant paths in a network unless they use special software or a special protocol.
- Bridges can prevent some applications from running over networks. Some applications need to use unique names on a network-wide basis. Such an application could malfunction if two copies of the application were running at the same time—each under the same name.

Bridges have a filter rating and a forward rating. When a bridge examines a packet to determine whether it should stay local or be sent elsewhere, it is filtering. If the packet is to be sent elsewhere, the bridge forwards it. Naturally, the higher the filter and forwarding rate, the faster the bridge.

11.2.2 Routers: Advantages and Disadvantages

The advantages of routers are as follows:

- Routers can select the best path from multiple options. Routers have the intelligence to make decisions about sending packets over different paths depending on user priorities and availability. They can also perform load-splitting.
- Routers can provide security. Since routers logically segment subnetworks, they can increase the security of confidential information.
- Routers provide a firewall between subnetworks. Routers can prevent incidents that happen on one network from affecting other subnetworks.
- Routers can support any topology. As a result, routers can more easily support network growth and complexity.

• Routers can segment packets. This allows routers to accommodate network protocols that have different packet sizes by dividing large packets into smaller ones.

The disadvantages of routers are as follows:

• Routers are generally more expensive than bridges. Routers cost more because they have more intelligence, requiring more software.
• Routers can be hard to set up and configure. While routers for NetWare networks are relatively easy to configure, routers for TCP/IP networks are difficult to configure.
• Routers are generally slower than bridges. They are slower because they use more software to make the decisions they are capable of making. However, when compression is used, many routers can match or surpass bridges in speed.
• With routers, moving end systems can be difficult. Since each network segment has a different network address, a new network address must be assigned to end systems that are relocated to a different segment.
• Routers are protocol-dependent, and not all protocols are routable. Routers can only communicate with other routers that support the same protocols. Protocols like IBM's SNA and NetBIOS and Digital's Local Area Transport (LAT) are not routable. This often requires users to purchase multiple solutions including several bridges and/or bridging routers.

IBM's NetBIOS cannot be routed because it has no routing information. NetBIOS uses a "user-friendly" network and device naming convention instead of 32-bit numbers. For example, it lets users use names like Joe's PC or Accounting LAN. A protocol dependent router would have no way of determining where and how to send this kind of packet. Some vendors use an encapsulating technique to handle IBM packets. For example, they insert, or encapsulate, the IBM packet into TCP/IP protocols and then work with the TCP/IP protocol. This, however, adds overhead and complexity.

Routers work at the network layer and maintain the logical identities of each network segment. An internetwork using routers consists of different logical subnetworks, each of which can be an independent administrative domain. A router needs to have appropriate software for each protocol that it supports. In fact, since so many sites today have many protocols installed, the trend is increasingly toward multiprotocol routers.

11.2.3   Summary of the Pros and Cons of Bridges and Routers

The more commonly mentioned advantages and disadvantages of bridges and routers are presented in the B
oxes 11.2 through 11.5.

Analysts offer conflicting opinions about the future of bridges vs. routers. Some analysts predict that the use of bridges will decrease in favor of routers—which are becoming more intelligent and less expensive all the time. Some say that simple bridges are now primarily used only in local environments—like within one building. However, others give evidence that bridges are holding their own.

At one time, bridging was considered the primary technique to connect Ethernet networks. However, as Ethernet networks expanded in size, they became "too big for their bridges" according to one analyst* who believes the bridge/router has come of age. Stand-alone bridges and routers are merging, allowing users to bridge, route, change back and forth, or do both.

Some analysts say it is not an issue of bridges vs. routers. Both are needed for different situations. These analysts say bridges are used at the departmental level, while routers are generally used to create enterprise-wide networks. Often, the main issue is how the tools are constructed.

11.3   VENDORS

11.3.1   New Vendors

There are thousands of Ethernet bridge vendors. Vitalink has been the leading bridge vendor for a long time. (Vitalink Communications Corporation, based in Fremont, CA, a subsidiary of Minneapolis-based Network Systems Company, also sells routers and a variety of other internetworking products.) For token ring bridges, IBM is the leading vendor since that is the LAN topology used by IBM. CrossComm (Marlboro, MA) is also an important token ring connectivity vendor.

Intellicom has a product line that includes a local Ethernet bridge, an Ethernet series of network interface cards, transceivers, adapters, the Long-Link interface extender system, as well as various PC and printer

---

*Edwin Mier, President of Mier Communications, a communications consultancy in Princeton Junction, NJ.

- Bridges are relatively easy to install.
- Bridges are generally inexpensive and offer good price performance.
- Bridges are transparent to different high-level protocols.
- Bridges are flexible, adaptable, and transparent to users.

Box 11.2 Advantages of bridges.

- Bridges cannot handle certain network problems and delays.
- Bridges offer little support for fault isolation.
- Most bridges are limited and cannot perform load-splitting.
- Bridges can prevent some applications from running over networks.

Box 11.3 Disadvantages of bridges.

- Routers can select the best path from multiple options.
- Routers can provide security.
- Routers provide a firewall between subnetworks.
- Routers can support any topology.
- Routers can segment packets.

Box 11.4 Advantages of routers.

- Routers are protocol-dependent, and not all protocols are routable.
- Most routers are more expensive than bridges.
- Routers can be hard to set up and configure.
- Routers are generally slower than bridges.
- Movement between end systems can be difficult.

Box 11.5 Disadvantages of routers.

connection devices.

Some highlights of Newport's family of products include the following: LAN2LAN/768, a multiport router for high speed LAN connections; LAN2PC which provides for interconnecting remotely located individual PCs to an internetwork of LANs; LAN2LAN with X.25, a NetWare compatible, multi-port router supporting X.25 network communications; LAN2LAN/Mega, designed for the highest possible LAN-to-LAN communications for large data and critical response times; and LAN2LAN/ Compression Router.

Some of the vendors for routers include Cisco Systems (Menlo Park, CA), Wellfleet (Bedford, MA), Proteon (Westborough, MA), 3Com (Santa Clara, CA), Network Systems (along with its subsidiary Vitalink, Fremont, CA), Advanced Computer Communications, (ACC in Santa Barbara, CA), CrossComm Corp., Microcom (Norwood, MA), Olicom USA (Richardson, TX), Andrew Corp. (Torrance, CA), and RAD Network Devices (RND, Huntington Beach, CA).

11.3.2 Traditional Vendors: Digital's Bridges and Routers

Digital has a wide variety of bridges, routers, and other network interconnection products. Its DEC Network Integration Server (DECNIS) family simultaneously handles multiprotocol routing, and local and remote bridging. The DECNIS 600 also handles X.25 gateway services and FDDI.

Digital says that with the DECNIS 500 and DECNIS 600, it has eliminated the either/or question related to bridging, routers, and gateways. The only disadvantage is that if a user only needed bridging capabilities, he would be paying needlessly for the additional functions. The DECNIS servers—a combination of hardware and software—also offer flexibility as the user's network changes. For example, if a user decided that he wants to interface to Ethernet, he would just put an Ethernet board into the DECNIS server.

The DECNIS 500 has two option slots, and the DECNIS 600 has seven option slots. The slots allow "hot-swappable" network interface cards to be inserted for Ethernet, token ring, etc. "Hot-swappable" means the cards can be inserted or removed without powering down the unit. This adds to network availability.

11.3.3 IBM's Source Routing

IBM has long used token rings in its LAN architecture. IBM uses a technique for connecting token rings called "source routing." However, since it operates at the data link layer, it is a bridging technology—not a routing technology. The technique is called "source routing" because the *route* is determined by the *source* station for each frame sent through one or more bridges to the destination address. The term "source routing" causes confusion, which is unfortunate.

In IBM's source routing, the routing information is contained within each frame of data. This routing information is used by each bridge to determine the next path to be followed by the frame. The routing information is acquired by the originating station by searching through the network for the destination address. If the originating station finds that the destination is not on the local ring, it sends an all-rings test broadcast frame.

Each bridge receives a copy of the test frame, inserts its address into the frame, and sends it on. Many copies of the test frame may exist, going through different bridges. When test frame copies are received by the destination station, the station sends them back to the source station using the same path by which they arrived. The source station then examines the multiple routes contained in the various test frames and selects a preferred one.

11.4 OTHER ISSUES

11.4.1 Importance of Compression

Compression is often used on networks to increase overall speed. Using compression techniques, it is possible to get about 24 Kbps across a dial-up line where you would normally only get about 9600 baud without compression. Baud is a variable unit of data transmission speed, usually equivalent to one bit per second.

The rate of compression depends on what type of file is being transmitted across a line. For example, files that have one character repeated many times or have a lot of spaces—characterized as having "a lot of air"—will compress into a smaller file. If a compression router discovers that it has 500 identical characters in a row on the sending side, it will not send all 500. Instead, it will send a code telling the receiving side that there are 500 iterations of the character involved. Achieving a compression ratio of 3 means that three times the usual amount of data is being sent over a line.

12

COMMUNICATING BETWEEN CLIENT AND SERVER MODULES

12.1 DIFFERENT TYPES OF COMMUNICATION

A number of different communication approaches are used in client/ server systems. The three most common ones are conversation, remote procedure call, and messaging. SQL is a higher-level approach and is usually built on one of these three models—often the RPC paradigm.

SQL and RPCs are quite familiar to developers due to their widespread use. This text will provide examples that will make developers feel quite comfortable with the conversational and messaging models, too. This chapter contains a basic overview of the conversation and messaging models and then provides a more in-depth discussion of SQL and RPCs. After a general description of SQL and RPC concepts, the advantages and disadvantages of each approach will be discussed.

12.1.1 Conversational Model

An example of the conversational model is found in IBM's APPC. In SNA, the term "conversation" refers to communication between peer application processes during a session. A somewhat comparable function is the "dialog" from OSI. OSI uses some different terms—for example, the word "association" is used instead of session. However, most of the concepts discussed here are quite similar in both conversations and dialogues.

In an APPC conversation, a logical connection is established between two partners. A particular conversation can only take place between *two* application processes. However either of these two processes can participate in conversations with other application processes—as long as there are only two parties in any one specific conversation.

The conversational model is particularly appropriate for situations that involve many interactions per transaction between the two partners. It provides tight control for detailed interactions. The conversational model provides and implements routines that permit overlapped execution. (RPCs, on the other hand, are usually restricted to synchronous operation.)

Application-to-application communication is usually achieved through the use of calls that are part of IBM's Common Programming Interface for Communications (CPI-C). Some of the more basic CPI-C calls are as follows:

- Initialize_Conversation—initialize the conversation characteristics
- Accept_Conversation—accept an incoming conversation
- Allocate—establish a conversation
- Send_Data—send data
- Receive—receive data
- Deallocate—end a conversation

There are many more CPI-C calls, including ones with advanced functionality for such things as procedure-oriented activities, set-up operations, and extract operations.

12.1.2 Messaging

Examples of products that use messaging approaches include Microsoft's Windows and IBM's IMS, CICS, and Presentation Manager. With Windows and Presentation Manager, message queues are used between the user interface and the many window processors. The broader concepts of messaging are familiar to anyone who understands the basics of electronic messaging—more commonly known as E-mail.

Using messaging, communication takes the form of a message. If a client module requests data from a database server, for example, the client module formats the request in the form of a message. In turn, the server provides the response in the form of a message also. As messages arrive, they are put into the queue (enqued); as the module is ready to process a message, a message is removed from the queue (dequeued). Message entries in a queue can be ordered in one of three ways: first-in, first-out (FIFO), last-in, last-out (LIFO), and according to the assigned priority of the message.

A client process can send a message to any number of servers. Queue managers make sure that a message is delivered to the appropriate queue. Queue managers are required at both the client and server ends.

Messaging has been fully developed by on-line transaction processing systems such as IMS and CICS.

12.1.3   Interprocess Communication (IPC) and "Middleware"

As mentioned in Chapter 2, this book avoids the use of the term "middleware" because it is used differently by different people. Some people use middleware to refer to SQL and RPC, while others use it to refer to communication techniques which are at a lower level on the OSI seven-layer model. The longer the term is used, the more consensus will develop on exactly how the term should be used.

Many terms are used in connection with communicating between modules or processes in a client/server environment. The term "interprocess communication" refers to techniques that can used between processes on separate machines, but the term very often refers also to communicating between processes that reside on the same machine. An example of such a term is "semaphores." Named after naval flags, program semaphores have the same intent: communication to avoid confusion and errors. A semaphore is an indicator or flag variable that helps maintain order among processes that are competing for resources. They are signals used to indicate the availability of resources and to prevent such things as one process writing to a memory location actively used by another process.

Pipes are another example of IPCs. A pipe connects items and permits the flow of something between the items connected; similarly, an IPC pipe connects two processes, permitting the output of one to be input to the other. The symbol that is used to indicate the presence of pipes is ¦. The Microsoft Press Computer Dictionary provides an example of how pipes work using the command *dir ¦ sort ¦ more*, which asks for a directory listing. Output from the *dir* command is piped to the *sort* command. In turn, the output from the *sort* command is piped to the *more* command which displays output one screen at a time.

Named Pipes is an interprocess communication facility in LAN Manager that permits data to be exchanged between applications that are in the same computer or in different computers connected with a network.

12.2   SQL

12.2.1   A Description of SQL

SQL was introduced by IBM. SQL is closely related to relational databases which were introduced in a paper by Dr. E.F. Codd in 1970. SQL was first proposed in 1974 and a prototype was implemented in System R by IBM Research in San Jose, CA. Its first commercial implementation was in SQL/DS, IBM's first fully supported relational product which was announced for mainframe DOS/VSE systems in 1981. In 1983 SQL appeared in DB2 for MVS/370. Since then, SQL use has spread and there are now a great many vendor implementations of it. It is very widely used in client/server database-oriented systems involving relational databases. In fact, entire systems can be built with SQL as the primary way that interaction takes place between the client software and the database server software.

SQL is not a full programming language. It is used primarily as a data definition language (DDL) and as a data manipulation language (DML). Some SQL statements are also related to data integrity, security, recovery, and the physical administration of databases. SQL commands can be submitted interactively by an end user from a PC or embedded in programs. It is often used in conjunction with a programming language like Cobol or C. Cobol or C instructions perform the basic application logic. When the program needs to access data, SQL calls are embedded within the application program to fill this need.

Most, if not all, database products that were specifically built to be database server products support SQL. Some databases may have started out as mainframe or minicomputer-based products and have been tailored to run on servers that feature a proprietary data handling language, but any vendor who is eager to be competitive is supplying SQL as well. While SQL is readily available for most database servers, the different implementations are not necessarily compatible with each other. Differences even exist in the SQL implementations provided by a particular vendor. For example, IBM's SQL implementations are not identical within all of its products.

The majority of SQL is similar from product to product. All SQL implementations will have capabilities like CREATE and SELECT. The differences are mostly minor. For example, the data type for date varies from one SQL product to another. Some implementations support concatenation (joining), while others do not.

Standardization efforts are being aimed at eliminating or reducing SQL incompatibilities. ANSI-standard SQL has been available since 1986, and ISO adopted the SQL standard in 1987. Most vendors do provide ANSI-standard SQL, but many also provide extensions to provide additional capabilities. If a site wants to be able to port its SQL applications from one platform to another, it would have to ensure that its programmers do not use any of the extensions.

There are other problems as well. The ANSI SQL standard is too broadly defined in some areas allowing different—and incompatible—interpretations of the standard to be implemented. This means that different vendors' SQL could be compliant with ANSI and still not interoperate. The SQL Access Group (SAG) consortium was formed in 1989 in an attempt to overcome some of the problems related to the SQL standard. SAG consists of over 50 software and hardware vendors, as well as representatives from the user community. One of SAG's major projects was to try to standardize error messages across SQL implementations. Other project areas included system catalog tables and association management statements. SAG's efforts at standardization refinements, as well as its extensions to SQL, are available in its Call Level Interface (CLI) and SQL Access Formats and Protocols (FAP).

Users must be aware of the differences in various SQL implementations to prevent problems. If an installation uses a vendor's SQL extensions because they provide added value, but later that installation decides to change the database server product, serious incompatibility problems could occur. As a result, some sites are adopting a strict policy of adhering to the SQL standard.

Several products are available to act as a middleman between different SQL implementations. An example is Jam from JYACC of New York, NY which can hide the differences between different SQL implementations. JYACC says Jam links transparently to Informix, Ingres, Oracle, Microsoft/Sybase, and Sharebase SQL servers, among others.

SQL is at the heart of IBM's DRDA which is described in Chapter 13. Briefly, DRDA is intended to help access data across heterogeneous environments. For example, DRDA provides facilities so other vendors can generate SQL requests to IBM's DB2. Vendors like Informix, Sybase, Oracle, and Computer Associates have announced support for IBM's DRDA.

Closely related to DRDA is IBM's Information Warehouse concept which represents the basic idea of obtaining data from wherever it is stored. IBM refers to the Information Warehouse framework as a set of database management systems, interfaces, tools, and applications for providing access to data wherever it exists in the enterprise. There are so many potential variations of heterogeneous database combinations today that IBM realized it could not provide all the answers itself. As a result, Big Blue announced the IBM International Alliance when it debuted its Information Warehouse concept in September of 1992. The International Alliance consists of Information Builders, Inc., Bachman, and IBM.

12.2.2   SQL Limitations

SQL is fine for what it is intended to do—database interactions in an RDBMS environment—but some interactions that need to take place between a client and server cannot be addressed by SQL. The RPC mechanism is used instead. As we mentioned earlier, these mechanisms are not mutually exclusive; SQL interactions can be built on top of RPCs.

A major distinction between SQL and RPCs is that SQL is database-specific, while RPCs are not database-specific. That is, RPCs can be used for database-related processing, but they can be used for other purposes as well. SQL, on the other hand, is intended only for processing directly related to databases. SQL can be used with a wide variety of databases, especially when its capabilities are extended with a family of products like EDA/SQL (described later in this chapter). However, SQL is not necessarily the answer for every installation. As always, each individual enterprise must examine its unique needs and long-term strategy to determine what is the best way for it to proceed.

For example, Larry Poleshuck, a vice president at Citibank in New York City, prefers to have his programmers use RPCs in their applications. He believes that relying on a database vendor is acceptable for relatively small systems, but not for complex ones.

Citibank has a large number of systems scattered around the world on different networks, hardware, and software platforms. These systems use various relational databases, indexed file systems, and other products. In addition, the bank has many requirements for interacting between these various systems. In the past, Citibank built point-to-point links between each application. Citibank's approach is different now. Poleshuck says his programmers are now developing a network of object-oriented servers with reuse of the server capabilities as a primary objective. The plan is to build the servers, put them on the network, and then have client/server applications interact with them. They believe that the RPC mechanism is the best approach for this plan. They will have more flexibility by using RPCs. Changing database design, for example, would be more difficult if they were using SQL statements that could be tied to the database design.

Poleshuck says Citibank is aware of the limitations of RPCs, and is working to counteract those limitations. For example, since RPCs do not provide transaction integrity, Citibank has transaction monitors to provide that functionality. The bank has chosen to implement OSF's DCE, and will use the RPC capabilities provided with that environment. Citibank has chosen the Encina transaction monitor from Transarc in Pittsburgh. (Each of these is explained later in this chapter and in subsequent chapters.)

12.2.3 Overview of Vendor Products

12.2.3.1 Information Builder's EDA/SQL

Information Builders, Inc., (IBI) plays a primary role in IBM's Information Warehouse concept with its Enterprise Data Access (EDA) SQL family of products. EDA/SQL provides an open API to which any front-end tool can link, and thereby provides access to over 45 different types of databases and file systems on over 35 different platforms.

EDA/SQL complements and extends IBM's own SQL solutions like DRDA, yet it provides the user with that very important access to non-relational and non-IBM platform data that heretofore has not been available directly from IBM.

IBI is probably best known for Focus. Focus started as an integrated 4GL/DBMS package and then became a 4GL that ran with multiple DBMSs. Eventually it became a client/server product where the 4GL could reside on one platform and the DBMSs on other, separate platforms. IBI was constantly working on the product's portability. Eventually Focus had the ability to read 45 different kinds of databases and files, both relational and non-relational. It now accesses VSAM files as well as IMS, IDMS, and other database systems.

As time went on and IBI realized the importance of SQL, as opposed to proprietary languages such as Focus, it wanted to open its architecture, incorporating SQL as the standard for data access. IBI also realized that it had developed some very valuable interoperability capabilities. The combination of these various capabilities and directions helped give birth to EDA/SQL. While the Focus 4GL can be used with EDA/SQL, Focus does not have to be present.

The EDA/SQL family of products consists of four client/server components that work together to provide SQL-based access to relational and non-relational data on interconnected multivendor systems. The four main products that make up EDA/SQL are as follows:

- EDA/SQL Server: The host component that processes SQL requests for data
- API/SQL: A call level application programming interface
- EDA/Link: A modular system of communication interfaces
- EDA Extender Products: Products that provide direct interfaces from popular SQL-based tools

The EDA/SQL Server forms the core of the EDA architecture. It manages the flow of data and keeps track of incoming requests and outgoing responses. When the product first came out there was an EDA/SQL Server for MVS with EDA/SQL Servers for VAX/VMS with CMS, VM, RS/6000, HP, Sun, and others available soon after. The EDA/SQL Server processes requests for both relational and non-relational data through EDA/Data Drivers. For non-relational data, the system converts SQL calls to the data manipulation equivalent in the source database. Utilities are provided to help the database administrator with data definitions and catalog services to set the system up.

The major components of the EDA/SQL Server for MVS include a scheduler/initiator subsystem, communications subsystems, the Universal SQL translator, a Data Access Engine, an EDA/DBA Facility, and data drivers.

Data drivers are individually designed to handle each unique data structure. IBI says its data drivers resolve any variations or idiosyncrasies in syntax, functionality, schema, data types, catalog naming conventions, and data representation.

The API/SQL component helps a developer incorporate Enterprise Data Access capabilities into a wide range of programs and tools including 3GL applications. API/SQL provides a library of modules which can be used to control numerous functions within the client/server environment.

Data access functions submit SQL statements to the server, define the data to be retrieved, and prepare SQL statements for later execution. RPC functions enable a client application to invoke a 3GL program on a server and pass data back and forth between the application and the program. The 3GL programs invoked can reside on a mainframe acting as a server. Thus, they could be existing production 3GL programs.

Control functions enable a client application to continue processing while SQL requests or RPCs are executing on the server. In this way, client/server multiprocessing is maximized. Environmental functions provide the ability to do things like limit the number of rows an application receives from a query. Trace and debugging functions permit the observation of a range of activities including low-level communications events, procedural execution, and high-level API calls.

Communication functions initiate and remove sessions on the server for a client application. Multiple servers can be accessed simultaneously and multiple sessions can be established on a single server. While the API/SQL component provides some communication functions, the real communication-level work is accomplished by the EDA/Link component.

EDA/Link is actually a modular set of many different communication interfaces. Popular protocols like LU2, LU6.2, DECnet, and LU0 are currently supported with TCP/IP and Asynch protocols to follow soon. A network administrator configures the communications environment using a series of pop-up menus.

Once configured and established, the EDA/Link interfaces generate and translate communication protocols, transmit and route messages, authenticate passwords, convert data, and detect transmission errors. EDA/Link also creates outgoing packets from the client applications and routes answer packets back. These functions are performed automatically, making communications transparent to the end user.

EDA/Extender Products provide interfaces between API/SQL and products like Lotus 1–2–3, HyperCard, and SmallTalk. The EDA/Dynamic Extender for DB2 lets existing DB2 applications and tools use EDA technology to access other relational and non-relational data. Existing applications using the Query Management Facility (QMF), an IBM query tool, can now access heterogeneous data sources.

The DB2 Extender intercepts DB2 calls, parses the SQL statements, and routes the statements to the EDA server where appropriate. Error and warning messages from the EDA Server are translated into their DB2 equivalents. The Data Lens Driver for Lotus 1–2–3 lets users of the popular spreadsheet transparently access data from almost any data file on leading computer platforms.

12.2.3.2 Lotus 1–2–3 DataLens Connects with SQL

The combination of Lotus 1–2–3 DataLens and EDA/SQL provides some very strong capabilities to end users. End users have long been interested in directly accessing data from various sources and moving it into Lotus 1–2–3 for analysis. Several years ago, a new version of Lotus 1–2–3 was released which had its own database engine as well as DataLens which provided access to external databases. When DataLens was first released, it could only access dBase. Soon after, access to Sybase/Microsoft SQL Server data was added.

Over time, more and more data drivers were added by Lotus and other vendors, permitting Lotus 1–2–3 to access additional databases. Novell provides data access from Lotus 1–2–3 to NetWare SQL (Btrieve files); Oracle Corporation provides access to the Oracle database on OS/2, UNIX, VAX, and IBM mainframes; various third-party vendors provide access to AS/400, Rdb/VMS, VAX/RMS, and Unisys systems.

DataLens provided a conduit that opened the door to EDA/SQL from Lotus 1–2–3. EDA/SQL broadens the scope of the data sources that can now be accessed by Lotus 1–2–3. Now with the EDA/SQL DataLens Driver for Lotus 1–2–3, users can access DB2, IMS, and VSAM data on the mainframe, which is welcome news for Lotus customers who have been asking for a door to IBM mainframe data. EDA/SQL offers the benefit of standard 1–2–3 menu commands to access data. This makes the product easy to utilize for end users familiar with Lotus menus. Most important, with IBI's DataLens support, people will not have to rekey mainframe data into their PCs.

The DataLens Driver supports all Lotus 1–2–3 functions and commands. EDA/SQL converts the Lotus command into an appropriate query for the target data source. Initially, Lotus users on DOS, OS/2, and Windows platforms were able to link to data servers on IBM mainframes and DEC VAX/VMS machines, while later releases included linkage capabilities for Hewlett-Packard, Tandem, Wang, and UNIX platforms.

Cigna Corporation, a leading provider of insurance and related financial services based in Philadelphia, has been using both EDA/SQL and DataLens. Donald Walker, director of technology strategy at Cigna Systems Division's Windsor, Connecticut Data Center, says that Cigna was looking for a way to provide end users with the self-sufficiency to access data by themselves. The goal was to let end users utilize tools they understood so they would not have to go to MIS every time they needed to access data. However, Cigna also wanted to insulate its end users from the details of physical data structures and data access mechanisms.

A number of years ago, the strategic planners at Cigna created an architecture with three layers to address this challenge. The first, or top, layer consisted of tools that end users were familiar with: Lotus 1–2–3, Paradox, and PC Focus. The bottom layer consisted of the databases and files where the data resides: DB2, IMS, VSAM, etc. It was the middle layer—the one to connect everything—that had been the challenge. And that is exactly where EDA/SQL fits in.

12.3   RPCs

12.3.1   A Description of RPCs

An RPC is similar to a local procedure call which programmers have used for a long time. With local procedure calls, frequently used code is often stored as a procedure or subroutine. When a program needs to execute that code, it performs a local procedure call which passes on any necessary parameters. It then executes the stored procedure. The RPC generalizes this model from a single system to a network of systems.

With RPCs, the procedure or subroutine is located on another machine in the network. Therefore, an RPC permits a program or process on one computer to execute a process on a different, usually remote, system. As with a local procedure call, any parameters that are needed are passed on by the calling program. The RPC mechanism builds this information into network messages and forwards the messages to the remote procedure. The remote procedure has code—built into it by the RPC mechanism—that understands what to do with the incoming message, how to respond to it, and how to get the requested results back to the calling procedure.

There are a variety of different RPC implementations. OSF's DCE is based on the Hewlett-Packard/Apollo Network Computing System (NCS) RPCs. Netwise's original RPC, which lost out on the OSF competition to the HP/Apollo RPC, is still widely used due to its many benefits. Netwise is also providing an OSF-compliant product as well.

RPCs are valuable because they take care of a lot of the details of distributed processing—making a lot of complexity almost irrelevant to the RPC user. For example, an RPC user does not need to know the location of the remote portion of the RPC. That knowledge—or the ability to determine it—is provided in the overall RPC mechanism. Also, the details of the transport mechanism used by the RPC are hidden from an RPC user even though that RPC may support several different transport mechanisms. The tools and capabilities of the RPC that hide these details of distributed processing are provided by the particular vendor's implementation of that RPC.

The types of tools provided generally consist of a language and a compiler that facilitate the creation of portable source code as well as a run-time facility—the portion that makes the operation of the RPC transparent. The application developer uses the language provided by the RPC tool to create a specification—or procedure declaration—describing aspects of the functionality to be accomplished with the RPC. The runtime environment handles all sending and receiving of data across machine boundaries and across the network. RPCs also locate the required computing resources on the network. While directory services used to locate resources differ, many vendors are evolving toward compliance with the OSI X.500 directory services standard. Another RPC responsibility is dealing with the different data representations of various machines on the network. Therefore it has to provide translating services or an intermediate data representation language.

12.3.2 RPC Limitations

Using RPCs may offer an application developer more flexibility, but RPCs are much more complex to code than SQL interactions. Writing applications using RPCs can also differ depending on different vendors' implementations of the RPC mechanism. Installations that have client/server implementations restricted to relatively simple database processing may do well with just the use of SQL.

If RPCs are to be used in database processing, the underlying facilities supported by the particular RPC implementation should be clearly understood. As was previously mentioned, an RPC can hide networking complexity from the developer and can even work over several different network transports. However, various network transport protocols work differently. Some network transports provide services to ensure that remote procedures take place, while other network transports rely on other network layers to provide that functionality.

Directly related to this issue is something called at-most-once semantics. Some operations can be performed many times without any harm, while others cannot. For example, if an application is changing the job title of an employee, it would be harmless if that operation took place several times. Operations that can be repeated without harm are said to be idempotent. If, however, $100 were being subtracted from a customer's checking account, repetition of that operation would be very harmful. Therefore, a developer needs to have some way of ensuring that this kind of operation takes place only once. As a result, developers need to know how the RPC mechanism works and what additional programming he or she may need to provide.

A transaction like subtracting money from a checking account may require additional considerations for an RPC. If money is being moved from a checking account record on one machine to a savings account record on another machine, protection against failure of one of the components will be necessary. RPCs have no notion of two-phase commit by themselves. If a two-phase commit procedure is required, that functionality will need to be added. This could be done, for example, by the application developer, or with the addition of a transaction monitor.

Some consider the lack of a universal standard to be another limitation of RPCs. The European Computer Manufacturers Association (ECMA) and ANSI are working together toward an RPC standard. One of the application services specified in OSI's application layer is the Remote Operations Service Element (ROSE), which could support an RPC facility. OSF says the modular design of its DCE RPC stub/run-time interface could permit the introduction of a new RPC protocol based on ROSE with no changes to existing applications.

Netwise and Sun both have popular RPC implementations. Among the differences between the DCE RPC and the Netwise RPC is the way that different data representations are handled. The Netwise RPC uses Sun's XDR (eXternal Data Representation) specification. This is an intermediate data representation language into which all communications between machines are translated. The argument against this approach is needless translation is necessary between like machines. The arguments for it say it provides a consistent interface and can integrate very different computing resources—a frequent need in large distributed computing environments.

An advantage of the Netwise RPC is that it was available before the DCE RPC. As a result, a large number of applications have been built using the Netwise RPC—more so than with the DCE RPC. Netwise enjoys a loyal base of users of its RPC implementation.

12.3.2.1 OSF's DCE RPC

The language provided with OSF's DCE, is called the Interface Definition Langu-age (IDL). Using the IDL, developers create an interface definition that specifies the data and parameters that need to be passed between procedures for their particular application. For example, if the procedure involves subtracting an amount of money from a savings account, the appropriate fields would be included in the specification. The IDL provides a syntax that is similar to the ANSI C language—as well as additional language constructs that are needed for a networked environment.

The IDL compiler translates this interface definition into client and server stubs which act as stand-ins for each other. The stub on the client side acts as a stand-in for the server procedure and the stub on the server side acts as a stand-in for the client procedure. What this means is that the stub on the client side looks to the client like the original subroutine, and the stub on the server side looks to the server like the original application. These stubs perform functions like copying arguments to and from RPC packets and call the RPC run time mechanism.

Some RPC mechanisms implement—and require—an intermediate form of data representation. All data is automatically converted to this intermediate form. That would be like saying everyone in an international meeting has to have their words translated into English. If a French person were talking to a French-speaking German, they would each still have to have all their words translated into English since that is the intermediate form. With the DCE RPC approach, conversion occurs only if necessary.

The DCE RPC tags all calls with a description of the calling machine's basic data representation. Capturing the required information in less than four bytes, it indicates, for example, how characters, integers, and floating-point data are represented. When the data is received, the receiving end compares the descriptor tags with the receiving machine's data representation. If the data representation formats are different, it is converted; if the data is in the same format, it is not converted.

13

DISTRIBUTED PROCESSING/ DISTRIBUTED DATABASES

13.1 OVERVIEW

Within the emerging area of distributed computing, the terms "distributed processing" and "distributed databases" are often used interchangeably, but they are two quite different terms. This chapter will compare the meaning of these two terms. It will use the term "distributed database" using its original, academic meaning. The final section of this chapter explores the possibility that the meaning of the term "distributed database" may be changing.

13.1.1 The Difference Between Distributed Processing and Distributed Databases

Distributed processing and distributed databases are *not* the same thing. They are similar—each one has certain elements that are distributed—but there are major differences, too. The terms themselves imply that something is distributed. Distributed processing implies that processing is distributed, and distributed databases implies that databases are distributed. Nothing is implied about the location of *data* in the term "distributed processing." The data could be distributed or all in one place. However, a distributed processing system could involve diverse databases in separate locations, and still not qualify as a true "distributed

215

database system." A system must have specific qualities like location transparency, replication transparency, and a single-site image before it qualifies as a distributed database system in the traditional, academic sense.

The increasing availability of LANs is giving a boost to distributed databases. General interest in distributed database systems seems to have increased in recent years, partly because the overall data processing environment is—or can be—more distributed now.

Distributed processing means that the *processing* is distributed. A distributed processing system consists of a number of autonomous processing elements interconnected by a network, that cooperate in performing their separate tasks. The data can be distributed, or it can all reside in one location. A distributed processing system could involve diverse databases that reside in separate locations, and still not qualify as a true "distributed database system."

In contrast, distributed databases mean that the *databases* are distributed. To qualify as a distributed database system in the traditional, academic sense, a system must have the afore-mentioned qualities of location transparency, replication transparency, and a single-site image.

A distributed database system is one form of a distributed processing system. Client/server, peer-to-peer, cooperative processing, and network-based systems are also forms of distributed processing systems. If one or more databases is involved in a distributed-processing, client/server system, some may consider the system a distributed database system. However, this would not necessarily qualify as a true distributed database system.

In some cases, an enterprise may have an IMS database on one machine, a DB2 database on another, plus an Oracle database down in engineering. Therefore, they argue, they have "distributed database systems." In fact, what they have is data "distributed" here and there, located in different places. But they do not necessarily have a "distributed database system." It could be argued that they have data "scattered" here and there. If, however, portions of one or more databases were located in different geographic areas, then it is closer to being a distributed database. For example, if West Coast data was located in Los Angeles and East Coast data was located in New York City but this geographic split of the data was transparent to the user, then we have a distributed database.

One danger of using "distributed processing" and "distributed databases" interchangeably is that it can create false expectations. While a distributed database may have many of the same capabilities as a distributed system, the reverse is not true. Distributed systems may or may not include distributed database characteristics. Most do not.

The qualities of a distributed database system described in this chapter represent the "textbook" version of a distributed database. Such a description could be considered an idealized view, since many commercial implementations fall short of this ideal. But a potential user should be aware of these characteristics to understand the true goals of a distributed database system.

13.1.2 A Definition of Distributed Databases

A simple working definition of a distributed database is: a collection of multiple, logically interrelated databases distributed over a computer network, with the distribution of data transparent to the users.

The key phrases in this definition are:

- logically interrelated
- distributed over a network
- transparently distributed

Transparency is one of the most important qualities in distributed database systems. "Transparency" makes something easier to work with. A transparent system hides the implementation details from the user; the user does not have to be concerned with them. When data has location transparency, users do not need to know where data is located; the system will find it for them.

In addition to location transparency, two other types are replication transparency and fragmentation transparency, among others. Relational database technology has made important contributions in creating these transparencies. In fact, many feel that distributed databases were not realistic until relational database management systems (RDBMS) became available.

Other important characteristics of a distributed database system are single-site or single-system image and site autonomy. Even though there may be many participating sites, the distributed aspect of the system should not be apparent to the user. The single-site image—one of the most important qualities of a distributed database system—gives the user the illusion that there is only one database site: his or her own. In addition, each site has everything it needs to be autonomous. It has its own processing elements, data, and DBMS. It does not need to be dependent on other sites within the overall distributed database architecture.

A distributed database system should also have a mechanism for ensuring that distributed data will be in a consistent state after transaction processing, if hardware or software failures should occur. For example, in a banking application involving a transfer of funds from a savings to a checking account, money should not be deducted from the savings account unless the checking account has money added to it. Both aspects of the transaction must take effect to reflect the desired results. A procedure that helps assure this is called two-phase commit.

For a long time, the lack of adequate two-phase commit procedures in commercial databases caused many companies to stay away from distributed database architectures. Other companies had their own programmers fill in the gaps left by inadequate two-phase commit implementations. Gaps were most noticeable in the area of recovery management. Many sites have designed distributed database systems in which only one major site has to be updated with the on-line transaction, while the rest of the sites are updated during overnight processing. This eliminates having to worry about some devices not being available during on-line transaction processing and eliminates the need for two-phase commit.

13.1.3 Early Distributed Databases

Computer Corporation of America (CCA), of Cambridge, MA, was involved in some of the earliest laboratory work on distributed database systems. CCA worked on the System for Distributed Database (SDD-1) under a DARPA-funded contract from about 1976 to 1980. SDD-1 was designed to run on a group of Digital PDP-10s interconnected with ARPANET.

Dr. Stonebraker and a group of researchers worked on Distributed INGRES starting in 1977 at the University of California at Berkeley. The project's biggest handicap was the overall lack of communications software available at that time. Distributed INGRES consists of multiple copies of a system called University INGRES and was designed to run on Digital PDP-11s.

IBM's R* (pronounced "R Star") project was the best known prototype of a distributed DBMS. Stonebraker says that R* benefited from insight into the mistakes of earlier prototypes as well as from the availability of VTAM software for communication needs. It was developed at IBM Research in San Jose, CA.

R* consists of multiple, cooperating copies of System R, IBM's earlier research database system. R* is designed to run on a group of IBM mainframes that communicate with the InterSystems Communication facility (ISC) of CICS (CICS/ICS.)

All of these research prototypes made valuable contributions to the state-of-the-art of distributed database technology. Many of the techniques developed in the laboratories are appearing in commercial products today.

13.2 DISTRIBUTED DATABASES HAVE UNIQUE REQUIREMENTS

13.2.1 The Transparencies

Some of the most important features of classical distributed databases are its transparencies. As mentioned above, three of these are location transparency, replication transparency, and fragmentation transparency, among others. The following sections will take a closer look at these three types of transparencies.

13.2.1.1 Location Transparency

The flexibility of the relational model helps to provide location transparency in distributed systems, so users do not have to track where data is located. Using SQL, programmers do not need to know on which pack and in which cylinder data is located. In addition, they do not have to know what the paths are to the data. The system catalog or dictionary/directory keeps track of the data location, and a database optimizer can determine the best path to the data, and then go and get the data.

In relational systems, data is stored in tables. A relation is a two-dimensional table with rows and columns. The idea of data tabularity provides great flexibility and independence. Programmers do not have to worry about pointers anymore. Therefore, it does not make any difference if tables are physically located on the same machine or on different machines.

If the requested data is not local, the system can handle it in the following ways: it can do the processing at the remote site and move the result to the local site; it can move the data to the local site for processing; or it can do some combination of these.

Location transparency significantly simplifies the job of the programmer, who does not have to code location into the program's logic. Also, there are no programming changes if the data is moved to a different site; for example, if its usage changes.

13.2.1.2 Replication Transparency

Replication transparency is another objective of distributed databases. Data replication means that a given data object may have several stored representatives at several different sites. This provides improved performance and reliability. Performance is maximized by locating the data closest to the site that uses it most often. Reliability is increased, since if one site is down, a user can still access the required data from another site.

Data may also be replicated to provide maximum availability. Although in a distributed database system, data is usually located closest to the source which needs it the most, there are times when two users in different locations have equally important usage needs for the same data. Not only is this a difficult technical decision, it is probably an even more difficult political decision. In this case, it makes sense to replicate the data and store it close to both users.

Replication can create problems, though. Retrieval operations should be directed to the copy closest to the user. Update operations, however, need to be directed to all copies. Special provisions must be made for copies that are not immediately available due to site or network failures. Replication transparency means that all details involved with locating and maintaining replicas are supported by the system, not by the user. Most database experts agree that some degree of replication transparency should be provided to realize the benefits of a distributed database system.

13.2.1.3 Fragmentation Transparency

Data in a distributed database can be partitioned or replicated. With partitioned data, one physically stored representation of a piece of data exists. With replicated data, there are multiple representations of data are in diverse locations. Data can also be fragmented (split up). Fragments are portions of a data representation. A database relation is divided into smaller fragments, each of which is treated as a separate data object. This approach is sometimes taken instead of data replication. With fragmentation, only a small part of the overall relation needs to be contained in separate locations.

The twin objectives of data fragmentation and fragmentation transparency together constitute two of the reasons why distributed database systems are almost always relational. Relations are easy to fragment, and the fragments are easy to recombine. Performing analogous functions in IMS or IDMS would not be easy.

Fragmentation transparency—which, along with replication and location transparency contributes to a single-site image—lets the user behave as though relations are not fragmented. Users are presented with a view of the data in which all fragments are combined. With the relational model, data can be fragmented and distributed in a variety of ways.

With the data stored as tables (relations), different fragmentations among the sites—such as vertical, horizontal, or combinations of both—are possible. With horizontal fragmentation, some relations are stored in one place, and other relations are stored in another location. With vertical fragmentation, a relation is separated into different sets of fields, and each set is stored at different locations. For example, suppose an employee relation (record) contained job skill codes and the employee's address. If this record were to be fragmented, the skill codes could be stored in one location and the employee's address could be stored in another location. Each fragment must contain enough information so the original relation can be reconstructed. Horizontal fragmentation is much simpler than vertical fragmentation, and it is used more widely.

13.2.1.4 Other Transparencies

Some additional transparencies are also important objectives and design issues for distributed databases. These include schema change transparency, network transparency, performance transparency, and transaction transparency.

Schema change transparency means that when a database object is added or deleted from a distributed database, the change needs to be made only once—to the distributed dictionary or catalog. The change does not have to be made to all sites in the distributed architecture.

Network transparency means that the existence of the network should not be apparent to the user. The user should not need to be concerned about any operational details related to the network. In fact, the user should not have to be aware that there is a network. This type of transparency is sometimes called distribution transparency.

With performance transparency, a distributed query optimizer finds an optimized plan before executing a distributed command. For example, if one wants to join 1,000,000 objects in New York with 10 objects in Berkeley, one wants to perform the join by moving the 10 objects to New York, rather than the reverse. While that is a simple example, many operations require real analysis. While SQL query optimization can be a critical factor in the performance of a non-distributed relational database, it becomes even more critical in a distributed relational database. The same query can take one second, or it can take many hours, depending on how it is executed.

Transaction transparency means that a user can run a transaction that updates data at any number of sites, and the transaction either commits or aborts at all sites. No intermediate states are possible. This, of course, is related to two-phase commit procedures.

13.2.2 Other Requirements of Distributed Databases

13.2.2.1 Updates

Updates have always presented the biggest challenge for the distributed database environment. Some of the greatest problems are update propagation, concurrency control, and recovery management.

An update to any local data item must be propagated to all copies of that data item. A problem occurs if one site is unavailable (due to network or site failure) at the time of the update. To solve this, one strategy is to designate one copy of the data item as the primary copy. That copy's responsibility is to apply the update to any data items that were unavailable during the update process.

Concurrency problems deal with the fact that in a shared, multiuser system, the possibility exists for concurrently executing transactions to interfere with each other, producing incorrect results. Concurrency control is often based on locking in distributed DBMSs. A mechanism must be provided to detect global deadlock. Global deadlock occurs when, for example, transaction T1 has a lock on object A in Chicago and requests a lock on object B in New York, and transaction T2 has a lock on object B in New York and requests a lock on object A in Chicago. In this situation, transaction T1 and T2 would both go into wait states resulting in a deadlock. A deadlock prevention mechanism averts this.

Recovery management has always been another challenge for distributed DBMSs. A transaction must be treated as a unit of operation. This quality is known as atomicity. Correct recovery must be made in the event of failure at one of the sites during the course of a multi-site update. While two-phase commit protocols are intended to solve this problem, different vendors may mean different things when they say "we have two-phase commit."

13.2.2.2 Two-Phase Commit

A two-phase commit should ensure that all the participants "go the same way" on a particular transaction. Either they all accept it (commit), or they all reject it (rollback). Two-phase commit is a complex and sophisticated procedure.

As the name implies, two steps are involved with a two-phase commit. The first step is a "prepare to commit" step. That is a signal to all the database sites that they have to get ready to perform the operation. If anything happens from that time forward, they must have enough information about the operation to recover in case of failure.

The following description provides a brief explanation of the two phases of the two-phase commit protocol. A system component called the coordinator is in charge. The action starts when software called the coordinator receives a commit-type request from the update transaction.

- •Phase one
  First the coordinator writes a begin.commit record in its log, then it sends a "prepare" message to all participant computer sites. This message asks each of the sites (that is, the software at each of the sites) to get into a state in which it can either commit the transaction or roll it back. When a participating site receives this "prepare" message, it determines if it can commit the transaction. If it can, it writes a ready record in the log and sends an "OK" message to the coordinator. If it cannot, it sends a "Not OK" message. All of this interaction is automatically taking place between the software components at each site, not among developers or operators at each site.

- •Phase two
  After the coordinator has received a message back from all the participants, it decides whether to commit or abort the transaction. If even one participant has sent a "Not OK" message, the coordinator aborts the entire transaction, sending out a "ROLLBACK" command. In this case, the participants would use their local logs to undo all local effects of the transaction. If all participants said "OK," the coordinator broadcasts the "COMMIT" command to all participating sites. The participants would then commit the transaction.

While a growing number of vendors are providing this capability, analysis reveals that not all two-phase commits are equal. The amount of coding a programmer has to provide to implement—and supplement— a particular two-phase commit can vary from vendor to vendor. For example, if the recovery management procedures are inadequate, the developer may have to provide them. In fact, a bare-bones, two-phase commit facility can put a great burden on the application developer to provide all the necessary functionality.

In a "true" distributed database system, application programs should be able to submit SQL statements that manipulate tables in diverse locations—and do that in a transparent way. They should not have to do anything differently in a distributed database environment than they do in a nondistributed database environment.

Surprisingly, in many installations, two-phase commit is not an important part of the distributed database system. These installations are performing distributed update as a two-step process. They are updating just one primary site with the initial on-line update transaction. Additional locations are updated as batch processes at night. That way, all sites are in synch by the next morning. For many applications this is acceptable. These installations are avoiding the problem that all sites involved may not be available at the same time.

13.2.2.3 C. J. Date's 12 Rules

Chris J. Date is well known for his work with databases. He may be best known for his work with relational databases and distributed databases, but he is knowledgeable in many aspects of database technology. He has also worked closely with Dr. Codd, the father of relational systems. C. J. Date published 12 rules that distributed database systems should follow in a 1987 article in InfoDB magazine. These rules and an explanation of each one are as follows:

1. Local Autonomy—Each site in a distributed database system should be independent of the others.
2. No Reliance on a Central Site—If a distributed database were to rely on a single central site, that site could become a single point of failure, something to be avoided in a distributed database architecture.
3. Continuous Operation—A distributed database should never require downtime. It should be capable of continuous operation with capabilities like on-line backup and recovery and full and incremental archiving.
4. Location Transparency and Location Independence—Users should not need to know where data is stored. It should seem that all data is stored locally.
5. Fragmentation Independence—Tables (in relational distributed databases) can be divided into fragments and stored at different sites. This should be transparent to users.
6. Replication Independence—Data can be replicated across different computers in the distributed architecture.
7. Distributed Query Processing—Performance of queries should be independent of the site from which it is executed.
8. Distributed Transaction Management—The system should be able to support atomic transactions. Atomic transactions, or atomicity, means that transactions must be performed as a whole, either entirely or not at all.

9. Hardware Independence—Data should be accessible from a wide variety of hardware platforms.

10. Operating System Independence—The distributed database should be able to operate with different operating systems.

11. Network Independence—The distributed database should be able to operate with a variety of network protocols or network topologies.

12. DBMS Independence—The ideal distributed database system would be able to support interoperability between different types of DBMS systems running on different nodes.

13.3   DIFFERENT ENVIRONMENTS AND IMPLEMENTATIONS

Many predict that use of distributed databases will spread in the future. In the past, distributed databases attracted limited interest. Now, with multiple servers available for storing data, far more people may begin to explore this approach.

13.3.1   Distributed Database in a Client/Server Environment

As sites run out of space on a server, they will upgrade the server. Eventually, they may decide to add a server and distribute the data. This is an area where some caution should be used. Before distributing any data, a company should perform the same careful analysis as they would when starting a new system. They should think through all the ramifications.

While database server software may behave fine with all the data on one server, it may not be adequate when the data is spread across two or more servers. The database server software may not have been built for distributed database processing. It would be wise to study the vendor literature carefully and work with database experts who are knowledgeable about the needs of a distributed database architecture.

Specialized software, called enterprise transaction monitors, are available to control transaction processing in a distributed environment. Examples of such products are Tuxedo from the UNIX Systems Laboratory in Summit, NJ, and Encina from Transarc in Pittsburgh, PA.

13.3.1.1   Help with Two-Phase Commit in C/S Systems

A relatively new product called Ellipse, from Cooperative Solutions, San Jose, CA, offers a unique application development environment that lets developers build distributed client/server applications with two-phase commit automatically generated. The product targets mainframe developers. Cooperative Solutions' management personnel say they wanted to give application developers a monolithic view of the system, since that is what they are accustomed to as mainframe programmers. This provides the programmers with a familiar model.

Therefore, Ellipse determines how to split the application into client and server modules. The product partitions the application without developers having to worry about it. Ellipse generates all the coding needed to perform two-phase commits. The generated coding is in C, but programmers do not need to know C, just Cobol.

Suppose many bank branches are using the same system. For most branches one server is enough, but some branches need more than one server. The same application code will work for both situations because Ellipse will generate appropriate code for the two different situations.

Cooperative Solutions' top management people are all former Non-Stop SQL gurus from Tandem who are familiar with the problems of transaction processing. They say that very few installations have taken advantage of distributed database processing in the past because it was so complicated; they believe this will change with Ellipse.

13.3.2 IBM's Approach to Distributed Databases

13.3.2.1 IBM's Unique Terminology

IBM's approach to distributed database has been a phased plan, with limited capabilities being released early, and more complex features released later. IBM's four levels of distributed database access are as follows:

1. Remote Request
2. Remote Unit of Work
3. Distributed Unit of Work
4. Distributed Request

With remote request, an application at site A can send a database request (SQL statement) to a remote site B. The request is executed and committed (or rolled back) entirely at site B. Each SQL statement is independent. The application at site A can send another request to site B regardless of whether the first transaction was successful. Only a single remote location can be specified in each SQL statement. In this context, "location" is a DBMS. If a machine has multiple DBMSs, only one can be included in each remote request SQL operation.

A remote unit of work allows an application at site A to send all of the database requests in a "unit of work" to site B. All processing for the unit of work is performed at site B. However, site A decides whether the transaction is to be committed or rolled back.

With the distributed unit of work (distributed transaction) at level three, an application at site A can send some or all of the database requests in a transaction to one or more remote sites for execution. Each request is executed entirely at one site; however, different requests can be executed at different sites. Site A determines whether the transaction should be committed or rolled back. Logs and a two-phase commit are required at this level. Either all of the related changes must be committed or else none of them can be committed.

Distributed request, the fourth level, includes the capabilities of the distributed unit of work. This level also allows individual database requests to span multiple sites. A request at site A can ask for a join to be performed between a table at site B and a table at site C.

IBM also provides some distributed CICS capabilities, permitting one workstation to access CICS-owned data and applications on another workstation or mainframe. For example, Distribute CICS Link enables a CICS OS/2 transaction to link to programs on any connected CICS system. An OS/2-based CICS system can access and use data on mainframe non-CICS database systems, such as DB2.

13.3.2.2 IBM's Distributed Relational Database Architecture (DRDA)

The Distributed Relational Database Architecture, announced in June 1990, is IBM's plan for accessing data in heterogeneous environments. The eventual goal is to be able to issue SQL statements on any of IBM's Systems Application Architecture (SAA) platforms (DB2, SQL/DS, OS/400, and OS/2 DBM) without regard to where individual tables are stored. IBM's Information Warehouse approach extends this concept to databases from other vendors as discussed in the previous chapter.

DRDA is a composite of various capabilities and relates back to many other types of services, functions, and architectures offered by IBM. Some of them are mentioned briefly here. Reader are advised to explore these concepts in more detail if they may become part of their client/server implementation.

Some of the things that DRDA builds on are the Common Programming Interface (CPI), the Distributed Data Management (DDM) architecture, the Common Communications Support (CCS) and LU6.2. The CPI defines a consistent set of languages and programming services that can be used in a variety of environments. This includes a SQL definition. The CPI specification permits programmers to use common interfaces to transparently access remote data. The communications interface portion of CPI is often abbreviated as CPI-C (pronounced "C-pick.")

DDM is an architecture which permits files to be shared among different IBM computing systems. CCS is a set of protocols, services, and standardized data stream formats used to interconnect applications.

The evolving ISO remote data access (RDA) standard defines a common set of database language statements and protocols for communication and transaction processing between a program and a remote database. IBM has promised to support the ISO RDA standard in addition to its own DRDA in the future in keeping with its commitment to open systems.

13.4   DISTRIBUTED DATABASE ISSUES

Database administration can be a tricky problem in a distributed database system. If a distributed system is set up with every node equal, the database administrator will have to establish a careful plan to ensure that appropriate procedures are implemented to take care of backup, recovery, change and version management, and creation and deletion of database objects. Security issues can be more complex in a distributed environment than in a centralized one. The usual issues are still present: protection of data from inadvertent change, destruction, or disclosure, along with new problems. If data is fragmented across two nodes, an individual may need to have security passwords that will be recognized on both network nodes, in addition to having access privileges to all fragments of the data.

A distributed database environment is characterized by having many end users on PCs accessing data that is distributed over several sites. A major security problem could be involved if end users in a distributed database environment download data to their PCs. If that data is given a high degree of security in its original environment, can that level of security be maintained in that end user's PC? If there is any doubt, then there must be restrictions on what data end users can download.

13.4.1   Pros and Cons of Distributed Databases

For many of the advantages of distributed database systems, a corresponding disadvantage often exists. The resulting problems must be overcome, or the distributed system loses its strength. For example, the ability to move data around is certainly an advantage, but it presents the problem of needing additional tuning to ensure optimal performance. Well-planned data placement and load balancing will be needed.

The advantages of being able to access and update data at remote sites brings with it the problems discussed earlier of concurrency control and recovery management. Overcoming these problems—as in other design situations—is often a matter of making trade-offs by deciding which capabilities are most important.

Distributed database is complex to plan and implement correctly. Obviously, an organization would not implement a distributed database system unless the reasons for doing so were compelling. The difficult part is determining whether the reasons are strong enough to warrant the extra work that will be involved. Additional resources will be needed as well, including networking capabilities. Is the need for distributed data strong enough?

Whether or not a distributed database is appropriate depends, of course, upon the unique circumstances of a particular situation. For example, if a company is small and highly centralized, it may not need distributed databases. Companies that are fundamentally distributed, on the other hand, may benefit handsomely from a distributed database architecture.

The politics of distributed database and distributed processing also must be addressed. People have pride of ownership of data. Often they do not want to relinquish control of what they consider to be "their data." It may be necessary to raise such issues to a high enough management level so that action can be taken. More than a few distributed database implementors have said that the technical side of implementation is easy compared to the political side.

13.4.2   Review of Reasons for Distributing Data

Some of the reasons why enterprises have installed a distributed data architecture are listed below:

- Matches the distributed need of the enterprise
- Permits data to be stored closest to where it is needed the most
- Enables database administrators to move data around easily
- Allows users to access and update remote data
- Provides improved data availability through replication of data
- Provides a "hot backup" through data replication, a safety factor
- Avoids a single point of failure

13.4.3 Are Definitions Changing?

Many people are using the term "distributed database" today to refer to client/server architectures where a payroll file is located on one server and a personnel file resides on another server or on a mainframe. Since the two data sets sit in different locations, people refer to them as being distributed. However, as the preceding material shows, many other features need to be present before a system is regarded as a distributed database in the classical sense.

However, people definitely are beginning to imply new meanings to the term "distributed database." Many English words—or words in any language—change in meaning over time. Maybe that is what is happening to the term "distributed database." Maybe in the future, distributed databases will not have to have all the requirements that are listed in the college textbooks. Maybe new times will bring new requirements. Maybe the textbook definition should be referred to as "classical distributed databases" to differentiate it from the more loosely, popularly used "distributed database" term. Purists and academicians would likely disagree with this proposal. However, everyone should be alert to the fact that many people today are using the term "distributed database" in a different way than the textbooks.

14

CLIENT/SERVER SYSTEMS MANAGEMENT

14.1 OVERVIEW

Some large companies already have tens of thousands of personal computers and workstations. Many companies now have hundreds of LANs and servers. As client/server configurations spread, to have many hundreds of LANs and even more servers will not be uncommon. If client applications are resident on tens of thousands of PCs, and database software is located on several hundred servers, how is all that software going to be accounted for, let alone maintained? Specialized software and a comprehensive plan to guide system administrators' actions will be needed.

14.1.1 Systems Management Considerations

14.1.1.1 Client/Server Systems Have Serious Management Issues

There are a number of management issues that need attention in a distributed, client/ server computing environment. Change management, configuration management, storage management, and network management are all more complex in a distributed environment than in a mainframe environment. These are the types of systems management issues with which this chapter will deal. The following paragraph describes how this book is using each of these system management terms.

Change management deals with keeping track of different versions of software components during the development phase and on through the life cycle of the system. Configuration management is concerned with making sure the correct components are used when performing a system build, compiling the separate modules into a comprehensive system. Configuration management procedures are often closely related to change management procedures. Storage management is related to where and how files and datasets are stored, and also to backup, recovery, and archiving procedures. Network management oversees networking hardware and software components, keeping them working, detecting and correcting problems, and optimizing service.

This chapter will deal with each of these management issues separately—pointing out many of the things that should be addressed in each area—and then it will review approaches that try to integrate them. Sometimes software packages support only one area of these management issues like, for example, backup and recovery. Increasingly, however, software products have capabilities that cover more than one of these areas, making a discussion of software products by category difficult. For the most part, therefore, discussion of specific packages will be deferred until the latter part of this chapter.

The reason why products cover several areas is because many of the issues in these management categories—change, configuration, and storage management—are so closely related. For example, change management and configuration management are so intertwined that many products offer capabilities in both areas. Now, with distributed processing, these issues are entwined with network management issues, too. Also, the fact that software that is located in different places across a network needs to be modified ties change management and network management together. Backing up files located in diverse locations and network-related files makes storage management and network management more related. In a similar way, all the other management issues are now impacted by network issues. It will become increasingly important that installations either buy integrated management packages or buy individual packages that will work with other packages they already own or plan to buy. Most vendors are aware of the need to work with other system management packages, and they are adhering to standards as they build new software packages.

Software that is mentioned in this chapter—as in other chapters—should be regarded simply as examples of software having various capabilities, not as a recommended approach. Every distributed client/server configuration will have unique requirements. Each installation must examine and study its own requirements in detail and make software selections according to its specific needs. Installations should also be alert to changes in the availability of features, because software which meets client/server system management challenges is evolving rapidly with dramatic improvements expected in the future.

14.2 THE PRIMARY MANAGEMENT AREAS

14.2.1 Change Management

Change management involves careful control of changes made to custom-built software components during the development phase as well as during production. Similar attention must be paid to purchased software, including proper distribution of purchased packages, vendor maintenance, installation of new versions, and licensing issues. (Distribution and licensing issues can be considered as configuration management issues, also.) An enterprise can be severely disciplined for the inappropriate behavior of just one or two careless employees when licensing issues are involved. If a site has a license agreement that permits ten users to use server software at the same time, managers cannot afford to let eleven or twelve users access it through an oversight.

With a mainframe computer or a minicomputer, software is generally kept in a single library. Software products, like Librarian from Computer Associates in Islandia, NY; Panvalet from Pansophic in Lisle, IL; and Endevor from Legent in Vienna, VA, have been used by mainframe installations for many years. Usually, all the software was located in one central place, so all changes were made in that one location. With client/server systems, software is located in many different places. All the complexities of keeping track of software changes in a mainframe environment are still present, and many new problems have been added. Now, not only will changes have to be made to all the locations where software resides, administrators will need to be certain where all the various versions are located.

Some of the capabilities that may be desirable in change management software products are as follows:

- To provide strong version control capabilities that are easy to use
- To lock versions of modules
- Locate software modules automatically, without programmer intervention
- To allow distribution of software across heterogeneous hardware and software
- To record changes made, by whom, date and time, and reason for change

- To retrieve modules by revision number, revision label, or other easy identifier

- To store any type of file: source code, object modules, binary code, design specifications, system requirements, data models, other graphics, documentation, etc.

- To track changes back to appropriate version of specification when code is generated from design specifications

- To produce a complete audit trail of all changes

- To maintain an archive of software with the latest version of each file and the changes (deltas) required to reconstruct any previous version of a particular software module

- To reconstruct a complete previous version of an entire system

- To ensure that no unlicensed users have access to inappropriate software

- To provide for electronic software distribution from a central location for software developed in-house and purchased from vendors

- To perform virus scanning of all new software or software updates automatically

- To permit retry of software distribution in case of error, with reporting of error conditions

- To support unattended distribution and vendor updates of software

- To support a workgroup of PCs or workstations as a unit

- To provide security measures to ensure appropriate access authority

- To maintain an audit trail of logons with any unauthorized logon attempts indicating terminal location, userid, date, and time of occurrence

- To enable safe parallel development and alternative lines of development where needed

- To work in coordination with other tools like CASE products, data dictionary/directories, and enterprise-wide repositories

- To provide a variety of standard reports

- To accommodate a variety of customized reports in response to queries or prompted responses

- To work easily with installation's backup and recovery procedures

Many times, large development projects are already underway when management realizes it is losing control over the changes. If management starts looking around for a different change management package at a time like this, it will want to be sure the new change management software can be installed without disrupting development of the project.

Some capabilities related to software licensing that are desirable in addition to the ones mentioned above include:

- To provide a complete audit trail and usage history of licensed products
- To accommodate different types of licensing agreements
- To adapt to changing licensing conditions
- To adapt to industry-wide licensing standards as they become available
- To maintain appropriate charge-back statistics as per installation procedures

There are many different types of considerations that need to be taken into account with software changes in a heterogeneous client/server environment. For example, while UNIX can run on many different platforms, binary compatibility of executable software across different hardware configurations should not be taken for granted. A site would not necessarily be able to compile software on one type of hardware platform and then distribute that code to different hardware systems. To overcome this problem, some companies have one of each of the hardware platforms in the enterprise installed in one central support location. Software is compiled on a machine in the support center that matches the target system and then is distributed to the appropriate location. This approach may have to be taken into consideration with regard to an installation's change management and configuration management procedures.

14.2.2 Configuration Management

Configuration management is important to any site, but it has been given special attention by DoD, space-related, engineering, and scientific enterprises. The DoD has mandated specific configuration management procedures for many years. During the Apollo moon program, NASA set up very comprehensive configuration management requirements. It was such a large program and had so many people working on it that precise control was essential.

As client/server environments become more complex, the number, type, and location of software modules in these systems will also become more complex. As a result, configuration management is expected to assume new importance, making precise control essential in all enterprises.

Due to their interrelationship, many of the issues described in the change management section also apply to configuration management. Maybe what really distinguishes them is more a matter of what issues are emphasized within each area. With change management, often the emphasis is on tracking different versions of software; with configuration management, the emphasis is on making sure the correct modules are put together during the process of creating the overall system—often referred to as a "system build."

This section will only address those issues related to configuration management that were not previously mentioned under change management, or which need special emphasis for some reason. As previously mentioned, many of the features listed in the change management section are available in configuration management software; however, a package that bundles both management areas may lack *specific* change or configuration features that could be critical to your needs.

Some of the issues that are specific to configuration management software products are as follows:

- Automate the work related to producing the appropriate executable code for a system, while providing a consistent approach and ensuring that:
  - the correct revisions of the source code are gathered
  - the right switches—if any—are set appropriately during a compile
  - any dependent object modules are also recompiled
  - all components are linked with the appropriate libraries
- Provide for parallel compiles on a network to speed up overall system compile time, if appropriate and desirable
- Facilitate the ability to reuse code in other applications on diverse systems
- Supply an identification footprint capability that ties compiled code to the related component modules
- Provide the capability to create "build scripts" that capture all the steps required to build a system permitting them to be repeated automatically in the future. Also:
  - Accommodate a syntax within the build script that makes it easy to read

- Provide the ability to include variations in build scripts to allow different performance under different conditions, for example, depending on which operating system the build is for
- Allow for other variations, sometimes referred to as dependencies, within build scripts
- Support nested "include files" within script subsections permitting multiple reuse of scripts
- Provide predefined macros to facilitate building scripts
- Provide debugging capabilities to aid in the testing of scripts

One of the desirable features listed for change management was the ability to work in coordination with other tools like CASE products, data dictionary/directories, and enterprise-wide repositories. The same requirement, of course, applies to configuration management tools. For a number of years vendors have had problems trying to determine exactly how to do this, what the best approach would be and what twists future directions will take. With configuration management software, it can be especially important for a vendor's products to work well with products from other vendors. This is especially true when one—or two—vendors have a large presence in the marketplace.

When IBM first announced its System Application Architecture, many vendors were concerned about being compliant with it since many IBM customers requested this capability. This happened again when IBM announced its AD/Cycle CASE tool—which presented new challenges for vendors. Vendors were once again faced with interoperability issues regarding their tools and IBM's Repository. Each of these products or environments added new twists and complexities for vendors. For example, IBM announced that configuration management services would be provided through its repository using its Software Configuration Library Manager (SCLM), and that IBM would permit other vendors to provide configuration management capabilities through tool services provided by the repository. However, many vendors did not fully understand what capabilities would be in different parts of IBM's separate packages and exactly where the linkage points were. And now, how will all this interworking of software apply as environments become more and more distributed?

Recently, vendors have had to think about fitting in with System View, IBM's comprehensive system management package. These vendors also need to be compatible with other vendors. In the future new interconnection challenges will arise. For example, many vendors are now reviewing how their products might be able to fit in with OSF's DME, the OSI

Common Management Information Protocol (CMIP), and the TCP/IP-related Simple Network Management Protocol (SNMP).

The requirement to be compatible with so many products and environments will be a challenge for vendors.

14.2.3   Storage Management

Storage management deals with how storage is managed, where files and data sets are located, optimizing storage and performance, and critical operations like backup, recovery, and archiving. These issues—like change and configuration management—have been addressed in the mainframe environment for over 25 years. As a result, excellent backup, recovery, and archiving procedures are available for mainframes. For a long time this was not true in the LAN environment. Yet for several years, some companies have had so much processing power and storage capacity on their LANs that they rivaled the power and capacity of the mainframes of just a decade ago. This meant that these companies had the need for backup and recovery procedures that were as good as mainframe products, though products of that quality did not yet exist. Such products, however, are beginning to appear.

The LAN products will have to deal with even more complexity than their mainframe counterparts, however. In the areas of backup, recovery, and archiving, the basic nature of the problem may be quite similar between mainframes and LANs, but the complexity of devices and locations needing these services increases significantly in heterogeneous, distributed LANs.

When PCs were isolated and alone, the end users made the decision whether or not to back up their data. If data was lost from a PC, only that end user's information that was gone. Now, however, corporate data—data used by a workgroup, department, or larger corporate group—could be lost. Generally the data kept on a server plays a more critical role in corporate client/server systems than does the data kept on a PC or workstation. Still, procedures for backing up personal computer and workstation data as well as server data should be established for any system.

Backup and recovery approaches for LAN-based files vary widely. Some sites rely predominantly on tape backups since tape is inexpensive and reliable. Other sites install a combination of tape, disk, and optical media. The predominant approach early in LAN usage was to do full overnight backups. Everything was backed up—whether it changed since the last backup or not. However, sites are increasingly moving toward incremental backups.

Some of the first backup and recovery tools to be available for networked systems started out as PC-oriented products. Vendors who had products that were originally written to back up a single PC extended them to be capable of backing up various network operating system and network-related files. Thus, the tools evolved from being for stand alone PCs to being "network-aware." As time went on, products began to appear that had the additional capability of providing backup and restore services for multiple servers and clients. Such products often include a database of related information to facilitate file restores and to provide file migration for aging files.

As with other products, the UNIX LAN market was ahead of the PC LAN market with storage server products. These UNIX storage servers could be configured as dedicated computer systems with high capacity disk drives and secondary storage in the gigabyte range. These servers would often sit on the network backbone and provide data management services for the entire network. Such products for PC LAN markets are appearing also.

Full system management services for LANs—similar to those currently available for mainframes—will certainly become available. Like mainframe products, they will be able to provide software that enables the system to automate much of the management of storage for the system administrator. Work is progressing so rapidly in this area that products with some mainframe-type capabilities are available now and others could become available very soon.

14.2.4 Network Management

Network management products have been available for WANs for decades and for LANs for quite a few years. The number of sites using network management tools is expected to increase dramatically as the use of client/server processing increases. Some of the network management tools that have been available for a number of years include IBM's NetView, AT&T's Unified Network Management Architecture (UNMA), Digital Equipment Corporation's Enterprise Management Architecture (EMA), Sun Workstation's SunNet Manager, System Center Inc.'s Net/ Master, and Hewlett-Packard's OpenView. Many of these are integrated network management systems, but they vary considerably in their inherent capabilities.

Network management tools like these are composed of a number of separate software packages to manage the numerous *elements*. Elements are components that make up a network. Network elements include devices like terminals, modems, switches, and multiplexors, among other components. In addition to the integrated systems listed above, there are also many individual element management systems. Element management systems often oversee a limited range of proprietary networking equipment like a particular vendor's line of modems or multiplexors.

Some systems are specifically meant to be used in LANs only, while other systems or tool packages are meant to be used in an environment where a number of LANs connect to one or more WANs or where a host is available to centrally manage everything.

Managing a large, heterogeneous mix of networks with individual element management systems can be far more difficult than using an integrated network management package. In fact, managing a network using a variety of tools has been compared to being responsible for a television store's display of 25 to 50 TV sets, each tuned to a different station. If every set lost its picture, the individual responsible would have to run from set to set, individually tuning and adjusting each one. Unfortunately, more than a few network management control rooms resemble such a scenario. In addition, each individual network management tool requires a hefty investment in staff training time. The ability to switch quickly from one network tool to a completely different one with its own distinct screen and unique operations can be not only difficult, but frustrating as well.

One of the most welcome features of an integrated network management system is the consolidation of network control functions. This consolidation results in a single interface to the overall system. For example, NetView's single presentation structure can alert the network manager to problems throughout a network. All of the individual element managers within NetView can be controlled from one centralized location. Use of integrated network management tools reduces demand for high-priced and hard-to-find network personnel, speeds up the resolution of network problems, and provides valuable data for assessing network productivity.

Additional benefits of an enterprise-wide network management system include tracking end-to-end traffic patterns to identify both low- and high-usage times and paths. This information is then used in load-balancing procedures. An integrated package generally reduces network downtime for end users. If a user reports an inability to access a resource and there is no central network management, the network administrator may have to test many lines before determining where the problem is. Meanwhile that user is out of luck—unable to use his or her equipment. With central network management, the administrator can reroute the user's access path resulting in little or no downtime for that user. The administrator can then restore the user's normal path after the problem is solved.

Integrated network management packages perform many individual functions. But the overriding objective of these integrated systems is to provide reliable communications services that meet the organization's performance needs in a cost-effective manner.

NetView was IBM's way of meeting that objective with IBM networks. What happens, however, when the system consists of a mix of networks from different vendors? IBM's initial attempt to assist in managing a heterogeneous mix of networks was in 1986 with its Open Network Management strategy and its Network Management Architecture. IBM opened its proprietary interfaces and defined service points which provided translation between SNA and non-SNA devices. Unfortunately, when vendors implemented products using these service points, each used data definitions, user interfaces, and application services that were different from the others. The profusion of different techniques, therefore, did not result in a harmonious integration of products.

IBM used a different approach in 1990 by embracing international standards for network and system management in its implementation of SystemView.

14.3   STANDARDS RELATED TO SYSTEMS MANAGEMENT

14.3.1   International Standards

The Common Management Information Protocol (CMIP) is part of OSI's standards work in systems management. OSI management consists of a group of standards and definitions comprised of numerous components. The overall OSI management model is too complex to describe in any detail in this book. However, this chapter will explain some of the basic ideas of the object-oriented approach that is used to permit products from different vendors to work together when they adhere to OSI standards.

The model uses the concepts of a managing process and an agent process. A managing process communicates with its peer, or agent, process in a remote part of the system. Interaction between a manager and an agent consists of operations that are related to specific systems management tasks, for example, configuration management.

OSI management is related to the OSI seven-layer reference model described earlier. Managing and agent processes are located at the OSI application layer, the top-most layer, which provides a software interface for application programs that use the network. ISO refers to the management communications parts of these managing and agent processes as Systems Management Application Entities. Each SMAE makes use of the underlying protocols provided by OSI.

Managing processes initiate network processes or transactions, and agent processes receive these transactions. An agent process can perform operations on managed objects. An agent process can also issue event reports to managing processes on behalf of other managed objects. A managed process can be responsible for one or more managed objects.

A very serious, concerted effort is being made to get international agreement on objects that will be permanent, widely-accepted objects to truly facilitate the management of heterogeneous distributed environments in the future. The fact that IBM uses OSI object concepts like managers and agents in SystemView permits other vendors' products to interact with SystemView.

14.3.2   De Facto Standards in Systems Management

The work of the Object Management Group (OMG), an industry consortium, on Object Request Broker (ORB) technology will undoubtedly impact system management standards. As defined by OMG, the ORB provides the means by which objects transparently make requests and receive responses. The ORB provides interoperability between different applications on diverse machines in heterogeneous distributed environments. It helps to seamlessly interconnect multiple object-based systems.

OSF's DME also uses OSI object concepts and a modular, building block approach so that products from a variety of vendors will be able to work together within the DME. The modular approach also is intended to facilitate the accommodation of older management applications.

A systems administrator generally manages by modifying information about resources or services and by performing operations on services and data. All management operations in DME can be carried out by communicating with objects. Third-party vendors will be able to create libraries of objects for specific management functions and have them interoperate with other management applications within the DME framework.

Management request brokers play a central role in DME. There are two management request brokers within DME. One makes an RPC-based management protocol available to provide a symmetrical, object-oriented environment for implementing management applications. The other management request broker supports established standard network management protocols like ISO's CMIP and the Simple Network Management Protocol (SNMP).

SNMP had its origins with TCP/IP and the Internet, a world-wide, massive internetwork of networks. As many companies begin to connect various LANs and internetwork them with their WANs, they frequently find that TCP/IP begins to play an increasingly important role for them. As a result, SNMP fits in very conveniently, despite shortcomings in the area of security. Some companies are using SNMP as an interim product until more products become available for OSI and/or DME approaches. Work on Secure SNMP, which addresses some of the security issues, may alleviate users' concerns somewhat.

The Simple Management Protocol (SMP) is a network management protocol that was developed by several independent consultancies and submitted to the Internet Engineering Task Force which oversees issues related to TCP/IP and the Internet. SMP has a different design which provides advantages over SNMP. It has an event-driven design which reduces network management traffic. As a result, a number of vendors are providing products to fit in with SMP rather than SNMP.

While CMIP is a de jure standard, SNMP and SMP are de facto standards. With X/Open's Open Management Protocol API, management information can be relayed through SNMP or CMIP. Being a consortium rather than an official standards body, the work of OMG will be considered a de facto standard unless it were to become accepted by official standards bodies, as many predict.

14.4 SOFTWARE DISTRIBUTION

Software distribution, as mentioned earlier, is a special problem in client/ server environments. Software distribution should be considered in its broadest context, involving procedures like updating software with new versions, installing new packages, and deinstalling packages that will no longer be used. These procedures must be followed for every client machine in the system and for every server. Software distribution includes not only client, application, and server software, but operating systems, network operating systems, all network software, and any other software that is in the overall system. Users must also make sure to adhere to all software licensing restrictions.

In a mainframe environment, nearly all of the software is in one place—the mainframe. A client/server environment is a much more modular and distributed environment. In this environment keeping track of all the different locations that need to be serviced and making all the necessarily changes that are required will be quite a challenge. Each enterprise should perform an analysis of what its software distribution needs will be. In searching for solutions, an electronic software distribution system would be most desirable in order to keep up with the work involved.

14.5 INTEGRATED PRODUCTS

14.5.1 IBM's SystemView

SystemView is IBM's system management strategy that attempts to encompass all the management issues that have been discussed in this chapter and more. Maybe one of the most important things about SystemView is that it uses OSI management objects. This will allow other vendors to share management data within SystemView and integrate their software into the overall SystemView structure.

SystemView has three dimensions which provide different ways of looking at the different tasks in systems management. The first dimension, the *end-use dimension*, determines how a systems management application should appear to an end user; in effect it defines a CUA-compliant end-user interface. A consistent interface reduces training time and overall efficiency.

The *data dimension* defines the format and content of systems management data. The data dimension features a data model to specify data definitions that represent the information processing resources of an enterprise. The data model states what data must be provided for SystemView applications and the format for that data. Complying with these data definitions will permit other vendors' tools to work with IBM tools within SystemView because it provides a consistent way to model, store, and retrieve systems management data. A number of databases such as the Enterprise Information Base and the Control Information Base, are used by SystemView specifically for storing management data.

The third dimension, the *application dimension* provides a way of classifying all the different system management tasks that exist. It divides all system management tasks into six different disciplines, each of which addresses a separate segment of systems management tasks. This provides a way to classify what kind of systems management task a particular management application addresses. The application dimension defines interfaces and services to support all the tasks that are needed to administer, coordinate, and operate large information systems.

The six disciplines in SystemView's application dimension are as follows:

- Business Management
- Change Management

- Configuration Management
- Performance Management
- Problem Management
- Operations Management

Figure 14.1 shows how the six disciplines fit into the three dimensions of SystemView.

14.5.2 Other Products

Many of the vendors who have had mainframe system management products are active in the client/server, distributed networking environment. In fact, many of them moved quickly, providing products with

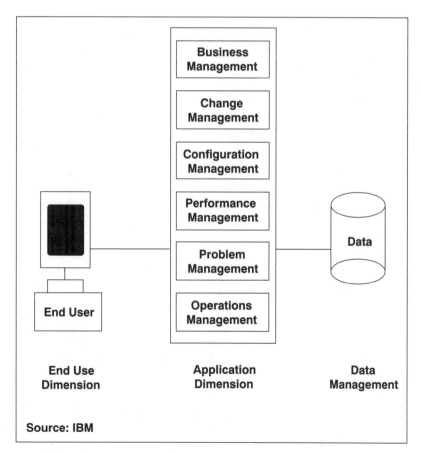

Figure 14.1 System view dimensions and the six disciplines within the application dimension.

expanded capabilities when sites first started using PCs as a development environment for systems that would be put into production on mainframes. Now, with sites installing these systems in client/server environments, the traditional system management vendors are expanding their products further. They are being joined by many new vendors who are also interested in this expanding market.

14.5.2.1 Many Vendors Offer Tools

Some mainframe change and configuration management vendors who are providing client/server tools include Computer Associates with Adlib, their PC version of mainframe-based Librarian, and Legent with Endevor/ PC as the PC version of their mainframe-based Endevor. Pansophic has a product called PAN/LCM—Pansophic Life Cycle Manager—which provides audit trails, controls, impact analysis, and similar types of capabilities for PC-based applications.

There are some particularly strong configuration and change control products available for the UNIX workstation and server market. Examples include the Domain Software Engineering Environment (DSEE) from the Apollo Division of Hewlett-Packard, Intersolv's Polytron Version Control System (PVCS), Cadre's Teamwork, Digital's Code Management System (CMS), and products from Aide-de-Camp in Concord, MA, and Softool in Goleta, CA, among others. Some products, like HP/Apollo's DSEE (nicknamed "Dizzy"), use parallel compiles on a network to speed up the compilation process.

Teamwork, Cadre's CASE product, is used in the development life cycle before coding takes place and therefore requires its own flavor of configuration management. Cadre's configuration management resources are embedded within Teamwork's processing, and Teamwork cooperates with other vendors' source code management systems. For example, Cadre's Teamwork can cooperate with HP/Apollo's DSEE for builds which are a collection of compiles.

Intersolv, based in Rockville, MD, has been active for years in both the UNIX markets and the IBM mainframe markets and provides both CASE and configuration management tools. Intersolv's Polytron Version Control System (PVCS) consists of a number of separate products with the overall package able to provide most, if not all of the features listed in the change and configuration management sections.

In the storage management areas, mainframe vendors like Legent in Vienna, VA, are active in the distributed systems management market. Legent believes that the future lies in distributed computing and that supporting these needs represents its strategic direction.

How do network operating systems help an installation with backup and recovery? It varies. For example, Novell provides backup capabilities with NetWare v3.11 using two utilities: NBACKUP, which backs up DOS client-based data and administrative information, and SBACKUP, which is intended to be used by a network supervisor for server-based backups. Using these two utilities, Novell says all network data can be backed up and restored. A variety of third-party backup solutions are also supported. NetWare for UNIX supports all of a host's backup utilities and file requirements so that all NetWare files can be backed up using the UNIX host's backup resources.

Microsoft did not write its own backup and recovery software for LAN Manager, but rather used a product from another vendor. Right from the initial shipping of LAN Manager, Microsoft packaged Sytron's Sytos Plus File Backup Manager with it. Sytos Plus performs full backup and restoration of network files including network security information.

Sytron Corporation, the vendor providing the Sytos Plus product for Microsoft, is located in Westborough, MA. Sytron has a full line of storage management products. Some additional vendors with storage management products include Irwin Magnetics in Ann Arbor, MI; Maynard Electronics in Lake Mary, FL; Epoch Systems in Boston, MA; and Tallgrass Technology in Lenox, KN.

Some of these tools overlap other management areas. For example, Tallgrass Technology's Performance Diagnostics Tool (PDT) is a system management tool that borders on being a network management tool. It can help sites optimize a network backup operation by determining the system feed rate (performance) that can be expected under a given set of circumstances. Networks often have equipment installed from a variety of vendors. The cumulative effect of the interaction of all this diverse equipment affects the overall throughput of the network. PDT simulates a backup on the network, measures it, and displays a chart that indicates the performance results. A site can then use this information to improve overall performance.

In the area of network management, many new tools and many new categories of tools are becoming available. Early in 1992, Novell announced its Network Management System (NMS) to monitor NetWare LANs across an enterprise. NMS is known as a LAN management platform which is slightly different from integrated network management tools—such as HP's OpenView and Sun's SunNet Manager—since network management tools do not provide the same breadth of capabilities for managing all the elements of an enterprise network. In comparison LAN management platforms like NMS are capable of managing an entire organization's diverse LAN's from a central site.

14.5.2.2 Other Tools from IBM

Some observers say that IBM has entered the LAN management platform market with its Distributed Systems Manager (DSM) products which feature SystemView for OS/2. These products can be linked easily to enterprise-wide managers like IBM's NetView and other SystemView components. But no matter how one classifies the new tools from IBM, they indicate how seriously IBM is taking the client/server market.

SystemView for OS/2 features the LANFocus Management/2 suite of software products. Basically, this is software that runs on an OS/2 workstation and provides centralized management of distributed LANs. When the product was announced in the fall of 1992, an IBM spokesman said that IBM wants to make it easier for administrators to manage LANs whether they have a mainframe or not. The suite of products includes LANFocus Manage/2 which will use both CMIP and SNMP to communicate with IBM and non-IBM devices on the LAN. LANFocus Manage/2 will use LANFocus Agents/2 Extended software to monitor IBM's LAN Server and Database Manager environments.

At the same announcement, IBM introduced new software distribution tools called Configuration, Installation, and Distribution (CID). These tools permit users to copy, modify, and update applications and/or operating systems and also to distribute the software across a LAN. The software resides on the LANFocus Manage/2 platform and can distribute non-IBM software as well as IBM software across the LAN without user intervention. IBM said that more than 150 vendors have said they will make their products compatible with CID technology.

DataHub is an IBM product line for managing distributed databases from IBM and, ultimately, from other vendors who conform to IBM's Distributed Relational Database Architecture. DataHub has an object-oriented graphical monitor that displays the status of data transfers between databases supported by DataHub. This and other capabilities should permit administrators to locate and resolve bottlenecks, thereby improving performance and reducing downtime.

14.5.3 OSF's DME

OSF offers its DME for management of open systems. DME is based on technology offerings submitted by such companies as Groupe Bull, Hewlett-Packard, IBM, and Tivoli Systems and can be used with both UNIX and proprietary systems.

There are two main components constituting DME: a set of application services and a framework. The application services provide some of the most basic management functions, while the framework provides

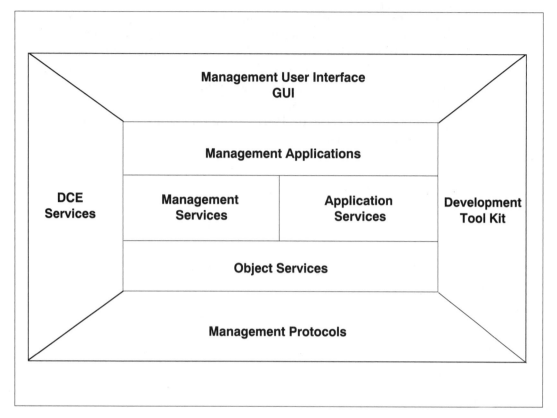

Figure 14.2 OSF's DME architecture. *Source:* OSF.

building blocks to develop software to manage heterogeneous systems. The DME architecture is shown in Figure 14.2.

DME uses object-oriented techniques to permit all network components to be represented by standardized, easily manipulated objects. All network components, including heterogeneous hardware and software, can be represented by objects. This object-oriented approach is at the core of DME and is called a Management Request Broker. This Management Request Broker is quite similar to the Object Request Broker proposed as a standard by X/Open and the Object Management Group.

Management among objects is accomplished by the Management Request Broker by using standard API formats. The standard API enables multivendor applications to talk to each other and to reuse application code. DME APIs are part of the Development ToolKit portion of DME shown in Figure 14.2. The APIs are based on the Consolidated Management API (CM-API) which was developed by Groupe Bull, HP, and IBM. The Consolidated Management API permits developers to continue writing software using traditional technology to develop DME applications, rather than being forced to write software in an object-oriented language. Software can be written in either C or C++. Communications protocols used by the DME applications can be the Simple Network Management Protocol (SNMP), the Common Management Information Protocol (CMIP), and/or DCE's RPCs.

An important feature of DME is that it simplifies many software distribution problems.

15

THE INCREASING ROLE OF UNIX

15.1   AN INTRODUCTION TO UNIX

UNIX systems actually consist of two kinds of software: the UNIX operating system and UNIX "application" or utility software. The word "application" is being used in the sense of word processing, electronic mail, and database systems being "applications" with accounts receivable qualifying as an example of a business application. Other UNIX applications are programming languages—with the most popular UNIX languages being C and Pascal, with Fortran running third—and an editor which lets the user write, change, and store text and data. Many people consider the UNIX operating system to be only one part of the UNIX system with the UNIX applications or utilities playing an important role. When reading about UNIX, the context will usually indicate whether the author is referring to the UNIX operating system only or to the UNIX operating system and the utilities as well.

Many traditional IBM shops are transitioning to UNIX whether they purchase IBM's version of UNIX—AIX (which stands for "Advanced Interactive eXecutive," a term which is rarely if ever used)—or another vendor's version. UNIX-proponents say many more would make the transition if they understood UNIX well enough. Certainly UNIX has been in the news enough that many non-UNIX users are very curious about it. In addition, the UNIX operating system is considered an open system, at least more so than proprietary operating systems. UNIX is the only operating system that can run on many different machines and was originally intended to do so. In that sense, it is definitely an open system. However, as mentioned in Chapter 4 on open systems, there are many differences between different implementations of UNIX. As a result, these different implementations and their associated applications and utilities are not quite so easy to port to other machines. Please see Chapter 4 for additional details on the relationship between UNIX and open systems.

IBM's introduction of their RISC-based RS/6000 gave many "true Blue" installations a chance to look at UNIX more seriously in the form of AIX. Many installations wanted to remain in the IBM camp but were also interested in benefiting from RISC architectures and UNIX. When the RS/6000 was introduced, IBM's AIX was its operating system, so these Big Blue users took a good look at both of them. Many of these users are now utilizing the RS/6000 and AIX.

15.1.1 A Brief History of UNIX

UNIX falls into a class of its own among operating systems. It was originally built by AT&T's Bell Laboratories in Murray Hill, NJ as an unofficial product. For a time, AT&T was prohibited from getting into the computer business by the consent decree governing the breakup of the Regional Bell Operating Companies. This complicated the UNIX picture. Certainly, if AT&T could not market UNIX, they had little motivation to improve it dramatically.

UNIX was originally built as a timesharing system, not a network operating system. However, as time went on, networking protocols were added to UNIX as was support for graphics. UNIX found its way into universities nearly right from the start due to its inexpensive licenses. It was popular with students who often added to the C code in which UNIX was written. Many variations of UNIX began to appear. As many as twenty different versions of UNIX existed. The two most commonly used versions were System V UNIX, the one from AT&T, and Berkeley UNIX, the one from the University of California at Berkeley. Berkeley UNIX is often referred to as BSD which stands for Berkeley Standard Distribution.

IBM and other vendors now have their own versions of UNIX. Since UNIX is a registered trademark of AT&T, other proprietary systems that are based on it must have different names. IBM has AIX; Digital Equipment Corporation has Ultrix; Xenix was built by Microsoft and The Santa Cruz Operation (SCO); and there are many others.

15.1.2 Some More Interesting History of UNIX

Ken Thompson at Bell Laboratories—the prestigious research division of AT&T—developed UNIX while he was working on a program called

*Space Travel.** No, he was not playing a game on company time. The program was intended to simulate the motion of the planets in the solar system. This took place in 1969, still very early in the computer's evolution. Thompson was using a General Electric computer, a GE645, with an operating system called Multics developed at MIT. Multics was one of the first multi-user systems; it could not handle many users and was an awkward system to use.

Thompson decided to try to move his space program over to a Digital Equipment Corporation computer called a PDP-7. In order to do so, Thompson had to write his own operating system. He did, and he called it UNIX. UNIX was quite successful and gained the attention of management who continued its development and implemented it as an operational system at Bell Labs in 1971. UNIX was used on various Digital computers by a number of Bell Labs' users but achieved widespread use within Bell Labs when used on Digital's larger machine, a PDP-11/70.

Thompson originally wrote UNIX in assembly language. Since each machine's assembly language is different, it was a significant programming effort to move UNIX to a different machine. Thompson decided, therefore, to rewrite UNIX in a higher level language called *B*. This language was subsequently modified by Dennis Ritchie, also of Bell Labs, and renamed *C* in 1973. If UNIX had not been rewritten in C, UNIX would undoubtedly not be as popular as it is today. C gave the operating system portability to other machines. Also, C is easier to write in than assembly language, and that contributed to other programmers being willing to add to UNIX.

Chapter 4 provided a brief explanation of how OSF was formed in response to some UNIX action taken by AT&T and Sun Workstations. Actually, much of the computer industry was surprised and alarmed by this action taken by AT&T and Sun. In the late 1980s, the two announced plans to completely rewrite UNIX and create a new, standard UNIX. Other major computer companies were afraid that AT&T and Sun would "corner the market" on UNIX, and these other companies formed OSF to compete with them. To counter the idea that the AT&T/Sun UNIX was a tightly-held operation, other vendors were invited to join AT&T and Sun to form a consortium, UNIX International (UI), to oversee development of the new UNIX. Over the years, there has been some bad blood between the two groups. It did not help that when OSF made selections from

---

*The source of the following information is The Waite Group's *UNIX Primer Plus Second Edition*, Mitchell Waite, Donald Martin, and Stephen Prata. SAMS, a Division of Prentice Hall Computer Publishing, Carmel, Indiana, 1990.

among the responses to its open Request for Technology for RPC technology, Sun was a loser. At one time Sun reportedly was saying that the letters OSF stood for "Oppose Sun Forever." Unfortunately, the result of all this is that the computer industry has two major and different UNIX standards: one from UI and one from OSF. The actual development of UNIX International's UNIX is performed at UNIX Systems Laboratories, formed by AT&T, and located in Summit, NJ. In another interesting development, Novell purchased USL and its UNIX software from AT&T in late 1992.

15.1.3 UNIX and Openness

Part of the UNIX dream was openness and portability. The idea behind the dream was to define a standard set of services to be provided by the UNIX kernel. The kernel of an operating system is the core portion that performs the most essential operating system tasks, like disk input and output operations and managing internal memory. The services that would be standardized in the kernel would be accessible through a shell which provides the interface to the user. All applications built for UNIX would use the same set of standardized services. And since UNIX was portable to a wide variety of machines, all those applications would be portable, too.

UNIX is indeed portable to many different computers. However, as mentioned earlier, many varieties of the UNIX operating system are available, and these different varieties are basically not interoperable with each other—which presents problems. Software that runs on one version of UNIX may not be portable to another version of UNIX.

15.1.4 Some UNIX Advantages and Disadvantages

UNIX—like any other software—has advantages and disadvantages. The primary advantage that most users would mention immediately is UNIX's reputation for openness, its scalability, and its wide portability. Many students are learning UNIX as part of their college training, so hiring people who are knowledgeable about UNIX is becoming easier all the time. Most graduates who have used UNIX in their studies seem to be avid fans and staunch UNIX advocates.

UNIX has some very definite disadvantages, however. UNIX is not user-friendly, and it is not easy to learn. It consists of very cryptic commands, like "rcp" and "rsh," which are entered into a command-line interface. Another disadvantage is that if a large enterprise has multiple UNIX implementations throughout its organizations, not many tools are available to perform systems management across the different versions of UNIX and their hardware platforms. Storage management and performance management are some of the areas that are problems in this regard.

Many installations with a mix of UNIX implementations are using CA-Unicenter from Computer Associates. The product covers nine functions, and all nine functions must be purchased together. CA-Unicenter is built in accordance with the CA90's architecture, offering similar functionality on dissimilar platforms. CA-Unicenter addresses the following nine management functions:

- Console automation
- Disk management
- Help desk
- Print spooling
- Report management
- Resource accounting
- Scheduling
- Security
- Tape management

Many of the large systems management vendors—companies like Candle Corp., Boole & Babbage, and Legent—are developing and/or improving current products for this area. Other vendors with products which enterprises are considering to address the problem of systems management across different UNIX platforms are shown below.

- Independence Technologies of Fremont, CA, resells the Tuxedo transaction monitor. It also provides some management tools for open systems transaction processing.
- Open Vision, Pleasanton, CA, offers a set of administration and operation software products for a UNIX data center.
- Raxco Software, Inc., in Rockville, MD, which has primarily offered products for MVS environments, is now branching into the UNIX environment.
- EcoSystems from Cupertino, CA, was formed in 1990 by executives from HP, Oracle, IBM, and AT&T. It originally targeted the market for Oracle systems in a UNIX environment. Tools produced by EcoSystems include EcoSphere, which supports manager/agent com-

munication using an active object model; EcoTools system management utilities; and EcoWorks, a kit for extending the system by creating additional utilities.

- DDS of Redwood Shores, CA, and Sydney, Australia, offers Patrol which is a framework for managing many different types of UNIX applications, databases, or systems. A primary feature of Patrol is its extendibility which permits users to put hooks into other tools and write their own scripts and modules.

Overall, UNIX is considered to have more advantages than drawbacks. Due to its scalability, companies have been able to move the same version of UNIX from a smaller machine to a larger one from the same vendor as they needed to add more users.

15.2   TECHNICAL FEATURES

UNIX is a multiuser, multitasking operating system. More than one person at a time can use the operating system, and it can perform more than one task at a time. With multitasking, users could be formatting a text file in the background while reading their E-mail at the same time.

15.2.1   UNIX Kernel, Shell, and Utilities

The UNIX system consists of three basic components: the kernel, the shell, and the utilities. Figure 15.1 illustrates their relationship to each other and to the user.

- The kernel is the core of the UNIX system and performs low-level functions like managing memory, files, and peripheral devices. It also allocates system resources, maintains the time and date, and launches applications.
- The shell is the command-line interpreter for the UNIX system. The shell is the part of UNIX with which an end user who is not using a GUI interface would interact. It accepts user commands and translates them into instructions that the kernel can understand so the commands can be executed.
- The utility programs come with the UNIX system because they are an integral part of the overall system. The utility programs take care of doing things like providing directory services for the user's files, as well as copying and moving files.

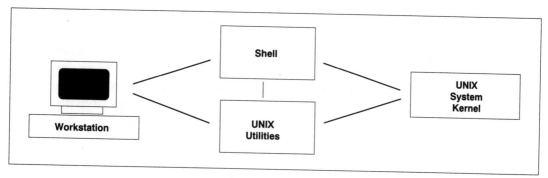

Figure 15.1 UNIX components.

Another way to picture the relationship between these three components is shown in Figure 15.2, commonly known as an onion drawing due to its similarity to the layers that make up an onion.

15.2.2 UNIX Daemons and Other Features

"Daemon" is a common term in UNIX. A daemon (pronounced "demon") is a program that performs a utility function without being requested to do so. The user (person or program) often is not aware of the daemon's action. A daemon sits in the background and is called when needed. The

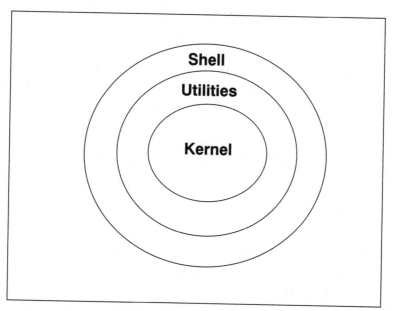

Figure 15.2 Layers of the UNIX operating system.

functions performed by daemons are generally of a housekeeping or maintenance nature, although they also perform functions like helping to correct an error from which another program cannot recover. Some individuals refer to a daemon with the term "demon," considering the former term a little archaic. The term *demon* is commonly used in artificial intelligence (AI) programs where the concept of a procedure that would become active when needed is similar to daemons or demons in UNIX.

15.2.3   UNIX Utilities Play an Important Role

The File Transfer Protocol is often used as one of the utilities on UNIX systems. FTP can be used to transfer one record, a group of records, or an entire file. Implementations of FTP often support some kind of character conversion (e.g., ASCII to EBCDIC) as part of the transfer. Other commonly used utilities with UNIX are Telnet and SMTP. Telnet provides terminal emulation over a network, and SMTP stands for Simple Mail Transfer Protocol. These utilities are available on non-UNIX systems as well.

15.3   UNIX E-MAIL

E-mail is one of the utilities provided with UNIX as explained below. E-mail systems in general—for a broad variety of client/server systems—are covered in Chapter 17 which is devoted to E-mail. However, E-mail for UNIX systems is covered in this chapter since E-mail is considered such an integral part of the UNIX environment and is automatically provided with most UNIX operating systems. The term "E-mail" stands for electronic mail which is sent from one computer to another over networks. The reader might find it helpful to refer to the introductory section of the E-mail chapter if they have had no experience with E-mail at all.

UNIX uses a mailbox type of system for its E-mail. UNIX uses the **mail** command to let the user enter the E-mail system. Entry of the **mail** command results in a response from the system of a display of a summary of the messages that have been received in the user's mailbox.

15.3.1   UNIX E-mail Systems

E-mail is built into the UNIX operating system through the UNIX-to-UNIX Copy (UUCP) capabilities and SMTP. As long as an end-user knows the path between his or her UNIX machine and the recipient's machine, he or she can send that person a message. Since any particular UNIX E-mail implementation is basically consistent with other UNIX E-mail implementations, nearly all UNIX systems can communicate with each other.

Differences exist in features such as user interfaces, routing, and delivery mechanisms.

The three most commonly used routing and distribution mechanisms for UNIX E-mail are Smail, Sendmail, and the Multichannel Memorandum Distribution Facility (MMDF). Smail is the simplest, and MMDF is the most complex. Sendmail is the one most commonly used, though it is difficult to use. Defenders of Sendmail point out that this routing mechanism is not the result of a carefully planned product plan. Rather, it is an example of the type of product that can be expected from the way many UNIX capabilities were developed—years and years of modifications, additions, and improvements added to software by a wide variety of academicians and other university inhabitants.

Actually, Sendmail originated as an experimental program and was subsequently distributed because it filled a need. However, gaining an understanding of how to modify Sendmail's addressing and routing rules can be quite difficult. A benefit of Sendmail is the simplicity with which new users can be added—a process of adding the additional sites to standard tables. This is also true of Smail, which is sometimes referred to as Sendmail's little brother. The problems occur when an administrator needs to add a *new kind* of connection, which in this increasingly heterogeneous world, is a growing need.

Adding local users becomes more difficult when utilizing the Multichannel Memorandum Distribution Facility—a process that involves editing and rebuilding tables. However, MMDF is generally flexible, and offers better organization and security, than Sendmail.

User interfaces for UNIX E-mail are generally quite simple, but third-party add-ons are available to facilitate usage. Some of the more elaborate front ends for UNIX E-mail include Next Computer's E-mail, S-Code Software's Z-mail, and Alfalfa Software's Poste.

15.3.2 Example of How to Use UNIX E-mail

Both the "mailx" front end originally from AT&T and the "Mail" front end from Berkeley consist of command-line interfaces. With such interfaces, users are notified that they have mail when they log in with a message that typically says, "You have mail." To access mail, a user types in:

mail

The user is then shown a list of message headers, with the most recent one shown first. Pressing the return key will provide the user with the text of the first message. Subsequent presses of the return key permit the user to read additional messages. A user may type "P" and a message number which enables him or her to read a specific message that appears later in the list of messages.

If a user wants to save a particular message, he or she issues the following command immediately after reading it:

mb

This will flag the most recently read message as one to be saved in personal mailbox when exiting from the mail system. Alternatively, he or she can save the message in a different file using the following command:

s

The **s** command should be followed by the name of the file where the message is to be stored. Mail to be deleted should be indicated with:

d

entered at the command prompt. Mail is not deleted until the user exits from the mail program, so if the user decides to save the message, or erroneously marks one for deletion, he or she can specify

u

to undelete it while still in the mail program.

Sending mail is quite simple, too. After entering the mail program, the user simply enters the mail command at the shell, followed by the names of the recipient/s. For example, someone sending mail would enter:

mail fsmith mjones

After doing so, he or she will be prompted as follows:

Subject:

The user has the option of entering a description of the message. After that, the user is automatically put into an edit-type of mode where the E-mail message is written. The edit capabilities of raw UNIX E-mail are not at all sophisticated, requiring that the user press the enter key after each line and preventing lines from being edited once the enter key has been pressed. Only words located on the same line where the cursor currently resides can be edited.

When the message has been completed, the system is notified by pressing <Ctrl-D>. This will cause the message to be sent, and it will print the following on the user's screen:

(end of message)

UNIX E-mail provides the capability to create mailing (distribution) lists as other E-mail systems do. Addressing mail to local users requires only the use of the user name (the login name). Addressing mail to remote users can be accomplished using either UUCP or Internet addressing.

Some of the packages that extend and make UNIX E-mail systems easier to use include Cymail from Cyantic Systems, Z-Mail from Siren Software, and Elm which is freely available and can be found on UNIX bulletin boards. Cymail and Elm provide full-screen user interfaces, while Z-Mail provides a command-line and full-screen interface and a GUI. One of the primary benefits to look for in UNIX E-mail extenders is the ability to edit all portions of a written message. Many new E-mail extender packages will certainly become available as the popularity of UNIX increases.

Usenet is an informal UNIX network established for exchanging mail and news. Usenet provides a network, and it also provides a set of programs that permits UNIX users to post and read messages on bulletin-board types of environments. These messages are generally divided into individual "newsgroups." Usenet networks are generally formed into a hierarchy with large computer sites connected to still larger sites. Usenet is connected to the Internet, an extremely large public internetwork of networks, which is discussed in Chapter 16.

15.3.3 Attaching Files to UNIX E-mail

The format of UNIX-based E-mail messages (which are closely intertwined with the UNIX operating systems software) is regulated by a message-format specification called RFC 822. This specification says that the message header and body can only consist of 7-bit ASCII characters. Users are interested in sending many different types of attachments to their electronic messages. These include not only binary program files, but also database, spreadsheet, and word processing files, as well as sound and video. In order to comply with the RFC 822 specification, a process of converting binary files to 7-bit printable character equivalents is used.

Another approach is one used by the Multipurpose Internet Mail Extensions (MIME) which is an emerging standard for attaching enclosures to E-mail. This approach does not send the binary file itself. Rather, it sends information saying where the binary file is located and how the recipient of the E-mail can go about retrieving the binary file.

15.4   USE OF UNIX IS INCREASING

While the UNIX strongholds have traditionally been engineering and scientific environments, many commercial business installations are beginning to turn to UNIX. The great majority of colleges and universities have UNIX installed. AT&T was smart to offer universities UNIX licenses at minimal cost early in UNIX's career. As a result, many computer science graduates come prepared with some degree of understanding of UNIX. No matter what level of understanding they bring, just about all of them have an appreciation of UNIX and would like to use it in their work.

An increasing base of knowledgeable UNIX developers is only one reason for its increasing use. The prominent place that UNIX has in the open systems market is another primary reason.

Some observers say that up until now, UNIX has won many client/server battles by default. They say that the other network operating systems that were available did not match up to UNIX. They indicate that with Microsoft's NT this will change because NT has all the capabilities that a sturdy network operating system needs for industrial-strength, mission-critical client/server systems. The September 1992 issue of Byte Magazine had "Is UNIX Dead?" written in big red letters across the entire cover. It was calling attention to the lead feature and cover story, written by Tom Yager and Ben Smith, which said that UNIX was at a crossroads, facing its most powerful adversary to date in Microsoft's NT. The article concluded that UNIX was not dead, but that it is facing a period of intense change in the marketplace.

16
UNIX NETWORKING

16.1   UNIX NETWORKING

The great majority of UNIX systems are networked today. Many of those networks are connected to the Internet, a public, widely-used network which permits the exchange of mail with UNIX and non-UNIX users all over the world. The Internet will be discussed in detail later in this chapter. Usenet is another popular public network which connects UNIX and non-UNIX machines and is used to send information to companies, government agencies, research laboratories, schools, universities, and individuals. Usenet offers E-mail and numerous newsgroups which are devoted to public discussions of various topics.

16.1.1   Overview

As stated earlier, UNIX was built as a multiuser system, but it did not originally have networking abilities. Its networking capabilities were built in later by many contributors. Since AT&T could not sell computer products when their Bell Labs employees first created UNIX, AT&T made the system available to universities through inexpensive licenses. The source code was made available to the universities, and the basic simplicity of the kernel made the whole system understandable to students. As a result, students thoroughly enjoyed adding to the UNIX system. Thus, students made many of the contributions to UNIX's networking capabilities.

16.1.2   Different Types of UNIX Networks

UUCP was probably the first UNIX networking capability. While in many ways it can be considered fairly primitive by today's standards, it remains the only UNIX network-related software that is available on practically all versions of UNIX running on different hardware platforms.

16.1.2.1 Early Networking: UUCP

UNIX-to-UNIX Copy (UUCP) at its most basic level is a copy program (cp) between UNIX machines. However, copying files from one UNIX machine to another is only one way UUCP is used. It permits other operations (like remote execution, remote administration, and remote maintenance). In some UNIX implementations, networked applications like E-mail and bulletin boards depend on UUCP.

UUCP was originally designed to work over serial lines and the telephone system, but it has been modified many times since it was first created. As a result, UUCP now works over a number of different low-speed and high-speed transmission systems. The most commonly used UUCP interconnections are direct dedicated lines, data PBX lines, the Internet, and dial-up telephone lines. UUCP has always been inexpensive, a characteristic which has probably contributed to its popularity and wide-spread use.

The creation of UUCP—during 1976—is attributed to Mike Lesk at Bell Labs. Part of the reason he created it was because he needed a way to automate administration of the constantly increasing number of UNIX machines in his center. In order to build such an automated system, he needed to have a way to automatically move files around among various machines.

Some say UUCP is a network while others say it is not really a network, it merely provides a capability to communicate between various UNIX machines. In fact, even in a set of machines which all use UUCP, there is no guarantee that all the machines will be able to communicate with each of the others. In addition, even if they can all communicate, there may be differences in the types of communication different pairs of machines will be able to execute. Information related to the device mechanism, for example, the device and login, must be listed in machine A for each of the other machines that machine A wants to access.

UUCP is a set of programs that gives one machine the mechanism to communicate with another UNIX machine. Two machines may each have the *mechanism* to communicate, but they may not have the *ability* to actually communicate successfully. Having the mechanism to communicate means they have the hardware and software capability; having the ability to communicate depends upon the mutual agreement between the administrators of the two sites. Therefore, a UUCP relationship between two UNIX machines is directly dependent upon the administrators of each of those machines.

UUCP has been modified by many programmers over the years. For the future of UUCP, its proponents predict that it will continue to prosper. They predict that UUCP will have more flexibility, better performance, better diagnostics, more automated maintenance, and more standardization.

16.1.2.2 TCP/IP and UNIX

The Transmission Control Protocol/Internet Protocol was described in Chapter 9; this chapter will explain why a fairly close bond has existed between TCP/IP and UNIX. Many people have considered TCP/IP as *the* networking protocol for UNIX for many years.

The DoD sponsored an experiment in 1969 that was designed to facilitate the sharing of resources. The research project was known as the DoD Advanced Research Projects Agency (DARPA). The network was called Arpanet, and it provided communication links between many major research sites at government, academic, and industrial laboratories. The early communication links were used for sending E-mail, transferring files, and logging into remote computers, and these links used leased, point-to-point line interconnections. DARPA was also sponsoring research in other technologies like satellites and mobile radio transmitters. Eventually, DARPA wanted a way to tie these various technologies together into a single network. It wanted to internetwork these individual networks—the result of which is often called an internetwork, or simply an internet. The result of that effort was the TCP/IP protocol suite which was first deployed on Arpanet in the late 1970s.

DARPA made implementation of TCP/IP available at a very low cost in order to encourage conversion to the protocol suite. This happened at the same time that many universities were using UNIX because it was available from AT&T at a very low licensing cost. Many of these universities were using the Berkeley version of UNIX. In addition, many universities were constantly increasing the number of UNIX machines they had installed. To encourage use of TCP/IP within these universities, DARPA hired Bolt, Beranek, and Newman, Inc. (BBN) to create a TCP/IP implementation that Berkeley could integrate with its version of UNIX so that it could distribute TCP/IP and UNIX together.

The fact that at that time universities were rapidly increasing the number of their UNIX machines and had a growing interest in communicating among them proved to be serendipitous for TCP/IP. The coincidence that there was a strong need for networking among UNIX machines when TCP/IP started to become widely and easily available, ensured the success of TCP/IP among UNIX university users. To make the TCP/IP protocols even more attractive, Berkeley provided application programs that used these protocols. The combination of UNIX and TCP/IP being available to universities for a very inexpensive licensing fee solidified the connection between the two technologies for many years.

16.2 NETWORK FILE SERVICES AND OTHER NETWORKING MECHANISMS

16.2.1 Sun's Network File System (NFS)

The Network File System was developed by the vendor Sun Microsystems, based in Mountain View, CA, to be an independent network service: independent of both operating systems and machine-types. The earliest implementation of NFS was in 1984 under a Berkeley UNIX-based operating system implemented by Sun called SunOS. Shortly thereafter, NFS itself was ported to a DEC VAX 11/750, DEC Ultrix on a Micro VAX II, DG/UX on the Data General MV/4000, as well as PC-DOS on an IBM PC. NFS has now been licensed and implemented on well over a hundred different platforms and provides service to well over 100,000 users.

The fact that NFS was designed to be machine and operating system independent means that any particular computer system can supply files to many different types of computers. The files of a remote computer system appear as though they are local to the user's own computer.

NFS is based on a number of key concepts, one of which is a mount. UNIX has a command called *mount* which makes a local disk available for use. NFS extends the concept of this local *mount* to permit users to access files and directories on remote machines from their own local machine.

Another key concept upon which NFS is based is the RPC. RPCs are one of the primary ways that NFS accomplishes its objective of being operating system independent. NFS uses RPCs to call a remote machine's software, bind to it, have it perform a service, and return the results to the calling machine. The RPCs also make use of an eXternal Data Representation Library (XDR) which aids machines in understanding other machines that use a different internal data representation.

NFS clients interact with NFS servers. As might be expected, a local NFS client makes a request of a service running on a remote machine, the NFS server. If the local machine has a hard disk drive that is available to other users on the network, then the local machine is both a client and a server. Machines that are used as NFS clients only are generally diskless machines. As in other client/server configurations, an NFS server platform is generally a larger, more powerful machine than an NFS client platform with a large amount of disk space attached.

16.2.2   The Transport Layer Interface (TLI)

The Transport Layer Interface is a programming interface to the transport network layer. AT&T's UNIX system TLI is constructed as a programming interface to any transport provider that follows the OSI standards. As a quick review, the seven layers in the Reference Model are as follows:

- Application
- Presentation
- Session
- Transport
- Network
- Link
- Physical

The TLI sits at the top of the transport layer, or in OSI terms, between the transport and session layers. The goal of the TLI is to allow higher layers, including specific applications for the application layer, to be developed independently of the details of underlying layers as implemented by various vendors. The intention is that users would be able to expect that any code which conforms to TLI specifications will run on any vendor's transport protocol.

Reportedly, in order to prepare a library of TLI routines, the requirements that a vendor must adhere to are not very demanding. These requirements are listed in a document called the Transport Provider Specifications. It is important to remember that TLI is not a transport provider itself; it is an interface to a transport provider.

16.2.3   RFS Overview

AT&T also provided—with the release of UNIX System V, Release 3.0, and subsequent releases—a Remote File System (RFS). RFS is an extension of the ordinary file system within UNIX. The theory behind it was to repeat what was a successful approach to dealing with storage on a single machine. RFS handles accessing data on remote systems in a similar way to local systems.

RFS is often referred to as Distributed UNIX, and it is often used in an environment with a collection of UNIX machines where the data on the various machines is treated as a unified whole. The important aspect of the "Distributed UNIX" appellation is that RFS operates by implementing remote system calls from inside the local UNIX kernel. An example may make this clear. As stated previously, a file in UNIX can be a device, a pipe, or one of many other things. Suppose that, using RFS, a system call is performed in a local kernel (on System A) and the local kernel detects that the call refers to a file on a remote machine (System B). System A will use the transport provider from inside the kernel, and it will arrange to have the system call continued on the remote machine and the results returned. As a result, this activity is very similar to normal UNIX kernel activity.

Other approaches can involve relinking of programs because the activity would be trapped at the library level. Thus, the programs would have to be relinked to use the new library. They may also involve special syntax to indicate that a file is located remotely.

16.3 UNIX INTERPROCESS COMMUNICATION

There are two popular application programming interfaces for network communications between applications in a UNIX environment: sockets and streams. Sockets dates back to 1983 when the University of California at Berkeley introduced them with UNIX 4.2 BSD. Streams were introduced in 1986 by AT&T with System V Release 3, though they were originally developed at Bell Labs in 1983. Sockets and streams are two examples of a larger class of processes known as interprocess communication (IPC) techniques. IPCs enable processes to communicate with each other to perform work.

While many client/server developers will not have to deal with streams and sockets, a brief description of these approaches are provided here.

The primary source used for the following description of sockets and streams is *Adventures in UNIX Network Applications Programming*, a book written by Bill Rieken and Lyle Weiman and published by John Wiley & Sons, Inc., in 1992. This book is an excellent source for additional information about UNIX network programming. Figure 16.1 is reproduced from that book with the permission of John Wiley & Sons.

16.3.1 Sockets

A socket can be thought of as a reference point to which messages can be sent and from which messages can be received. Any process can create

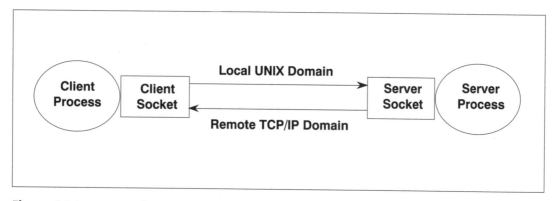

Figure 16.1 UNIX sockets.

a socket to communicate with another process, but both processes must create its own socket, since the two sockets are used as a pair.

The reference to "Local UNIX Domain" and "Remote TCP/IP Domain" in the figure means that the communication can be taking place locally (within the same system) or between remote systems over a TCP/IP network.

When users create a socket, an integer "file handle" is returned to them. The concept of a handle is similar to a name or a label in that it permits the user to identify a particular resource.

A client process creates a socket using the **socket ( )** system call. It then attempts to **connect ( )** to a server. A daemon in the server would automatically respond by creating a socket on the server side. The server daemon will also bind this new socket to an address or port associated with the server with a **bind ( )** call. The server will then **listen ( )** on this port. When it detects a connection request from the client, it executes an **accept ( )** system call. The accept call basically accepts the connection request and creates a new socket which is used for actual communication with the client. This new socket is called a child socket, and nearly all communication goes through this socket. Only an occasional quick service is performed using the original, parent socket.

16.3.2 Streams

Streams are more closely related to device drivers. The UNIX kernel is responsible for finding the addresses of streams drivers and modules in a table called a "character device switch" table.

A primary concept associated with streams is that of stacks. There are systems calls and commands for adding modules to the top of a stack and for popping modules off a stack. The upstream direction flow of the stack is toward the user and associated with a read system call. The downstream direction flow is toward the device and associated with a write system call.

In addition, each stream's module consists of two queues: an upstream (or read) queue and downstream (or write) queue. Both of these can queue messages for later service processing. If necessary, the two queues can communicate with each other.

The module in the stack that is closest to the top is called a stream head. Its purpose is to move data between user space and internal messages which flow through the streams modules. The driver end has a driver module to interface with the device control and status registers. Even though modules can be added to the top of the stack and get popped off it, the stream head module always stays where it is. When a module is added to the top of a stack, it gets added just below the stream head.

The modules are basically network protocol layers. In fact, streams technology is recognized for its ability to provide a framework for stacking different network protocol layers on top of each other. Streams permit a programmer to build protocol stacks.

16.4   THE INTERNET

As mentioned earlier, the Internet is the word's largest computer network with over 8 million users. It consists of over 8,000 separate networks which are interconnected with such protocols as Telnet and FTP into the huge, world-wide internetwork, called the Internet. The Internet is growing constantly with usage estimated as having doubled every year since 1988. Its growth is expected to continue. While the Internet is generally regarded as an internetwork for universities and research organizations, it is widely used by private business as well. In fact, misconceptions about the Internet are so prevalent that this discussion of the Internet will begin by dispelling some of these erroneous perceptions.

Occasionally, large enterprises refer to their internetworks as Internets (capital I) instead of as internets (small i). Therefore, determining whether an individual is referring to his own enterprise's internet or the large, international Internet described above can be confusing. Often, the context of the conversation or written material helps one to determine which one is meant.

16.4.1   Misconceptions about the Internet

Of the many misconceptions about the Internet, the biggest is that the whole Internet is owned by the government. The Internet's growth does, indeed, owe a debt of gratitude to the U.S. government which was active in its sponsorship, particularly through Arpanet, but the government does not own the entire Internet.

ARPANET was a computer network which consisted of tens of thousands of computers developed by the Advanced Research Projects Agency (ARPA) in the 1960s to permit universities and research organizations to exchange information. Though part of the DoD, ARPANET was not a classified network, nor was it dedicated to military research only. Due to its obsolescent technology, it was retired in 1990. However, in 1977, the ARPANET was one of the Internet's backbone networks. The protocol research sponsored by ARPA made a significant contribution to the evolution of TCP/IP on which the Internet is based.

Another misconception is that the Internet is restricted to university and scientific communication and is not open to commercial business use. The Internet is owned by over 18,000 organizations throughout the world, including large corporations, as well as civilian and military government organizations. Though the U.S. government was influential in its early days, it currently owns only a relatively small part of the overall Internet. There are over 40 countries that participate in the Internet and that number is expected to grow significantly.

The Internet, in addition to many university and government networks, also consists of thousands and thousands of LANs located in private companies which use the Internet to conduct business communication. Such connections from private companies are growing more quickly than connections from universities. While parts of the Internet are restricted to research and educational use, many privately-owned wide area Internet connectivity vendors will provide communication for whatever traffic customers are willing to pay.

16.4.2 General Information

E-mail is the most common usage of the Internet, though it can be used for other services as well. The Internet provides an economical approach to E-mail for a number of reasons one of which is that connection costs often consist of a monthly flat fee for dial-up or leased line access. In combination with that, the Internet can deliver E-mail much more quickly than other E-mail services. This is attributable to its overall structure which includes mail protocols which automatically handle queue congestion and flow control. There are reports that messages which can take up to hours to be delivered on other E-mail systems have been delivered in seconds or minutes on the Internet. A 56K bit/sec connection to the Internet by a large corporation may cost in the range of $12,000 a year.

For enterprises that can make good use of its capabilities, the benefits of an Internet connection can more than repay that cost many times over.

An additional factor that can make use of the Internet less expensive than other approaches is its use of TCP/IP which multiplexes messages across common links. This approach results in maximizing the use of available bandwidth, minimizing cost while permitting continuous connection. The fact that such a connection is available to so many recipients throughout the world is another factor that contributes to the economic value of the Internet.

Security is a concern on the Internet, but this issue can be addressed in a number of ways. Security was not one of the features emphasized in the early days of the Internet, since it was mostly used for the open sharing of information among universities and research organizations. Password protection is available, of course, for Internet users. Users have also established procedures to either limit or prohibit specific incoming network connections. For example, certain hosts or networks may be considered as off-limits for incoming messages from the Internet. Work is progressing on an Internet feature called Privacy Enhanced Mail (PEM) which will use encryption techniques. Messages can be encrypted and encryption keys will be available to ensure that users can authenticate the sender of a message.

The National Research and Education Network (NREN), which is supported by President Clinton and Vice-President Al Gore, is likely to become part of the Internet, however, it will only be one of more than 8,000 networks that are part of the overall Internet structure. When built, it is expected to be the fastest wide area network on the Internet. While the overall Internet is international in use, the NREN may be limited to U.S. use since the U.S. government will be funding it.

16.4.3   Additional Internet Services and How to Use Them

Although E-mail constitutes the largest volume of its traffic, the Internet offers many other types of services, too. Many of these services are related to permitting or facilitating research activities.

Some of the many capabilities offered by the Internet include the following:

- Access to libraries
- Access to many informational and specialty databases
- Access to newsgroups
- Ability to be included on mailing lists to receive specific types of information

The Internet has a capability called Multipurpose Internet Mail Extensions (MIME), which is able to encapsulate other types of correspondence with a written message. With MIME, the following can be encapsulated with an E-mail message: fax, sound, video, foreign character sets, and Postscript files (from Adobe Systems, Inc.).

16.4.4 Research on the Internet

Libraries, of course, are used by many people doing research. Researchers using the Internet have access to the standard reference books and other research facilities of libraries (as opposed to access to specific books which are protected by copyright laws). However, efforts are underway to make access to books through the Internet possible also. The Internet's OnLine Book Initiative (OBI) and Project Gutenberg are both working on providing free access to books for which the copyright has expired. Also, another service called the Online BookStore will provide access to books with copyright protection for a fee. The Online BookStore pays royalties to the authors of the books or whoever else may hold the electronic rights. This service also provides access to illustrations.

One of the networks on the Internet is named the Research Libraries Information Network. Libraries available through the Internet include those for Harvard University and the University of California, among many others. The Library of Congress Catalog can be searched through use of the Internet.

16.4.4.1 Database Research

A wide variety of specialty-type databases can be accessed and searched using the Internet. While services such as CompuServe also offer access to many research databases, the Internet offers a wider variety, including many that have only a limited audience. While providing access to databases with very limited appeal would not be economical for a vendor like Compuserve, the Internet provides such access.

More than 400 databases which may be used for research are located on servers throughout the Internet. Topics range from computer processing to molecular biology. Index and search services are available to help users find what they are looking for.

Archie, for example, is a service that indexes more than 1000 servers. A user provides the name of a specific program or other package, and Archie will provide a list of server locations where it can be found. With another package, the Wide Area Information Servers (WAIS), a user can provide a piece of text with key words, and WAIS will provide the user with text where these key words can be found; additionally, WAIS has a specific service that will search the Bible for specific passages and key words.

A package called Gopher helps users keep track of various information sources. Listings from Archie and WAIS are available through Gopher, as are other information services. Gopher brings them all together into one menuing system.

16.4.4.2 Patent Research

A number of companies use the Internet's information database services to find out more about what their competition is doing. Searches of patent databases has increased 40 percent in recent years according to Advanced Network and Services. An examination of patent databases can be used in any number of ways. In its simplest form, it can tell an enterprise what its competitor has patented recently. It could point out areas where its competition is active and where they should become active as well.

In addition, information database services can tell a firm whether a competitor has already patented something for which it is about to apply for a patent. This can do two things. It can save the researching firm the time and expense of applying for a patent on something that is already patented. In addition, the information provided may give the researching firm enough information to permit it to modify its product so it may also obtain a patent on its particular product or technique.

One enterprise, which prefers to remain anonymous, stated that its research of patent databases using the Internet has saved it over $15,000 in costs for patent research which it previously performed in other ways. Further, the firm says that it expects that the more thorough and reliable information it now receives on other patents will permit it to apply for up to three times more patents than it had applied for previously.

16.4.5 Internet Newsgroups

Users can utilize newsgroups in a number of ways. A user can be a member of a newsgroup related to a particular topic, ensuring that he or she will receive new information about that topic as it becomes available. The Internet carries many newsgroups that are available through USENET, one of the many networks connected to the Internet. Companies have used newsgroups to keep up-to-date on items ranging from changes in trading regulations with a specific country to the daily price of various commodities. A service called Clarinet will connect a user—for a fee—to news wire services, sports lines, business news, and syndicated columnists, among other items.

Some new groups provide services that go beyond providing access to information. One example is a service that provides software updates. Another is a classified service which lists job openings. This is reportedly a particularly popular service.

Some users combine the features of newsgroups with the capabilities of mailing lists (a distribution list of people who should receive messages when the list name is referenced). Firms have used this combination to obtain and send product-related reports directly to customers. Such reports may concern a bug that was discovered and describe a temporary fix users can apply until the vendor permanently corrects the problem. These reports can also contain information related to benefits or new uses of the products. In turn, firms use such a combination to obtain feedback from their customers. The vendor can either pose questions to which users can respond or just provide a general way for customers to express their positive or negative experiences with the product.

16.4.6   Free Software from the Internet

A lot of software is available for free over the Internet. This primarily derives from its roots in the university and research world where many people mutually benefited by sharing the results of their work. In today's world, many private corporations are also able to benefit from the fact that much free software is available via the Internet.

One of the most widely used software packages is GNU Emacs, a popular UNIX text editor and formatter. It is provided free of charge by the Free Software Foundation. It can be obtained from a machine called *ftp.uu.net*. GE's Research and Development division, for example, has hundreds of people who are benefiting from use of GNU Emacs.

Many university research groups make the software they create freely available to industry as well. A systems engineer in a division of the energy company, Unocol Corporation in Brea, CA, says Unicol received an advanced technology software program from Caltech for modeling seismic data. Other private enterprises report that such research-based software they receive for free was worth well over the cost of their connection to the Internet.

16.4.7   How Companies Have Benefited from the Internet

A few of the companies that have benefited from use of the Internet include the following:

- General Electric
- SRI International, a research and consulting firm
- Various publishing firms such as Addison-Wesley Publishing Company, the Oxford University Press, and Editorial, Inc.
- Tadpole Technologies, a network vendor
- Various newspapers including the Houston Chronicle, The Village Voice, the New York Times, and The Economist.

Various research divisions within GE use the services provided by the Internet to assist in their work. SRI International uses the Internet to communicate between its offices in California and London. The Internet permits SRI to send E-mail and other types of information more economically, and therefore, more frequently, than they could previously.

The Oxford University Press uses the Internet to coordinate the work of over 7,000 contributors. Using the Internet, the publisher coordinates text contributions from writers. Addison-Wesley uses the Internet to keep in touch with both writers and potential writers. Addison-Wesley also reviews proposals submitted via the Internet by potential authors. Editorial Inc., uses the Internet to exchange drafts and subsequent iterations of writers' work via the Internet. Correspondence and editing changes that used to take days or a week using postal services or more can now be completed within one day using the Internet's communications facilities.

Tadpole Technologies, Inc. uses the Internet to keep in touch with salespeople on the road. While traveling, salespeople carry a notebook and connect via the Internet at locations such as the customer location, their hotel room, and even airport lounges.

The newspapers and publishers mentioned above—and probably many others—have used the Internet to get feedback as well as ideas from readers and other sources. They have used it to ask readers their opinions on different topics. They have also used it to ask for knowledge and/or experiences related to specific topics, significantly aiding in the writing of stories.

16.4.8   Additional Information about the Internet

While this book provides a fairly extensive bibliography of sources for additional information on a broad range of topics related to client/server environments, this chapter will provide a list indicating which ones of those books are related to the Internet for those individuals who are particularly interested in this topic. They are as follows:

- Kehoe, B.P., *Zen and the Art of the Internet: A Beginner's Guide*, Prentice Hall, 1993.
- Krol, E., *The Whole Internet User's Guide and Catalog*, O'Reilly & Associates, Inc., 1992.
- LaQuey, T., *The Inernet Companion: A Beginners' Guide to Global Networking*, Reading, MA, Addison-Wesley, 1993.
- Tennant, R., et al., *Crossing the Internet Threshold: An Instructional Handbook*, Library Solutions Institute and Press, 1992.

17

E-MAIL AND CLIENT/SERVER SYSTEMS

17.1   OVERVIEW OF E-MAIL

17.1.1   E-mail Concepts

Some of the earliest servers used in client/server environments were E-mail servers. File servers and print servers, of course, appeared early, too, but once the concept of a server caught on, all three of these types of servers were quickly in widespread use. E-mail systems use the basic client/server model. The client end allows the user to communicate with the E-mail software on the server system and the server sends the message to the recipient or recipients.

The purpose of E-mail is to send messages to other computer users through the use of networking capabilities. In the past, the implementation of E-mail within an enterprise has often opened the door to client/server computing. In turn, the introduction of networks for application-oriented client/server systems has often opened the door for E-mail within an enterprise. If a network is installed for production client/server systems, that same network can be used for E-mail, and vice versa. In fact, as we will see shortly, E-mail and business application client/server systems can work together very well in other ways, too.

E-mail can take the place of paper interoffice memos, faxes, telephone calls, or mail sent through the postal system. Of course, it is not really fair to compare the speed of E-mail and the postal system; E-mail is practically instantaneous. However, some E-mail enthusiasts enjoy referring to the postal mail system as "snail mail."

17.1.2   Store-and-Forward Messaging

E-mail uses the store-and-forward communication technique of client/ server messaging. Basically, this means that computers or LANs can transmit messages from a terminal or workstation on one system to a terminal or workstation on another LAN through the use of intervening systems. Store-and-forward refers to the manner in which a message is sent to its destination. The message can be temporarily stored at intermediate sites before it is forwarded to the next node on its way to its final destination.

Another important feature of the communication techniques used in E-mail is that recipients do not have to be at their machine and ready to accept a message when it is sent. The message can be stored until they are ready to read it.

When an E-mail system is for a small, local group, a LAN and appropriate E-mail software will suffice for the exchange of messages. For large geographic areas, a WAN will need to be involved as well.

17.1.3   Evolution of E-mail

When networks started appearing in companies, each different department or division would often have its own separate network. When E-mail was installed, it often serviced just the needs of that particular division or department. Therefore, each division installed E-mail software that met its particular needs. As a result, many large companies wound up with a broad mix of different E-mail packages installed throughout the enterprise. The different E-mail packages generally use different addressing schemes and different ways of performing translation and conversion of data.

Early E-mail systems generally dealt with messages that consisted of text. A useful extension to E-mail text was the addition of "attached files" which could contain graphics and/or numeric data. Now, attached files can consist of video, voice, and other media. Some of the items that most E-mail systems have in common are the concepts of an inbox where incoming mail is stored, an outbox where outgoing mail is "sent," a filing cabinet where important mail that has been read can be stored, a waste basket where E-mail recipients can dispose of mail, and a mechanism to carry the mail.

As the use of LANs spread, so did the use of E-mail. In the early days of LANs, some claimed that E-mail was the primary reason for the growth of LANs. Firms like Banyan and 3Com sold E-mail packages with their network packages. Other software firms such as Consumers Software, Da Vinci, Higgins, and PCC Systems (later renamed as cc:Mail) offered E-mail for the most widely-used networks.

Another big boost for E-mail was the advent of multitasking. This meant that an E-mail system could constantly be running, checking for the arrival of new mail, and notifying the user (who could also turn off the announcement of new mail, if desired). Prior to multitasking, users had to end a particular job to see whether or not any new mail had been delivered.

When E-mail systems reside on different LANs, interconnection problems arise. Standards now exist to facilitate the interconnection of different E-mail systems. Two of the most popular are the Message Handling Service (MHS), a defacto standard currently promoted by Novell, and the de jure X.400 message exchange protocol.

With wireless networks and pocket-size computers, E-mail services are now becoming quite portable. Such advances and the popularity of E-mail is boosting the use of worldwide E-mail. It is apparent that a universal E-mail addressing scheme is needed for world-wide E-mail. The telephone system provides a familiar example of an addressing scheme which permits telephone access to anyone in the world who has a telephone. The de jure X.500 Directory Services standard provides such a universal E-mail addressing scheme with universal directories.

17.1.4   The Advantages of E-mail

E-mail provides many benefits in addition to speed of delivery. The message can be created at any time at the sender's convenience. In fact, many people create and send E-mail messages using their modem-equipped home computers late at night. A corresponding convenience is that the recipient can read the message at his or her convenience as well. While the recipient would not be happy to receive a late night phone call, it does not matter to the receiver when E-mail is sent. Even if E-mail is sent during the business day, the recipient is not forced to interrupt what he or she is doing as when responding to a ringing telephone.

Another advantage of E-mail is that the sender can send the same message to many people very easily. Most E-mail systems have a provision for establishing distribution lists that can be used many times. The user simply lists the individuals who should be on a particular distribution list and assigns a name to the distribution list. Most users have multiple distribution lists. It is easy to add and delete users from a distribution list.

E-mail can also be filed in an orderly fashion by category. This can provide a user with a sort of audit trail of what was said by whom and when. If users cannot remember the specifics of a particular E-mail message, they can retrieve it and reread it. In addition, the recipient of an E-mail message can forward it to someone else with an additional new note attached if desired. Most E-mail systems are private to the individual user. However, some companies feel they have a right to read any employee's E-mail, since the employees are using company equipment.

Another advantage of E-mail is that it can also be printed out. The user is not restricted to having an electronic copy only. Printing an E-mail message is often done if someone wants to post a message he or she received on an employee bulletin board. Users should be wary, however, of printing out (e.g., for sentimental reasons) any personal E-mail they may get from an avid admirer since someone else may get to the shared network printer before they do. The person who got to the printer first would probably find the E-mail more interesting reading than what he or she was originally looking for on the printer.

17.1.5   Drawbacks of E-mail

Despite the many advantages of E-mail, there are some disadvantages as well. E-mail can become over-used and, therefore, abused. It seems to have an addictive power for some people. There are users who will send lengthy E-mail messages to someone who is sitting in the next cubicle— while the sender is aware that person is at his or her desk. Some people are such E-mail addicts that they would rather send a mail message than get up and walk over and deliver the message verbally, which in the great majority of cases would be much faster. Such advocates have defended their action saying that in delivering the message in person, they could get involved in another topic, keeping them from their current work. However, the individual could certainly control this situation. Addictive use of E-mail is a common phenomenon, can be counter-productive, and should be carefully managed.

Overuse of E-mail can also result in people sending messages that are not really important enough to send. This can result in more "FYI" (for your information) or "thought you might be interested in knowing" messages than most recipients need to read. While this information might be "nice," the recipient does not have time to sit at his or her desk and read all kinds of nice, interesting bits of information.

Overuse of E-mail can result in having too many messages pile up while one is on a business trip, vacation, out ill, or on other leave. In many companies an individual can return after a relatively short absence to find over a hundred E-mail messages waiting to be read. Some sites have a priority code to indicate how important it is for the reader to read any particular message. Priority codes and message descriptions can be extremely useful in those cases where hundreds of E-mail messages can pile up.

Some E-mail packages have message management capabilities such as sorting, filtering, and filing capabilities to address this specific problem. Some of these packages permit users to sort incoming mail in a variety of ways including sender, date sent, subject, size, and other characteristics. For example, a package like Z-mail is able to alert the recipient to specific messages. A company that uses Z-mail says that some of its managers receive 300 mail messages a day. Such a high number of E-mail messages could require that an individual spend many hours responding to them all. Z-mail's filtering and rule-based system helps assist with properly dealing with such a high-volume of messages.

When overuse becomes too abusive, enterprises often establish usage standards for E-mail. If too many "fun" type messages are being sent, severe limits may be installed, or these types of messages may need to completely be disallowed. While fun and humor have their place in the office—and, in fact, have been known to increase productivity—excessive use of funny E-mail messages is not an appropriate use of business equipment and time.

Speaking is much faster than writing. Therefore, for many situations, voice mail can be much faster than E-mail. If a great deal of information needs to be conveyed to another individual and both parties have voice mail, verbalizing this information is much faster than writing it all out on a keyboard. Even if the sender needs some response, voice mail can handle that, too. Many companies have sophisticated voice mail that makes responding to in-house voice mail as easy as responding to E-mail, if not easier. With these voice systems, the recipient of the in-house call just needs to press a particular button on his or her telephone to provide an *immediate* voice response to meet the caller's needs. If the call is from another company, a voice E-mail response can be returned with a simple phone call. If an individual does not care to get into an interactive conversation just then, he or she can sometimes go through the voice mail system in a particular way which just puts the caller directly into the recipient's voice mail system.

Like any tool, E-mail should be used appropriately for true effectiveness. Enterprises may need to monitor how E-mail is being used to make sure it is not being used ineffectively through inappropriate use.

17.2   E-MAIL ARCHITECTURE AND UTILIZATION

17.2.1   Architecture of E-mail

The architecture of E-mail software is a client/server architecture. E-mail consists basically of two components: a front-end user interface (the client), and a back-end which provides the E-mail service (the server). In between is the communication mechanism that connects these two components, as in any other client/server system.

The front end, the user interface, is often called the user agent, or UA, while the back end is referred to as the transport agent (TA) or message transport agent (MTA). When a site buys an E-mail package, it often purchases a system which offers both the front- and the back-end components. However, E-mail is becoming more modularized. In the future, users will probably purchase the front-end and back-end separately. The site often has the communication component installed already or installs it separately. Of course, it must ensure that the E-mail system it purchases will work with the communication capabilities the site has or plans to install.

The client module provides the interface to permit a user to interact with the E-mail system. As with other user interfaces, E-mail interfaces should be consistent for end users, to facilitate their use of the system. The network provides the communication mechanism. Generally, both the sender and the recipient must share the same protocol, transport mechanism, or approach. The server module for E-mail runs under the operating system on the server and provides the basic E-mail engine which generally provides the following primary functions:

- The database or store of messages
- The software that moves messages around
- The directory services (addressing)

E-mail architectures are in the process of changing. The basic E-mail configuration described above consists of a user interface, a network, and an E-mail engine. Early (and still existing) E-mail packages had all of these components as part of one package. As mentioned above, that is changing as E-mail components become more modularized.

The E-mail server software that moves messages around, the transport services, will begin to be packaged more and more in operating system software such as Microsoft Windows, IBM's O/S, NetWare NLMs, and certainly in Microsoft's NT. The client user agents, or user interfaces, will then be the primary capability that competing E-mail vendors will offer—with more and more services to lure customers. E-mail vendors may also be able to compete by offering better directory services and authentication services. The term "electronic signature" is used in connection with authentication in E-mail systems. At this stage of the technology, authentication in E-mail systems is quite similar to authentication in any other system. Vendors, however, are working to implement special types of authentication for E-mail systems. Examples are Apple Computer's Open Collaborative Environment (OCE) standard and Bellcore's digital time stamp. The recipient can use the time stamp to see if the message has been read or altered while in transit.

Generally when E-mail systems are purchased, two packages of software are acquired. One component is the basic server and related system administration software. The other consists of the user packages. These can be purchased for a specific number of users, i.e., ten, twenty, fifty, or for an unlimited number of users. Prices will vary with the number of users, of course. Occasionally, the server, administrator, and end user software are all included in one package. Transport services are not generally purchased with E-mail packages; transport services are installed separately. However, users must be sure that the E-mail package they purchase will indeed run with the transport services that are available to them.

An attractive feature of E-mail is the ability to cut-and-paste information from other documents (e.g., word processing documents, spreadsheets, graphics) and include it as part of the E-mail. (Many packages permit the "attachment" of such information.) A Windows-based E-mail system could enable such a feature, but not all Windows-based systems offer this capability. This ability is sometimes referred to as a Multiple Document Interface (MDI) with a clipboard.

17.2.2 End User Utilization

While back-end features are often considered the most important aspects of an E-mail system, the ease with which an end user can access the system using the front end is an important factor also.

17.2.2.1 How to Use E-mail

Users generally access an E-mail system by logging in with their user name and confirming their identity by entering a password. Users can check their inbox to see if they have any mail. If so, they may access their messages right away or later. After accessing and reading them, users generally either save, or discard them. Before doing so, however, they can reply to any of the messages. Most E-mail systems have a clearly marked method for replying to an E-mail message as soon as it is read. After reviewing the subject matter of each electronic message, in the listing of new E-mail messages, readers may decide to read only a few messages—saving the rest for later. Requiring all E-mail users to utilize the Subject entry within the E-mail header can be a significant time-saver.

If a user wants to send mail to someone, he or she can define the recipient by selecting a name from a directory or by responding to an E-mail prompt with the recipient's user name and network location. Many E-mail systems also permit a user to send a message to everyone on the network through use of a "broadcast" mode or to selected individuals through use of a mailing list.

The actual message itself can be created in the text editor provided with the E-mail software or in a separate word processing package. If the latter technique is used, the user tells the E-mail software the name of the document containing the appropriate E-mail message. As soon as the user tells the E-mail system to send the message, it appears in the computer mailbox of the recipient. Some E-mail systems notify recipients that they have new mail immediately; others inform recipients when they are finished with their current application.

17.2.2.2 Saving, Filing, and Disposing of Messages

After E-mail messages are read, the recipient may either immediately delete it, or save it. It is interesting to note that when individuals first begin to use E-mail they have a tendency to save most or many of their messages. More experienced E-mail users tend to immediately delete most of their messages after reading them. Why the difference? Probably because the seasoned E-mail users have learned how quickly these already-read messages can pile up, taking what usually amounts to needless space. In addition, without sophisticated filing and organizing tools, quickly determining what is contained in the great bulk of these accumulated messages is difficult. Better to just get rid of each after its message has been read.

When messages are saved, they can either be saved in a user's inbox or outbox—depending on the particular E-mail system. Some systems will save E-mail messages on the E-mail server if the recipient does not specify otherwise. This can eventually result in many messages being stored on the server, slowing it down. If a recipient has a diskless workstation, the alternative would be to print out important E-mail messages.

Different E-mail systems offer a variety of ways to save messages ranging from keeping them in the directory provided by the E-mail system to permitting users to create their own directories and subdirectories for organized filing purposes.

An advanced feature related to storing E-mail messages is the ability to link related messages, sometimes referred to as "threading" information about messages. This capability can provide an important asset if the sequence of events must be recalled related to a particular set of correspondence.

Other features related to saved messages include the capability to tag them and index them according to the information they contain. For example, Folio's Mailbag permits tagged messages to be routed to a queue until the Mailbag server program can route them to an "infobase" where they are compressed to save on storage space. Subsequently, messages sent to that infobase can be searched according to common criteria, like sender and subject, and they can also be searched for specific words, phrases, and/or combinations of both.

17.2.2.3 The Basic Structure of Messages

The structure of every E-mail message consists of a header and a body. The header contains the address. The body, also known as the envelope, contains the actual message or readable text of the E-mail.

The address portion of E-mail is generally divided into the following parts:

- To: The recipient's name
- From: The sender's name
- cc: Additional recipients of the message
- Subject: An optional message description
- Time: Time the message was created
- Date: Date when the message was created
- Message #: A unique message identifier

Some systems have a "bcc:" capability. This is used for sending a message to additional recipients without having their names appear as recipients on the message. A frequent use of this is for the sender to send themselves a copy of the message they are sending to others so they may store it in their files.

The E-mail system generally fills in the sender's name, the time, date, and message # automatically.

17.3 E-MAIL FEATURES

Various features of E-mail are discussed throughout this chapter. This subsection will review some of them and will also call attention to a few E-mail features that—in many cases—should be carefully considered by many sites. Some features of E-mail are "nice to have," while others are extremely important. Having the right degree of security is important to any E-mail installation. There are other features that may be "nice to have" for some sites, but may make an extremely valuable contribution to other sites. Then, there are new features, such as wireless E-mail, that could be nearly useless to some organizations while providing such a strategic benefit to others that they mean the difference between success and failure.

E-mail options can include such capabilities as mailing and distribution lists, providing printed copies, the organizing and archiving (storing) of messages, and the relatively new forms and forms-routing capabilities. Some E-mail systems allow users to encrypt messages to protect the contents.

Additional features can include the following:

- Audible notification of received messages
- Ability to assign priorities to messages
- Provision for rule-based management where messages are received, handled, and/or stored according to logical rules established by the user.

Mailing, or distribution, lists can be quite handy. There are some distribution lists that are established by the E-mail administrator for use by many people. Such a distribution list may contain everyone in a particular division or work group. It may also designate a group of people who are following a specific technology. Other distribution lists are set up by private users for their own unique needs. To send a message to everyone on a particular distribution list, the sender only has to provide the name of the list as the recipient when sending the message.

An example of forms-based capabilities can be found in Microsoft's Electronic Forms Designer package. This software allows users to create and distribute—with E-mail—forms that range from telephone slips to purchase orders.

17.3.1 Security

Most E-mail systems are protected by the security features that are built into the network operating system they are using. Some additional security features are also available to E-mail users. Encryption, used to protect many types of files, is an obvious one that comes to mind. A more unique one is a dial-back system. Using this approach, a remote user dials in to the network. The network will recognize the dial-in, but rather than granting access, it disconnects the remote caller and then dials the stored phone number for that remote user itself. If connection is made in this manner, then the connection is permitted. Using this scheme, an unauthorized user would not be able to get into the system just by knowing a remote user's password. Of course, if the unauthorized user also has access to the authorized user's equipment, they would be permitted to connect.

When users log into their network operating system, they enter a password that verifies who they are. E-mail systems also require a password to uniquely identify specific users. It can be a wise idea for users to have an E-mail system password that is different from their network operating system password.

Encryption (encoding) of messages extends to stored messages and to messages while in transit. The former is offered by more E-mail systems than the latter. Decoding a stored message that is encrypted involves use of the encryption password.

The encryption of messages while they are being transmitted prevents their exposure to cable-tapping attempts. While this may not be necessary for casual E-mail, at times such security is important. Some systems even have provision for the encryption of the sender's name, permitting only the recipient to be privilege to that information.

Security features generally come with a price. Installing them and using them can be time-consuming. However, when tight security is not needed, many of the installed security features can be disabled by E-mail users. This will make their system easier to utilize for casual use.

17.3.2 Authentication

Authentication is a special type of security feature which is becoming more important, especially as E-mail is used in combination with EDI and EFT transactions. However, it can also be important with any high security use of E-mail. Authentication—sometimes referred to as an electronic "signature"—validates the sender's authenticity, ensuring the recipient that the sender of the message really is the person the recipient thinks he or she is.

Authentication uses a mathematical password and code. When the stored code matches the one from the sender, the sender's authenticity is validated.

Apple Computer's Open Collaborative Environment (OCE), an E-mail enabling system, provides a dual-encryption system for authentication. Under this system, users have two keys or numbers. One is private, known only to the sender; and the other is public, which the sender will provide to recipients of documents requiring authentication. Based on the contents of a specific transmitted message, OCE will create a unique "fingerprint" for the document. This "fingerprint" is encrypted along with the sender's private key and attached to the transmitted message. Using OCE features, the recipient is able to generate a second fingerprint from the contents of the document. When matched, this fingerprint in combination with the sender's public key will provide authentication of the sender of the document. This authentication capability can also be used with program-to-program communication.

As the importance of E-mail usage increases, additional security mechanisms are sure to be provided by many vendors. Bellcore offers a data integrity service that inserts a digital time stamp on a document. As mentioned earlier, this is a tamper-detection provision which permits recipients to determine if the document they have received has been read or altered during transmission.

17.3.3 Wireless E-mail

E-mail can be accessed while the user is on a business trip. Some of the options are as follows:

- A modem on any PC can be used to dial-in to the user's network using compatible modem software or an E-mail remote capability
- Public Phone 2000 equipment with color monitors and keyboards, provided by AT&T
- Wireless E-mail

While wireless E-mail is in its early stages, significant advances can be expected in the future. The early adopters of wireless E-mail are likely to be those who currently use pagers. A pager can let a user know that someone needs to contact him or her and provides the phone number to call. Wireless E-mail can provide the user with an entire message. This could be a tremendous asset, particularly where a home-office is paging someone to tell them they need to call someone else and why they need to call that person. Wireless E-mail is able to store the transmitted message to be read at a later time as well as immediately.

Some of the vendors who are actively working on wireless E-mail systems include Hewlett-Packard, Anterior RadioMail, Motorola, and— of course—AT&T. HP provides wireless E-mail in its 95LX palmtop computer. Connected to a Mobidem wireless modem, the 95LX palmtop can receive E-mail anywhere. No telephone line connections are needed.

Some pager-users from Oracle Corporation use Anterior RadioMail wireless E-mail to have messages transmitted to their pagers which can store several hundred characters from each of the 20 most recent messages received. Anterior RadioMail connects public and private E-mail services, and so these messages can come from such services as CompuServe, the Internet, and AT&T Mail.

Motorola's evolving contribution is their E-mail Broadcast to a Roaming Computer (Embarc). This is a radio-based, hand-held E-mail system which uses the DataStream receiving unit to receive messages by means of a radio signal sent by transmitters on satellites. Interfaces to this capability are being provided by Motorola and other vendors for existing E-mail systems.

AT&T and SkyTel are combining resources to provide E-mail/pager capabilities for AT&T's Safari notebook computer. Early plans involve having interested users equipped with a Windows-enabled Safari which includes a wireless mailbox and a small pager adapter. This would enable users to receive messages through services such as the EasyLink commercial E-mail service and read them right on the screen of their palmtop Safari computer. Plans include providing the capability for users to send messages to other users by means of a cellular telephone link.

17.4   E-MAIL SOFTWARE

There are many different kinds of E-mail packages available for different platforms. The capabilities of E-mail packages vary widely, too. More and more vendors are beginning to add new features to what used to be simple, basic E-mail software. Some of the simpler features include such capabilities as automatic filing abilities. But far more advanced features are also being added to E-mail, giving birth to the term "smart E-mail." The concepts of smart E-mail and mail-enabled software are discussed in Chapter 20. Various E-mail software packages are described in that chapter. The product descriptions in that chapter will point out which E-mail packages have various types of "smart" capabilities.

17.4.1   Tips for Selecting an E-mail System

As with any other technology, many factors are involved in selecting an E-mail system. An enterprise may have to give serious consideration, for example, to E-mail systems that are already installed. However, looking to the future (the enterprise's strategies and goals) may be the most important consideration. This is especially true for enterprises which can foresee that they could benefit from combining E-mail capabilities with other technologies.

Some of the factors that can be considered when reviewing E-mail systems could apply to the selection of any technology. Some key considerations to keep in mind when purchasing an E-mail system are listed in the E-mail Checklist section which follows.

17.4.2 E-mail Checklist

- A careful analysis of the enterprise's needs.
- Check that the E-mail package will be able to communicate with all the platforms with which it will need to interact. For example, ensure that the E-mail package selected can operate on the available network operating system.
- E-mail should be easy to use because people at all levels within the firm may need to use it—including some who are computer-phobic.
- Determine what additional features such as mail filtering, mail-enabled applications are needed.
- Pay attention to directory needs. This is often overlooked by new E-mail users. Directory capabilities can determine the ability of the E-mail system to meet the enterprise's needs in the future.
- Determine whether to connect the E-mail capabilities to fax, voice E-mail, EDI, and other services.
- Establish in-house procedures for E-mail use. Excessive use of E-mail can lower productivity.
- Make clear to employees that company-provided E-mail is for company use only; not for private use.
- Tell employees whether their E-mail will be monitored by management.
- Give careful thought to strategy with regard to standards and open systems, both for the short-term and for the long haul.
- Look to the future. What will the company's E-mail needs be in a few years, in five years? Plan to be able to interconnect local E-mail systems. Plan also to interconnect to systems outside the enterprise.

17.5 REPRESENTATIVE E-MAIL PACKAGES

Far too many E-mail software products are in existence for this book to mention them all. This section will only be able to mention a few of the more widely-used systems or systems with unique features. Different E-mail packages are available for the diversity of platforms on which they can run. For example, different E-mail systems are available for mainframes, minicomputers and LANs. In addition, packages for public E-mail and the Internet are available. While some E-mail systems can run on a variety of these platforms, others are meant specifically for one platform.

This discussion of E-mail packages will be separated into (1) LAN-based and (2) mainframe and minicomputer systems. UNIX E-mail is described in the introductory chapter on UNIX, and public E-mail systems are discussed in the next section. Special considerations related to E-mail systems for the Macintosh are also described in this section. The information on mainframe, minicomputer, and public E-mail systems is provided because these systems will have to interconnect with E-mail software found in client/server environments.

Some of the E-mail packages described have workgroup and workflow capabilities built into them as will be occasionally pointed out. The concepts behind workgroup and workflow software are described in Chapter 19 and 20, respectively.

17.5.1 LAN-based E-mail Systems

Two of the most popular E-mail systems are Lotus Corporation's cc:Mail and Microsoft Mail for PC Networks. There are many other products, however, with new ones appearing all the time.

17.5.1.1 cc:Mail

The small letters in "cc:Mail," the most popular E-mail system, are not a typo. The original vendor of this package was a company called cc:Mail, also spelled with a small "c." The vendor was purchased by Lotus Corporation in 1991, but the original cc:Mail management, sales, and development team was left largely intact. Adding to the prestige of cc:Mail, IBM agreed in 1992 to license and distribute cc:Mail. They marketed it to IBM mainframe users who were migrating to LANs, instead of the mail product that was integrated with IBM's Office Vision product.

Users with Windows, DOS, OS/2, UNIX, and the Macintosh can all use cc:Mail. It can even be utilized by Hewlett-Packard's palmtop 95LX computer and wireless radio E-mail users with the help of memory cards. cc:Mail also offers a wide range of gateways for connecting to other E-mail systems. It is relatively inexpensive, easy to use, and has a fair number of administrative and security features considering its price and ease-of-use.

The owner of cc:Mail has mail capabilities in its Notes package described in both the groupware and combination software chapters of this book. Lotus provides directory synchronization and other integration capabilities between the two E-mail systems.

Many add-on products were provided by other vendors for cc:Mail as a result of its wide-spread use. For example, Powercore provides a calendar and scheduler called the Network Scheduler II program. A list of such third-party add-ons is published and available from Lotus Corporation.

17.5.1.2 Microsoft Mail for PC Networks

Microsoft acquired this E-mail product in 1991 from Consumer's Software which called it "Network Courier." Microsoft modified it and changed its name to Microsoft Mail. This name initially caused a little confusion because Microsoft was already marketing an E-mail package for Macintosh AppleTalk networks named "Microsoft Mail" which was quite different.

Microsoft Mail provides numerous gateways for connecting to other E-mail systems. While software prices frequently vary, Microsoft Mail has had a history of being more expensive than cc:Mail. Microsoft Mail offers a generous array of diagnostic tools for maintenance. Microsoft, like Lotus, publishes a catalog of available add-on programs for its E-mail package, including Schedule+, a scheduling and calendaring capability.

Microsoft has made it clear that it believes that E-mail should be an integral part of operating systems like NT. This involves building the E-mail engine right into the operating system. This, of course, could have ramifications on the way E-mail is currently developed and sold. Users who purchase an operating system from Microsoft which incorporates an E-mail engine obviously would not need to purchase an E-mail engine from another vendor. (Though they may prefer to stay with their existing E-mail system if that system is other than Microsoft Mail.) Vendors of other E-mail engines could still compete based on additional features or the capability to combine with technologies not directly offered by Microsoft. They could also devote their energies to excelling in front-end interface software for E-mail users. Software vendors are also known for their ingenuity and may come up with other ways to compete as well.

Microsoft offers forms designer capabilities with its Electronic Forms Designer software package. This software lets users design forms for simple things like telephone slips to more complex forms like purchase orders. The package includes form templates. Once forms are created, they can then be distributed to others by E-mail. The forms tool will have an intrinsic knowledge of the capabilities and constraints of Microsoft Mail, but it can also be used with AT&T's EasyLink and Hewlett-Packard's OpenMail systems, and any future E-mail systems that support Microsoft's MAPI.

One of the strengths of Electronic Forms Designer lies in its ability to be programmed. The package comes with a set of run-time libraries based on Microsoft's Visual Basic. This allows programmers to create a detailed routing scheme that permits data from other Microsoft applications to be inserted into the form that is being routed. For example, an enterprise-wide sales report could be routed to various sales managers in different locations who would insert their sales figures from Excel into the sales report. The completed sales report could then be distributed to all managers who need this information. This is a good example of how new tools are letting us find new ways to work.

17.5.1.3 DaVinci Mail

While DaVinci Mail is not nearly as widely-used as cc:Mail and Microsoft Mail, it has loyal users in what is considered a solid market share. DaVinci Mail is known for its ease-of-use and excellent support, and it also has many features that are comparable to the two top runners. Also in its favor is that Novell—with its large LAN market-share—owns a large percentage of DaVinci which was built based on Novell's MHS technology.

DaVinci Mail has some interesting features. One example is a spelling checker, which is surprisingly rare in E-mail programs. Another is its ability to search for a particular word or term and replace it—also unique in E-mail systems. DaVinci Mail also offers a feature which permits users to sort and search old messages by their context to other messages. This archiving capability is enabled by "conversation message threading" records.

DaVinci Mail is becoming more modularized. This will permit users to utilize DaVinci portions that they want and use other modules from operating systems or other E-mail packages. This seems like a smart move on the part of its developers.

17.5.1.4 BeyondMail

BeyondMail is available for DOS and Windows-based clients. BeyondMail supports Banyan Vines and Novell MHS mail engines. While it offers traditional E-mail features like mailing lists, basic editing, encryption, and administrative capabilities, it is primarily interesting for some of its more forward-looking aspects. These include the incorporation of forms, rules, and the ability to launch other programs.

The blending of rules and BeyondMail's ability to launch other programs can be a powerful combination and extremely useful for workflow projects. The combination of these two features permits the establishment of a system that could detect a particular type of message, manipulate the message's contents, and then automatically forward either the original message or its results to another E-mail user. Such a system could automate numerous operations that are repetitive in nature. Many workflow systems are based on concepts like these.

BeyondMail comes with some basic forms that are commonly used. It also comes with a form designer which permits users to design any unique type of form they may need. These forms are then used as the basis for E-mail messages. For example, a telephone message form can quickly be filled out to relay phone messages via E-mail. In the same way, forms for meeting minutes, customer support, or a variety of other purposes can also be quickly filled out by an individual and sent on their way.

BeyondMail's rules capability can be used in a variety of ways also. Many users utilize this language of rules and commands to manage incoming mail, providing instructions for sorting mail by subject, sender, or other criteria. The rules can also be used to enhance the message security of the system. One of the most interesting ways that the rules are being used is in connection with workflow and groupware projects.

17.5.1.5 Mail Packages for the Macintosh

Microsoft also provides a version of its E-mail package for Apple Computers. It is usually simply referred to as Microsoft Mail for the Mac. It provides connection between PCs and Macs through Apple Computer's AppleTalk protocol.

Another E-mail package for the Macintosh is QuickMail from CE Software. QuickMail is an AppleTalk-based E-mail system. Macintosh clients go through AppleTalk to communicate with the dedicated Mac mail server for QuickMail. The mail server stores messages and can be equipped with gateways to other networks. The system can communicate with PC clients with the installation of a LocalTalk card.

This communication can also occur through the use of separate mail servers, but communication is limited since the two mail servers are indeed quite separate. While users on the two separate mail servers can send each other mail through the use of a shared file area, they face some limitations. If Joe Smith is set up as a user on the DOS mail server and Jane Dow is established as a user on the Mac mail server, Joe can only read his mail from a DOS client, and Jane can only read her mail from a Mac client.

17.5.1.6 Other LAN-based E-mail Packages

The primary strength of the Network Mail for Vines package, the E-mail system for Banyan VINES, is its StreetTalk directory technology. This is a global naming service which many observers predict could be adapted to other network operating systems in the future. It is available for DOS, Windows, OS/2, and Macintosh clients, and it does not require a dedicated mail server on the network. Optional gateways connecting to mainframe, minicomputer, and X.400 E-mail systems are available.

WordPerfect Office constitutes WordPerfect's attempt to capitalize on having the world's most widely-used word processing software and extend its market presence. WordPerfect Office has a Windows version, but WordPerfect for DOS makes a good attempt to make DOS easier to use by providing menus that facilitate the use of other WordPerfect packages such as DrawPerfect. The WordPerfect Office package offers an E-mail system which offers some unique features such as subject security and the ability to delete a message that has been sent but not yet read.

Enable Software's Higgins software is probably best known for being one of the first groupware packages ever offered. As an E-mail package, one of its primary advantages is the fact that since it can be loaded as a simple TSR utility, it is easy to switch back and forth between Higgins and other programs.

Syzygy from Syzygy Development (pronounced "Sizz-a-gee") is another product that has some unique features. It is actually a combination of many programs or software modules that can facilitate the management of people and projects. Syzygy uses MHS to send and store messages and offers a variety of typical E-mail capabilities.

17.5.2 Mainframe and Minicomputer E-mail Systems

As mentioned earlier, our focus on mainframe and minicomputer systems will be on how they relate and interconnect with E-mail systems found in client/server environments. E-mail originated on mainframes and minicomputers since they were the first computers in wide-spread use. Now, many enterprises need to interconnect their mainframe E-mail users with the growing number of LAN-based E-mail users.

17.5.2.1 IBM E-mail Systems

3270-type terminals on IBM mainframes were used to send and receive E-mail messages. There are two E-mail systems offered by IBM:

- The Professional Office System (PROFS) runs under VM/CMS and is used on many 4341 and 4381 mainframes.
- The Distributed Office Support System (DISOSS) runs under MVS and DOS and is found on many 308x and 309x series mainframes.

Although PROFS and DISOSS were quite dissimilar in appearance originally, IBM has worked to make them look more alike and share similar features. Much of this effort was due to IBM's effort to have most of their systems follow the Common User Interface guidelines established by their System Application Architecture. Using Systems Network Architecture Distribution System (SNADS), IBM is also internetworking PROFS and DISOSS nodes to permit the two packages to exchange messages and computer files.

A number of third-party packages are available to link IBM mainframe E-mail systems with LAN-based ones. But the best-known one is Soft*Switch from a vendor also named Soft*Switch. The package runs on an IBM mainframe and connects to over 50 different E-mail packages. Soft*Switch also has software that integrates directories from various E-mail systems by converting them to common format.

Retix and Touch Communications are other vendors that are active in connecting mainframe and minicomputer E-mail with other mail systems. They both provide gateway software that is used by many E-mail vendors. Digital Equipment Corporation provides software to connect various E-mail packages as well.

ADR/E-MAIL from Applied Data Research (ADR) runs under IBM's MVS, DOS, and OS operating systems, but requires either CICS or ADR's ROSCOE teleprocessing monitor to operate. Another example of third-party E-mail for IBM mainframes is provided by Verimation, a subsidiary of Volvo, which created MEMO for in-house E-mail purposes. Verimation made the product available in the market after other companies expressed interest in it.

OracleMail from Oracle Corporation also runs on IBM mainframes—as well as on a variety of computing platforms. This product is also available for wireless and portable E-mail systems. It is capable of connecting, via Oracle's PalmLink, with Sharp's Wizard which is a pocket-size organizer. The PalmLink technology connects Wizard with either a Windows-equipped PC or Macintosh as long as Oracle's OracleCard program is also installed. Using the PostCard API, E-mail functions can be added to send copies of Oracle database documents to others on the network. This configuration can also be used not only for E-mail, but also as a data entry vehicle for Oracle databases.

17.5.2.2 Digital Equipment Corporation E-mail Systems

Digital Equipment Corporation also offers two different E-mail systems. Rather than being aimed at different computers within the corporation, however, the difference is in the features:

- •VMSmail is a simple E-mail system
- •All-in-One is an integrated office package offering more than just E-mail

In addition to E-mail, All-in-One offers such capabilities as word processing, database access, and decision support tools. Along with its multiplicity of features, All-in-One can be used by more than just VMS clients, including such platforms as DOS, OS/2, and the Macintosh. It is capable of running not only on DECnet, but also on LAN Manager, MS-Net, NetBIOS, TCP/IP, and AppleTalk. Gateways are available for connecting to PROFS, Telex, MCI Mail, X.400, VMSmail, SMTP, and SNADS. Portable PCs equipped with Mobilizer can use All-in-One's E-mail services using a modem or other line that supports Digital's Local Area Transport protocol.

Digital provides All-in-One Desktop for MS-DOS which permits PC users to access all of the All-in-One applications. There are also a number of third-party vendors who provide software connectivity between All-in-One and other systems.

An example of a third-party vendor that provides E-mail for Digital computers is Alisa Systems with its AlisaMail. This product offers X.400 gateways as well as gateways to PROFS, DISOSS, and UUCP mail.

17.5.2.3 Minicomputer E-mail Systems

Hewlett-Packard provides HPDeskmanager for its line of 9000 minicomputers. This integrated office package offers such capabilities as time management and filing software as well as E-mail services. Gateways can connect HPDeskmanager with X.400 and Telex among other systems.

Data General provides a package called Comprehensive Electronic Office (CEO) for its minicomputers equipped with DG's AOS/VS operating system. It has gateways for DISOSS, MCI Mail, and, of course, X.400

among other E-mail systems. CEO is also an integrated office package offering word processing, business graphics, decision support tools and database access.

17.6   PUBLIC E-MAIL SYSTEMS

Many public E-mail systems can be accessed from a variety of platforms including personal computers, workstations, minicomputers, and mainframes. A user can connect to them through a dial-up modem or a packet-switching network. The great majority of users of public E-mail systems are private individuals. However, many businesses use public E-mail as well. An example of why a business would use a public E-mail system is to obtain information from various databases and to make business travel arrangements. Some of the public E-mail systems have excellent airline reservation systems available, permitting small (and large) businesses to gain access to the best pricing and scheduling information for their needs. Many financial and news sources—such as stock market prices—are available through public E-mail systems which are used by businesses as well.

17.6.1   EasyLink

Despite all the advertisements for Compuserve, MCI Mail, Prodigy, and others, EasyLink is one of the most widely-used public E-mail system in the U.S., carrying over eight million messages a month for its owner, AT&T. This reportedly accounts for about 30% of the public E-mail market.

Actually, a figure like this may be comparing apples and oranges since these different systems offer a broad variety of other services in addition to E-mail. Some people may use a particular system just to access its information resources rather than to send electronic messages to other people. But for those individuals primarily interested in E-mail, EasyLink seems to have the lead.

Some of the information bases that it provides access to include the following:

- The Official Airlines Guide (OAG) providing airline schedules and reservation capabilities
- The FYI news service
- Infocom information databases

17.6.2   MCI Mail

MCI Mail from MCI International provides only messaging services. Using MCI Mail, one can be connected via MCI Mail gateways to many other messaging systems. End users have an 800 number they use to reach MCI Mail and payment is make by the number, size, and types of transactions, rather than by the month or the time spent on-line as with other services.

MCI Mail was originally aimed at private individuals. However, MCI International is also aiming for corporate customers by adding capabilities like bulletin boards where a company can post and update information for all of its employees to read.

There are some PC programs that automate MCI Mail usage. Two are Lotus Express from Lotus Corp, and Desktop Express which was purchased by MCI from Solutions, Inc. These programs permit users to do such things as work off-line on their messages and then upload outgoing messages in a batch operation. Incoming messages can also be downloaded in a batch operation. There are also MCI Mail front ends like Future Soft Engineering which operate as scripts for popular communications packages.

17.6.3   CompuServe

CompuServe, from CompuServe Inc., offers both E-mail and other types of services. Some of the things that can be accomplished with CompuServe are making travel reservations, reading news services, checking financial statistics, searching databases, getting technical support for computer packages, and joining conferences on a wide variety of topics. CompuServe offers the InfoPlex E-mail system for corporations. CompuServe also connects to the Internet.

18

E-MAIL STANDARDS AND PROTOCOLS

18.1 THE IMPORTANCE OF STANDARDS IN GENERAL

The use of standards can make a significant difference in how well something is accepted. Standards can make a technology or an infrastructure easier to use and therefore, more useful. International standards ensure that a worldwide date and timing system is in place. If it is 9:00 A.M. on January 1, 1994 in New York City, international standards let us determine what time (and day) it is in Tokyo or Singapore. Standards play a vital role in commerce by establishing weight and measurement systems.

18.1.1 Standards Benefit the Interstate Highway and Railroad Systems

The U.S. interstate highway system was built according to a number of established standards that individual states followed. One simple example is that interstate highways that run east and west end with an even number (e.g., Interstate 80), while those that run north and south end with an odd number (e.g., I-95).

Train tracks adhere to a standard as well, so that trains can run on the tracks of different railroad companies throughout the U.S. Tracks were not always built according to one standard. Even after rail companies realized the importance of establishing a standard, two competing standards fought it out for a while. A few tracks which adhere to the abandoned standard still exist in some parts of the country. They are only local lines and are retained simply for local transportation and for their tourist value.

303

18.1.2   Standards Facilitate Telephone Communication

When telephone technology first became available, multiple companies provided telephone service. A telephone company providing communication services in a city like Boston in the early days of telephones was primarily interested in connecting as many individuals and businesses in the Boston area as possible. The systems and techniques they were providing were different from those provided by companies in other large cities. These communication companies were in their infancy. They had many problems trying to promote their new technology and make a profit. Coming to a decision regarding which particular company's technology should be established as the standard for all of them was more than could be handled by the separate firms. It took U.S. federal government intervention to settle the matter. Telephone standards permit us to call anyone in the nation, and in other countries easily.

18.1.3   Lack of Computing Standards Delay Progress Significantly

The lack of communication standards in the computer industry has severely delayed the progress that could have been made if standards had existed. Ever since WANs have existed, proprietary communication systems offered by individual vendors have not been able to communicate readily with proprietary communication systems from other vendors. The same is true with LAN technology and with E-mail technology.

Different E-mail systems can more easily communicate with each other if they adhere to international standards which have been established for this specific purpose. If the E-mail systems do not adhere to these standards—that is, if they are proprietary in nature—then special gateway software must be provided for one vendor's E-mail system to communicate with another vendor's system.

Some large corporations have between fifteen and twenty different networking technologies installed in different locations throughout the enterprise. They may have up to a dozen or more different E-mail systems on them—systems that were originally installed just to meet the local needs of a particular department or division. Now it is becoming increasingly important for these individual local E-mail systems to be able to communicate with each other.

Companies that are just now beginning to install E-mail systems should think about their long-range needs and look at systems that adhere to standards. Companies that already have a wide variety of different E-mail systems should begin to consolidate them. Many enterprises have already analyzed their needs, selected the two, three, or four

E-mail systems they feel they need, and are replacing the remaining E-mail systems with one of the selected enterprise-standard systems.

18.1.4 Standards for E-mail

As in any other area, E-mail has its de facto and de jure standards. The Message Handling Service offered by Novell is a de facto standard for transporting E-mail messages, while X.400 is a de jure standard. X.400 is sponsored by the CCITT and supported by the ISO MOTIS Messaging Standards. X.500 is a de jure standard for directory services that is sponsored by CCITT. Additional defacto E-mail and messaging standards include Vendor-Independent Messaging (VIM) and Microsoft Messaging (MAPI)—both described later in this chapter—while related ones are also appearing.

Use of International standards like X.400 and X.500 in products is expected to grow dramatically. A program management director for electronic messaging at International Data Corporation said they expect to see X.400 passing the use of proprietary approaches by 1996.

Large corporations and government enterprises like the U.S. Navy consider the X.400 and X.500 standards as critical elements in their long-range strategic plans. For example, Luther Blackwell, a spokesman for the U.S. Navy's Integrated Interior Communications and Control Project, and a network systems engineer with that project, said that X.400 is vitally important from a communications point of view because a ship is envisioned as a node in a global network. The Navy will use X.400 as the common protocol to permit messaging to take place between many different kinds of ships as well as huge numbers of shore installations which already have many different E-mail systems installed. X.400 will be the intermediate mechanism permitting the diverse systems to inter-communicate.

18.2 THE X.400 E-MAIL STANDARD

The X.400 Interpersonal Messaging System standard was established so that any E-mail system that adheres to it would be able to interconnect and exchange messages with any other E-mail system that also adheres to it. X.400 was developed by CCITT. The X.400 standard is considered as residing at layer seven—the application layer—of the ISO Open Systems Interconnection Reference Model.

In X.400 addressing, every destination has only one X.400 address. This address is stored in the header of the X.400 E-mail message. An X.400 address works its way down from identifying the country right down to identifying the individual user. The obvious advantage of the

X.400 standard is the interoperability that it promises. Anyone in the world hooked into the system could be reached.

X.400 is large and complex which contributes to both its advantages and disadvantages. In its thoroughness, X.400 specifies—in detail—how a message should be structured and handled. The X.400 specification is also designed to permit the integration of voice mail, fax, and telex services.

X.400 specifies both a public and a private mail service.* Administrative Domains (ADMs) are for public mail service and Private Domains (PRDMs)—as the name implies—are for private mail. Administrative Domains are public mail services that are meant to be administered by authorized government or telecommunications organizations, for example, the Postal, Telephone, & Telegraph (PT&Ts) of many foreign governments. This role is important because the Administrative Domains maintain a directory of all the Private Domains that are registered in their region. Private Domains are maintained by private organizations such as universities, companies, and individual government agencies.

Among the disadvantages, there are slightly different versions of X.400; for example, the standard specifications adopted in 1984 are different from those adopted in 1988. The 1984 standard could only move text information; movement of binary information was added with the 1988 standard. Also, there are different implementations of the different versions. Fine-tuning, however, generally smoothes out these incompatibilities.

Another disadvantage of X.400 is that it does not have the widespread acceptance of other E-mail approaches such as the Message Handling Service (MHS) and the Simple Mail Transport Protocol (SMTP). These are widely used defacto standards. However, the problem of lack of widespread acceptance could certainly be overcome in time.

Additionally, directory services were not built into X.400 when it was conceived. The international standards for directory services are specified by X.500. However, there are many concerned parties who are working to ensure that the two standards will work together and evolve more smoothly together in the future.

18.2.1 Organizational Support for X.400

The X.400 standard is given support by ISO through its MOTIS (Message-Oriented Text Interchange Systems) protocol which is quite similar to the X.400 series of recommendations.

---

*X.400 is a *voluntary* international standard. Therefore, it is implemented to various degrees by individual enterprises and countries.

Additional support for the X.400 standard comes from the X.400 API Association (XAPIA). The goal of XAPIA is to establish a set of multiplatform common Mail Calls to permit various E-mail front ends to communicate with various E-mail back ends.

18.2.2   Industry Support for X.400 and X.500

There are many large enterprises that take an active stand in the support of de jure standards like X.400 and X.500. General Motors and The Boeing Company, active in supporting ISO standards, are also active in supporting the X.400 and X.500 standards from CCITT. They feel it will be a tremendous advantage to large enterprises like themselves when products can more easily interconnect because they adhere to international standards.

Making a blanket statement saying that all sites should pursue a specific approach is always difficult, but an installation that adheres to international standards such as X.400 and X.500 within its E-mail system is bound to be better off in the long-term. The international standards for messaging and for directory services will permit an enterprise to participate fully in the future growth of inter-enterprise messaging. While X.400 may not be as widely-used as other transport services today, it is gaining ground. X.500 use is growing, too.

18.3   DE FACTO E-MAIL STANDARDS

There are de facto standards for various aspects of E-mail. For example, there are de facto standards for E-mail front ends and for E-mail transport agents.

18.3.1   Transport Services

The primary transport agents on existing E-mail LANs are the Message Handling Service (MHS) from Action Technologies and the UNIX-based Simple Mail Transfer Protocol (SMTP), though there are additional proprietary ones, as well as some X.400-based ones. X.400 and SMTP are often regarded as coming the closest to establishing a "common language" for E-mail systems. MHS and SMTP are the most widely used defacto E-mail transport standards.

18.3.1.1   Message Handling Service (MHS)

The Message Handling Service (MHS) is a protocol translation program that was originally developed by Action Technologies. The vendor originally sold it to be used on Novell networks. However, Novell now develops and sells MHS for NetWare. Novell runs MHS as a NetWare loadable module on its own network PC, called the MHS server. Action Technologies now sells MHS for network operating systems other than NetWare. Novell's predominance in the networking world has made MHS a widely-used E-mail system.

The MHS server must be set up by an administrator with information about local and remote users, applications, and any additional services such as MCI Mail or a fax gateway. A gateway can be set up on the MHS server permitting it to communicate with remote systems. Different types of devices can share E-mail through an MHS server including combinations of DOS, OS/2, Microsoft Windows, and Macintosh platforms.

Many E-mail programs support MHS one way or another. Some come with built-in support for MHS, while others require an MHS gateway. Some packages require that MHS already be installed before they will function. Buyers should check carefully with vendors to determine what the current requirements of their E-mail software packages are. CompuServe, the commercial-service E-mail network, offers an MHS hub, as does Novell. Such hub configurations mean that anyone with an MHS-supported E-mail system can exchange messages with other MHS-supported users.

While MHS is used in many installations today, there are a number of reasons why it may not maintain its market lead. Competitive pressure from other vendors is certainly one important factor; however, the growing, world-wide interest in international standards may be an even more important one. Just as standards contributed to the success of the telephone, standards could also make a vital contribution to permitting E-mail to be as convenient to use as telephones are today. As a result, MHS may lose a lot of ground to the X.400 international E-mail standard in the future.

18.3.1.2 The Simple Mail Transport Protocol (SMTP)

The UNIX-based Simple Mail Transport Protocol is the established transport agent for E-mail on the Internet. SMTP has the following two basic addressing methods:

- •UUCP
  UUCP stands for UNIX-to-UNIX Copy. This approach is also called "Bang," the name being derived from the exclamation point that separates the individual elements in the address of the message—which can be quite numerous. UUCP is an asynchronous communi-

cation link through which messages jump from one machine to the next as the systems make connections.

In the UUCP approach, the sender must specify the user's name and the entire path that the message will take. This requires a knowledge of all the names and hierarchies of all intervening "hops" or intermediate store-and-forward stations. An example of the format is "hub1!regionalhub2!regionalhub3!recipient." If there are twelve or fifteen separate store-and-forward stations, an address in the UUCP approach can become quite cumbersome. There is the additional problem that one of the specified links could be out of operation temporarily.

• DNS

DNS, the Domain Name System, also known as Internet addressing, maintains a directory of unique node names. Using this approach, the sender needs to specify the user name and that user's home machine. A simplified example of the format is "recipient@homemachine." In reality, the format is more complicated because the "homemachine" portion generally consists of the server or host used by the recipient— a domain and subdomain which specifies exactly where the recipient is located. Therefore, a more realistic example of the format of DNS is "recipient@host.subdomain.domain." Elements within a DNS address are separated by periods as opposed to the exclamation points used in the UUCP approach.

18.3.1.3 Current E-mail Interconnection Techniques

Until the X.400 standard is widely-used, various gateways will be the primary way to connect different E-mail systems to each other. As mentioned earlier, many vendors provide gateways to MHS and X.400 for their E-mail products.

There are also some independent E-mail gateway-vendors—that is vendors who provide E-mail gateways only, not an E-mail package. Their E-mail gateway is used with E-mail systems from other vendors. For example, Computer Mail Services (CMS) based in Southfield, MI, offers a gateway called M-Bridge which is an SMTP to MCI Mail gateway and S-Bridge which is an MHS to SMTP gateway. By providing these gateways, CMS is able to let sites interconnect UNIX-based E-mail systems with PC- and LAN-based E-mail systems.

The primary role of gateways is to translate address headers between two different E-mail systems. This must be accomplished while leaving the actual message intact. The problem of providing gateways for many distinctly different E-mail systems is that when individual packages change, the corresponding gateways must change also. Some sites report that some gateway approaches can seriously degrade in performance when traffic requirements become very heavy.

18.3.1.4 Backbones

E-mail backbones are also being used to solve the problem of interconnecting different E-mail systems. When a backbone approach is used, each individual E-mail system needs to have a gateway to the backbone connection.

An example of how this works is provided by Retix's Open Server 400 mail server. Each individual E-mail system's Retix gateway maps the addresses of its own mail system to that of X.400. This scheme makes the whole process seem simple to the end user. As far as the end users are concerned, they are able to connect to remote E-mail systems using the same familiar techniques they use to connect to local E-mail users.

18.3.2 De facto Front-end E-mail Standards

Some of the de facto standards that are most well-known refer to front-ends such as Microsoft's proprietary MAPI for windows and the multivendor-supported cross platform approach known as the VIM API. The primary difference between these two approaches is that while MAPI takes a more generic approach which requires compliance with various Microsoft APIs, VIM provides individual specifications for connecting with specific E-mail engines—regarded as a more vendor-independent approach. Users do not have to be compliant with one specific vendor's API on both the front-end and back-end software modules.

VIM's approach is illustrated in Figure 18.1.

18.3.2.1 Vendor-Independent Messaging (VIM)

In order to make the VIM approach work, each individual vendor who wants to be involved will need to provide the "hooks" or interconnection software specified by VIM. These hooks will connect to that vendor's back-end E-mail service, or E-mail engine—which provides services such as message store, transport, and directory services. (See Figure 18.1) For example, Lotus Corporation offers implementations of VIM for Windows and OS/2 clients to connect with the cc:Mail engine and with Lotus Notes.

Apple Computer provides its own Open Collaborative Environment (OCE) E-mail enabling system. (Apple Computer's authentication system

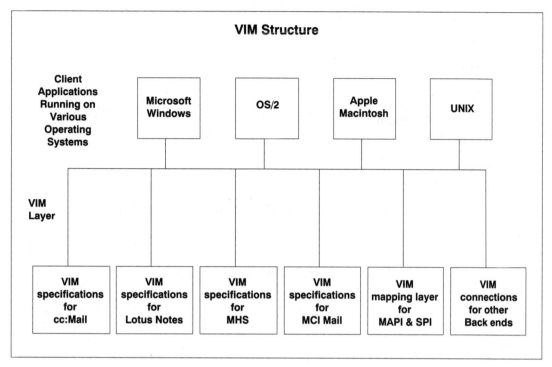

Figure 18.1 Basic structure of VIM.

was discussed in the introductory E-mail chapter.) Apple also provides support for VIM so that Apple users can access mail engines on other platforms.

18.3.2.2 Microsoft's MAPI

The MAPI approach consists of the following software components:

- An API that specifies system calls for invoking such E-mail functions as send and receive,
- Dynamic Link Library routines which enable E-mail services and interfaces to E-mail engines,
- The Service Provider Interface (SPI) which is the component which actually performs the interface to E-mail back ends.

The MAPI architecture (see Figure 18.2) is designed so that any Windows application that is compliant with MAPI is able to use capabilities in the DLL to connect with any E-mail backend that is compliant with

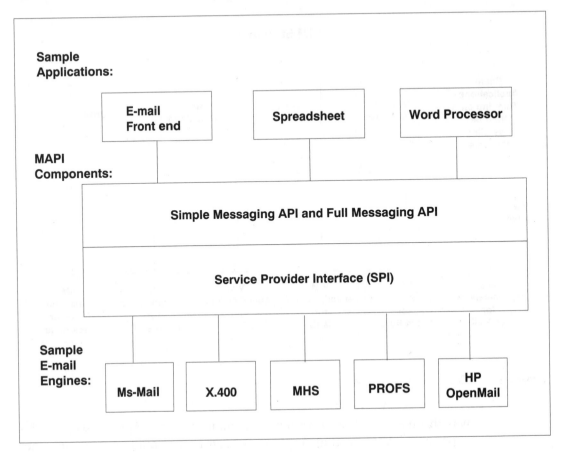

Figure 18.2 Basic structure of MAPI.

SPI. MAPI specifies over 60 operating-system calls that invoke common mail actions such as send, receive, and management services. A subset of these calls—referred to as "Simple MAPI"—was built into Workgroup for Windows, but it only works with the Microsoft mail engine. The full MAPI implementation—appropriately referred to as "Full MAPI"—is available in Windows for DOS and in NT.

Lotus Corporation and other firms plan to support both VIM and MAPI. Lotus, for example, provides a system that permits VIM-compliant applications to talk to MAPI-compliant mail engines. It accomplishes this by remapping VIM-specified calls to MAPI requirements.

Vendors that have committed to providing SPI support for their E-mail engines include AT&T, Banyan, Digital Equipment, Hewlett-Packard, Novell, SoftSwitch, and WordPerfect.

Some observers feel that what the end-user portion of E-mail does or does not do is not the critical factor in E-mail. They feel that the most important feature of an E-mail package is the ability of that particular E-mail front end to be able to connect with a variety of E-mail back ends as these packages become more and more modularized.

18.4 DIRECTORY TECHNIQUES

18.4.1 Directory Services

The purpose of a directory service is to find out where users are located. Directories contain user names and information related to how to find individual user names. With small networks there are few addressing problems since a directory can easily list the name of every user. As systems grow larger, so do the problems.

If a system has several "post offices" (mail or directory centers), each post office can stay current by exchanging messages about changes in their individual directories. But the addressing problems become very significant as the size of systems continues to increase. As additional users are added, a large portion of network traffic can be consumed by such a system because of excessive messages to change directories.

Another problem is that in many of today's systems, a user's network address is not necessarily the same as his or her E-mail address. This means that as users move around in an organization, administrators have to update two separate addresses for each user: the network address and the E-mail address. This can become a time-consuming, labor-intensive process.

Various approaches to directory services are quite unique. For example, the ability of an E-mail system to read network operating system files can facilitate the work of maintaining a directory of users. Another example in this regard is provided by Novell. Novell has a Bindery file—a file that the NetWare network operating system uses to identify its users—which contains basic information about each user's directories and other network setup information related to each user. If a site has NetWare and the site's E-mail system can access the NetWare Bindery file, information for its E-mail directory can be accessed from there, saving the E-mail administrator a lot of work.

Other approaches include Banyan VINEs distributed naming service called StreetTalk and Lotus's cc:Mail which has evolving directory update propagation features. One important aspect of Banyan's StreetTalk is that users' StreetTalk ID is both their network address and their E-mail address, simplifying network synchronization just as Novell's bindery file does.

The primary solution to trying to interconnect and/or synchronize directories from different E-mail packages is to use E-mail gateways. The most widely used gateways are from Soft Switch, in Wayne, PA, and Retix, based in Santa Monica, CA. Retix is becoming an important vendor, not only for its E-mail gateways, but for its other interoperability solutions as well.

SoftSwitch provides programs that can integrate directories from a variety of systems. These programs bring in the directory listings from the diverse systems, translate them into a common format, and then export them again.

If an E-mail user wants to send a message to a recipient and does not know his or her address, this can be quite a problem. On well-maintained local systems, questioning the local directory may reveal the address. But no single solution exists if the intended recipient is outside the local site. Often, E-mail users utilize the telephone to obtain the recipient's E-mail address.

Most of the large enterprises that have many diverse E-mail systems installed in different parts of the organization are actively consolidating them. At one time, Aetna Life & Casualty Insurance in Hartford, CT had nine different E-mail systems installed in different locations. That is not unusual for a company as large as Aetna where there are many sophisticated computer users who want to use technologies like E-mail. Aetna is in the process of consolidating the number of E-mail packages, and in 1993 it had reduced the number from nine to five. The five remaining systems were cc:Mail, Digital Equipment's All-in-1, IBM's PROFS, Microsoft Mail for DOS, and Microsoft Mail for the Mac. To connect the different E-mail systems internally, Aetna uses a SoftSwitch messaging backbone. They use X.400 gateways to communicate with outside companies.

18.4.2 A Global E-mail Directory

Work is actively progressing on a global addressing system that could be accessible to everyone world-wide. It would contain the E-mail (and other) addressing information of everyone who *wanted* to be listed. The address of the intended recipient would be provided to the questioning sender very quickly and address updates would not consume an excessive amount of overall network traffic. The system would not be an invasion of privacy since only individuals who want to be part of the system would be included in it.

These are just some of the goals of the X.500 Directory Service from the CCITT. It is still in its early stages, but its future importance cannot be denied.

18.5   THE X.500 DIRECTORY STANDARD

Whether a discussion of the X.500 Directory Standard should be included within an E-mail discussion is certainly debatable. The reason it is debatable is because the directory standard can be used for much more than E-mail. It can be used to locate people, computers, and networks in a variety of distributed computing applications. The reason why the discussion of X.500 is being included here is because a useful integration of E-mail message delivery techniques and the X.500 directory standard could become a powerful combination.

18.5.1   X.500 Goals

As mentioned earlier, one of the goals of the X.500 Directory Service is that anyone listed in it would be accessible to everyone else using this service on a world-wide basis. It would provide the E-mail and any other addressing information of people wishing to be listed.

The naming capability of X.500 goes beyond E-mail, encompassing system messages such as file and printer commands. Observers speculate that the X.500 specification could contribute to such services as on-line "Yellow Pages."

X.500 is designed to be able to service extremely large, distributed systems and provide many services. In order to meet its ambitious goals, X.500 is a large and complex protocol. As the technology improves and more vendors provide X.500 products, X.500 implementations are expected to become less expensive.

The obvious advantage of such a global addressing scheme is the increased accessibility of intended-recipients. However, critics claim that is also one of its disadvantages.

18.5.2   Concerns About X.500 and How They are Being Addressed

While a company may want their suppliers and customers to have access to their employees, they may not want to provide such access to competitors. This can be controlled by managing the directories like internal telephone directories.

Addressing such concerns, a consortium of seventeen E-mail vendors formed the North American Directory Forum (NADF) and issued a User Bill of Rights related to listings in the X.500 Public Directory. The rights are as follows:

- To not be listed
- To be informed when a user's entry is created

- To examine the entry
- To correct any errors in the entry
- To have remote access to data in the entry
- To be assured that the listing will comply with national laws (U.S., Canadian, etc., as the case may be) regulating privacy and access to information
- To receive timely fulfillment of all these rights

18.6   WHY SOME VENDORS AVOID DE JURE STANDARDS

Vendors are in the business of making money. They generally provide products for which they see the greatest need. Many vendors say that is why they have not provided products that meet international de jure standards. They say that they cannot detect a great demand for such products from the bulk of the marketplace.

Vendors also provide products which may keep customers buying their specific products. Another way of putting that is that customers would be *required* to continue buying their products. It is known as "customer lock-in" and some of the most well-known, prestigious, and wealthiest vendors have been criticized as using this tactic. Seemingly, though, as long as customers are willing to buy such products, vendors will continue to use this approach.

These are not the only reasons why vendors provide proprietary products. Sometimes, they themselves are "locked into" product lines that have evolved over the years. In addition, vendors are often able to provide services within their own proprietary lines that would be extremely difficult for them to provide in products that were compliant with de jure standard products. Also, while many users hope for the success of de jure standards, many of these standards do not seem to provide the best approaches, and they certainly do take a long, long time before they are available. As a result of all these factors, this book will certainly not be too harsh on vendors who are providing their own proprietary approaches. However, neither will this book defend vendors who purposely "lock-in" customers. Customer loyalty which must be forced via "lock-in" sounds more like a "bullying-type" of company rather than a talented one which attracts customers through creative innovations.

Many vendors are providing proprietary products because they believe they truly provide unique added-value. Telling the true motives of vendors is difficult, but at times vendors are more easily able to provide additional capabilities through proprietary systems than they are through ones that strictly follow de jure standards. The primary point that many vendors make with E-mail systems is that packages built to work across multiple platforms forfeit the specificity and, therefore, the richness of advanced features. They claim that installations working with relatively new combinations such as complex workflow systems will probably prefer to work in an overall environment where all components are offered by a single vendor. Enterprises should take a careful look at that suggestion, depending upon their own needs. The reverse might be true. An enterprise may not be able to gain all the functionality it requires by staying within the confines of a single vendor's offerings.

Although many vendors who primarily provide proprietary products are beginning to offer products that are compliant with de jure standards, a few vendors stand out with their strong support of de jure standards. The following section will indicate those vendors who have made the strongest contributions to products that are compliant with dejure standards. Some of these companies have dedicated their work to creating standards-compliant products and to helping to promote the use of international standards.

18.6.2   Vendors Taking a Pro-Active Role with De Jure Standards

While most major E-mail vendors either currently provide gateways to the X.400 standard, or have plans to do so, a number of vendors have been particularly active in providing products that comply with international, de jure standards. Retix is one name that comes to mind immediately. This company has been active in providing numerous communications products that comply with standards. Retix provides compliance with X.400 messaging standards. The vendor is providing a migration path to X.500 as well. Retix does not provide end user interface software for E-mail, rather, it specializes in providing connectivity and other features.

The Wollongong Group is another vendor active in international standards. Wollongong's PathWay Messaging system incorporates integrated X.400 message handling and a full implementation of the X.500 Directory standard, introduced in March, 1993, PathWay Messaging, targeted E-mail users currently utilizing TCP/IP as a backbone for network transport but interested in moving to open systems based on the OSI architecture. PathWay Messaging will permit administrators to expand their E-mail systems continually without constantly having to add complicated gateways in order to connect dissimilar proprietary E-mail systems.

18.7   THE FUTURE OF E-MAIL

The future for E-mail is quite exciting with new "smart E-mail" packages and mail-enabled applications. Vendors are adding capabilities to their

E-mail packages all the time. For example, many vendors are adding E-mail capabilities to other types of software packages like spreadsheets. Software that has had E-mail capabilities added to it is referred to as mail-enabled software. Such software is generating a whole new area of application software as described in Chapter 19 and particularly in Chapter 20, which discusses new combinations of software.

19

GROUPWARE AND WORKGROUP COMPUTING

19.1 NEW COMBINATIONS OF SOFTWARE AND WORK SHARING APPROACHES

Among the most exciting developments in computing today are the new combinations of technologies that are being developed. After all, one of the key characteristics of client/server and peer-to-peer, networked, and distributed computing is the combination of new technologies. The emergence of new ways to combine various modules of technology to achieve new goals is certainly going to increase significantly over the next few years.

Equally important is the ability for people to work *together* more easily as a result of these new technologies. Since people's desktop computers can be networked together, the projects they are working on can now be networked together. An employee's workplace no longer has to be an individual, isolated desk where he or she works alone to accomplish an objective. That employee's workplace now can be an electronic desk where the work objective is shared by co-workers. Software such as groupware and workgroup computing packages demonstrate this new ability for co-workers to work cooperatively to accomplish business objectives.

Primary enablers of these new combinations are the advances in messaging and other communication techniques. Messaging and E-mail are generally the basis for various workgroup computing packages. Groupware is possible because networking and software that uses networking approaches can connect separate individuals into a communicating, cooperative group. This concept carries with it tremendous ramifications. The use of networking will expand dramatically and change the way business is done. A primary example is Electronic Data Interchange where E-mail is being combined with transaction processing, offering tremendous advantages to companies.

Packages that combine various computing technologies are referred to by different names. Sometimes the names refer to approaches that are quite different, but sometimes different names are used to refer to basically the same approach. Again, during a time when technology is still emerging, one must define terms to ensure that everyone is using the same language—or referring to the same concepts. Some of the most common terms being used to refer to new software combinations are workgroup computing, groupware, collaborative computing, workflow, and intelligent E-mail. This chapter will concentrate on groupware and workgroup computing; the next chapter will discuss workflow, intelligent E-mail, and mail-enabled packages.

Research on collaborative computing under the name Computer-Supported Cooperative Work has been continuing in universities and other research centers for many years. E-mail, teleconferencing, and office information support systems were among the earliest research efforts of CSCW. Subsequent work included research into tools that would support work operations performed in separate locations and work that was spread over a period of time.

Such tools and techniques are an important part of the re-engineering process going on in many companies today. Firms are using these approaches to redesign outmoded business procedures that are no longer efficient. Of course firms must be alert to the dangers of using these new techniques to automate all procedures only *as they now exist*. These firms must also examine existing procedures to see if all of the currently existing steps are still needed. Newly available techniques may permit some steps in the business procedure to be eliminated completely, while many other steps are automated, creating a completely new way to achieve the business objective.

19.2   AN OVERVIEW OF GROUPWARE

A variety of packages referred to as groupware are currently available. Groupware and workflow packages (which are discussed in the next chapter) are quite similar. Notes from Lotus Corporation was the first prominent example of groupware software. When first introduced, it was greeted with great interest, but firms needed several years of experimenting with it to realize how useful this approach could be.

Due to its unique nature, Lotus Corporation's Notes will be covered in more detail than other products. Notes provides a good indication of the kind of direction that this type of software is taking. Notes also shows how groupware can combine different types of applications and share information. Other groupware packages are available, but Notes has specific characteristics—such as being based on a database concept—that make it unique.

19.2.1 A Definition of Groupware

Groupware is basically software that is designed to facilitate the work of a group of users who are connected by a network. The users cooperate with each other using the capabilities of the groupware software which acts to coordinate the activities of the group. One example of groupware is software that permits collaborative writing. Each participating user can make changes to the document, subject to the approval of other members of the group. Users can also insert comments into the document. Other examples include software that permits members of the group to create a database of shared documents or to retrieve documents from a database of shared documents.

E-mail functions are an important part of groupware. Standards are emerging to facilitate the use of E-mail within applications. Standard ways of moving messages across a network and standard programming techniques for implementing E-mail in programs will further encourage the growth of groupware products and the integration of E-mail within a wide variety of applications.

19.2.2 Groupware Features

Most workflow or collaborative computing systems are not delivered, ready to use, with a flow of work carefully outlined. This type of software is available with tools and features that permit the using site to *tailor* the tools and features to accomplish what it wants to achieve. Enterprises adapt the tools to their own specific needs. The tools and capabilities of workflow packages provide facilities that can be worked into the unique needs of the organization.

All kinds of existing packages are beginning to be equipped with automated, intelligent features like routing and the ability to initiate other actions. Triggers are now being built into server databases (triggers can automatically initiate other programs and actions). Similar types of capabilities will be built into more database, word processing, spreadsheet, document management, and desktop operating systems. The process of building cross-communication intelligence into different types of software as well as integrating different types of software is just beginning. It will become an important trend in the future.

19.2.3 Scripting

Most workflow packages today involve the use of scripting, which is basically a set of instructions to an application. Scripting could be considered a type of programming language, but it is not quite the same. A script generally tells an existing application (like a spreadsheet or word processing program) to perform a series of steps. A script is similar to a macro which in the PC environment is a series of steps that are recorded and stored using a short key code.*

Scripting generally involves the talents of a programmer, though some end users are becoming adept with writing scripts also. Certainly, we will see packages that enable end users to develop their own workflow routines easily. GUI-type tools for scripting that an end user can use are already available. The results of the GUI-type tool are generally processed by another software product which generates scripting type statements. Additional ease-of-use approaches for permitting end users to create their own workflow packages are expected in the future.

19.3 NOTES

What makes Notes unique among other groupware packages is that it uses a combination of a high-security E-mail and database capabilities. These two features permit users to share, organize, and archive ideas with others in a workgroup. The database capabilities combined with E-mail let users build message databases for transmission over enterprise-wide networks.

The initial version of Lotus Notes offered basic routing and workflow capabilities. A subsequent version, Version 3.0, included capabilities to facilitate the coordination of people working in different database environments. It also provided centralized forms templates, forms-based action buttons, additional signature control, and macros that allow

---

*In assembly language and C coding, a macro is a series of instructions which can be called and executed by invoking the name of the macro—a short name assigned to the series of instructions.

periodic updates. Although the initial version of Notes required that users continually query it for updates, Version 3.0 automatically sent messages to users based on their profiles or activities. Version 3.0 also permitted Notes to operate on Macintosh and UNIX platforms as well as on OS/2 and Microsoft Window's platforms.

One of the largest users of Notes is Anderson Consulting. In fact, Anderson Consulting was one of the early pioneers with this type of technology, and it has really been profitable for them. Anderson Consulting is a $2.3 billion management and information processing consulting firm with over 25,000 employees world-wide. Anderson Consulting and its parent firm, Arthur Anderson, the large accounting consulting firm, purchased 20,000 copies of Lotus Notes. Their interests went beyond E-mail to knowledge sharing and timely information sharing.

With Notes, users at Anderson Consulting can ask the system for information related to projects they are working on. This can take the form of general information or information of a competitive nature. A basic software infrastructure is evolving within Anderson Consulting to facilitate use of Notes. This infrastructure includes a database directory to centralize information. While accounting and consulting firms like Anderson consulting and Coopers and Lybrand are big users of Notes, many other types of industries are also using Notes.

Financial companies are big users of Notes for its real-time news feeds from financial wire services and its capability to replicate databases. One way Notes is used by financial services firms is to pass trading information from one office (for example, one in London as it is closing for the day) to another office (such as one in New York, which would be beginning its business day).

J.P. Morgan and Co., Inc. was one of the earliest financial firms on Wall Street to make wide use of Notes. This bank uses Notes to give analysts immediate online access to market research. Previously, these analysts had to wait their turn while the research reports were circulated by means of a distribution list. In addition, the company uses Notes to file status reports about projects. This means that information previously available only to managers is now available to peers.

The Patricia Seybold Group, a market research company, uses Notes not only for research, but also to create and deliver its information products to its clients. Consultants associated with the Patricia Seybold Group insert information related to upcoming newsletters in a Notes database. Colleagues, often on the road, add comments to the database. Finished products are available to subscribers through the Notes databases.

A defense contractor uses Notes to distribute documents to a dozen of its office locations around the United States. Not only does this save on paper costs, it also enables employees who frequently travel to other office locations to keep in touch. This contractor has reported that when its employees tap into the Notes database, they feel they are in the familiar surroundings of their home office.

Lotus provides a Notes-based Document Manager program which allows users to access Notes through desktop applications like word processors. A version control capability permits users to track changes in a document easily. This program can automatically create a new version of a document whenever a change is made and save the older one for reference. Document Manager has a file-lock feature that works across an entire WAN; the file-lock feature in most document management packages only works across LANs.

19.4   COMPETITIVE PRODUCTS

While no product performs exactly the same functions that Notes performs, competition is appearing in a number of ways. First and foremost is the fact that many vendors are adding such features as mail-enabling capabilities to their application software. We are bound to see more and more "combination" packages that include the ability to communicate with others and to share information.

Other products that offer somewhat similar groupware capabilities include Digital Equipment Corp.'s TeamLinks, NCR's Cooperation, and WordPerfect Corporation's WordPerfect Office. These products work with different network operating system servers. Users should check with each vendor to determine what networks each vendor is currently supporting. Software vendors are constantly adding new capabilities to their products, but when these products first came out neither Notes, TeamLinks, or Cooperation were able to run with NetWare. NCR's Cooperation ran with LAN Manager and OS/2, while TeamLinks required Digital's Pathworks network package. A subsequent version of TeamLinks that runs on a UNIX server was provided by Digital.

19.5   UNIX-BASED GROUPWARE

As mentioned earlier in this book, UNIX is equipped with a built-in E-mail system. Additionally, access to the many different databases and research facilities on the Internet have probably satisfied most, if not all, research needs of UNIX users. Still, the lack of groupware-types of products has been noticed, and various vendors are now filling that void. Lotus and WordPerfect were among the earliest of these vendors, with many others sure to follow.

When first introduced, Notes was available only on networks with OS/2 as the server and either OS/2 or Microsoft Windows on the client stations. Now Notes is also available on UNIX. The first introduction of UNIX-based Notes was for Sun Microsystems Inc.'s SPARC systems.

WordPerfect Office Version 3.1 was available on UNIX platforms such as SPARCstations; Version 4.0 was initially made available only on DOS, Microsoft Windows, and Apple Macintosh platforms with UNIX-based versions following. While WordPerfect Office 3.1 was file-based, Version 4.0 has an underlying database that integrates its messaging and calendaring capabilities.

WordPerfect Office Version 4.0's rule-based message handling may be its most important feature. The recipient of a message can forward or delegate messages and let the sender know when and how the message was handled through acknowledgment procedures. With 4.0's status tracking and task management features, a manager can create a task, send it to an employee, and then know when the task is completed by the employee placing the task in a "completed" box.

19.6   LIMITATIONS OF GROUPWARE AND RELATED ISSUES

19.6.1   Limitations

So much excitement and enthusiasm has been generated about products like Notes that, to some degree, more has been expected from these products than they can currently deliver. Users must remember that certain products are meant to help with specific types of work situations—and that is all. None of these products are a panacea at this point. None of them can do everything that a specific enterprise might wish it to do. Even more important, since these products are still in their early stages, users frequently find that a particular feature they would expect a product to have (since it has related features), is surprisingly absent from it. Therefore, a company must plan in advance what its needs are and will be in the near future when considering buying such products.

19.6.2   Issues Related to Groupware

Some stumbling blocks can occur when implementing groupware. One is that people are accustomed to working alone and may have difficulty making the transition to working within a group. Another is that if not managed properly, groupware could result in information overload, exposing workers to information and procedures they do not need to know. This could take up their time without contributing to the accomplishment of their work objectives.

20

SOFTWARE COMBINATIONS: WORKFLOW, SMART E-MÁIL, EDI

20.1   WORKFLOW SOFTWARE

As mentioned in the previous chapter, many new combinations of software are being put together to create new approaches to accomplishing business objectives. Workflow and smart E-mail, or mail-enabled software, are just some of the new mixtures that are offering benefits to many enterprises. EDI has been around for a number of years, but it provides another example of how networking and messaging software can change the way business is done. This chapter will describe how these combinations of software are being used. Workflow and other new combinations of software are very similar to groupware. After offering a definition of workflow software, this chapter will indicate differences between workflow software and groupware.

Workflow software facilitates work processes by digitally replicating existing business processes that involve routing forms (or any other type of information on paper) among multiple employees. Many are projects where several people often work together on potential candidates for groupware. These projects could be, for example, processing expense reports or creating mutli-author documents. Companies that have made the most significant investment in workgroup products seem to have several characteristics in common, including:

- Having procedures that involve more than one person to complete
- Needing a variety of personnel to be knowledgeable about aspects of the business
- Being physically dispersed
- Having world-wide operations
- Needing quick reactions to rapidly changing market conditions
- Having a critical need to share information on a timely basis, among themselves, and/or with their clients

These new software packages are being used by enterprises for such wide-ranging items as advertising campaigns, sales proposals, and strategic plans.

20.1.1 Difference between Groupware and Workflow Packages

Workflow tools are sometimes considered as a subset or a form of groupware. One of the primary differences between groupware and workflow software is that groupware is passive while workflow tools are more active in nature.

For example, groupware packages do not track who gets specific information or what is done with that information. Workflow packages, on the other hand, take a very active role in determining who gets particular data, and they are concerned with what the recipients do with that data.

20.1.2 Workflow Package Architectures

Some industry observers categorize workflow packages into three primary architectures* for workflow packages:

- User or client-based
- Object or agent-based
- Server-based systems

These are useful categories which will be used here, noting, however, that some observers categorize workflow software by the *way* it is used.

---

*When interviewed for a *Software Magazine* article in 1990, Esther Dyson, editor of the *Release 1.0* newsletter and a well-respected industry observer, described these three categories of workflow surface.

For example, an observer might say one category of workflow software is used for document preparation, while another category is used for automating administrative functions.

20.1.2.1 User-, Object-, and Server-based Systems

User or Client-based Tools

User- or client-based tools are intended to help individual users to automate their interactions with other individuals as well as with applications. An example is BeyondMail which has a rule-based engine for filtering and sorting mail.

Spokespersons from Beyond say that BeyondMail has a bottom-up approach to automation through the use of its scripting language and FormsDesigner package. With these tools users can establish rules for tasks that range from simple personal mail management to complex forms routing. This contrasts with other packages that use a top-down approach. In a top-down approach, specific processes are selected for automation and then an automation plan is developed for those processes. Reportedly, with BeyondMail's approach, users can more easily add incremental functions over time.

Object- or Agent-based Tools

Object- or agent-based tools contain the required intelligence (built into them by the user or developer) to correctly process the forms involved in a specific procedure. These tools regard data in the forms as objects. The values of these objects can be viewed by the user through the use of various forms. The forms contain "active fields" which can automatically activate specific actions such as calling an external database. The placement and functions of these active fields are built into the form when it is designed.

Server-based tools

Server-based tools are generally built around a single logical center through which an administrator can monitor the status of tasks throughout a system, making the job of tracking work flow much easier for the administrator. These systems are often able to use the capabilities of an existing relational database, including the RDBMs tools for managing transaction processing. Action, from Action Technologies, is an example of a server-based tool.

With Action software, task status and workflow are monitored and controlled by a central database. The knowledge of what should be done is coded into its design by a developer. This approach offers much more control than the approach offered by client-based workflow tools. An-other advantage of having the definition of routing and other knowledge in a central location, as server-based tools do, is that this information can be replicated and the functions can be used elsewhere.

Advocates of server-based tools feel that these tools are more valuable when it comes to re-engineering businesses. With a server-based tool, more thought is likely to be given to the overall process and its objectives than simply to automating the existing steps of an old process.

Action's Workflow Management System provides a workflow designer and an applications builder. These tools can be used to connect work flows with external packages such as E-mail or databases. The status of work is stored in a convenient relational database, and reporting tools permit the user to inspect what is happening and manage the work flow by altering it.

Action's workflow software products are available on an OEM basis. Action developed The Coordinator and the MHS E-mail transport service which is described in Chapter 18. LaserData, a vendor of document-imaging systems in Tyngsboro, MA, resells the Workflow Management System and incorporates workflow technology into its document man-agement system.

20.1.2.2 Categorizing Workflow Software by Functionality

Since so many different terms can be used for situations in which many people use software to accomplish a common objective, this type of software is sometimes more easily characterized by its functionality. Some observers categorize workflow and other types of group software by the different types of objectives being performed.

For example, a group approach to software is often used in document preparation and in other office automation functions. A group approach is also used to perform other types of objectives such as business trans-actions. Not only is groupware involved in business transactions, but multiple technologies are being combined as witnessed by the combina-tion of EDI and E-mail. A group approach also is frequently used for objectives such as speeding up the process of accomplishing repetitive office procedures like approving travel requests and processing expense reports. Without a doubt, the use of groupwork computing will expand dramatically.

The fact that information can be shared through capabilities like DDE, DLL, and OLE will further promote sharing information among groups of people. Many packages which were originally intended to be used by multiple people currently use capabilities such as DDE and DLL as standard parts of their package.

20.2   HOW THIS SOFTWARE IS USED

As mentioned above, this kind of software is being used in a wide variety of ways. Image processing is also being used with workflow software, and a variety of multimedia combinations are available as well. Many of the most common uses of this kind of software—areas like document preparation, office automation, and administrative functions—are a result of users looking for better ways to do their job.

Most companies report that workflow implementation is being initiated by the users who are currently doing the repetitive tasks that the workflow package will automate. The actual E-mail and communication networks are being installed by the networking groups. However, once E-mail is installed and end users begin to learn about the additional ways that messaging software can aid their work processes, they are the ones who are taking the initiative to analyze various packages and implement them. In fact, many vendors have reported that this is one instance where vendors are not pushing products for end users to buy, but rather it is one where end users are pushing vendors to provide additional capabilities to facilitate their work even more.

More uses for this software will very likely be invented by end users themselves who have the creativity to see ways of doing their work more efficiently using such tools. The term "transaction-oriented workflow" is being used to describe systems created by users to automate their office procedures and other business processes.

20.2.1 Document Preparation

Many office documents are written as a group project. One individual may be an expert in one area, while others have other specialties. Each may be assigned to write one or more chapters of the document. An overall technician who has a good basic knowledge about all aspects of the document may be assigned to verify the accuracy of the individual parts. In addition, a technical person who has good writing skills may be assigned to oversee the project, ensuring that the completed document reads as though it were written by one person. Reading a document that has one consistent style of writing is easier than reading one that consists of dramatic style differences.

For years, group-effort documents have been prepared manually, with each participating individual reading a paper copy of the work of others, manually marking the copy, and then giving the work to someone else to make the changes.

When the writers are connected by means of a network, changes can be made directly to the electronic copy rather than being hand-written on a paper copy to be entered by someone else. Word packages have capabilities which permit the individual making changes to the document to turn on a "revision indication" feature. Using this feature, any changes the person makes to the document will be clearly indicated. Most packages have a choice of ways to indicate the revision. For example, text that is added can be indicated with a horizontal bar in the margin to the left or right of where the material appears. In addition, the new words can also be highlighted with such features as bold printing, italics, underlining, and double underlining. Words to be deleted are indicated with a horizontal line drawn through them.

An individual can make revisions to a computer copy of a document and send the electronic image back to the original writer or to others in the group project. The others will be able to immediately see what the proposed changes are.

The Boss Document Manager (BDM) is often used to facilitate the creation of multi-authored documents by combining messaging, imaging technology, a distributed document database, and other aspects of workflow technology. Other features include routing, notification, project schedules, and approval lists. The tools provided by BDM permit users to assign tasks to specific individuals, outline the document's life cycle, establish project due dates, and monitor and modify all of these elements during the course of the project. The product offers links to Microsoft's Dynamic Data Exchange and Object Linking and Embedding capabilities. It also offers a C language API as well as links to other products.

20.2.2 Office Automation and Administrative Functions

Procedures such as filling out the paperwork to attend a seminar or filing business trip expense reports are two examples of how workflow automation techniques are becoming widely used. Many companies have used E-mail and its extensions to automate the paperwork involved in attending seminars or going on other business trips. More recently, companies are adding the expense report portion as well. For example, firms are providing scanners which employees use to scan receipts from their trip. These receipts are then electronically attached to the electronic expense form filled out by the employee. The manager can review the electronic data, affix his or her digital signature, and then route it to the accounting department.

Some automatic operations could be performed when the data comes into the accounting department, such as entering the data into a variety of weekly and/or monthly reports which manage trip expenses according to various criteria. After the form has met all qualifications, the accounting department could create a check to reimburse the employee for his or her expenses or bill the employee for funds left over from an advance.

This process can be managed, permitting various individuals to determine where the "paperwork" is in its travels. Certain people would have access only to the kind of information they need to know, of course. "Time limits" can also be assigned to each location on its route. If this time limit is exceeded, either the individual at that location or a designated person could be notified that immediate action is requested.

As mentioned earlier, many E-mail vendors are adding features to their products to facilitate the use of their packages beyond just sending a message to someone. Many have now added various forms features. Forms impose a structure on an electronically sent message. The different portions of a form are filled out by the various people to whom the form is routed. In some cases, the sections of the form that are pertinent to the recipient are highlighted, calling attention to the action to be taken regarding this particular form. WorkMan from Reach Software is one of the various vendors who provides this feature.

Many packages provide some standard forms that come with the package, some permit these standard forms to be modified, and some permit users to design their own forms from scratch. With WorkMan, for example, users can design their own forms using either a GUI-based tool or a scripting language. Sometimes the end user uses a high-level scripting tool, which is then processed by a program generator, which creates a lower level scripting language, which may be modified by the end user, although more often, if modified at all, a programmer will do the modifications. The program generator also processes the results of the actions taken using the GUI-based tool, creating a low-level scripting which can also be modified.

Reach's WorkMan also offers a feature called "handlers." Handlers are sections of script language which define such things as what happens if the user presses a specific button. Handlers can also be used if a user wants to view or modify the workflow. There are often a dozen or so default handlers when this feature is present. Default handlers can usually be changed by someone who knows the script language.

Some packages can be protected by security features so the wrong people do not tamper with the appropriate flow of work. In addition, some packages (e.g., Reach's WorkMan) provide an audit trail of where the form or document has been, as well as other administrative functions. Reach stores audit trail information in its Status Tracker database.

Digital Equipment also provides a package for use with forms. Its TeamRoute provides a GUI to help users define forms and delineate the route the form should take. TeamRoute includes user administration features and capabilities such as a status query tool and history log. The package also provides a C language interface to run-time routines which can be used by programmers to perform specific activities.

NCR offers a package called ProcessIt which offers many of the features mentioned above, but also offers openness. NCR says the product can be customized by C, C++, any popular 4GL, as well as by software such as spreadsheets, word processors, or graphics packages.

Borland is concentrating heavily on providing tools with object-oriented capabilities, finding ways to combine applications with object-oriented and E-mail capabilities. The vendor's goal is to permit users to send electronic messages without exiting from a specific application. The vendor has a software architecture called Object Exchange (OBEX) which is built on Borland's Object Component Architecture. This architecture, in turn, is built on top of Interbase, Borland's database engine.

20.2.3   Image Processing Combined with Workflow

FileNet Corporation provides an image management capability with its WorkFlo product. Pacific Mutual Life Insurance Company in Newport Beach, CA, is using it to obtain loan documents quickly, providing faster service for its customers. Prior to installing this system, the insurance company had to wait for the results of a mainframe-based batch processing system to respond to a customer. Previously, after a customer filled out a loan request, a loan officer could only process the request through his or her 3270-based batch-oriented system, which was dependent on when the batch operation was scheduled to run.

FileNet's WorkFlo product provides support for 3279 and 5250 terminal emulation to assist sites in migrating from older production systems to new techniques. It also provides support for Digital Equipment's VT terminal standard, and for IBM's LU6.2 communications. Of course, DDE and DLL are also supported as are standard SQL interfaces.

In the case of Pacific Mutual Life, the 3270 emulation feature is making itself useful. Programmers are using it to connect the FileNet system with the company's 3270-based policy issuing system. End users will be migrated to WorkFlo interfaces by means of FileNet's forms and scripting languages which will be used to build common interfaces. Users can build forms using WorkFlo's scripting language or with AutoForm, a Visual Basic-type of toolbox which has drag-and-drop capabilities. Management reports can also be generated with WorkFlo.

20.2.4 Preventing $10,000/Hour Overcharges

Many companies are coming up with innovative ways to use messaging to expedite their business processes. An interesting example is provided by Texaco Inc., which is headquartered in Tulsa, OK. Texaco is using messaging to notify workers when a tanker pulls into port. Seaport overtime charges are in the area of $10,000 an hour, so it is important to avoid such costly charges. Since a carefully orchestrated series of activities among a wide variety of oil terminal workers occurs when a tanker arrives, messaging helps by sending automatic assignments and updates to employees as the work progresses. The work can then be carefully tracked to make sure all assignments get done when they should, making sure the company can avoid any excess dock charges of $10,000 an hour.

20.3 SMART E-MAIL AND MAIL-ENABLED SOFTWARE

The term "smart E-mail" refers to E-mail services that go beyond what are currently considered the expected range of E-mail capabilities. Mail-enabled applications are applications with E-mail capabilities built into them. Some people refer to this as "hiding" the E-mail capabilities within an application, thus making transmission easier for users. Both "smart E-mail" and mail-enabled applications are expanding in use—with end users eager for the assistance they provide. Falling somewhere between smart E-mail and mail-enabled applications are situations where applications send E-mail to each other. Such applications are sometimes referred to as "virtual E-mail users."

So many vendors are providing "smart" extensions to their E-mail packages that expectations are sure to change over time. This means that more and more users will expect their E-mail packages to automatically provide many of the features that are now contained in what are currently referred to as "smart E-mail" packages.

Intelligent routing capabilities are one example of smart E-mail. Banyan Vine's StreetTalk permits encoding of rules to perform various functions. For example, such an encoded rule could be used to permit a user to instruct the system to send a copy of the E-mail message to the recipient's immediate supervisor. The system is set up in such a way that it is able to locate the supervisor's E-mail address "on-the-fly" as the message is transmitted.

Other examples of smart E-mail features are the ability for mail to be routed and to trigger events. BeyondMail for Beyond Inc. is one of the leading examples. Others include Lotus Notes from Lotus, TeamLinks for Pathworks from Digital Corporation, Microsoft Mail from Microsoft, and The Coordinator II from Deviance. Each of these products has a different area in which it excels. For example, Microsoft Mail is noted for its filtering capabilities, while BeyondMail is noted particularly for its powerful and easy to use mail management features. On the other hand, some packages are more powerful than BeyondMail, but they are also more difficult to use.

20.3.1 Examples of Mail-Enabled Applications

An example of a mail-enabled application is a spreadsheet program that would list Mail in the File menu right along with the Print option. The user would pull down the File menu, select the Mail option, and then be provided with a dialog-box which would facilitate the composition and sending of the message. The spreadsheet the user was working on would automatically be attached to the transmitted message. If the recipient had the same spreadsheet package on his or her PC, the spreadsheet software could be launched automatically via the E-mail message attachment. The recipient could potentially make a modification to the spreadsheet and retransmit it to the original sender. Many mail front ends provide the ability to view the spreadsheet even if the appropriate spreadsheet software is not available on the recipient's machine. Of course, in this case, the recipient could only view the spreadsheet, he or she would not be able to modify it.

Other software applications that are appearing in mail-enabled versions include word processing, database, and graphics packages. Mail-enabled programs that can communicate with each other will be able to exchange information in a manner similar to DDE and OLE types of information exchanges.

Deloitte & Touche, the consulting firm, uses smart E-mail and mail-enabled applications built on cc:Mail in a number of ways. For example, company auditors and other employees can register for in-house seminars through E-mail. Automated audit software is another example. Using this capability, field staff employees can exchange audit work papers with each other, expediting their work.

Lotus's 1–2–3 for Windows provides embedded E-mail capabilities.

The technology, called Version Manager, facilitates the sharing of worksheet data. Version Manager lets users import and export cell ranges as objects which have attached properties such as author name and version number. One spreadsheet user is able to mail a range object to the in-box of another spreadsheet program. The recipient of the spreadsheet program would obtain the range object from its in-box and incorporate it into the appropriate worksheet.

Another feature of Version Manager will permit multiple workers to make contributions to a worksheet that is being constructed, *as it evolves*. This permits the workers to see intermediate results as they become available instead of waiting until all users have completed their specific portion. Elements that make this possible are the software's ability to store cell ranges as separate entries into the Lotus Notes database, combined with other Notes features, such as its ability to replicate data across servers. Individual users can make their contributions and then view the incremental changes instead of having to wait until all contributors have added their figures.

20.4   MORE VENDORS

Among the many vendors not mentioned in this chapter which also provide workflow or mail-enabled types of products are:

- Delrina in Toronto, Ontario which provides forms-routing packages
- FileNet in Cost Mesa, CA which markets workflow document image processing systems
- JetForm in Ottawa, Ontario which provides form-routing packages
- Keyfile in Nashua, NH which markets workflow document image processing systems
- Powercord, based in Manteni, IL which merged with Finansa in London and provides a general workflow package
- Quadratron System Inc. offers Cliqmail which provides mail-enabled applications
- Recognition Equipment/Plexus (Dallas) provides the UNIX-based technology contained in NCR's ProcessIt workflow system
- Workhorse (Dublin, Ireland) which markets workflow document image processing systems

This list is not all-inclusive, and new vendors of this type of software will appear constantly due to the exciting new capabilities it offers.

20.5 ELECTRONIC DATA INTERCHANGE (EDI)

Electronic data interchange is another example of an application that shares many characteristics with both client/server and E-mail systems. EDI is the ability to exchange and process data between a computer in one company with the computer (or computers) of a trading partner. The primary purpose of EDI is to reduce or eliminate the delays in order processing that are related to paper processing, mail, and/or other delivery services. Standard messaging services like X.400 are often involved in EDI exchanges.

As mentioned in Chapter 17, the introduction of client/server systems is often a prelude to EDI processing. The establishment of a network for client/server systems makes getting started with EDI easier since networks enable both of these technologies. Of course, the reverse is also true as well: the installation of EDI often leads to the introduction of client/server systems.

A similar correlation can be observed between EDI and E-mail. E-mail frequently allows for the debut of EDI. Many firms get started with EDI by using the messaging abilities—such as store-and-forward techniques— provided by E-mail and LANs. As EDI volume increases, value-added networks (VANs) and special EDI software are often added to the overall configuration.

Some of the most common types of EDI are as follows:

- Trade Data Interchange—The business exchange of data like purchase orders
- Electronic Funds Transfer—Financial transactions such as those performed by automatic teller machines
- Interactive Query Response—An example of this is airline booking
- Graphics Transmission—Plans and drawings are often exchanged this way

20.5.1 How Client/Server and EDI Systems Work Together

Client/server systems and EDI systems have many things in common. The most obvious is that both are related closely to networking. EDI is basically a form of E-mail. Many client/server systems use E-mail to accomplish their objectives. But client/server systems are much more than E-mail and much more than networking. Client/server systems are modular systems that accomplish the work of a system using the most appropriate platforms. That is another similarity between client/server and EDI systems. EDI systems also are modular and use different, appropriate platforms to accomplish the work at hand. Most importantly, both of these technologies benefit from recent advances in networking technology.

Interestingly, one of the primary differences that observers have pointed out as existing between E-mail and EDI is the nature of the recipient. They point out that with E-mail, the business-related messages transmitted are generally sent to an individual, while with EDI, the information in the message or form is sent to software at the recipient's site such as a database. However, as we have seen in Chapters 18 and 19, many mail-enabled applications now communicate with each other directly via E-mail. Therefore, this reduces the ability to specify the nature of the recipient of the message as the primary difference between E-mail and EDI. Reflecting back on the discussions of "smart E-mail" in the earlier chapters, EDI sounds very much like smart E-mail that is dedicated to carrying out specific business transactions.

20.5.2 The Growing Importance of EDI

Many large companies are demanding that their trading partners install EDI systems if they want to continue doing business with them. Sears Roebuck is an example of this. Sears expects any supplier of substantial size to have EDI capabilities. Not only do they expect it, they insist upon it.

The most common form of EDI in use today is the Trade Data Interchange (TDI) which is a business transaction that involves documents like purchase orders and invoices. In these situations, the electronic data transmitted by the sender is sent to the recipient's database for processing rather than to an individual. The system is designed and set up so the recipient's database knows what to do with specific transaction types and automatically performs the required functions. The system is then likely to initiate further actions. These additional actions could be activities performed by another database stored procedure (note the similarity to triggers and event alerters), the generation of another electronic form, and/or the transmission of a message to another database or another electronic or personal participant in the business transaction.

A second widely used type of EDI transaction is electronic funds transfer (EFT) which involves the automatic transfer of funds between a bank and another organization or individual. Various forms of EFT have been in use for many years. Since 1986, the Social Security Administration has made EFT transfers to recipients' bank accounts. During that time, the Social Security Administration has saved over $60 million in postage costs alone.

A third form of EDI is known as Interactive Query Response. A primary use of this form of EDI is in the travel agency business. Using Interactive Query Response, a travel agent can review flight schedules, request additional information about flights, book reservations, and print the airline ticket for the passenger.

Another form of EDI is the automatic transmission of graphics materials. This can be used by a number of industries that require the use of graphics in performing their business. Such business projects can range from design engineers working collaboratively or facility planners reserving space for a tenant, to dealers displaying alternative kitchen cabinet designs and configurations to potential customers.

20.5.3   The Interesting History of EDI

The birth of EDI is directly related to the Berlin Airlift when there were massive efforts to fly relief supplies into the blockaded city just after World War II. Edward A. Guilbert, the traffic director for American operations, began using telex systems to alleviate the mammoth amounts of paperwork related to the airlift. He designed and used standard forms and procedures to further facilitate the operation.

His introduction of the telex into the overall operation was so successful that he later formed the Transportation Data Coordinating Committee to further develop this approach. The committee started publishing standard computer formats for data exchange between companies in the late 1970s. The initial formats dealt with forms such as bills of lading and other shipping-related information. Today this committee is called the Electronic Data Interchange Association and is involved in creating EDI standards for over 150 different types of transaction sets.

An EDI standard, X.12, is a result of the work of this committee. While X.12 is supported by ANSI, ISO supports the EDIFACT standard which is used by most other nations in the world to perform EDI transactions. ISO is working on trying to merge the two standards.

EDI and client/server systems work together in a manner similar to the way that E-mail and client/server systems work together. Network connections are involved in both of these technologies, and the presence of one technology encourages use of the other. In an EDI environment using the Trade Data Interchange approach, an end user can initiate an electronic transaction using client software sitting on his or her desktop computer. The data on the electronic form can be transmitted to a database sitting on a server at the trading partner's site. In this scenario, the three basic components of a client/server architecture are present: a client (end-user) module, a network, and a server component. Of course, both the initiating software and the database at the trading partner's site could also be on mainframes.

The use of a client/server architecture is certainly not an integral part of EDI. The networked computing model does, however, lend itself nicely to the procedures involved in EDI. Since start-up costs are often a consideration in whether or not EDI is implemented, the lower costs of a client/server architecture could make adopting EDI feasible and show a return on investment more quickly. Although the example used above referred to the Trade Data Interchange model of EDI as being a good candidate for a client/server architecture, the same is true for the other uses of EDI as well.

20.5.4　Benefits and Obstacles to EDI

There is one fact about EDI that can be looked at as an advantage or a disadvantage, depending on a user's attitude. That fact is that EDI will reduce an enterprise's costs dramatically (an advantage); however, it will take a little time before the investment in EDI pays off (the disadvantage).

20.5.4.1　Benefits of EDI

A survey by Coopers & Lybrand reveals that a company's initial investment in EDI will pay for itself over time.* Typical respondents to the survey indicated that EDI investments can pay for themselves after a period of three years. However, the payoff can be substantial. Typical survey respondents indicated a savings of $1 million a year and more. One might wonder if only the most successful users of EDI responded to the survey. Still, it certainly indicates the potential of this technology.

The reason why cost savings can be so high is because it costs so much money to process transactions with existing systems. Even though computers are used in many of the systems with which EDI gets involved, often the computers are used to generate paper documents that are sent to the business partner. This is where the expense comes in, and this is where the savings result when the paper steps are eliminated. Also, with EDI, data is entered into computers just once. With many existing computer systems, data related to business transactions are entered into computers several times. Reduced data entry saves money.

Additional cost savings are possible because Just-in-Time inventory

---

*Richard H. Baker, *EDI, What Managers Need to Know About the Revolution in Business Communications*, TAB Professional and Reference Books, a Division of TAB Books, Blue Ridge Summit, PA, 1991.

and manufacturing practices can be implemented with the use of EDI. Instead of having a warehouse of inventory ready whenever the time comes that you need it, EDI permits users to order the inventory just before the time when it will be needed. As a result, warehousing costs can be reduced.

Along with cost savings in the kinds of situations described above are time savings. Since EDI transactions are practically instantaneous, one merely has to imagine how long it might take to process a paper purchase order (PO), send it through the mail, and have the PO processed by the recipient to realize the extent of the time savings. Some enterprises have reported that the before and after figures are five weeks to three days.

Additional benefits are that errors can be reduced and service can be improved. Since data about business transactions is entered only once— not several times—data entry errors are significantly reduced. Errors related to the previously existing manual handling of paper purchase order and billing paperwork is also reduced. This reduction in errors cannot help but result in better service.

One of the most interesting benefits of EDI is that it generates new ways for enterprises to conduct business, and it could potentially create entirely new business opportunities. Airline reservation systems are also taking advantage of EDI to provide hotel and automobile reservations for their airline clients. Baxter Health Care is also using the technology innovatively enabling hospitals to automatically order supplies from Baxter. Baxter was one of the first companies to use EDI. In fact, it was using EDI before the technology was referred to as EDI. No doubt, enterprises like Baxter will continue to invent ways to increase their business opportunities using EDI.

20.5.4.2 Obstacles to EDI

One of the biggest problems with EDI is that a company cannot use this technology alone. By its very nature, a company's business partners must be able to participate or the whole effort is impossible. Generally, if a company's business partners are large, this is not a problem. Company A simply has to convince Company B that B will also benefit from the transition to EDI. Most large corporations are already either performing some business transaction using EDI techniques, are installing such systems, or are analyzing the approach.

The difficulty arises when business partners are small and perceive the expense of installing EDI as being beyond their capabilities. If a firm is small enough, it may be many, many years before an EDI system will pay for itself. Of course, in some of these situations, installing EDI may open up new business opportunities for a small firm. Unfortunately, on the other hand, there may be some situations where the EDI system will never pay for itself.

The other primary obstacle is to ensure that the computer systems of the business partners are compatible with the company's. Even though they may have the same application software and database product, serious difficulties can arise if these products are installed on different hardware platforms or connected to a different networking architecture. This problem also calls to mind the difficulties that arise when different standards are encountered. This is particularly true when enterprises that are performing national EDI transactions want to start processing international transactions. They will have to adjust to the different EDI standards that are used in the rest of the world.

21

SECURITY IN CLIENT/SERVER SYSTEMS

21.1   SECURITY IS AVAILABLE FOR CLIENT/SERVER SYSTEMS

IS managers and mainframe developers are often unwilling to fully accept a client/server architecture for important production systems until they feel assured that the same degree of security that surrounds mainframe systems are in place for the client/server environment. As systems management tools for the client/server environment become available, as discussed in Chapter 14, sufficient security tools are also available to make production client/server systems as secure as their mainframe counterparts.

In reality, many of the same security mechanisms and procedures that are used in mainframe systems are used in client/server systems. Security approaches like using personal IDs (identifications), passwords, data encryption, and adequate backup and restore procedures used on mainframe computer systems are used in client/server architectures as well. A client/server system is more modular than a mainframe system, so security procedures may have to be placed in several, separate modules. Client/server systems generally involve networking, so network security will need to be present. But many mainframe systems use networking as well and have network security in place.

Some differences are certain to occur between security for mainframe systems and security for client/server systems. While mainframe systems often have just one networking protocol involved, such as SNA or DECnet, client/server systems often involve numerous LAN protocols. Kerberos, discussed later in this chapter, is an authentication protocol that is often used in multiprotocol environments.

Another significant difference is that security for mainframe systems in existing installations is firmly established and has been in place for many years. Client/server systems are relatively new. Adequate security measures may not be in place for the client/server environment.

21.1.1 Taking Responsibility for Security

Just as implementors of production quality client/server systems need to be more aware of networking concepts than mainframe developers, they also need to be more aware of security measures. The early designers of production-quality client/server systems will have to think through and plan adequate security for their new systems. They should coordinate all security measures with any existing security groups within their enterprise. Ideally, however, they should be willing to bear the ultimate responsibility for ensuring that their client/server systems have adequate security.

In fact, before the first production client/server systems are built, designers should perform a risk analysis to determine the proposed system's security needs. Areas to check include the client hardware and software, the server hardware and software, as well as the networking hardware and software.

Passwords, access rights, and data encryption procedures are just some of the techniques of which a client/server developer should have knowledge. Since many client/server developers may find themselves on their own for the first time in their career with regard to developing security, this chapter will discuss some basic concepts related to security that should go into any computer system (e.g., passwords, authentication, encryption) and will point out some special security needs of client/server systems (e.g., client, server and network security).

In many cases, it might be necessary for the client/server developer to take the lead in developing security for their new systems—especially if the managers of mainframe development are not yet taking an active role in designing client/server systems. In a mainframe environment, application developers know that security is built into the overall configuration: in logon procedures, operating systems and other software. Policies and procedures for mainframe security in the majority of shops were clearly established years ago. However, client/server systems are still relatively new. Many shops do not have all the necessary security measures installed yet. As a result, some of this responsibility will fall on the shoulders of the early client/server application developers. They should be up to the task of analyzing the security needs and making sure adequate protective measures are installed for their systems.

21.1.2   Balancing Security and Ease-of-Use

A careful balance is always important with security. Excessive security can make computer systems difficult to use. This can lead to frustration for users as well as developers. Client/server systems are supposed to make computer systems easier to use, not more difficult. If excessive security makes systems too hard to utilize, interfering with end users' ability to get their job done, they will find ways around it. The ideal objective is that security for a system should be as invisible as possible when a user is authorized to use a system, while the same system should be impenetrable for someone who is not authorized to use it.

Some database server packages and networking packages have security measures built into them and many third-party (independent) vendors provide security software to go with the more widely-used client/server software components. It might be a good idea for developers to examine what security features are present in the software that will be used in the client/server system and plan their overall security in conjunction with it. Even if the software being used provides good security mechanisms, chances are that additional security measures for the overall client/server environment will still need to be developed.

21.2   ALL COMPUTERS NEED SECURITY

Security is always an issue in any computer system. It is a rare computer system that does not have any security needs. Even if the computer system is one used at home for personal finance and word processing tasks, the individual would at least want to know that his or her system was secure from viruses. Even if a PC in one's home does not have a modem and only uses software that is purchased from a reputable source, the system is not guaranteed to be virus-free. Unfortunately, there have been instances where a brand new software disk has been infected at the software publisher's site—possibly by a disgruntled employee. Fortunately, such situations are few and far between. However, this points out the importance of protecting all PCs and workstations with virus-scanning software—no matter where the computer is located and no matter what it is used for.

Simple physical security is another consideration that applies to any computer no matter where it is located. Whether it is located in a small business in a friendly community or in a large business office, there should be some degree of physical security. In a small business, this can simply mean locking doors, knowing who is on the premises, and why they are there. In a large business office, similar measures are generally taken. "Locking doors" often equates to employees having a pass-key card that will open a locked, outer entrance door to the building. Receptionists can be located at main entrances where the public is generally permitted to enter. Buildings that have a lot of traffic involving the general public should take special precautions. Physical security risks for desktop computers range from having someone copy files to having someone dressed as a repairman walk off with the entire machine.

21.2.1 Security to Fit the Situation

Whether on a PC, LAN server, or mainframe, the more important the data involved, the greater the security measures that must be taken. Some defense sites have two or more completely different computer systems. That way they are able to establish greater security measures to protect their most vital data.

The Department of Energy (DOE) in Albuquerque, NM, provides an example. They have two separate computers: one is a classified mainframe computer with numerous, extremely strict security measures and the other is a mainframe with just normal security measures. All classified data resides on the classified computer which is accessed only by those who have a direct need to do so. Everyone who is permitted to be physically present where the two computers are located is required to have a security clearance, whether he uses the classified computer or not. *So, without a security clearance, you cannot be anywhere in the vicinity of the classified computer center.*

The classified computer is protected by many security measures ranging from internal measures like encrypted data to *armed security guards* located in the general vicinity where the computers are located. Some of the security measures even have a cloak of secrecy about them. While this may sound excessive, there is a reason for all this security.

The Department of Energy (DOE)—among other assignments—is responsible for the administration and security of the entire U.S. nuclear weapons program. The office in Albuquerque is responsible for many aspects of the nuclear weapons program, ranging from research to manufacture, transportation, record keeping, and storage of all the nuclear weapons in the country. (Employees who drive trucks transporting nuclear weapons are heavily armed and extensively trained in combat techniques and the martial arts. When in transit, the exact location of every truck is constantly monitored by satellites and a variety of hi-tech devices in Albuquerque.) DOE takes its job very seriously. Other enterprises which value the competitive nature of their data guard it with as much zeal—though the armed guards may be absent or less obvious.

21.2.2 "Hackers"—The Term Takes a Nasty Twist

The term "hacker," unfortunately, has now taken on a sinister meaning in the mind of the general public. The term originally just referred to someone who enjoyed working and playing with computers and was generally very talented with them. Unfortunately, some of these extremely talented computer people took it as a challenge to see if they could "break into" highly secure systems. Since they were exceptionally talented, some of them found that they *could* do so—and so they did. Many regarded it as a simple prank. It is no such thing. It is a criminal act and the law enforcement agencies are now taking it very seriously. Unfortunately, the term "hacker" has become associated in the public mind with individuals who break into secure computer systems either for fun or devious purposes.

21.3 SECURITY ASSESSMENT

Many firms perform a risk evaluation and security assessment before they implement any new computer system. A security assessment should certainly be performed before the firm proceeds with the implementation of production client/server systems. If some client/server systems are already installed, and a security assessment has not been performed, it should be performed before additional systems are added to the client/server environment. If a firm is now planning its first production-quality client/server system, this is the best time to perform a security assessment. Some of the basics of performing such an assessment are explained here for the benefit of firms where mainframe developers are thrown into the job of creating production-quality client/server systems when inadequate security measures exist and there are no in-house security experts to guide the way.

A risk/exposure assessment consists of such things as determining what could go wrong, estimating what it would cost, and deciding how much the firm can afford to lose in various situations. The assessment is often performed by a team of security experts (as described in Section 21.3.1 below).

21.3.1 Potential Risks

Some potential risks that are common to many firms' evaluation of risk assessment include the following:

- Equipment theft (common theft): high
- Vandalism (damaged equipment): medium
- Equipment failure: medium
- Virus damage: medium
- Screw-ups (Improper use of hardware/software): low
- Earthquake damage: low
- Unauthorized access: low
- Data theft: low
- Fire damage: very low
- Fraud (e.g., computerized embezzlement of funds): very low

This list—and portions of other material appearing in this chapter—is taken from *The Stephen Cobb Complete Book of PC and LAN Security*, written by Stephen Cobb and published by McGraw-Hill. Another recommended book on computer security is *Computer Security Basics*, written by Deborah Russell and G. T. Gangemi, Sr., published by O'Reilly & Associates, Inc.

The list shows threats, ranked by risk factor, as estimated by a hypothetical small firm that does not have extensive connections to outside computers. The firm has well trained employees and good fire protection. It does not consider its equipment to be reliable, yet it is very optimistic that its employees will not screw up too often. A variety of categories of data loss is presumably included under improper use of equipment.

21.3.2   Example of Calculating Risk Exposure

Cobb goes on to have the site create a spreadsheet (Figure 21.1) showing these risk threats and he assigns a numeric risk factor to the terms high (4), medium (3), low (2), and very low (1).

The spreadsheet is then expanded by assigning a third column which shows an estimated potential per incident loss (PPIL) figure, given in units of $1000, for each threat. The last column in the spreadsheet is derived by multiplying the risk factor by the potential per incident loss, which yields a loss exposure.

The results are then sorted according to the loss exposure column (Figure 21.2). Figure 21.2 shows the firm that the highest risk factors do not always create the largest exposures.

21.3.3   The Need for Security Experts

Large enterprises which value their data must have a group of individuals who are security experts and who concentrate their time and energy on

Threat	Risk Factor	PPIL (K)	Loss Exposure
Fire	1	$5.0	$5.0
Equipment Theft	4	$5.0	$20.0
Vandalism	3	$5.0	$15.0
Failure	3	$3.0	$9.0
Screw-ups	2	$5.0	$10.0
Virus	3	$1.0	$3.0
Earthquake	2	$5.0	$10.0
Leaks	2	$50.0	$100.0
Data Theft	2	$70.0	$140.0
Fraud	1	$10.0	$10.0

Source: PC and Lan Security by Stephen Cobb

Figure 21.1 Risk analysis—loss factors.

always keeping abreast of the newest security measures. This is not an area that can be reduced or eliminated in a time of cost-cutting or downsizing. In fact, if an enterprise is downsizing computer systems

Threat	Risk Factor	PPIL (K)	Loss Exposure
Data Theft	2	$70.0	$140.0
Leaks	2	$50.0	$100.0
Equipment Theft	4	$5.0	$20.0
Vandalism	3	$5.0	$15.0
Screw-ups	2	$5.0	$10.0
Earthquake	2	$5.0	$10.0
Fraud	1	$10.0	$10.0
Failure	3	$3.0	$9.0
Fire	1	$5.0	$5.0
Virus	3	$1.0	$3.0

Source: PC and LAN Security by Stephen Cobb

Figure 21.2 Risk analysis—sorted by exposure.

from mainframes to smaller systems, it should have employees who are making sure that the newly designed systems are secure and that migration procedures are secure as well.

The need for security experts will be indicated several times again throughout this chapter in appropriate places. The more modular that systems are—as in client/server systems—the more separate places there are for security intrusions to occur. As enterprises build and interconnect more and more client/server systems, the more heterogeneous (having a mixture of systems and protocols) the overall environment will become. Heterogeneity will be discussed in the section on network security, but having an in-house staff of security experts will become more important as firms interconnect a great variety of different components in their expanding client/server architectures.

Many sites have the security experts provide a strategy paper that outlines the overall approach to security taken for the entire enterprise. This strategy paper should have a section dedicated to how these security measures apply specifically to client/server systems. Client/server developers should be aware of what the strategy paper contains if it is already written. If the client/server section is not yet written, developers should work with the security experts to develop it. If it is written, but the developer feels it is inadequate, he or she should work with the security group to strengthen the client/server section.

21.3.4 Security Lines of Defense

The various categories of security measures are sometimes referred to as the lines of defense against intrusions and security breaches. Some of the major lines of defense are listed below. Most of them are also discussed in more detail in later sections of this chapter. They include the following:

• **Physical Security**—This is the most basic line of defense. Also, it is one of the simplest of security measures. Network and server equipment can be locked in a special room. Wiring hubs, bridges, routers and various telecommunications access equipment can be locked in a wiring closet. (And be sure to keep it locked. Users have returned from an extended trip and found that they were no longer connected to the network. Someone else had been hooked up using the connection—which was deemed "spare" since the user was not using it at the time.) Desktop computers can be protected with keyboard locks and passwords.

• **Backup and Recovery**—Another major line of defense is backup and recovery. All systems from the smallest to largest should have adequate backup and recovery procedures. Databases that are constantly being updated online may need to have an audit trail of update transactions. In this scenario, the main database is backed up every night, and then a file of all update transactions is created as the transactions update the main database. If something happens to the newly updated database, it can be recreated from the previous backup and the update transaction file.

- **Passwords**—This is another primary line of defense and is considered as a basic security measure. We will discuss passwords more in the next subsection.

- **Authentication**—Authentication often works "hand in hand" with passwords. In other words, the individual user is authenticated by entering the correct password, login and password, or other identifiers. Other types of authentication include simple measures like a pass card or security card to more sophisticated measures like using biometric devices to analyze the person's retina or verifying a physical characteristic like a fingerprint. Authentication in a client/server environment includes having the user or server process be authenticated by each server invoked. Kerberos can simplify that operation. Kerberos is also often used for authentication in systems that have a mixture of network protocols.

- **Ensuring Network Security**—Any computer system that includes networks involves more security risks than one that does not. However, these risks can be dealt with. For example, to provide additional security when modems are being used, telecommunications access can be limited to certain directories and servers only. Modems that call users back at specified numbers can be used to reduce the chance of intrusion by strangers.

- **Securing UNIX Remote Services**—Kerberos or a similar authentication scheme can be used to prevent illegal use of the rlogin and rshell commands. These commands are sometimes used as a mechanism to break into a system since they permit individuals to move from one machine to another, gaining access rights as they go.

- **Encryption**—Encryption is a secure way to protect data travelling over a network. Encryption is the scrambling of data so that it becomes meaningless to those not knowing how to unscramble it.

- **Fiber Optic Cabling**—In addition to its many other benefits (See Chapter 9, Benefits of Fiber Optic Cabling), fiber optic cabling is also a more secure medium than copper wire. Using a radio frequency receiver to eavesdrop on an electromagnetic conversation travelling across a copper wire is relatively easy. However, eavesdropping on a light-based conversation travelling across a fiber cable is more difficult because the intruder needs to physically tap into the cable. The resulting reduction in light levels can be detected.

21.3.4.1 Passwords

Passwords are always part of the primary line of defense. If a firm has a group of security experts, the developer of production-quality client/ server systems will not need to establish a password system from scratch. Developers only need to coordinate their work with that of the security experts. If a firm does not have a security group or adequate security measures, the developers may need to provide them. Passwords should be high on their priority list.

The general rules that have long been followed for passwords on mainframe system apply to client/server systems, too. For example, a user should not pick obvious passwords like their nickname, spouse's name, child's name, or their own birth date. So many people have done this that such names are the first guesses made by individuals who try to break into someone else's computer system. Someone who has such knowledge is likely to be someone who works within the company. However, these names might appear on photographs on the worker's desk. That brings up another danger. Users should not write down their passwords. This is a frequent mistake which is taken advantage of by individuals who search the individual's desk and then break into the computer system.

Security administrators usually establish procedures that require users to change their passwords periodically. This period varies from monthly to a period of several months. This is a decision of the specific installation.

If an installation has separate application server hardware devices, consideration should be given to putting them in a physically protected room as described above for database server hardware.

21.3.4.2 Backup and Recovery

Backup and recovery procedures are an essential component in any computer system. Backups can restore data whether the loss was due to an intruder, a software or hardware failure, a mistake on the part of a user, or physical loss from any disaster like fire, flood, storm, vandalism, or earthquake damage.

A great deal of literature on backup and recovery procedures is in existence. Many of these procedures can be used in a client/server environment the same way they are used in other computer architectures. Many backup and recovery products are also available. Many products are built to work with a specific hardware or software environment, while others are more for general use.

Systems documentation should be created that tells how and when backups are taken. Specific people should be assigned to perform backups and recoveries. If these people would feel more comfortable with training, it should be provided for them. If many different individuals are responsible for backing up different systems, some way of checking to make sure all backups are actually performed on a regular basis should be established. It should be considered a severe infraction of company policy if backup procedures are not followed. In some companies, it can cost a person his or her job. Many systems will perform backups automatically. These systems should be checked regularly to ensure they are working properly.

Some companies do a full backup of data files every night. Other companies perform a full backup on a periodic basis, like once a week or once a month, and then—on a daily basis—do incremental backups of everything that has changed since the full backup. Some companies have both policies—one for some files, the other for other files. Backups can be encrypted for particularly sensitive data. A backup copy should always be kept at a secure, off-site location.

An absolute wealth of backup hardware and software products are available for use in client/server architectures. Developers should do some research using current trade journals for existing products and then monitor future issues of trade journals for new developments. Additional information related to backing up systems in general is provided in the sections in Chapter 8 on disk mirroring, disk duplexing, fault tolerance, and RAID.

21.4 SPECIAL NEEDS FOR SECURITY IN CLIENT/SERVER SYSTEMS

Client/server systems are particularly impacted by security issues in a number of different ways. For example, the fact that client/server systems are modular in structure means security measures might have to be installed in several places. System designers who have only built systems for mainframes will need to learn about new security procedures and products to incorporate into the client/server systems they design. Again, this is another reason for having special security personnel. They could become the experts on client/server security and then serve as a welcome resource for client/server designers.

21.4.1   Desktop Computer Security

First, a site needs to determine whether it wants to install security systems which need to be satisfied before an individual can gain access to a desktop computer. In many installations, the majority of personal computers and workstations—ones that are used only by one individual for his or her own "personal" business usage—are not protected by security systems. This might involve desktop machines in client/server systems that only provide a shared print server. However, PCs that let an individual gain access to data in production client/server systems should be protected by security measures. And increasingly, PCs that are used *only* for "personal" (individual) business purposes are also being protected by security measures. If there is a chance that employees could lose several week's or day's worth of work—or even one day's work—a security procedure would be a welcome asset.

Again, if the desktop computer is connected to a production client/server system, it must have security protection. Each user of the client/server system must have a personal ID and password. The ID is used to assign authority and track access to the system. In addition, the IDs can be used to assign specific procedures to various individuals for unique backup procedures, prompting, and access times.

Generally, sensitive data is not stored on desktop computer systems. If the desktop computer has no security protection, then, of course, no sensitive data should be stored on it. Some sites that have installed security measures to prevent access to desktop computer systems by unauthorized users do permit some sensitive data to be stored on these computers. Other sites, however, do not permit this because desktop computers can be removed from the premises fairly easily.

21.4.2   Application Security

The term "application security" can have a variety of meanings. It may refer to applications like word processing, spreadsheets, and E-mail. The measure of security applied to these types of applications can vary widely depending on the installation, the data involved, and how these applications are used. Often, there are no security requirements to access word processing software applications. On the other hand, these security procedures are generally *always* involved in order to access E-mail. In some situations, even after an individual is identified with a user name and password to gain access to the network, he or she will have to go through the process again to gain access to his or her own E-mail system. This is for the user's own protection. Users should be sure to use a different password for their E-mail system than they use to gain access to the network. That way if an unauthorized person figures out one password, that person will not automatically know both passwords.

In a client/server environment, "application security" can refer to the client portion of the system or to the overall application that is designed with a client/server architecture. Making sure the front end of applications are secure generally means having users sign on and identify themselves. It often also involves assigning specific profiles to different users who can access different portions of the overall application.

21.4.3 Server Security

Sometimes the fact that an individual has gained access to the network automatically gives him or her access to the database that resides on the database server. Sometimes it does not. In either case, additional security measures are often built into the server database by the database administrator (DBA) or related staff members. For example, some users have access only to certain data fields. They may have access to the job assignments of various personnel, but not to other personal information about the employee. For example, they may not have access to salary data. Sometimes personnel or payroll employees do have access to salary data, but only up to a certain limit. They may not, for example, have access to the salary data of executives or those who are making over $100,000 a year. DBAs are able to secure specific fields so that the user profile indicates which fields each user can access. This situation is quite similar to mainframe database access and minicomputer database access. The important difference is the client/server developer *should make sure* that procedures similar to mainframe and minicomputer database access *are* in place, rather than merely assuming so.

Additional personalized security measures can be designed to track the access of specific individuals to particular systems or components of systems. This can be vital in determining who had access to systems or components at particular times if something is amiss. Personalized security procedures can also be established to manage such additional things as specialized backup procedures for certain individuals.

Servers are an example of a situation where physical security can be useful. The end users who utilize the data on a database server do not need physical access to the server hardware. As a result, database server hardware is generally kept locked in a secure room. In fact, most servers are kept in a room that is or was used—or could have been used—by the mainframe computer. Large enterprises which rely heavily on a client/server architecture have more than one server. For example, Microsoft performs most of its processing with client/server systems. As a result,

Microsoft literally has racks and racks of servers. The servers are stacked three and four high and are lined up in row after row of multiple columns of stacked servers. These servers are physically secured in a locked, protected room that resembles a traditional mainframe computer center. Often the input/output devices such as the monitor, keyboard, and disk drives are removed from the server even though the server resides in a locked room. If a disk drive is needed to reboot the server, the drive is disabled when the server is up and running.

21.5 NETWORK SECURITY

Many of the security features discussed elsewhere in this chapter relate to network security. In a client/server system, the data generally resides on a server that the client module accesses through the use of a network. Therefore, security measures that apply to data in general and specifically to servers also apply to the "networked data." Securing the data while it travels over the network is also important. This can be done by encrypting the data.

Many network operating systems have special security and redundancy features built in. For example, Novell's System Fault Tolerant (SFT) Features attempt to prevent data loss by keeping a second copy of all data on a separate disk. The sections in Chapter 8 on Fault Tolerance and RAID disk systems cover techniques that are used to protect data that resides on a server in a LAN environment.

Security on a LAN should include assurance of availability of the network in addition to protection against intrusion. Developers should review the network design, look for devices that might be a single point of failure, and consider having a second device installed to serve as a hot backup.

See Section 21.7 for a discussion of Kerberos which is becoming popular for use with a wide mix of client and server hardware and software in multi-network environments.

21.5.1 Network Passwords

Everyone should have to "sign on" to the network to gain access to it. All network users should identify themselves with a user name and a password. This applies to everyone in the company. There can be no exceptions. A high-level manager cannot think that he or she should be excused because of his or her prominent position. While one human can recognize another and know who he or she is, the typical desktop computer is not able to do that. Advances are being made, so that computing devices are now being equipped with a variety of ways to recognize different individuals—for example, through fingerprints or retinas, as mentioned earlier. However, this is certainly not the norm for the usual desktop computer at the present time. Therefore, everyone must identify him- or herself with a user name and password to gain access to the LAN.

If additional networks are installed, it is sometimes necessary for an individual to identify him- or herself again to the additional networks. This, of course, depends upon the software capabilities between the networks and the particular circumstances of the installation, among other factors. It is always better to have only one or two passwords than many passwords. Tools like Kerberos assist in the process of having each user be approved by each server without forcing the user to enter multiple passwords.

21.5.2   Network Fault Tolerance

Fault tolerance is often achieved by having duplicate hardware/software configurations. With LANs, enterprises often duplicate key portions of the network. The most common advice to developers and administrators is to examine the network and make sure there are no single points of failure. If such points of failure are found, sites should think about duplicating equipment to add safety. Sites often have a "hot backup"— one that is "ready to go"—for critical network devices. In case of failure, the hot backup is activated, and LAN operation continues. The theory behind duplicate pieces of equipment is, of course, that two are better than one. Having two of critical devices can make the difference between halting all operations or being able to continue processing.

Items like bridges, routers, brouters, and gateways are frequent candidates for redundancy. In addition, many enterprises have duplicate sets of wiring for local sites as well as dual FDDI rings. The most frequent type of redundancy in networks is duplicating the file or database server. However, developers should be aware that duplicate servers entail duplicate writes. Everything that is written to one server needs to be written to the other server. This will, of course, involve more network traffic which will take more time, thus slowing down the overall operation. If speed is critical, then a faster network configuration should be given consideration.

21.6   DATA ENCRYPTION

Data or file encryption is accomplished by using a formula, often referred to as an algorithm, which can be simple or quite complex. The degree of complexity of the algorithm affects how long it takes to encrypt and decrypt data. The degree of complexity also affects how long it would take a computer system to "break" the code. Some simple codes can be broken by a personal computer. Other codes might require a mainframe or a super computer working many weeks to break the code. The Data Encryption Standard, sponsored by the U.S. Government, offers a secure encryption procedure and will be discussed below.

21.6.1 Cryptography

Cryptography has its own unique terms and tricks of the trade. *Encryption,* or *enciphering,* is the process of scrambling data according to some formula and *decryption* or *deciphering* is the process of unscrambling the encrypted data. The data before encryption is called *plaintext*, and the encrypted data is called *ciphertext*. The science of designing systems for encrypting and decrypting information is called *cryptography* while the history and study of codes and ciphers is known as *cryptology*. The actual process of deciphering encrypted data is called *cryptoanalysis*.

Cryptography provides a method to encrypt plaintext into ciphertext that looks like a purely random collection of data. Stephen Cobb, in his book *PC and LAN Security*, points out that a simple cryptographic approach is to replace every character in the original plaintext with a different character in the ciphertext. An early example of cryptography is attributed to Julius Caesar in Roman times. Caesar's cipher shifted the letters of the alphabet by three places—making three the key to this text—as shown below.

```
A B C D E F G H I J K L M N O P Q R S T U V W X Y Z
X Y Z A B C D E F G H I J K L M N O P Q R S T U V W
```

21.6.1.1 A Message to Decode

Readers who would like to try to decipher an encoded sentence that might have been written in this code, can try the following one. The code should be decrypted by substituting the appropriate letter in the encrypted message with the one shown above it in the top row. For example, the Y in the encoded should be replaced with a B, the B should be replaced with an E, the T should be replaced with a W, etc.

```
YBTXOB QEB FABP LC JXOZE*
```

The decoded message is revealed in the footnote on the next page for those who do not care to try to decipher it.

The technique used here is known as a substitution cipher. Substitution ciphers can be far more powerful than this, however.

21.6.1.2 Breaking Codes

To break codes, a cryptoanalyst uses certain established techniques and tricks of the trade. For example, one trick is to count how many times each letter occurs in the text. The cryptoanalyst then develops a list showing which letters were used the most frequently. This list is written in the order of most frequently used letters to least frequently used letters. Suppose this is list A.

Next, the cryptoanalyst reaches for his or her table of frequencies, a list showing the relative frequency with which the letters of the alphabet occur in plaintext, or uncoded text (also known as plain English). Two lists showing the relative frequency of letters used in the English language is shown in Tables 21.1 and 21.2. Table 21.1 is shown with the letters in alphabetical order. Table 21.2 is shown by frequency of use.

The cryptoanalyst compares the letters in list A (above) to the list shown in Table 21.2. Notice that Table 2.1 reveals that the letters E, T, R, I, etc., are the most frequently used letters in the English language. Stephen Cobb offers the following example of a message that is decoded using the frequency lists.

The encrypted message is as follows:

```
YZYG JKZO RZOY XZRR KZRK XUXR JXRZ XUYK
```

Notice that the encrypted message is divided into equal letter groups. This is done to further complicate the process of figuring out the message.

21.6.1.3 Frequency of Letters

Cobb points out that when the frequency of each letter in this particular encrypted message is counted, we come up with the following list:

R	Z	X	Y	K	J	U	O	G
6	6	5	4	4	2	2	2	1

Correlating this list directly with the most frequently used letters shown in Table 22.2 will render almost the exact translation. The R is replaced with an E, the Z is replaced with a T, the X is replaced with an R, the Y is replaced with an I, the K is replaced by an N, the J is replaced with an O, and the U is replaced with an A. So far, the code has been broken by going straight down the list of most frequently used letters and

---

*The decoded message is "Beware the Ides of March."

Table 21.1 Letter frequency with letters shown in alphabetical order.

A	7.25
B	1.25
C	3.50
D	4.25
E	3.00
F	3.00
G	2.00
H	3.50
I	7.75
J	0.25
K	0.50
L	3.75
M	2.75
N	7.75
O	7.50
P	2.75
Q	0.50
R	8.50
S	6.00
T	9.25
U	3.00
V	1.50
W	1.50
X	0.50
Y	2.25
Z	0.25

Source: Stephen Cobb, *PC and LAN Security.*

making a corresponding substitution. The next letter needs a little trial and error. The O is not replaced with an S, but with an H. The final letter falls back into the original pattern, with the G being replaced by an S. If the computer were to count the frequency of letters in a large piece of text, it would be likely to come up with a close correlation between the frequency of letters used.

Cobb's example develops a scenario where a customs officer has raided the offices of an arms dealer. The officer finds the encrypted message starting with YZYG shown above while inspecting the computer files, trying to determine when an illegal weapons shipment will enter the country. The translation of the code yields the following:

```
YZYG  J  KZO  RZOY  XZRR  KZRK  XUXR  JXRZ  XUYK
ITIS     ONTH  ETHI  RTEE  NTEN  RARE  ORET  RAIN
```

Table 21.2 Letter frequency with letters shown by frequency of use.

E	12.75
T	9.25
R	8.50
I	7.75
N	7.75
O	7.50
A	7.25
S	6.00
D	4.24
L	3.75
C	3.50
H	3.50
F	3.00
U	3.00
M	2.75
P	2.75
Y	2.25
G	2.00
V	1.50
W	1.50
B	1.25
K	0.50
Q	0.50
X	0.50
J	0.25
Z	0.25

Source: Stephen Cobb, *PC and LAN Security.*

Changing the spacing yields the following:

        IT IS ON THE THIRTEEN TEN RARE ORE TRAIN

Passwords are used to establish the ciphering scheme. Individuals or systems that are entitled to decipher data are made aware of the password. The password used in the above example is TRICK. The way that passwords are used is interesting. First, the password is written out, followed by the regular alphabet, minus the letters in the password. The following illustrates this.

  T R I C K A B D E F G H J L M N O P Q S U V W X Y Z

The above line is the plaintext. To create the cipher, the entire alphabet is written out—backwards—immediately below the plaintext. The plaintext and ciphertext, shown together, are as follows:

```
T R I C K A B D E F G H J L M N O P Q S U V W X Y Z
Z X Y W V U T S R Q P O N M L K J I H G F E D C B A
```

21.6.2 The Data Encryption Standard (DES)

The Data Encryption Standard (DES) is an algorithm that uses a personal key to make data unusable to anyone who lacks that key. The data is encrypted when it is stored and decrypted when it is retrieved. The data becomes meaningful only when the correct DES key is provided.

DES originated with work done by IBM in conjunction with universities. IBM was concerned about encrypting data used in automated funds transfers, especially those involving communication between on-line terminals. In the early 1970s, NIST started work on a national encryption standard and placed a notice in the Federal Register of May, 1973 inviting vendors to submit data encryption techniques. At first, no adequate responses were received. In August of 1974, NIST tried again, prodding IBM to submit the encryption algorithm on which it had been working. This algorithm met with NIST's approval. The National Security Agency was also involved in the evaluation and approval process. DES is an official U.S. standard. It was originally published as FIPS PUB 46, and later updated and revised as FIPS PUB 46-1 in 1988. DES was subsequently adopted as an ANSI standard, too. It is the official way of protecting unclassified data in the computers of U.S. government agencies.

Export restrictions have been placed on products that have DES security built into them. As a result, some products will have DES security in versions of their products for domestic sales and a different security scheme in those versions of their products intended for export.

Details about the DES can be obtained from the U.S. Government and are also described in a number of books about security, like *Computer Security Basics*, a book by Deborah Russel and G. T. Gangemi Sr.

21.7 KERBEROS

Kerberos is an authentication system that was developed by Project Athena at the Massachusetts Institute of Technology. Project Athena was one of the first distributed, client/server systems to be built. It provided campus-wide access to numerous servers for students, instructors, professors, and administrators. Project Athena developers faced the problem of how to obtain and maintain system security with insecure workstations after login. To meet this need, they developed an authentication service. True to the client/server architecture, Kerberos sits on an authentication server. It provides a trusted, private key, network authentication system. Authentication is the confirmation that particular information was sent by a particular user. The name Kerberos comes from the many-headed dog in Greek mythology who was the servant of Pluto and guarded the gates to the underworld, thus earning himself immortality.

21.7.1 Kerberos Overview

With Kerberos, each user and network server has an encryption key which is known only to it and the Kerberos authentication server. To establish authentication, Kerberos securely makes and distributes a session key for each server-client instance. Then, each server uses the key in a manner that is consistent with its individual authentication policy. The server has several choices of action. Based on various criteria, it can decide on any of the following:

- Authenticate and encrypt all transmissions
- Use just authentication on all transmission
- Use authentication on only the first request
- Not use authentication at all

Kerberos is often used with multi-protocol environments and with open systems. Originally implemented for TCP/IP and UNIX networks, Kerberos can also be used to help secure UNIX, VMS, OS/2, DOS, and Macintosh machines. It is used by a number of different vendors and by the OSF's OSF/1 operating system.

As mentioned previously, authentication in a client/server environment should include having each user or server process be authenticated by each server invoked. Kerberos provides this ability. Kerberos authenticates users, but it does not determine what the users can do. Each individual Kerberos server is responsible for determining that.

One of the most important advantages of Kerberos is that it provides a way to authenticate users without having users send their passwords—even in encrypted form—over the network. Sending passwords over a network opens the system to the risk of invasion by intruders with protocol analyzers who may be able to snoop passwords off the wire.

One of the problems with Kerberos that users report is its lack of ability to scale. The OSF has recommended various enhancements to

Kerberos to address this problem, but many enterprises are not satisfied with this area of Kerberos.

21.7.2   Shared Secrets and Tickets

To provide authentication, Kerberos uses a combination of DES keys which are called "shared secrets," and a system of "tickets." To decrypt a message, it is necessary to know the key. A user's password is encrypted and kept in a highly secure machine called the Kerberos key server. This encrypted password is the client's (user's) key. The keys are called shared secrets because the secret of the keys is shared between the client and the server. There is Kerberos software on both the client end and on the Kerberos server. However, the client user can use the Kerberos protocol to log onto any server that is under Kerberos protection.

"Tickets" involved in the Kerberos protocol include a "ticket-granting ticket." This brief explanation of how Kerberos uses ticketing will start with a user who types a password into the client machine, requesting access to a server. The Kerberos client software does not send the password anywhere. Instead, it asks the Kerberos server to issue a ticket-granting ticket to the client. (A ticket-granting ticket is a ticket that grants the client another ticket. Let us call that other ticket, the internal ticket.) The Kerberos server responds with an encrypted message which contains the ticket-granting ticket. This message is encrypted using the client's key.

Essentially, the fact that the client software can decrypt the message from the Kerberos server, thus obtaining the internal ticket, proves to the Kerberos server the authenticity of the user. In this manner, clients are able to prove their validity without ever sending passwords over the network. The client software then sends requests to the Kerberos server, encrypting the requests using the shared key. The Kerberos server provides the necessary tickets to the client software for all the services it needs to use.

21.8   GOVERNMENT SECURITY: THE "RAINBOW SERIES" OF MANUALS

When building systems for government agencies, developers will need to perform some research on the government's special needs for security. Non-military agencies like Housing and Urban Development generally have less security than the military agencies which have very definite, specific security requirements. However, any system being developed for the government should be checked to determine what special security needs that particular branch of the government has.

The federal government has a series of manuals that are available free of charge describing the various security measures sponsored by the government. The entire set of manuals is often referred to as the "Rainbow Series" because of the colorful covers of the manuals. There are about 30 manuals in the entire series, and each one seems to be a different color or shade. A box full of the entire series can be obtained by writing to the following address:

INFOSEC Awareness Division
ATTN: IAOC
Fort George G. Meade, MD 20755–6000
or by calling (410) 766–8729

These brightly colored manuals cover many aspects of security from password management and authentication to understanding audit in trusted (secure) systems. A glossary of computer security terms is available as well as manuals on design documentation, trusted distribution, configuration and facility management in trusted systems, and other topics.

21.8.1 The Orange Book

The best known books in the Rainbow Series are probably the Orange Book and the Red Book. These books were some of the earliest in the Rainbow Series and came about as a result of the growing need for security on the part of the government and industry. In addition, the federal government needed standards for purchasing and using computers. In 1983, the government developed its *Trusted Computer System Evaluation Criteria*—the TCSEC—which became known as the Orange Book due to the color of its cover. This document defines four divisions of security protection as follows:

D Minimal Security
C Discretionary protection
B Mandatory protection
A Verified protection

Each division contains one or more numbered classes, with successively higher classes of security. For example, B1 is the lowest class of security in the B division; B2 is a higher class than B1, and B3 is the highest class of security of the three. The C division currently has two classes, C1 and C2, while the A division only has one class at the present time. Each class has a specific set of criteria which must be met for a system to be awarded a rating in that class. The criteria consist of four general categories:

- Security policy
- Accountability
- Assurance
- Documentation

Class D is reserved for systems that are submitted for evaluation but fail. The following information provides examples of systems which have been in existence for quite a while, and which have been awarded various security ratings by the government. IBM's early MVS/RACF system was awarded a C1 rating, while a later version was awarded a C2 rating. Other systems with a C2 rating include Computer Associate's ACF/2/MVS, Digital Equipment's VAX/VMS 4.3, and Hewlett-Packard's MPE-V/E. IBM's MVS/ESA and Unisys' OS 1100 both earned a B1 rating, while Honeywell Information System's SCOMP and Boeing Aerospace's SNS have an A1 rating, the highest possible.

21.8.2 The Red Book (Network Security)

Many of the concepts in the Orange Book apply to networks, but there are gaps. First, the Orange Book primarily deals with single-system security. In addition, it does not deal with availability—ensuring that a system or network keeps running—and authenticity. These gaps, and a variety of concerns over the security of data sent over communication networks, led to the development of standard criteria to be used in evaluating the level of security—or trust—that can be placed in a computer network. These criteria were published by the National Computer Security Center (NCSC) in 1987 in a document called the *Trusted Computer System Evaluation Criteria* which became known as the Red Book.

Computer Security Basics, a book by Deborah Russel and G. T. Gangemi Sr., provides a good overview of both the Orange Book and the Red Book.

Client/server developers should check the security ratings of systems with both the vendor and the government if they plan to use the vendor's products in secure client/server systems they are building for the government.

A fascinating book about computer espionage is *The Cuckoo's Egg: Tracing a Spy Through the Maze of Computer Espionage*, by Clifford Stoll. It is a story about how the astronomer-turned-detective author stumbled upon an intruder and spent the next year tracking and eventually trapping a system cracker from West Germany. The intruder breaks into 30 computers of his intended 450 before being apprehended. He uses worldwide networks including the Lawrence Berkeley Laboratory where Stoll worked. This true story reads like a well written espionage novel.

21.9 UNIX SECURITY

UNIX was originally created as a time-sharing system at Bell Laboratories. UNIX was widely used at universities and among Bell Lab employees in large measure to help researchers *share* information rather than keep information secure. Still, it had some degree of security, and as UNIX grew to become used in other types of computer systems, additional security was built into it.

The UNIX concept of a superuser with unlimited privileges is one of UNIX's biggest security problems. The superuser concept could permit someone to breach an entire system with only one password.

The fact that a variety of protocols, file systems, and other tools are used with UNIX also complicates the UNIX environment. For example, each network interface like the File Transfer Protocol (FTP) or the Network File System (NFS) from Sun Microsystems has its own mechanisms that must somehow integrate with the UNIX file protection mechanism.

The first encryption scheme for UNIX was based on the German World War II Enigma cipher. UNIX is now supplied with the Data Encryption Standard. Since export of DES to non-friendly countries is restricted, a special version of UNIX System V called the *International Edition* exists for export purposes. It has a crypt command and other extensions which use portions of DES.

Special techniques can be used to increase security when UUCP is used. A UNIX administrator should be aware of these techniques. They are discussed in a number of UNIX books such as *UNIX Networking*, a collection of writings edited by Stephen G. Kochan and Patrick N. Wood and published by Hayden Books.

21.9.1 RPC Security

There are numerous implementations of RPCs. Developers will need to research what security provisions are provided by the RPC implementations they are reviewing for use in their systems. This section will use Sun Microsystem's NFS RPC as an example of how security is related to this interprocess communication mechanism.

The NFS RPC has features which permit a developer or programmer to generate credentials to verify that the client has appropriate access right to a server. It is also necessary to set the server with knowledge of the appropriate credentials that the client should present. The credentials contain the user ID, group ID, and a list of groups to which the user belongs. The NFS server takes on the credential of the user as it tries to access the server requested by the user. When using this scheme, clients on non-UNIX machines must also generate a UNIX credential to access a UNIX-based server.

At one time, remote users with access to the root password on their local hosts could impersonate another user through the *su username* command. That command changed the effective user ID to *username*, thereby permitting the user to defeat the UNIX credential-passing ability. However, that problem was fixed in "Secure NFS," a new feature in a more recent release of NFS. Secure NFS uses a more secure RPC mechanism that passes the real user ID of the client, not the effective user ID. Secure NFS also authenticates the NFS client, assuring that the real user ID is coming from a trusted source.

Additional information on how NFS RPC security works can be obtained from Sun Microsystems' *Security Features Guide*, part number 800–1735–10.

21.9.2   Additional Help and Information with UNIX Security

Some companies offer analysis of UNIX security. Examples are Lachman Associates, Inc., and Spectrum Technology Group, Inc. One of the services Lachman Associates and Spectrum Technology will perform is to run programs that try known UNIX loopholes. Commercial products are also available for users to test their own UNIX systems for security problems. Examples of these are SystemAdmin from UniSolutions Associates and USECURE from Unitech Software Inc.

Books on UNIX security include *UNIX System Administration* by David Fiedler and Bruce Hunter, and *UNIX Survival Guide* by Elizabeth Nichols, Sidney Bailin, and Joseph Nichols. The February 1988 issue of *UNIX REVIEW*, (Vol. 6, No. 2), contains a selection of highly regarded essays on UNIX security. Another good article is "Stalking the Wily Hacker" by Clifford Stoll, in *Communications of the ACM*, vol. 31, no. 5, May 1988. A good on-going source of information about UNIX security risks is a newsgroup on Usenet known as comp.UNIX.wizards.

22

EXISTING PRODUCTION-QUALITY CLIENT/SERVER SYSTEMS

22.1 MANY FIRMS ARE IMPLEMENTING CLIENT/SERVER SYSTEMS

Statistics vary on the number of firms that have already implemented client/server systems. Most polls indicate that the majority of enterprises have installed, are installing, or are planning to soon install client/server systems. How are these enterprises solving their business problems with a client/server architecture? How did these enterprises get started with client/server systems? How are they handling some of the issues related to client/server systems? This chapter will answer these questions and more with examples of how various enterprises installed production-quality client/server systems to address business needs. Many of the business problems revolved around providing better access to enterprise data for end users, expanding business operations without adding to staff, and providing better customer service for both in-house and external customers.

22.1.1 Different Types of Systems

There are many different types of client/server systems in production today. Many of them use database servers on a LAN as a place to download data from the mainframe. Other client/server systems run mission-critical systems for their enterprise. In situations that use servers to download mainframe data, the database server provides a convenient and inexpensive way for many users to access data that they need. Many companies are using this approach to get started with client/server systems.

There are many types of hardware and software configurations in existing production client/server systems, too. Some systems consist of just UNIX, while others have no UNIX in them. An increasing number have a mixture of UNIX and non-UNIX systems working cooperatively together.

First, this chapter will describe some client/server systems which were installed relatively early, in the late 1980s. Baxter Healthcare and Textron Financial were early experimenters with client/server systems. Their efforts were successful and have led to both companies installing additional client/server systems. These two pioneers, like many other early users, continually upgrade the hardware and software they use for their client/server systems.

22.2   MISSION-CRITICAL CLIENT/SERVER SYSTEMS

We often think of high-volume transaction processing applications as being the most important systems; however, many different types of client/server systems can qualify as "mission-critical" systems. Individual companies must determine which of their systems are mission-critical to them. A system may be a mission-critical system to one enterprise, while its twin system in a second enterprise is only of medium importance to the second firm.

Hyatt Hotels uses a client/server architecture which includes an Informix database with fault-tolerant hardware and software to record and keep track of hotel reservations nationwide. That is certainly a mission-critical system to Hyatt Hotels. Its entire business depends on reservations at their many hotels and resorts.

22.2.1   OLTP Hotel Reservation System

Many thousands of people use Hyatt Hotels and Resorts' online reservation system each day. The system provides round-the-clock support for hundreds of concurrent users. Within moments a reservation agent is able to book and confirm a reservation that will even take into consideration the guest's preferences for a non-smoking room or king-size bed if he or she has stayed at Hyatt before. (Such preferences are stored by Hyatt in its customer history database.)

Before moving to a client/server architecture, Hyatt ran its reservation system on an IBM 4381 mainframe. The system was a modified version of a United Airlines reservations system that had been written in the mid-1970s. Over the years, Hyatt MIS management became increasingly aware that the 4381 mainframe was expensive to operate, inflexible, and did not offer ease-of-use to end users. Hyatt started a search for a more productive, functional, and lower cost environment. It did not take them long to decide they wanted a UNIX environment. That became one of the requirements when searching for a software and hardware solution. They were also interested in using a 4GL and a relational database.

Hyatt selected the Informix-Star database and other Informix software which is now running on AT&T's System 7000 RISC-based symmetric multiprocessor computers and other UNIX-based processors from AT&T. The size of the database is four gigabytes. The system provides sub-second response for most transactions, which are retrieving, creating, and updating database records which number in the millions. Hyatt has experienced a cost savings of over 25 percent as a result of this change in hardware and software.

Hyatt is taking advantage of a number of Informix products and services. These include Informix OnLine, Informix-Star, Informix-4GL Compiler, the Informix-4GL Rapid Development System, Informix-4GL Interactive Debugger, Informix-SQL, Informix-ESQL/C, Wingz, Client Services, Regency Support, and Training Services. Informix's Client Services group worked with Hyatt in designing the application to make sure that a system written with a 4GL and RDBMS would deliver the kind of OLTP performance required for a reservation system. AT&T worked with Hyatt to benchmark and fine-tune the overall system to make sure it met performance requirements.

The system has been a tremendous success. Not only does it meet all of the performance requirements, Hyatt feels it gives mainframe-caliber performance at a fraction of mainframe cost. In addition it offers flexibility, ease of programming, and ease of use. Hyatt has also developed a number of other client/server systems including a marketing system, a hotel management reporting system, and an executive information system. More client/server systems will follow.

22.2.2 Outsourcing Systems

Many major companies are turning to outsourcing to get a faster start with client/server systems. Consulting firms like EDS, Anderson Consulting, SHL Systemhouse, Inc. are winning many new outsourcing contracts due to their client/server knowledge. Bethlehem Steel outsourced its entire data processing operation to EDS with the intention of having EDS eventually lead Bethlehem Steel into client/server systems.

Flour Daniel Inc., a construction and engineering subsidiary of Flour Corporation, had developed some client/server systems itself before it made the decision in 1992 to sign a five-year outsourcing agreement with SHL Systemhouse. The systems it installed itself were for its engineering operations, which had to have information systems installed at client sites very quickly. Flour MIS management said it chose a client/server architecture because client/server systems put the work closer to customers and permit easier ad-hoc reporting than mainframe systems.

Flour also implemented a client/server system that linked computer-aided manufacturing programs with procurement, project control, and accounting data before signing the outsourcing agreement. It expects the migration from the mainframe to client/server to move faster with the outsourcing plan. Flour expects that its overall costs will decline as more processing is moved off the mainframe and onto servers.

22.3   IMPROVING CUSTOMER SERVICE

Many companies are interested in improving customer service. They see that information technology can help them do this. Many of these companies are turning to a client/server architecture to improve customer service because various characteristics of this architecture can help the firm be more responsive to customer requests. GUIs, distributed architecture, and networking capabilities all add to this responsiveness. This section will describe the experiences of two MIS departments who pursued a client/server architecture to meet their needs to be more responsive to both in-house customers (users) and external customers.

In 1988, Providence, RI-based Textron Financial Corporation, which provides a wide variety of financial services, wanted to improve customer service. It wanted to start by expanding the inventory finance operation. Textron Financial management wanted to permit 30 percent growth in the inventory finance operation without increasing the MIS or overall finance operation workforce. After the system proved itself successful, management planned to expand the implementation to additional departments.

Sprint was also interested in improving customer service. This included MIS developing a closer relationship with various divisions within Sprint—its in-house customers. If MIS provided better service for its in-house customers—many of them marketing units—these units could provide better service for Sprint's external customers. Some of Sprint's in-house customers used to go outside for help with various IS projects when there was an appropriate fit. However, since the Business Systems Development (BSD) in Sprint's information systems department has been working with client/server systems, these units turn to BSD for new systems.*

22.3.1 Textron Explored Other Options First

At first, Textron** called in a major consulting firm that recommended Textron use DB2 with the Easel development tool software from Easel Corporation in Burlington, MA. The utilization of Easel was to improve the 3270 interface. However, MIS managers at Textron—seeing this as a safe, but not an advanced approach—turned down this recommendation. They went to Textron senior management for funding to implement what was then (1988) still a relatively new client/server architecture.

In fact, in keeping with good practice, Textron performed a buy-or-build analysis. Should it buy a packaged application system or build one? It quickly found that in 1988 not many packaged application systems were available for a client/server environment. (That has changed. An increasing number of packaged application systems are available for client/server environments.) Textron had no choice at that time but to build its own system in-house.

22.3.1.1 "Client/Server is the Future of Computing"

After studying the client/server architecture, Textron believed in 1988 that client/server systems represented the future for computer systems. Fortunately senior management was supportive. Textron's senior management is known for being fairly to very aggressive in investing in information technology in support of the business. Senior management knew that the existing systems were inadequate and gave MIS the go-ahead to proceed with the proposed client/server system. Management has not regretted that decision. It put Textron Financial on the road to developing more and more client/server systems.

Textron Financial chose SQL Server for its database server, the Micro Decisionware Gateway to download data from the mainframe, and LAN Manager as its network operating system. Additional tools used by Textron Financial included NetGateway and Open Server for CICS from Sybase;

---

*Information for this section came from Damian Rinaldi's article, "Mining Business Nuggets" in Software Magazine"s *Client/Server Computing*, November, 1992, vol. 12, no16.
**Information for this section came from John Desmond"s article, "Firm Opted for a More Risky—But True—Solution," in *Software Magazine*, August, 1991, vol. 11, no. 10.

Application Manager from Intelligent Environment Inc. (Tewksbury, MA); PC Telon from Pansophic Systems Inc. (Lisle, IL); Micro Focus Cobol from Micro Focus Ltd., (Menlo Park, CA); DB2 from IBM; and tools supplied by Anderson Consulting.

At first Textron used IBM's AIX software (IBM's version of UNIX) on an IBM RS/6000 computer for their server. However, IBM's AIX and RS/6000 were both new at that time, and Textron experienced bugs in IBM's operating system which caused delays, frustration, and other problems. As a result, Textron switched to a UNIX-based SPARCstation workstation from Sun Microsystems as their server.

Textron Financial used OS/2 and IBM's Presentation Manager for its GUI on the client desktop computers. Textron's MIS management said it originally chose Presentation Manager because Windows 3.0 was not out yet and it felt the earlier version of Windows was not adequate for their needs. While Textron did experience some difficulties with Presentation Manager, after a while the software stabilized and met the company's needs quite well.

22.3.1.2 Expect Heavy Training Costs

Textron Financial recommends that other companies be prepared for hefty training costs. Textron MIS management said a lot of money was spent on training. The learning curve it experienced was quite steep when it implemented its early client/server systems. The learning curve included training the MIS department to use client/server technology and training end users to utilize the new systems. Interoperability issues also contributed to the learning curve.

Textron said that another factor in the learning curve was that the developers had to be multi-disciplinary to build client/server systems. That is, the client/server development process combined what were previously separate operations and technologies. With mainframe development, one could be a database expert and that was sufficient. However, Textron Financial found that client/server developers had to know not only database technology, but also application development, GUI, and communications technology concepts.

22.3.2 Sprint Gets More Proactive With Customers

In improving its customer service, a major goal of the National Service Organization within Sprint was to be more proactive with its customers, small- to medium-size businesses. This meant providing faster service and the ability to provide service to more customers each day. Each

Sprint representative typically handled 250 accounts, each one of which usually had anywhere from 50 to 100 separate locations. The previous system permitted only a limited ability to respond to customers—each representative could only handle a few proactive calls each day. It would take approximately three hours for a representative to gather information from over 1000 3270 screens before he or she could call the customer back and help him or her. The goal of Sprint was to handle customer service in a high-quality, expedient fashion.

22.3.2.1 Sprint's Development Choice was Foundation

When looking for solutions, Sprint examined several possibilities. Its choice was Chicago-based Anderson Consulting's Foundation for Cooperative Processing (FCP). Integration, service, and support capabilities played important roles in the choice of Foundation. Another important factor was Anderson Consulting's long-term plan to evolve Foundation.

Sprint's Business Systems Development Group found that with Foundation, the need for IS developers to learn specialized communications skills for the client/server environment was significantly reduced. In addition, the fact that Foundation is a repository-based toolset facilitated coordination among the developers. Training was provided on Foundation for BSD developers. Training was also provided for OS/2 and for developing windowed applications. Also addressed was the end users' learning curve with the windowed applications.

In addition to using the software package, BSD was able to benefit from the service arm of Anderson Consulting. Nearly half of the development team's 31 people consisted of consultants from Anderson. BSD employees were able to learn from Anderson Consulting employees. Later, the BSD employees were able to use those new skills on future client/server projects and, in turn, train co-workers. As the project progressed, that aspect of the plan and Foundation's repository-based toolset became very important parts of the overall approach.

22.3.2.2 Challenges, Surprises, and Accomplishments

One of the challenges that Sprint's Business Systems Development group overcame was data capture from multiple mainframe sources including Adabas, DB2, and VSAM. The system had to integrate data about average monthly bills, customer cost per minute, receivables, late payables, and open disputes. The data sources were spread over several locations and tied to separate applications.

Another challenge was that end users were so accustomed to 3270 terminals that they continually expressed their requirements in terms of 3270 screens. To change this, BSD established focus groups that discussed what the end-user representatives did each day and what could be automated. The positive side of this was that the end users became very involved in the overall prototyping and development process. When the prototype for the first group was nearing completion, a second group within Sprint expressed interest in having a similar system. Interest throughout the company has grown, so that now plans are being made to deploy the system widely within Sprint.

One of the surprises that Sprint's BSD group encountered was that the cost of the new system was not as low as had been expected. The group found that costs were equal or higher than those of previous 3270 systems. However, the higher costs included the additional training and the fact that IS support for the new applications will be more labor-intensive than they were for the 3270 applications. Some of these costs may diminish over time. BSD management says the system could have been made less expensive by having fewer screens and data sources, but that would have limited the new system's functionality.

Cost benefits have been realized, however. Sprint has experienced compensating savings and customer service benefits from the system. The fact that there have been cost savings on the business side makes the technology investment worthwhile, says Sprint management. Since the system has been installed, Sprint has experienced less turnover in the external customer base due to the higher level of service now being provided.

22.3.3 Providing Server Access to Mainframe Data

Providing better "customer service" also means providing better service for in-house customers—employees—of the enterprise's information systems. Baxter Healthcare, in Deerfield, IL, has been doing just that by moving rapidly into client/server systems. Baxter liked the idea of moving mainframe data to LANs. Baxter looked at it as a way to share mainframe data, thus letting its employees "work smarter." The new architecture let many people access data they needed without slowing down the mainframe. In addition, Baxter liked the low cost of server Mips.

After experimenting with the client/server architecture to spread access to needed data, IS professionals within Baxter Healthcare liked what they saw and believed that LANs would play an important role in overall enterprise computing in general. They started the process of building an infrastructure to move more data from the mainframe to LANs. They were primarily interested in letting employees have access to historical sales data for analysis and decision support.

The users who were given access to the sales data on LAN servers already had access to that data on the mainframe. Baxter felt that these users were the rightful owners of that data. Baxter's IS professionals made sure when moving the data from the mainframe to servers that they provided security and implemented the system following good business practices. They required a password to gain access to the LAN, and thus to the data. They also used various security measures that were provided with LAN Manager, the network operating system from Microsoft.

Among the security measures that Baxter developers installed were the use of diskless workstations to access data on the database servers. Diskless workstations ensure that sensitive data is not inadvertently left on a desktop machine's disk. It is a precaution that numerous sites take when critical data is available to many users. Since each workstation has access to the data on the LAN database server, no workstation should have the need for its own hard disk. In fact, users generally get better performance from the LAN server than they would from hard disk of their own because the LAN servers are so much faster. Of course, end users who need to store personal business data can have hard disks installed for office systems usage. End users who use the servers and their own hard disk usually realize and appreciate how much faster the server is. Client/server developers from Baxter said that their end users often wind up moving their own personal business data from their PC's hard disk to a server to benefit from the speed.

22.3.3.1 Using a Gateway to Access Mainframe Data

Baxter Healthcare's early systems used Compaq 286s as desktop machines. Later, Compaq 386/SXs with 5Mb of memory were used, followed by 486s. Baxter continues to upgrade its systems' configuration. Early servers were SystemPro 386/33s from Compaq Computer, Houston, TX with 840Mb of hard disk memory.

Exact configurations within Baxter vary from LAN to LAN. Sometimes there is one Compaq SystemPro to run SQL Server and another SystemPro to run the network. Most of the LANs are equipped with LAN Manager and the DCA/Microsoft Communications Server. Divisions that do not need SQL Server receive the downloaded mainframe data in the form of flat files.

Baxter Healthcare used DOS with Windows on the desktop machines and SQL Server and OS/2 on the database servers. The database servers also have the Database Gateway from Micro Decisionware, Boulder, CO. The Database Gateway accesses data from the mainframe while SQL Server provides a staging area for the data. The Database Gateway software has its own security features and has the ability to take care of mainframe security. Baxter uses the Database Gateway to access data from IMS, DB2, and VSAM files.

When a request for data comes from the Database Gateway, it triggers a whole series of activities on the mainframe. Mainframe transactions that were created in-house perform IMS queries to respond to the requests, and then send the resulting data from IMS to DB2 for staging.

Fifty percent of the updates to the IMS System comes from end users on Compaq desktop machines. The other fifty percent comes directly from external customers' systems. Some of these customers are using EDI and some are not. Baxter has permitted external customers to enter orders themselves since the days of teletypes. Since those early days, Baxter has constantly updated its order systems installing PCs, touch tone telephones, bar code readers, and mainframe-to-mainframe connections. More and more EDI software is being installed all the time.

22.4 CONNECTIVITY AS A CRITICAL SUCCESS FACTOR

Many MIS managers have identified corporate-wide connectivity as a critical success factor for their enterprises. Two companies' connectivity experiences that will be discussed in this section are Motorola in Schaumberg, IL, and Foxboro Corporation in Foxboro, MA. Many other companies agree that corporate-wide connectivity provides a strategic benefit and are installing or have installed interconnected networks throughout their enterprise.*

22.4.1 Motorola Sees Network as Strategic Benefit

MIS Managers at Motorola determined that having a worldwide network would provide the company with strategic benefit. This worldwide network would be an internetwork, or internet, of many different LANs. Motorola, like many other large enterprises, found it had a complex combination of networking products and protocols which had to work together.

---

*Information about Motorola's implementation came from "Motorola's Massive Internet Poses New Type of Security Challenge," by Damian Rinaldi, in Software Magazine's *Client/Server Computing* supplement, May, 1992, vol. 12, no. 7. Information about Foxboro's implementation came from Damian Rinali's "Foxboro Co., Transforms Standards Vision to Reality," *Client/Server Computing*, January, 1993, Vol. 13, No. 2, pp. 55–57.

22.4.1.1 Motorola's Three-Tier Network

Motorola's overall network consists of three tiers. The first tier is a high-speed network which carries voice and data and consists of 150 T1 lines, some T3 lines, spots on three satellites, and a number of ground stations. The second tier is made up of FDDI rings transmitting at 100M bits per second which have workstations and LANs tied into it with twisted-pair connections. The third tier includes a variety of LAN technologies including Novell's NetWare, Microsoft's Lan Manager, IBM's PC LAN, Banyan's VINES, and HP's Apollo Domain system. 30,000 desktops, including IBM PCs, UNIX workstations, and Macintosh computers are able to communicate over Motorola's internet. Notebook computers can also use the communications internetwork.

Motorola's goal is eventually to have an OSI-compliant network. In an effort to move in that direction, Motorola switched from its IBM SNA network to TCP/IP. The TCP/IP internet has over 500 Cisco Systems' routers to handle traffic to major campus locations.

22.4.1.2 Security, Scalability, and Interoperability

Motorola has conquered some of the security issues that have come up in connection with its massive internetwork. However, Motorola security management says that new issues always arise. For example, the requirement to support notebook computers is growing rapidly. Notebooks, portable by nature, represent unique security requirements.

One of the problems Motorola is facing is getting Kerberos to scale large enough. Many other security managers in other firms are concerned about this—especially when they start to connect large numbers of workstations to internets, for example, in the thousands and tens of thousands of workstations. OSF—which uses Kerberos in its DCE—has proposed enhancements to Kerberos, but Motorola management says they are not sufficient. As a result Motorola is looking at third-party security packages to extend Kerberos' security functions.

Another concern is what to do about scaling and integrating E-mail systems in large and growing internets. Many enterprises have diverse E-mail systems used by different divisions. Now, with enterprise-wide internets, users want to be able to send messages to anyone in the company. Therefore, handling 50,000 or 100,000 E-mail IDs becomes a problem. At Motorola, one manager is dedicated to the problem of enterprise integration. Motorola's goal is to incorporate and follow standards like the X.400 OSI messaging and mail protocol as much as possible. However, some of Motorola's developers have had to write specialized code to assist in translating from proprietary E-mail implementations to the format of the X.400 standard.

Another interoperability problem Motorola is dealing with is assisting its users with exchanging spreadsheet files and combining data from multiple, diverse sources. In-house developers provide translation software where translation software does not exist. So far, all of the challenges have been met. End users are happy with the new internetworking capabilities that they have, and they are looking forward to more.

22.4.2   Foxboro Cuts Costs in Half

In 1987, Foxboro had a five year plan to build an interconnected network and to cut operating costs. At the time, Foxboro had a terminal-based broadband network of Digital VAX systems that did not interoperate with their other VAX-based networks and systems. In addition, the president of the company did not believe the existing systems were accurate enough to help launch a new product line or meet his vision of the future.

Five years later, a cohesive network was installed, Foxboro had reduced the total IS budget by fifty percent—from approximately $28 million to a little over $14 million—and had reduced the IS staff from 225 to about 115. Many of the IS staff members were reassigned to other positions within Foxboro. Overall, it was a successful five years for the company.

Today, the company's MIS department has been renamed to the Corporate Information Services (CIS) Group. The group oversees a TCP/IP network which connects more than 3,000 intelligent devices worldwide. The network is based on the Open Network Computing (ONC) environment from Sun Microsystems. It includes the following equipment:

- Macintosh
- IBM and compatible PCs running MS-DOS and Sun's PC-NFS
- Hewlett-Packard midrange systems and workstations running MPE, MPE-XL, and HP-UX
- One IBM 4381 running MVS
- VAXes running Ultrix and VMS
- Sun servers and workstations running Sun OS
- NetWare and AppleTalk LANs

Each of the servers runs a version of NFS—some from the server manufacturers, others from third-party vendors. PCs in the network rely on the Network Driver Interface Specification (NDIS) from Microsoft and 3Com Corp to connect to the backbone network. NDIS lets the PCs access any server in the network because it is able to run multiple protocols over the same Ethernet board.

Putting the basic network infrastructure in place was only part of the overall five year plan. Other important parts of it were to replace or upgrade all of the company's application software packages and to make sure everything was interconnected. For example, management said that without an order entry interface to manufacturing, it could wind up with a two-week cycle time. With the order entry package from Cardinal Data Corporation, a division of Ross Systems, Inc., in Waltham, MA, the cycle time is less than 22 hours. Foxboro will switch from the McCormick & Dodge financial software it bought in 1987—before M&D's acquisition by D&B—to D&B's UNIX client/server implementation of its financial software as soon as modules become available. Foxboro will also implement D&B's UNIX client/server human resource applications.

22.4.3   Distributed System Helps School System Downsize

Many client/server systems qualify as distributed systems. Some sites say establishing a distributed system was their primary goal in developing client/server systems, while other sites say the fact that their final system was a distributed one was minor related to other goals they were achieving. The Tucson Unified School District (TUSD) in Arizona and the Massachusetts Institute of Technology were two enterprises who had a specific goal of establishing a distributed client/server system.*

The Tucson Unified School District (TUSD) in Arizona had an important reason for moving to a distributed system. It wanted to empower each individual school site so it could more easily meet the growing reporting and data manipulation demands of federal and state governments. To meet the government requirements, the individual school sites needed to have excellent access to the necessary data. A distributed system could provide that.

TUSD also experienced a welcome side benefit from their new distributed system. It was able to retire its DECsystem 10 mainframe from Digital Equipment Corporation not long after it started developing its distributed client/server systems. At the same time, it could see that the days of their IBM midrange System 38 were numbered as well.

---

*The information about TUSD is from John Desmond's article, "Building Around Unknowns of Client/Server" in *Software Magazine*, March, 1992, Vol. 12, No. 3, pp. 68–69. The information about Project Athena was taken from the book, *A Model for Distributed Campus Computing*, by George Champine.

From the start, the goal of TUSD was to move from a centralized system to a distributed system of PC LANs running NetWare from Novell, Inc. on the servers and Windows on the desktop machines. TUSD felt that the advantages of a distributed system were as follows:

- Better hardware price performance
- A more attractive user interface
- Faster development times
- An ability to develop the system incrementally

Not all the software that TUSD needed for its long-term plans was available when it started its distributed client/server approach. This did not bother TUSD which said it was accustomed to the unavailability of software because the mainframe environment did not meet all of its software needs, either. TUSD IS management says it is looking forward to building more systems on the client/server foundation it has established.

22.4.4 Workflow Software Increases Productivity

CareAmerica HealthPlan, a health insurer in Chatsworth, CA, is using workflow software from WorkFlo provided by FileNet Corp., in Costa Mesa, CA to streamline its everyday operations like processing insurance claims. In 1990, CareAmerica started searching for a better way to process its paper insurance claims. It had nearly 30 cabinets filled with paper that employees had to search through to respond to customer inquiries. Employees used microfiche slides to discover where insurance information was stored.

One of the reasons why CareAmerica selected the WorkFlo software was because WorkFlo had many programming functions that enabled CareAmerica's developers to build their own customized applications more easily. The software is running on an Ethernet LAN using Microsoft's LAN Manager network operating system. CareAmerica management said it expects to recoup its $1 million investment in three years. The new software system permitted the company to keep its employee headcount low because existing employees were able to process claims more efficiently.

22.5 USING PACKAGED-APPLICATION CLIENT/SERVER SYSTEMS

Foxboro is not the only one implementing client/server application packages. Many companies have made the transition to a client/server architecture by first installing a client/server application package. A company sets up the required hardware, buys a ready-built client/server financial or human resource application package, gives its staff the necessary training, and is fairly quickly operating with a client/server environment. Employees get acclimated to the new environment this way, and then the company either buys additional client/server application packages and/or starts building client/server systems itself.

22.5.1   End Users Go Around MIS

Some end users and other business people are taking matters into their own hands when they feel that MIS is not able to meet their needs. Fifteen financial analysts at Esco Corporation in Portland, OR, a manufacturer for the construction and mining industries, convinced management to allow them to be "guinea pigs" for implementing a client/server architecture. The analysts bought networked financial applications from IMRS in Stamford, CT. The financial application packages run consolidated reporting systems on 386 PCs connected to a NetWare network.*

Business managers know their overall requirements. These business managers may not have been able to express their processing requirements in terms of mainframe processing because mainframe computers were an unknown to them. However, business managers and end users have had a decade or more of experience with PCs. They understand PCs, and they understand the software that comes with PCs. They have seen what they can do with stand-alone PCs. It is not much more difficult for them to realize what they could do with networked PCs and servers—the basic foundation of client/server systems. Now that vendors are coming out with good application packages, like financial software for client/server architectures, business managers and end users in many companies are installing their own client/server systems.

22.5.2   Pepsi Seeks Better Functionality

The primary motivation for moving to client/server application package software by Pepsi-Cola International, in Somers, NY, was not to save money on mainframes but to gain better functionality. Pepsi has end users accessing data from many different time zones around the world. MIS personnel at Pepsi said it would be a problem to have someone in India online, accessing data on a mainframe in New York during normal

---

*Information in this section was obtained from John Desmond's and Jack Gold's "Financial Client/Server Applications Empowering Non-Technies" in *Client/Server Computing*, March, 1993, Vol. 13, No. 5, pp. 51–52.

business hours. Yet the individual in India had to have access to the data he or she needed. A worldwide network of servers will provide relief for that situation.

To get better functionality, Pepsi chose to use the modular SunSystems financial management accounting package from Systems Union. It runs on a Compaq SystemPro 486/50 server with 16Mb RAM and several gigabytes of storage. The SystemPro is running OS/2 while the client machines run DOS and are connected to the servers with a Token-Ring network. The client machines are 386s and 486s with 8Mb of RAM.

After the first SystemPro was installed in Somers, NY and proved successful, Pepsi made plans to install six more SystemPro servers at division offices and larger area offices located in various parts of the country. Pepsi also planned to install servers at international offices in various countries. All of the servers will be connected to each other by means of WANs. This configuration provides much more responsiveness than a centralized mainframe. Pepsi management says that the combination of the financial application package and the client/server architecture will provide the additional functionality it needs.

22.6 CLIENT/SERVER AND OPEN SYSTEMS

Many enterprises have lost patience with proprietary systems. They know they can save money with open systems, and they are determined to move to open systems as soon as they believe it is feasible for their specific circumstances. Many companies already have moved to open systems. For many of these companies, switching from proprietary operating systems to UNIX started their open systems venture. Others are starting or planning to implement software from OSF, which is dedicated to open systems.

Some enterprises that have had IBM's proprietary MVS installed for many years took a wary approach to UNIX. An example is U.S. West, which for years had production systems on both MVS and UNIX machines in the same data center. A U.S. West system architect said that for a time there was a "line of death in the middle that we never crossed." Now, however, the architect says that U.S. West has the same reliability and availability on the UNIX side of the line as it does on the MVS side of the line.

22.6.1 Millipore is Dedicated to Open Systems

Millipore Corporation, a leader in fluid analysis and purification, is a proponent of open systems. A number of years ago, Millipore decided that it could save money if it moved its computing systems from proprietary systems to open systems. In evaluating various products, Millipore first selected Oracle, a database which can be ported to many different hardware platforms. Its next decision was to go with UNIX. Its choice of hardware was Sequence Computer's Sequent symmetric multiprocessor which is based on multiple Intel Corp. chips. Sequent Computer, Inc., in Beaverton, OR, has a UNIX operating system called Dynix/ptx, based on UNIX System V, which Millipore is using.

Millipore initially installed two Sequent multiprocessors—one with 18 processors and one with 14 processors. At this time Millipore has a total of 60Gb of storage—that is 60 *billion* bits of storage. Millipore's network consists of 3000 PCs, workstations, terminals, and Apple Macintoshes connected by Ethernet cabling, DECnet and TCP/IP, and 128K T1 leased lines. Multiple plants, offices, and laboratories located in various parts of New England are connected to ones on the West Coast.

Millipore has its order entry system in production in its open system client/server environment. Oracle Corporation co-developed the system in the Oracle language for Millipore and then wrote additional coding, evolving the software to be its standard order application offering.

As systems are built in Oracle for the Sequent, Millipore is phasing out the hardware and software it previously had. This includes an IBM 4381 mainframe running VM and VSE, a 3000 Model 70 from Hewlett-Packard running MPE V, and an Eclipse MV10,000 from Data General Corp running AOS/VS. More than hardware and software is changing, however. The move to open systems caused a lot of evaluation within Millipore which included a restructuring for the corporate MIS group.

The combination of the new approach, attitude, and hardware/software of the restructured MIS group has caused a rejuvenation of its reputation within Millipore. Formerly, the business units avoided it, but now MIS is considered a partner. This has had a very positive impact on both MIS and the business units.

22.6.2 Burlington Plans to Shut Off the Mainframe

Burlington Coat Factory in Hanover, NH plans to get rid of their mainframe after it has moved enough systems to its open systems client/server environment. Burlington uses Sequent computers on which it is currently running new systems in parallel with the older mainframe systems. The mainframe is a DPS 8 machine from Bull HN Information Systems, Inc., in Billerica, MA, which was installed in 1981. The mainframe was running the proprietary DTSS operating system. In the late 1980s Burlington decided to pursue an open systems environment. That was when the Sequent was brought in. Burlington is running Dynix/ptx,

Sequent's version of UNIX.

It has been inventing its own solutions to running large-scale UNIX and client/server data centers. Management at Burlington said it had to invent its own solutions because no satisfactory, established policies and procedures for running large UNIX client/server environments had been developed at the time.

22.6.3 The Importance of Openness

Open system qualities will become an increasingly important aspect of client/server systems. The more open client/server systems are, the more quickly the technology will be implemented. Along with increased productivity and responsiveness, cost-effectiveness, and user friendliness, openness will become a major attraction of client/server systems.

The modularity of the client/server architecture provides the perfect environment for potential portable "plug-in" components. We are still a long way from achieving this ideal—but it is certainly a very worthwhile goal.

ACRONYMS

ACE Advanced Computing Enviornment

ACF Advanced Communication Function

ACM Association for Computing Machinery

ACSE Association control service element (Prounounced ak-see)

ADR Applied Data Research

AFIPS American Federation of Information Processing Societies

AI Artificial intelligence

AIX Advanced Interactive eXecutive (IBM's UNIX)

AMS American Management Systems

ANDF Architecture Neutral Definition Language (OSF)

ANSI American National Standards Institute

API Application programming interface

APP Application Portability Profile (NIST)

APPC Advanced Program-to-Program Communications

APPN Advanced Peer-to-Peer Networking

ARPA Advanced Research Projects Agency

ARPANET Advanced Research Projects Agency Network

ASCII American Standard Code for Information Interchange

ASM Association for Systems Management

ASN.1 Abstract Syntex Notation 1

ATM Asynchronous Transfer Mode

ATMI Application Transaction Manager Interface (X/Open)

A/UX Apple's UNIX for the Macintosh

BBN Bolt, Beranek, and Newman, Inc.

BIOS Basic I/O System

BIPS Billion instructions per second

BLOBS, Blobs Binary Large Objects

BRI Basic Rate Interface

BSC Binary Synchronous Communications

BSD Berkeley Software Distribution (UNIX)

CA Computer Associates, Inc.

CAD Computer-aided design

CAD/CAM Computer-aided design/ computer-aided manufacturing

CAE Common Application Environment (X/Open)

CAI Computer-assisted instruction

CALS Computer-Aided Acquisition and Logistics Support

CAM Computer-aided manufacturing

CASE Computer aided software engineering

CBEMA   Computer and Business Equipment Manufacturers Association

CBT   Computer-based training

CCA   Computer Corporation of America

CCITT   Consultative Committee for International Telephony and Telegraphy

CCS   Common Communications Support

CDA   Compound Document Architecture

CDDI   Copper Distributed Data Interface

CGA   Color-Graphics Adapter

CGI   Computer Graphics Interface

CGM   Computer Graphics Metafile

CICS   Customer Information Control System (Prounounced "kicks" or "C-I-C-S")

CID   Configuration, Installation, and Distribution (IBM)

CIM   Computer-integrated manufacturing (Pronounced "sim")

CISC   Complex instruction set computing (Pronounced "sisk")

CLI   Call-level interface

CM-API   Consolidated Management API

CMIP   Common Management Information Protocol

CMIS   Common Management Information Services

CORBA   Common Object Request Broker Architecture

COS   Corporation for Open Systems

COSE   Common Open Software Environment

COSI   Corporation for Open Systems International

CPI-C   Common Programming Interface for Communications

cps   characters per second

CRC   Cyclical Redundancy Checking

CSCW   Computer-Supported Cooperative Work

CSMA/CD   Carrier Sense, Multiple Access with Collision Detection

CSTP   Client/server transaction processing

CTG   Computer Task Group

CUA   Common User Access (IBM)

DAL   Data Access Language

DARI   Database Application Remote Interface (IBM)

DARPA   DoD Advanced Research Projects Agency

DASD   Direct Access Storage Device

DAT   Digital Audio Tape

D&B   Dun & Bradstreet

DB2   DataBase 2 (IBM)

DBA   DataBase administrator

DBMS   DataBase Management System

DCA   (1) Document Content Architecture
(2) Defense Communications Agency
(3) Digital Communications Associates, Inc.

DCE   Distributed Computing Environment (OSF)

DDBMS   Distributed DataBase Management System

DDE   Dynamic Data Exchange

DDL   Data definition language or Data description language

DDM   Distributed Data Management

DECmcc   DEC Management Control Center

DES   Data Encryption Standard

DIF   (1) Data Interchange Format
(2) Document Interchange Format

DISSOS   DIStributed Office Support System (IBM)

DLL   Dynamic Link Library

DME   Distributed Management Environment (OSF)

DML   Data manipulation language

DNS   Domain Naming System

DOE   Department of Energy

DOD   Department of Defense Sometimes shown as DoD

DOS   Disk Operating System

DP   Data processing

dpi   dots per inch

DPMA   Data Processing Management Association

DRDA   Distributed Relational Database Architecture (IBM)

DSA   Distributed Systems Architecture

DSEE   Domain Software Engineering Environment (HP/Apollo)

DS/DD   Double sided/double density

DS/HD   Double sided/high density

DSM   Distributed Systems Manager (IBM)

DSS   Decision Support System

DTE   Data Terminating Equipment

DTP   Distributed Transaction Processing

DUA   Directory User Agent

DXT   Data eXTract (IBM)

EBCDIC   Extended Binary Coded Decimal Interchange Code

EC   European Community, European Commission

ECMA   European Computer Manufacturers Association

EDA/SQL   Enterprise Data Access/ Structured Query Language (Information Builders, Inc.)

EDI   Electronic Data Interchange

EDIFACT   Eletronic Data Interhange For Adminstration, Commerce and Transport

EDS   Electronic Data Systems

EFT   Electronic Funds Transfer

EGA   Enhanced Graphics Adapter

EIS   Executive Information System

EISA   Extended Industy Standard Architecture

ELF   Extremely Low Frequency

EMA   Enterprise Management Architecture (Digital Equipment Corporation)

EMACS   Editor MACroS (UNIX)

E-Mail   Electronic Mail

EPROM   Erasable Programmable ROM

ES   Expert system

ESCON   Enterprise Systems CONnection

EVGA   Extended VGA

FCC   Federal Communications Commission

FCP   Foundation for Cooperative Processing (Anderson Consulting)

FDDI   Fiber Distributed Data Interface

FIPS   Federal Information Processing Standard

FLOPS   FLoating Point Operations Per Second

FTAM   File Transfer Access and Management

FTP   File Transfer Protocol

Gb   Gigabits; Billion bits per second

GB   Gigabytes; Billion bytes per second

GDI   Graphics Device Interface

GEnie   General Electric Network for Information Exchange

GIF   Graphics Interchange Format

GKS   Graphical Kernel System

GNMP   Government Network Management Profile

GOSIP   Government Open Systems Interconnection Profile

GUI   Graphical user interface

HDLC   High-level Data Link Control

HIPPI   High Performance Parallel Interface Channel

HLLAPI   High Level Language Application Program Interface

HP   Hewlett-Packard Company

HP-UX   HP's Version of UNIX

HPFS   High Performance File System

IBI   Information Builders, Inc.

IC   Integrated Circuit

I-CASE   Intergrated CASE

ICCP   Institute for Certification of Computer Professionals

ICS   InterSystems Communication facility (IBM's CICS/ICS)

IDAPI   Integrated Database Application Programming Interface

IDC   International Data Corporation

IDG   International Data Group

IDL   Interface Definition Language (OSF's DCE)

IEEE   Institute of Electrical and Electronic Engineers

IEF   Information Engineering Facility (Texas Instruments)

IEW   Information Engineering Workbench (Knowledgeware)

IFIP   International Federation of Information Processing

IGES   Initial Graphics Exchange Specification

IGOSS   Industry and Government Open Systems Specification

IMS   Information Management System (IBM)

I/O   Input/Output

IP   Internet Protocol

IPC   InterProcess Communication

IPL   Initial Program Load

IPX   Internet Packet Exchange (Novell)

IRDS   Information Resource Dictionary System

IRM   Information Resource Management

IS   Information Systems

ISA   Industry Standard Architecture

ISDN   Integrated Services Digital Network

ISO   International Standards Organization

ISV   Independent software vendor

IT   Information technology

ITAA   Information Technology Association of America

JAD   Joint Application Development

JITC   Joint Interoperability Test Center (DCA)

KBps, Kbps   KiloBytes Per Second, KiloBits Per Second; Thousand bytes/bits per second

LAN   Local Area Network

LAP   Link Access Procedure

LASER   Light Amplification from the Stimulated Emmission of Radiation

LAT   Local Area Transport

LEC   Local Exchange Carrier

LED   Light Emitting Diode

LEN   Low Entry Networking

LIPS   Logical Inferences Per Second

LISP   LIST Processing

LLC   Logical Link Control

LM/X   LAN Manager/X (Microsoft)

LU   Logical Unit

LU6.2   Logical Unit 6.2

MAC   Media Access Control

MAN   Metropolitan Area Network

MAP   Manufacturing Automation Protocol

MAPI   Messaging Application Programming Interface

MAP/TOP   Manufacturing Automation Protocol/Technical and Office Protocol

MAU   Multi-station Access Unit

Mbps   Millions of bits per second (Megabits)

MCA   Micro Channel Architecture

MCI   Media Control Interface

MDI   Multiple Document Interface

MHS   (1) Message Handling System (2) Message Handling Service

MHz   Mega-Hertz

MIB   Management Information Base

MIDI   Musical Instrument Digital Interface

MIMD   Multiple Instruction stream Multiple Data stream

MIME   Multipurpose Internet Mail Extensions

MIPS   Millions of instructions per second

MIS   Management Information System

MIT   Massachusetts Institute of Technology

MMDF   Multichannel Memorandum Distribution Facility (UNIX E-Mail)

MMS   Manufacturing Messaging Specification

MMU   Memory Management Unit

modem   MOdulator-DEModulator

MOTIS   Message-Oriented Text Interchange Systems (ISO)

MTA   Mail Transport Agent

MUA   Mail User Agent
MVS   Multiple Virtual Storage
NADF   North American Directory Forum
NAS   Network Application Support (Digital)
NBS   former National Bureau of Standards (now NIST)
NCC   National Computer Conference
NCP   Network Control Program (IBM)
NCS   Network Computing System (HP/Apollo)
NCSC   National Computer Security Center
NDIS   Network Driver Interface Specification (Microsoft)
NetBIEU   NetBIOS Extended User Interface. (Pronounced "net buoy")
NetBIOS   Network Basic Input/Output System (IBM)
NFS   Network File System (Sun Microsystems)
NIC   Network Interface Card
NIST   National Institute of Standards and Technology (formerly NBS)
NLM   Netware Loadable Module
NMS   Network Management System (Novell)
NOS   Network Operating System
NREN   National Research and Education Network
NSA   National Security Agency
NSAPS   Network Service Access Points
NT   New Technology (Microsoft)
NTFS   NT File System (Microsoft)
NVLAP   NIST National Voluntary Laboratory Accreditation Program
OAI   Open Application Interface
OBEX   Object Exchange (Borland)
OBI   OnLine Book Initiative (Internet)
OCA   Object Component Architecture
OCE   Open Collaboration Environment (Apple Computer)
ODBC   Open Database Connectivity (Microsoft)

ODA   Office Document Architecture
OEM   Original Equipment Manufacturer
OLCP   On Line Complex Processing
OLE   Object Linking and Embedding
OLTP   On Line Transaction Processing
OMA   Object Management Architecture
OMG   Object Management Group
OMI   Open Messaging Interface
ONA   Open Network Architecture
ONC   Open Network Computing (SunSoft)
OO   Object-oriented
OOA   Object-oriented analysis
OOD   Object-oriented design
OODB   Object-oriented database
OODBMS   Object-oriented database management system
OOP   Object-oriented programming
OOPL   OOP language
OOPS   Object-oriented programming system
ORB   Object Request Broker
OS   Operating system
OSE   Open System Environment (NIST)
OSF   Open Software Foundation
OSI   Open System Interconnection (ISO)
PABX   Private Automatic Branch eXchange
PARC   Palo Alto Research Center (Xerox Corporation)
PBX   Private Branch eXchange
PC   Personal computer
PCB   Printed Circuit Board
PD Software   Public Domain software
PDES   Product Date Exchange Specification
PDL   Page Description Language
PDT   Performance Diagnostics Tool (Tallgrass Technology)
PEM   Privacy Enhanced Mail
PHIGS   Programmer's Hierarchical Interactive Graphics Standard
pixel   Picture element
PM   Presentation Manager (IBM)
POS   Point-Of-Sale

POSI   Promoting Conference for OSI (Japan)

POSIX   Portable Operating System Interface for UNIX

POTS   Plain Old Telephone Service

pph   pages per hour

ppm   pages per minute

PRI   Primary Rate Interface

PROFS   PRofessional OFfice System (IBM)

PROM   Programmable Read Only Memory

PSN   Packet-Switched Network

PTC   Prepare-To-Commit

PTT   Postal, Telegraph, & Telephone (European agencies)

PU   Physical Unit

PU 2.1   Physical Unit 2.1

PVCS   Polytron Version Control System (Intersolv)

QBE   Query By Example

QMF   Query Management Facility

RACF   Resource Access Control Facility

RAD   Rapid Application Development

RAID   Redundant Arrays of Inexpensive Disks

RAM   Random Access Memory

RBOC   Regionall Bell Operating Company

RDA   Remote Data Access

Rdb   Relational database (Digital Equipment Corporation)

RDBMS   Relational Database Management System

RFS   Remote File System (AT&T)

RIFF   Resource Interchange File Format

RISC   Reduced Instruction Set Computing (Pronounced "risk")

ROM   Read-Only Memory

ROM BIOS   ROM Basic Input Output System

ROSE   Remote Operations Service Element (OSI) (pronounced "rose")

RPC   Remote procedure call

RPG   Report Program Generator

RS-232-C   EIA Standard for Serial Interface

RS/6000   RISC Based Workstations (IBM)

SAA   System Application Architecture (IBM)

SAG   SQL Access Group

SCO   Santa Cruz Operation, Inc

SCSI   Small Computer System Interface

SDK   Software Developer's Kit

SDLC   Synchronous Data Link Control

SFT   System Fault Tolerance

SGML   Standard Generalized Markup Language

SIG   Special Interest Group

SIM   Society for Information Management

SMA   Software Maintenance Associaton

SMAE   Systems Management Application Entities (OSI)

SMB   Server Message Block

SMDS   Switched Multimegabit Date Services

SMP   (1) Symmetric Multiprocessing (2) Simple Management Protocol

SMTP   Simple Mail Transfer Protocol

SNA   Systems Network Architecture (IBM)

SNADS   Systems Network Architecture Distribution Services (IBM)

SNMP   Simple Network Management Protocol

SONET   Synchronous Optical NETwork

SPAG   Standards Promotion and Application Group (European)

SPI   Service Provider Interface (Microsoft)

SPX   Sequenced Packet eXchange (Novell)

SQL   Structured Query Language

STP   Shielded Twisted Pair

SVID   System V Interface Definition (UNIX)

SVR4   UNIX System V Release 4

TA   Transport Agent

TCP/IP   Transmission Control Protocol/
Internet Protocol

TCSEC   Trusted Computer System
   Evaluation Criteria (U.S. Government's
   Orange Book)

TDI   Trade Data Interchange

TDM   Time Division Multiplexing

TIFF   Tagged Image File Format

TLI   Transport Level Interface

TOP   Technical and Office Protocol

TTI   Technology Transfer Institute

TP   (1) Transaction processing
   (2) Teleprocessing

TPC   Transaction Processing Council

TPS   Transactions per second

TPM   Transaction processing monitor

TSR   Terminate and Stay Resident

UA   User Agent

UAE   Unrecoverable Application Error

UCA   Utility Communications
   Architecture

UDP   User Datagram Protocol

UI   UNIX International

UNMA   Unified Network Management
   Architecture (AT&T)

USENET   USEr NETwork

USL   UNIX System Laboratories, Inc.

UUCP   UNIX-to-UNIX Copy

VAN   Value-added network

VAP   Value-added process

VAR   Value-added reseller

VGA   Video Graphics Array

VIM   Vendor-Independent Messaging
   Interface

VINES   VIrtual NEtworking System
   (Banyan)

VM   Virtual Machine

VS   Virtual Storage

VSE   Virtual Storage Extended

VSAM   Virtual Storage Access Method

VT   Virtual Terminal

VTAM   Virtual Telecommunications
   Access Method (IBM)

WAIS   Wide Area Information Service
   (Internet)

WAN   Wide Area Network

WIN INI   WINdows INItialization

Windows NT   Windows New
   Technology (Microsoft)

WORM   Write-Once Read-Many

WPS   Workplace Shell (IBM OS/2)

WYSIWYG   "What you see is what you
   get"

XA   X/Open Resource Manager

XAPIA   The X400 API Association

XDR   eXternal Data Representation
   (Sun)

XGA   Extended Graphics Array

XNS   Xerox Network Services

XPG   X/Open Portability Guide

XPG3   X/Open Portability Guide Issue 3

3GL   Third Generation Language

4GL   Fourth Generation Language

GLOSSARY

Most words and terms in this glossary will be found spelled out rather than in acronym form. The reader should check the Acronyms Section to determine the meaning of a term if only the acronym is known. A few words which are used primarily in letter or acronym form will be found that way in this Glossary. For example, IBM's UNIX operating system, Advanced Interactive eXecutive, is usually referred to as AIX; therefore, it is listed as AIX in this Glossary.

active Window In an environment where multiple windows can be displayed, the window that will be affected by user actions. Only one window is active at a time; the other windows are inactive. The user can change the active window.

ACTOR PC-based object-oriented programming language that runs under Windows and features a Pascal-like syntax. From The Whitewater Group, Inc.

Advanced Communications Function (ACF) IBM's product name for SNA programs such as VTAM (ACF/VTAM) and NCP (ACF/NCP).

Advanced Peer-to-Peer Networking (APPN) Communications capabilities available within IBM's SNA that offer intermediate node routing, dynamic network services, and improved administration. It is implemented in SNA Node type 2.1 and uses LU6.2 protocols.

Advanced Program-to-Program Communications (APPC) IBM's term for communications between programs using IBM's SNA LU6.2 protocols. APPC is a peer-to-peer protocol in which devices are equals.

Advanced Program-to-Program Inter–face An IBM networking protocol that permits devices to exchange data directly.

AFS Distributed file system for large UNIX networks from Transarc Corp. Based on Carnegie Mellon's Andrew File System, it is easy to administer and expandable.

Agent Software that waits in the background and is activated when a specific event occurs. For example, a monthly sales report could be generated by an agent on the final day of each month.

AIX Advanced Interactive eXecutive is IBM's version of UNIX. It is based on AT&T's UNIX System V with Berkeley extensions.

Alias An alternate name.

Allocate To reserve a resource such as a disk drive or memory.

American National Standards Institute (ANSI) A U.S. organization of industry groups devoted to the development of standards to facilitate trade and communications. These voluntary standards are geared at both public and private sectors. ANSI is a member of the ISO international standards group.

Anomaly Term used to describe abnormal or inexplicable output from complex systems.

Application Traditionally, the term applies to software that performs a specific function or "job" for users, such as payroll, accounts receivable, accounts payable, inventory, word processing, or spreadsheets. Applications differ from systems software, which is more concerned with running the computer, or utilities, which perform maintenance, tuning, and other activities. In recent years, the term "application" is used to refer to end-user software like spreadsheets and word processing programs.

Application developer Generally refers to a person who creates a business application. Duties can include systems analysis, design, and programming.

Application generator Software that generates programs from descriptions of the problem rather than from traditional program code.

Application layer The highest layer within the OSI Reference Model protocol hierarchy (layer 7). It is concerned with interaction at the user or application program level.

Application package Software designed for a certain task that is sold by a software publisher or vendor.

Application program Software that processes data for a single user or group of users.

Application program interface (API) An interface that occurs at the programming level, permitting two pieces of software to interact. An API is generally a formally defined language interface that permits an application program to gain access to system-level tasks and resources. For example, an API could help a developer access GUI resources from an application program. Another example is

that use of IBM's NETbios API can help a developer gain access to networking services.

Architecture The structure of a computer system and the details for how it functions and how its components interact. An architecture may include both hardware and software systems.

Archive To copy data, often compressed, and save it on tape or a different disk for either historical purposes or as a backup.

ARPANET Advanced Research Projects Agency Network. A computer network that consisted of tens of thousands of computers developed by the Advanced Research Projects Agency in the 1960s to permit universities and research organizations to exchange information. Though part of the Department of Defense, it was not a classified network, nor was it dedicated just to military research. Due to its obsolete technology, it was retired in 1990.

AS/400 Application System/400. IBM's minicomputer series introduced in 1988 that supersedes the System/36 and /38.

Asymmetric modem Full-duplex modem that transmits data in one direction at one speed, and simultaneously transmits data in the other direction at another speed. For example, data flows at high speed in one direction, while acknowledgment is returned at low speed in the other.

Asymmetric multiprocessing In multiprocessing, devices that are physically attached to only one processing unit; each CPU is generally dedicated to one specific function. (Also see Symmetric Multiprocessing.)

Asynchronous operation Unsynchronized events; events not happening at the same time.

Asynchronous protocol Communications protocol that controls asynchronous transmission. Examples include ASCII, TTY, Kermit and Xmode.

Asynchronous transmission Transmission of data where information is sent one character at a time. Generally used with modems, the time between character transmission is variable.

AT Advanced Technology. IBM PC based on

Intel's 80286 processor. It runs about three times faster than its predecessor, the XT, which was based on Intel's 8088 processor.

Atomicity A quality of an operation that says it must be performed in its entirety. Atomicity is associated with two-phase commit in distributed database update operations. (See *two-phase commit*.) If any participating member of the transaction cannot complete, all other members will be rolled back (restored) to their original state.

Audit The process of studying a data center's computer systems, programs, and procedures for efficiency, security, and data integrity.

AUX Auxiliary. DOS name for the first connected serial port.

A/UX Apple's version of UNIX for the Macintosh. A/UX is based on AT&T's UNIX System V with Berkeley extensions.

B1 Level of security established by the Department of Defense.

Backbone A networking term used to describe that portion of a network that plays the major role. It often refers to that part of the network that handles the majority of traffic—especially between subnetworks.

Background Computer processing that is noninteractive. (Also see *Background Processing*.)

Background processing (1) In a multi–tasking operating system, processing that takes place noninteractively and invisibly to the user while the primary program is working. (2) In a non-multitasking system, processing that takes place when foreground (primary) jobs are idle.

Background program A program that runs in the background.

Back-end processor A slave processor that performs specialized tasks. (Also see *Database Machine*.)

Back up To copy data onto a different storage medium in case the main system loses power or somehow corrupts the data.

Band A range of frequencies used for transmitting a signal.

Bandwidth Transmission capacity of a communications line, channel, or bus.

Baseband A communications technique, usually limited to a couple of miles, in which digital signals are placed onto the transmission line without change in modulation. It uses the full bandwidth of the channel and does not require complex modems as needed for broadband transmission. Token Ring and CSMA/CD (Ethernet) are examples of baseband LAN techniques.

Batch A group of data items processed as one unit.

Batch processing The processing of transactions that are grouped together. One example is transactions that are processed against master files at specified periods, such as daily, weekly, or monthly. Most information systems use both batch and transaction processing.

Batch program A program that does not interact with the user. (See *Batch session*.)

Batch session A session that transmits or updates an entire file. It implies a process that is not interactive and is not normally interrupted while running.

Batch stream A collection of batch programs scheduled to run in a computer.

Baud The signaling rate of a line, specifying the number of transitions (voltage or frequency changes) that are made per second. At low speeds bauds are equal to bits per second; therefore 300 baud is the equivalent of 300 bps. However, baud and bps are not always the same. For example, a device may generate 1200 bps at 600 baud. With baud and bps so often used interchangeably, baud is usually used to specify bits per second for modem speed. Thus, with modems, 1200 baud means 1200 bps.

Baud rate The term "baud" is actually a rate. While the term "baud rate" is redundant, it is frequently used.

Bell Labs AT&T's world renowned research and development center.

Berkeley Extensions Extensions to UNIX, developed by the University of California at Berkeley. These extensions include networking and larger file names.

Beta test   A user test of hardware and software, typically performed before a product is generally available for purchase. During beta test, problems are often detected and corrected before the product is placed on the market.

Betaware   Software a user is testing for a vendor before that product is generally available in the market.

Big Blue   A nickname for IBM.

Bindery   The NetWare Bindery file is a file that the NetWare network operating system uses to identify its users.

Binding   The linking of two routines or objects.

BIOS   Basic I/O System. A very basic piece of software that is written into a chip within a personal computer. It provides a connection between the operating system software and the hardware.

Bisync   Binary Synchronous. A communications protocol used in mainframe networks. Before data is transmitted, both sending and receiving devices must be synchronized.

Bisynchronous   See bisync.

Bitmap   (1) A term in computer graphics for an area in memory that represents an image. Monochrome screens have one bit per pixel, while gray-scale color or color screens have several bits per pixel. (2) A binary representation in which each bit or set of bits corresponds to an object or condition.

Bitmapped graphics   A matrix of dots that represents an image.

Boot   As a verb, to start a computer. As a noun, the process of starting a computer. A "cold" boot is when the machine is first turned on; a "warm" boot is when the user presses the Control, Alternate and Delete keys at the same time (Ctl-Alt-Del) on an IBM machine or chooses Restart from the Special Menu on an Apple computer.

Bps   Bits Per Second. Measurement for data transfer speed in a communications system.

Bridge   A devices that connects two similar networks. It functions at the data link level (layer 2) and is independent of higher protocols.

Broadband   Communications technique that uses high frequency transmission over coaxial cable or optical fibers. It can transmit large amounts of data, voice, or video over long distances.

Brouter   A device that functions as both a bridge and a router in a multiple network system. (See *bridge and router*.)

BSD UNIX   Berkeley Software Distribution UNIX. One of the earliest versions of UNIX. Developed at the University of California at Berkeley, the term often appears in literature to identify more recent versions of UNIX that stem from BSD UNIX.

Btrieve   A database management system included with Novell's NetWare network operating system.

Burst mode   A method of high-speed transmission in a communications or computer channel which permits a burst of data for some period of time.

Bypass   A term that refers to avoiding the local telephone company by using satellites and microwave systems in communications.

Byte   A unit of computer storage made up of eight bits (eight binary digits). A ninth bit is sometimes added as a parity bit for error checking.

C   A programming language that manipulates the computer at a low level. Many client/server applications are developed with C. The language was originally developed at Bell Labs.

C++   An object-oriented version of C that combines traditional programming with object orientation.

Cache   A reserved section of memory, either on the controller board (disk cache) or between memory and the CPU (memory cache).

Call   A programming statement that references an independent subroutine or program.

Carrier Sense Multiple Access/Collision Detection (CSMA/CD)   Communications ac-cess method that uses a collision-detection technique.

When a device wants to transmit data across the network, it checks to see if the network is in use. If it is, the device waits a random amount of time and then tries again. If two devices start transmitting at the same time, they both must stop, even if a collision has not yet occurred. Each then waits a random amount of time before trying again.

Class In object-oriented programming, a category to which specific objects (members) belong. The class defines specific characteristics or services that each member of that class possesses.

Class library A collection of object-oriented programming classes, often provided by third-party vendors.

Click (As in "click on an icon") To press a button on the mouse, for example, to select an object or procedure. The cursor should be pointing to the desired option when the mouse button is pressed.

Client (1) A software module that makes a request for services. (2) A computer, such as a PC, that acts as a client in a client/server network system.

Client/server architecture An architecture that consists of a client module that makes requests from a server module, which fulfills these requests. In popular client/server systems, the client module often resides on a PC or workstation and is connected to a server via networking.

Client/server platform The hardware/software combination where a client/server system resides. The term can also refer to software alone or hardware alone. For example, a relatively inexpensive microcomputer is often used as a client/server platform.

Closed architecture A software or hardware system whose technical specifications are not made public by the vendor.

Color Graphics Adapter (CGA) The first graphics standard for the IBM PC, which provided low-resolution text and graphics. It has been superseded by EGA and VGA.

Common carrier A government-regulated company that provides communications services to the public.

Communications channel A data transmission pathway between remote devices. It can be a physical medium, such as a telephone line, optical fiber, or cable, or it may be a frequency transmitted within the medium, such as a radio or satellite channel.

Communications controller A peripheral device connected to a host computer that handles data transmission and reception, and other communications tasks, relieving the host of these jobs. Communications controllers are typically nonprogrammable units, but some can be programmed.

Communications program Software that manages data transmission between computers.

Complex Instruction Set Computer (CISC, pronounced "sisk.") Traditional computer architecture that requires complex circuitry. A characteristic is that it uses microcode to execute very comprehensive instructions which may be variable in length and uses various addressing modes.

Computer Aided Software Engineering or Computer Aided Systems Engineering (CASE) Software tools that automate any or all development phases of an information system.

Computer-supported cooperative work (CSCW) A term for groupware often used in research environments.

Concentrator A device that joins several communications channels together.

Concurrency control The management of simultaneous accesses to a database by more than one application to prevent multiple users from editing the same record at the same time. It is also concerned with serializing transactions for backup and recovery.

Concurrent operation (or processing) The processing of two or more programs in what seems like the same time, but in most cases is not simultaneous. However, concurrent processing *can* occur in one computer with two or more processors, or when two or more computers are used.

Configuration   The sum of all the hardware and software components making up a system.

Connection-oriented   A communications technique that requires an established session or a direct connection between nodes for transmission.

Connectionless   A communications technique that does not require the establishment of a direct connection between nodes. Each packet contains its source and destination addresses to enable proper delivery.

Consultative Committee for International Telephone and Telegraphy (CCITT)   Geneva-based international organization for communications standards.

Contention   When two devices simultaneously vie to use a single resource.

Contention resolution   The process of determining which device can use a resource when more than one device requests the resource.

Context-sensitive help   A help screen that provides information about the program's condition at the time a user requests help.

Continuous carrier   A carrier frequency that is transmitted over the line even when no data is being sent.

Control program   Software that controls a computer's operation and has highest priority.

Conventional programming   Programming that uses a procedural language, such as Cobol, C, Pascal, Fortran, Basic and Ada and is primarily sequential in nature. The term is used to contrast with other techniques like object-oriented and event-driven programming.

Cooperative processing   A smaller computer, such as a PC, processing a system in cooperation with a larger system, usually a mainframe. IBM is credited with coining the term.

Corporation for Open Systems (COS)   A consortium of user and vendor organizations promoting a worldwide open network architecture. It supports systems that conform to open standards, including OSI and ISDN.

Cps   Characters per second.

Customer Information Control System (CICS, which is pronounced "kicks.")   IBM's transaction processing monitor that was originally developed for its mainframe and midrange computers, but is now also available for client/server applications using OS/2.

Daemon (Pronounced "demon.")   A program that waits in the background ready to perform a certain function when a particular event occurs, usually unbeknownst to the user. Typically associated with UNIX systems.

Data compression   Encoding text, machine language files, or graphics files to take up less storage space.

Data integrity   Data that is uncorrupted in any way.

Data link layer   The second layer of the OSI Reference Layer. It is concerned with providing reliable data transmission from one node to another.

Data link protocol   Provides for the transmission of a unit of data from one node to another while ensuring that the bits received are the same as the ones sent.

Data rate   The speed with which data is transferred within a computer, between a peripheral and a computer, or between devices in a network.

Data transmission   The sending of data over a network.

Data transparency   Data that can be accessed by a user without the user needing to know where the data is located or which application it originated from.

Database machine   A specially designed computer for database access that often uses multiple processors to perform fast disk searches.

DataBase Management System (DBMS)   Software that controls the organization, storage, retrieval, security, and integrity of data in a database. Major DBMS features include data entry and updating, data integrity, data security, and interactive query.

DB2   IBM's relational database management system (DATABASE 2) with SQL interface that was originally written for the mainframe.

De facto (1) Exercising power as if legally constituted. (2) In standards, a de facto standard is one that is so widely used that it is recognized as a popularly established "standard."

De jure (1) Exercising power by right. (2) In standards, a de jure standard is one established by official national and international standards organizations.

Desktop computer Same as personal computer or microcomputer.

Developer's toolkit A set of software routines used in writing programs for an application, operating system, or interface.

Development system Programming language and other tools for developing software applications.

Distributed Computing Environment (DCE) The Open Software Foundation's standards based environment for developing and implementing client/server applications on a network.

Distributed database A collection of multiple, logically interrelated databases distributed over a computer network, with the distribution of data transparent to the users and which meets a set of transparency requirements.

Distributed file system Software that keeps track of files stored across network nodes or multiple networks and makes these files available as though they were local. Files are identified by name rather than location.

Distributed function Distribution of processing functions within a system or throughout an organization.

Distributed intelligence The distribution of processing ability among multiple devices which can work independently, but also work together as one unit.

Distributed Management Environment (DME) A set of integrated programs from the Open Software Foundation for systes and network management.

Distributed processing A number of autonomous processing elements interconnected by a network, that cooperate in performing their separate tasks. The *data* used in the processing can be distributed or reside all in one location.

Distributed Relational Database Architecture (DRDA) IBM's blueprint for allowing data to be distributed among DB2 and SQL/DS databases.

Distributed Relational DBMS (DDBMS) A relational DBMS that manages distributed databases.

Downsizing Converting systems that run on a large computer to a smaller computer; for example, from a mainframe to a minicomputer or PC local-area network, or from a minicomputer to a PC local area network.

Downward compatible When smaller or earlier models of a computer system can run the same software as larger or newer models. Also called backward compatible.

Dpi Dots Per Inch. Measures printer resolution.

Drag & drop Executing a function by selecting an icon by clicking with a mouse and dragging it across the screen.

Dynamic Refers to operations performed immediately and concurrently as needed, while the program is running.

Dynamic allocation Allocation of a resource such as memory while the application is running, according to its needs. For example, memory is allocated when the program needs the memory, and is usually deallocated during those times when the program does not need that memory.

Dynamic binding Linking a routine or object while a program is executing, based on current conditions.

Dynamic data exchange (DDE) A message protocol used in Microsoft Windows that permits applications to exchange data dynamically. For example, use of DDE could permit a spreadsheet to be dynamically updated with fluctuating stock market prices it receives from a communications channel.

Dynamic SQL SQL statements that are interpreted by the SQL database at runtime, rather than prior to runtime by a compiler. Dynamic SQL may be generated by a program or entered interactively by a user.

Electronic Data Interchange for Administration, Commerce and Transportation (EDIFACT) The ISO standard for EDI. While it is widely used in most countries in the world, the U.S. still performs most of its EDI transactions using the ANSI X.12 standard. The two standards are expected to merge to some degree, with eventual transition to EDIFACT.

Electronic data interchange (EDI) The electronic exchange of business transactions between organizations, such as purchase orders, confirmations, and invoices.

Electronic mail (E-mail) A message that is sent over a computer network to one or more recipients.

Electronic messaging Often used as a synonym for electronic mail, though it can also refer to the messaging mechanism used to send e-mail.

Embedded SQL SQL statements inserted into a high-level language source program.

Encapsulation (1) In object-oriented programming, making both data and processing private ("hidden" or enclosed) within an object. This allows the object to be modified without creating problems elsewhere in the program. (2) In communications, adding protocol headers and/or trailers from a higher- level protocol to the data frame of a lower-level protocol.

Encipher To convert data into code for security against unauthorized access.

Encode To assign a special code to represent data for security purposes. Same as encipher or encrypt.

Encryption For security, converting standard data code into a special proprietary code that must be decoded.

End user computing Work accomplished by users in an organization who use personal computers. Many years ago, end users used to receive

just the output from computer processing which was performed by a specialized department; today many end users perform their own computing.

Engine (1) A specialized processor. (2) Software that performs routine or specific functions. A database engine is an example.

Enterprise data Generally refers to data that is shared by many users throughout an organization. As a result, it is often centralized.

Enterprise model An organization's model for doing business. Ideally, the basis on which information systems are implemented.

Enterprise network A network that serves an entire enterprise. It is generally a geographically dispersed network that often contains systems from several (or many) vendors.

Environment The surrounding circumstances or elements. For example, it could mean a configuration of computer systems, including the CPU model, system software and programming language used. Environment may also refer just to the operating system.

Ethernet IEEE 802.3 LAN standard that uses the CSMA/CD access method. It can connect up to 1,024 nodes and transmits at 10Mbps.

Event-driven Application that is driven by choices that the user makes. It needs to respond to input from the user or another application at unregulated times. Windows programming is an example.

Extended Edition IBM version of OS/2 that includes communications and database management. The Communications Manager has built-in LU6.2 and X.25 protocols. The Database Manager uses IBM's SQL.

EXtended Graphics Array (XGA) High-resolution video display standard from IBM optimized for graphical interfaces.

Extended Industry Standard Architecture (EISA) A bus "standard" introduced in 1988 by a consortium of nine vendors: AST Research, Compaq, Epson, Hewlett-Packard, NEC, Olivetti, Tandy, Wyse, and Zenith. EISA maintains backward compatibility with ISA, but also offers new capabilities offered by IBM in its Micro Channel Architecture. (Pronounced "e-suh.")

Extensible Virtual Toolkit   See XVT.

Fault tolerant (or fail safe)   Operation that does not halt when a software or hardware failure occurs, thus preserving all programs and data. A fault-tolerant system can correct or avoid a failure by utilizing one or more backup computers that duplicate processing. The duplicate systems may reside in disparate locations.

Fiber Distributed Data Interface (FDDI)   An ANSI standard for a 100Mbps token passing LAN that uses optical fiber. It is compatible with OSI layers 1 and 2, the physical layers. FDDI permits transmission speed that is significantly greater than Ethernet, Token Ring, and other LANs techniques.

Fiber optic   Communications system through which light beams are transmitted. Optical fibers are thin filaments of glass that are insensitive to electromagnetic interference and can carry more data at a greater distance than other methods.

File manager   (1) Software that manages and controls access to data files. (2) Software that manages files on a disk.

File server   LAN-based computer that provides a way for users to share files.

File transfer protocol   Convention for transmitting files over a communications network, between programs, or between computers, without losing data.

Footprint   The desk or floor space occupied by a computer or peripheral.

Foreground/background   In a multitasking windows environment, the foreground program has the priority and is affected by commands from the user. The background has the lowest priority and often performs its tasks transparently to the user. In a personal computer, the foreground is the program a user is working with, such as a word processing program, and the background is the print spooler.

Fourth-generation computer   Contemporary computers that incorporate thousands of circuits on one chip.

Fourth-generation language (4GL)   A computer language with English-like commands, often used with relational databases, that is more advanced than third-generation languages (high-level languages) such as Cobol, Basic, and C. Query language and report writers are considered 4GLs.

Frame relay   High-speed packet switching protocol that provides faster transmission than X.25; used primarily for data and image transfer rather than voice.

Front-end processor   Computer that han–dles mainframe communications processing by connecting to the communications channels on one end and the mainframe on the other. In a LAN, network adapters perform the functions of the front-end processor.

Full-duplex   Simultaneous transmission and reception of data.

Function   In programming, a subroutine that carries out a task.

Function library   A collection of program routines.

Gateway   A node (computer) on a network that connects two incompatible networks via protocol conversion.

GBps, Gbps   Gigabytes per second; Gigabits per Second. (Giga = billion.)

Gigabit   A billion bits.

Gigabyte   A billion bytes.

Government Open systems Interconnection Profile (GOSIP)   U.S. government mandate that after 8/15/90 all new network procurements had to comply with OSI. Compliance testing of products is performed at NIST. Recent developments indicate the possibility that TCP/IP may be included under the GOSIP umbrella.

Graphical Kernel System (GKS)   ANSI and ISO accepted graphics standard for developing and porting graphics applications.

Graphical Programming Interface (GPI)
Graphics language in IBM's OS/2 Presentation Manager.

Graphical User Interface (GUI) A display format that typically resides at the client end (front end) of a client/server system and facilitates use of the application by the end user. A stand-alone system can also have a GUI.

Graphics Interchange Format (GIF) Raster graphics file format that handles 8-bit color (256 colors) and achieves compression ratios of 1.5:1 to 2:1.

Groupware Software that is designed to be used by groups, typically connected by a LAN.

Half-duplex The ability to send and receive data, but only in one direction at a time.

Handshaking Predetermined signals exchanged between two communications devices when a connection is first established.

Heterogeneous environment A configuration of computer systems and software from a variety of vendors.

Hierarchical communications A communications system that is controlled by a host computer. The host is responsible for managing all network connections.

High-level Data Link Control (HDLC) ISO communications protocol (used in X.25 packet switching networks) that provides error correction at the data link layer.

High Level Language Application Program Interface (HLLAPI) IBM programming interface that allows a PC application to communicate with a mainframe application through the use of micro to mainframe 3270 emulation.

High Performance Parallel Interface channel (HiPPI) ANSI-standard high-speed (100 Mbytes/sec) supercomputer channel.

Hooks A term applied to software provided by one vendor so its product(s) can interconnect with other vendors' software.

Host-based A communications system that is controlled by a large, central computer system; generally a mainframe.

Hub A central point in a network where numerous circuits connect.

Hypermedia A storage and retrieval system that integrates data, text, graphics, video, and voice.

Hypertext The linking of related information that allows a user to browse through related topics in a nonsequential way.

Icon A small, pictorial representation of an object such as a file, program, disk, etc. Commonly used with GUIs and windowing software.

Independent Software Vendor (ISV) Developer and marketer of a software product. This term is used to differentiate these vendors from vendors like IBM or Digital who write software for their hardware lines.

Industry Government Open Systems Specification (IGOSS) A unified OSI procurement document that merges four major OSI standard profiles: GOSIP, MAP, TOP, and UCA. The goal of this unity is to remove confusion generated by OSI profiles which overlap each other.

Industry Standard Architecture (ISA) An unofficial designation for the bus design of the IBM PC/XT. It allows the addition of various adapters by plugging cards into expansion slots. In 1984, ISA was extended from an 8-bit data path to a 16-bit data path to accommodate the new IBM PC/AT. The term "ISA" is frequently used to refer specifically to the expansion slots. (Pronounced "i-suh.")

Information Technology Association of America (ITAA) A computer industry membership organization that works to improve management methods, define performance standards, and monitor government regulation in the computer services field.

Inheritance In object-oriented programming, a class of objects passes properties down to its descendants.

Instance In object-oriented programming, an object that belongs to a class.

Instantiate In object-oriented programming, to create an instance of a class.

Institute of Electrical and Electronic Engineers (IEEE) A membership organization of engineers, scientists, and students involved with setting standards for computers and communications, among other things.

Integrated Computer Aided Software Engineering (I-Case) CASE systems that generate application code directly from design specifications. Features include support for rapid prototyping, data modeling and processing and drawing logic diagrams.

Integrated Database Application Programming Interface (IDAPI) An API intended to provide a de facto standard for accessing and manipulating both relational and nonrelational data, with support for joins across SQL and navigational data sources. It is a superset of the SQL Access Group's Call Level Interface and is somewhat similar to Microsoft's ODBC.

Integrated Services Digital Network (ISDN) Telecommunications standard for transmitting voice, video, and data over digital communications lines. ISDN services come in the following two forms: Basic Rate Interface (BRI) provides a 144Kbps services, and Primary Rate Interface (PRI) provides a 1.54Mbps service.

Intelligent hub A network hub that can perform numerous functions, allowing connection to a variety of cable types and routing. The fact that it can make decisions differentiates it from a passive hub.

Interactive Dialog between the user and the computer interface.

Interface A place where two elements (e.g., hardware and software, or user and software) meet and interact. There are a wide range of interfaces, from high-level display graphics that help a user interact with the computer system (GUIs) to low-level physical devices that connect pieces of hardware internally. In the modular client/server architecture, there are numerous interfaces (e.g., between the client process and networking software, between the server process and networking software, between different types of networking components).

Interface adapter A device that connects a computer or terminal to a network.

International Organization for Standardization (ISO; anglicized, International Standards Organization) Geneva-based organization that sets international standards, except electrical and electronics. ANSI is the U.S. member body.

Internet/internetwork (1) The interconnection of many individual networks. (2) Communication between networks.

Internet The world's largest computer network with over 8,000 connected networks and over 8 million users. The retired Arpanet was originally part of the Internet. The Internet is owned by over 18,000 worldwide organizations, including private companies and military and government organizations.

Interoperable The ability of computer hardware or software to function with other hardware and software.

Interprocess communication (IPC) Allows two processes or tasks to exchange data through mechanisms such as semaphores, queues, shared memory, signals, mailboxes, and pipes, among others.

Interrupt driven Computer or communications network that uses signals, passed by either software or hardware, to get the CPU's attention.

KBps, Kbps Kilobyte per second; kilobit per second.

Kernel Memory-based core of an operating system or program.

Kilobit (Kb or Kbit) One thousand bits.

Kilobyte (KB or Kbyte) One thousand bytes.

Legacy data Data used by a legacy system.

Legacy system Systems that have been in operation for a long time and have been built with what some now consider as "old" technology. Legacy systems are often quite complex, expensive to maintain, and are not user-friendly, but they serve as important production systems for an enterprise.

LAN Manager Microsoft's LAN operating system originally built to run under OS/2 on a server and connect computers running MS-DOS, OS/2 and UNIX operating systems. It enables client/server systems and permits users to share files and system resources such as hard disks and printers. It uses the NetBIOS protocol for its transport mechanism, Named Pipes for interprocess communications, and the Microsoft File Sharing Protocol (Server Message Block, abbreviated SMB) for file sharing.

LAN Requester LAN Server software that resides in the workstation.

LAN Server IBM's version of Microsoft's LAN Manager.

LAN station Workstation in a local area network.

Laptop computer Battery operated, lightweight portable computer that typically has a flat screen.

Latency The time it takes to begin transferring data after the initial request to do so.

Leased line A private telephone channel leased from a common carrier.

Local area network (LAN) The IEEE de-finition of a LAN is a data communication system allowing a number of independent devices to communicate directly with each other, within a moderately sized geographic area, over a physical communications channel of moderate data rates.

Local bypass Direct interconnection between two sites without the use of the local telephone company.

Local loop Communications line between an enterprise and the telephone company's central office.

Logical Unit (LU) In IBM's SNA, one end of a communications session.

Logical Unit 6.2 (LU6.2) IBM's SNA peer-to-peer protocol that permits network devices to communicate directly as equals, rather than forcing one to be a primary station and the other a secondary station. It is sometimes referred to as Advanced Program-to-Program Communications (APPC).

Long-haul A modem or other communications device that can transmit data over long distances.

Machine dependent Describes software that runs in only one kind of computer.

Machine independent Describes software that can run in a variety of computers.

Mail box A user's assigned storage space for electronic messages.

Mail Transport Agent (MTA) The back end of E-mail systems. Includes such functions as transport services, directory services, and message store.

Mail User Agent (MUA) The user interface or front end of E-mail systems.

Manufacturing Automation Protocol (MAP) Communications protocol for factory automation introduced by General Motors in 1982. It specifies which of the many options within the OSI Reference Model vendors should use. Often used in conjunction with TOP (Technical Office Protocol).

Massively parallel processing (MPP) Parallel processing architecture that uses hundreds or thousands of processors that do not share memory. Contrast with Symmetrical Multiprocessing.

Megabit (Mb or Mbit) One million bits.

Megabyte (MB or Mbyte) One million bytes.

Megahertz (MHz) One million cycles per second.

Menu Onscreen list of user options.

Menu-driven The use of menus to command the computer.

Menuing software Software that provides a menu for running operating system commands and for launching applications.

Message (1) Data and control bits that are transmitted as a whole over a communications line. (2) A unit of communication between processes or stations, with a beginning, content, and ending. It can be composed of a single packet or a series of packets. (3) In object-oriented programming, communication between objects, similar to calling procedures in traditional programming, except that message sending is more dynamic.

Messaging Application Programming Interface (MAPI) Microsoft's cross-platform API for writing mail-enabled applications.

Message Handling Service (MHS) E-mail system that Novell licenses from Action technologies to be used with the NetWare operating system. It provides for the transfer and routing of messages between users and provides store and forward capabilities.

Message Handling System (MHS) (X.400). The OSI protocol, based on CCITT's X.400 international message protocol, for the exchange of electronic messages in E-mail systems. It sits at the application layer in the OSI Reference Model.

Method In object-oriented programming, an operation that manipulates the instances of a class. A method is invoked by sending a message to the instance.

Metropolitan Area Network (MAN) A communications network for a specific geographic area, such as a city or county.

Micro Channel Architecture The design of the bus in IBM PS/2 computers except Models 25 and 30. The bus functions as either a 16-bit or a 32-bit bus. It is incompatible with the IBM PC/AT bus.

Microcomputer A computer that uses a single-chip microprocessor for its CPU. Same as personal computer.

Micromainframe A term used for a microcomputer with mainframe or near mainframe speed.

Millisecond (ms or msec) One thousandth of a second.

Minicomputer A midrange computer that generally functions as a multiuser system with up to several hundred terminals, though it can also be used as a single workstation. For many years, minicomputers were considered more powerful than workstations, but less powerful than mainframes. As microcomputers increase in power, distinctions become more blurry.

MIPS One million instructions per second. A computer's processor speed.

Motif The Open Software Foundation-endorsed graphical user interface for the X Window system.

Mouse A handheld device used for actions like drawing or commanding the computer using icons and menus. It is an alternative to typing keys on the computer keyboard. As it is rolled across a mouse pad, the screen cursor moves correspondingly.

Mouse pad A rubber pad covered with fabric that provides an excellent surface for rolling a mouse. Usually nine inches square.

Multimedia A mix of text, audio, graphics, animation, and video.

Multiple Document Interface (MDI) The capability to use "cut-and-paste" capabilities and combine information from applications such as spreadsheets and graphics directly into E-mail rather than as attachments to the E-mail message.

Multiprocessing system A system designed to allow execution of multiple programs simultaneously.

Multiprogramming See multitasking.

Multistation Access Unit (MAU) A central hub in a token ring LAN.

Multitasking system A system designed to allow execution of multiple programs nearly simultaneously. While the tasks appear to be executing simultaneously, each is assigned a discrete time slice for execution.

Multithreading Running several processes in one program.

Named Pipes An interprocess communication facility in LAN Manager permitting data to be exchanged between applications over a network or running in the same computer.

Nanosecond One billionth of a second.

National Institute of Standards and Technology (NIST) U.S. government agency responsible for defining standards. Formerly National Bureau of Standards (NBS).

Native operating system The basic operating system of a workstation or PC, e.g., DOS or OS/2. This term is often used to distinguish between the

PC's basic operating system and the network operating system.

NetBEUI (NetBIOS Extended User Interface, pronounced "net buoy") The NetBIOS transport protocol as implemented within LAN Manager and LAN Server. It communicates with the network adapter using Microsoft's Network Driver Interface Specification (NDIS).

NetBIOS Network Basic Input Output System. Protocol for PC LANs that provides applications with a uniform way to request network services. It was developed in 1984 by IBM and Sytek for PC connectivity. Some consider it as sitting at the OSI session layer, while others see it as an interface between the transport and session layers. It provides application parograms with a uniform set of commands for requesting lower level network services needed to transmit information and conduct sessions between network nodes. It is regarded as a de facto standard due to its support by IBM and NetBIOS' support for EtherNet, Token Ring, serial port, as well as other types of LANs. Supported by Microsoft for many years, that may or may not continue as Microsoft's new operating systems begin to diverge from IBM's OS/2 and as Micorosft develops more networking capabilities.

NetBIOS Extended User Interface See NetBE*UI*.

NetView IBM SNA network management software that provides centralized monitoring and control for both IBM and non-IBM devices.

NetView/PC IBM software that interconnects NetView with Token Ring LANs and other devices while maintaining host control.

NetWare Novell Inc.'s network operating system.

NetWare Loadable Module (NLM) Software that provides additional server functions in a server running NetWare 386. Most database vendors provide NLM versions of their databases to run with NetWare.

Network administrator Individual responsible for managing a communications network.

Network architecture The structure of a communications system, including hardware, software, protocols, and access methods and which defines the method of control and connectability to it.

Network Basic Input Output System See NetBIOS.

Network Driver Interface Specification (NDIS) A Microsoft specification often used when writing hardware-independent drivers at the data link layer.

Network layer The third layer of the OSI Reference Model. It is primarily concerned with routing. It establishes, maintains, and terminates a network connection between two points.

Network management Process of monitoring a network for troubleshooting, performance tuning, and capacity planning.

Network operating system (NOS) A server-based operating system in a LAN that responds to requests from multiple workstations.

New Technology (NT) Microsoft's 32-bit operating system for 386 and higher speed machines. There is a client version of NT, called Windows NT, and a server version, called Windows NT Advanced Server. NT is based on the Mach variation of the UNIX kernel. It supports multiprocessor systems and multiple threads of execution. All application threads, including the Windows NT kernel, are able to run on many different kinds of processors in a multi-processor configuration. Multiple threads of execution can operate simultaneously to complete a task.

Node A connection point in a network.

Notebook computer A battery operated, portable computer that is smaller and lighter than a laptop.

Object (1) In object-oriented programming, a module of data and programming treated as a single entity. (2) In compound documents, a block of data, text or graphics created by separate applications. (3) In computer graphics, a discrete entity, such as an image.

Object-oriented database A database that incorporates the object-oriented paradigm in a database management system.

Object-oriented interface A graphical user interface that uses icons to represent system elements. Not necessarily related to object-oriented programming.

Object-oriented programming (OOP) A method of programming that uses object-oriented approaches. Programs are regarded as a collection of objects that interact with other objects.

Object-oriented technology Paradigm that views the world as objects rather than procedures.

Offload To move work from one computer to another, usually a smaller computer. Can be related to cooperative processing.

Off-the-shelf Refers to software products that are sold as a package and used pretty much as purchased (without being modified).

OLE Object Linking and Embedding. A Microsoft Windows' protocol for compound documents, whereby a "server" application creates an object within a "client" application document. When a user double clicks on this object in a client application, the appropriate server application is loaded.

OMG Object Management Group. An international standards organization for object-oriented applications.

OMI Open Messaging Interface. Lotus-developed application programming interface for writing mail-enabled applications that is now incorporated in the VIM API. (See VIM.)

Open Collaboration Environment (OCE) An extension to Apple Computer's System 7 operating system providing E-mail and document sharing across platforms.

Open Look Sun-developed X Window-based graphical user interface for UNIX.

Open system Standards-based hardware or software that can work with products from multiple vendors.

Operating system The software that runs the computer.

Optical disk A storage medium for digital information. The direct access disk is read by light.

OS/2 IBM's multitasking PC operating system for Intel 286 computers and up. IBM co-developed the 16-bit version with Microsoft, but the joint venture split when Microsoft began promoting its competitive Windows operating system. IBM developed the 32-bit version independently.

OS/2 PM OS/2 Presentation Manager. The graphical user interface for IBM's OS/2 operating system.

OSF Open Software Foundation. A Cambridge, Mass.-based organization of vendors and users that promotes a standards-based open computing environment. Technology is solicited from members.

OSI Reference Model Open Systems Interconnection. A seven-layer standards model from the International Standards Organization (ISO) for exchanging information over a network. Each layer builds on the standards set by the lower layer. From lowest to highest, the layers are: physical, data link, network, transport, session, presentation, and application. It is described in Chapter 9.

Outsourcing Refers to when a data center contracts with an outside consultant or vendor to handle some or all of its operations.

PABX Private Automatic Branch Exchange. Same as PBX.

Packet A unit of data transmitted as a whole from one device to another on a network.

Packet switching A technique for handling high-volume network traffic. Messages are broken into small packets and then sent to their destination via the best available route. When the packets arrive at their destina-tion, the receiving computer reassembles them. In packet-switching, a packet contains both data and a header consisting of an identification number, source and destination addresses, and, sometimes, error-control information.

Palette (1) In computer graphics, the range of colors available for display, although they usually cannot all be used at once. (2) Range of tools available in a paint program. (3) A set of modes or functions.

Palmtop A portable computer that can fit in the

human hand. It may have a specialized keyboard or keypad.

Paradigm A model or pattern, such as for software development or hardware design.

Parallel computing A single computer that uses several processors working together, or multiple computers working together.

Parallel processing Dividing a task among several processors working simultaneously on one computer.

Parallel transmission Transmitting multiple bits simultaneously. Can be accomplished with frequencies operating in parallel or multiple transmission lines.

Private Branch Exchange (PBX) Inhouse telephone switching system that connects enterprise telephones to the outside telephone network and to each other within the enterprise.

PC LAN A network of personal computers.

Peer Functional units in a communications network that are on the same protocol layer.

Peer-to-peer communications Communications in which either side can initiate the session. Neither device has to play the role of a primary station.

Peer-to-peer network Local area network that allows equal access to data on all workstations or other devices for all users.

Personal computer A computer designed for a single user, either for business or personal use. Same as microcomputer.

Physical layer The lowest layer of the OSI Reference Model (layer one). It is concerned with delivering bits from one end of a wire to another.

PIF file Program Information File. A Microsoft Windows' data file (file extension is .pif) used to hold requirements of non-Windows applications.

Pink Code name for a cross-platform operating system under development by Apple Computer and IBM.

Pipes A pipe connects items and permits the flow of something between the items connected. A computer pipe connects two processes, permitting the output of one to be input to the other.

Pixel Picture Element. A dot or cluster of dots among numerous dots that together comprise a video display image.

Pixel graphics The representation of an image as a matrix of dots.

Platform Architecture of computer hardware, an operating system, or other systems software.

Pointing device An input mechanism, such as a mouse, used to move the cursor on the screen in order to select a menu item, highlight text or choose spreadsheet cells.

Polymorphism In object-oriented programming, the ability of a language construct to assume different types or manipulate objects of different types. Thus, it can produce different results based on the object that it is sent to.

Port (1) In computer hardware, a pathway into and out of a computing device. (2) In software programming, the ability to modify software so that it runs on a different hardware platform.

Portable In programming, refers to software that can move easily to a different hardware platform.

POSIX Portable Operating System Interface for UNIX. Specification from IEEE that defines the language interface between application programs and the UNIX operating system.

Power user Individual who is adept at using personal computer hardware and software.

Preemptive multitasking Multitasking that shares processing time with all programs that are currently running.

Preprocessor Software that performs some preliminary processing on an entity or input before it is processed by the main program.

Presentation graphics Graphics used in business presentations such as bar charts and pie charts used to represent business data.

Presentation layer The second highest layer in

the OSI Reference Model (Layer 6). It is concerned with the syntax and semantics of the information transmitted.

Presentation Manager   See OS/2 PM.

Private line   Dedicated line leased from a common carrier.

Procedural language   A programming language that creates procedures or sequences of code such as a routine, subroutine or function. Examples are Cobol, Fortran, Basic, C, and Pascal.

Procedure   In programming, refers to a subroutine or function.

Process bound   Having excessive processing requirements that limit performance, either in a personal computer or multiuser system.

Production database   An enterprise's database that is used to run the business. It usually has master files and daily transaction files. It generally contains data that is vital to the on-going operation of the enterprise.

Production system   A computer system that processes work that is vital to the operation of an enterprise.

Program-to-program communications   Protocol-based communications between two programs. May or may not have peer-to-peer capability.

Protocol   An agreement on how an exchange will take place. In communications, guidelines governing data transmission and reception.

Protocol stack (or suite)   The hierarchy of protocols used in a communications network. Examples of three different protocol stacks are: (1) Named Pipes, NetBIOS, NetBEUI, IEEE LLC, Token Ring; (2) RPC, XDR, Sockets, TCP/IP, Ethernet; and (3) APPC,LU6.2, PU2.1, SDLC.

Prototyping   Building a working model of a software application or computer system that will be tested and refined before a final system is developed. The prototyping process can help clarify system requirements.

PU   Physical Unit. In IBM's SNA, software that manages the resources of a node. A PU supports a connection to the host that is used for gathering network management statistics.

PU 2.1   Physical Unit 2.1. In IBM's SNA, software that provides peer-to-peer communications between intelligent physical devices. PU Type 2.1 nodes are supported by LU6.2 sessions.

Pull-down menu   A menu the user "pulls down" from the menu bar using a mouse.

Query   To request and/or extract data from a database.

Query language   A language that is easy to use and allows end users to select records from a database. Techniques used for expressing matching conditions can vary from a menu or query by example (QBE) format to a command language. Query languages are often included in DBMSs, but standalone packages are also available.

Raster display   Display terminal that generates dots line by line on the screen. Televisions and the majority of computer screens use the raster method.

Raster graphics   The representation of an image as a matrix of dots.

Reboot   To restart a computer. (See boot.)

Redirector   Software that routes workstation requests for data to the server.

Reduced Instruction Set Computer (RISC.)   An architecture that limits a microprocessor's instructions, thus reducing complexity. It is designed to process simple instructions very rapidly. For simple instructions, RISC machines are much faster than CISC machines, but much slower when processing complex instructions.

Remote communications   The interaction of computers over long distances via some type of communications line.

Remote Procedure Call   A form of task-to-task communication that allows one procedure to make a call to another procedure that resides, and will be executed, in a remote location.

Repeater   In communications, a device that extends the distance of the transmission by amplifying or regenerating the data signal. In long distance communications, it prevents signals from losing their strength.

Reusability   The ability to use all or part of the same programming code in another application.

Rich E-mail   Electronic mail that includes voice messages.

Ring network   Network topology that connects terminals and computers in a continuous, closed loop or ring.

Rollback   A DBMS procedure that returns that database to its previous state if a transaction is interrupted and fails to complete.

Router   A device in a communications network that selects the best route among multiple pathways for a message to reach its destination.

RPC   See Remote Procedure Call.

Run under   To run within the control of a higher-level program, such as an operating system. Some use the terms "run under" and "run on top of" synonymously.

Runtime   The execution time of a program.

Runtime version   The form that program code is in when it is ready to be executed.

Scalable   The ability to expand a system in size and/or configuration with minimal change.

SCO Open Desktop   Multiuser graphical operating system from The Santa Cruz Operation that runs on 386 and higher machines with UNIX, XENIX, DOS, and X Window applications.

Screen capture   An onscreen image transferred to a text or graphics file.

Scroll   Continuous forward, backward, or sideways movement through data or images on a display terminal screen.

Scroll bar   Horizontal or vertical bar that contains an arrow at each end, and rectangular box. To scroll the screen, the user clicks on one or the other arrow to move the image in the corresponding direction, or clicks on and drags the rectangular box in the desired direction to scroll the screen.

Seamless integration   The addition of software

or hardware that works well with a current system, with few or no modifications required.

Semaphores   Named after naval flags, program semaphores have the same intent: communication to avoid confusion and errors. A semaphore is an indicator or flag variable that helps maintain order among processes that are competing for resources. It is a signal used to indicate the availability of resources and prevent such things as one process writing to a memory location actively used by another process.

Serial transmission   Sending data one bit at a time over a single wire.

Server   (1) A computer in a local area network that controls access to other resources on the network. Multiple users share a server. (2) In a client/ server approach, the client makes requests of the server, and the server services those requests. Servers and clients may be either hardware or software or both.

Server application   A software program that runs in the server.

Server Message Block (SMB)   Microsoft's message format (protocol) for file sharing. It is used to transfer file requests between workstations and servers. It is also used within a server for internal operations.

Session   (1) In communications, the active connection between a user and a computer or between two computers. (2) Time between starting up and ending an application program.

Session layer   The fifth layer of the OSI Reference Model. It is concerned with establishing sessions between different machines. Dialogue control is one of the services it provides.

Shell   A software layer or add-on program that enables easy communication between the user and the operating system.

Simplex   One-way data transmission.

Single-system image   The perception of distributed databases, multiple networks, or multiple computer systems as if they were one system.

Single threading   Running one transaction from start to finish before starting another process.

Single-tasking A system designed to support only one task or program running at a time.

Smalltalk Object-oriented language and operating system developed at Xerox Corp.'s Palo Alto Research Center. It was one of the earliest object-oriented languages.

Smalltalk V Version of Smalltalk from Digitalk, Inc. for PCs. Versions exist for DOS, OS/2 Windows and the Mac.

Smart hub Same as intelligent hub.

Smart (or intelligent) terminal Video terminal with a CPU and some memory for basic processing. It has built-in display characteristics and may contain a communications protocol.

SMTP Simple Mail Transfer Protocol. The primary E-mail protocol used in TCP/IP networks.

SNA Systems Network Architecture. IBM's networking strategy for exchanging data between computers. The framework is divided into layers, with each passing control to the next highest layer.

SNADS SNA Distribution Services. IBM's electronic mail system for SNA networks.

SNMP Simple Network Management Protocol. The primary network management tool used in TCP/IP networks. It uses databases called Management Information Bases (MIBs) that define what data can be obtained from networked devices and what can be controlled. Data is passed between SNMP agents and the workstation used to oversee the network.

Sockets An abstraction used in UNIX to provide a file-like interface to networks (all UNIX devices have file-like interfaces that are quite similar to each other). For the most part, the semantics of sockets are the same as those of files, permitting the seamless integration of networks into the general UNIX environment. Socket descriptors are "handles". When an application creates a socket, it returns a handle which is used in all further socket-related commands. The handle is interchangeable with the file descriptor used in read and write commands.

Software Developers' Kit (SDK) See developers' toolkit.

Software IC (Software integrated circuit) Coined by The Stepstone Corp, the term refers to an object-oriented programming class packaged for sale.

Software interface Same as API.

Software tool Software program that a developer uses to create software.

SONET Synchronous Optical Network. International standard for broadband transmission through fiber optic cables. Operates in the 50Mbit to 13Gbit per second range.

SPARC Scalable Performance ARChitecture. A 32-bit reduced instruction set computer microprocessor developed by Sun Microsystems.

Specification (or spec) A description of the details of a hardware system, operating system, data records, programs, or procedures.

SQL Structured Query Language. A language used to interrogate, update, and manage data in a relational database. SQL commands can be entered interactively or embedded into a programming language. Derived from an IBM research program, it is now an accepted standard which is automatically included with many databases. Since there are now many different SQL implementations, standardization efforts are ongoing. (Pronounced "seequill" or S-Q-L.)

SQL Server A relational DBMS from Sybase, Inc., Emeryville, CA, that was designed for network use with UNIX. It can be accessed by applications using SQL or from Sybase's QBE and decision support utilities. Microsoft markets an OS/2 version, known as Microsoft SQL Server.

Stack See Protocol Stack.

Standards Guidelines for instituting uniformity among hardware and software products and development methods. Informal standards (de facto) are established through marketplace acceptance and proliferation of a product, such as DOS or Windows. Formal (de jure) standards are established through a formal qualification process most often spearheaded by an organization devoted to promoting standards in a specific technical area.

Static allocation Allocation of a resource such as memory for the duration of program execution.

For example, memory is allocated when the program begins and remains allocated as long as the program continues to run.

Store-and-forward In communications, the transient storage of a message between sender and receiver, before it is sent to its destination. Although store-and-forward routing can take longer than direct connections, it avoids network traffic jams and allows for routing over networks that may not be accessible at the time the message is sent.

Symmetric MultiProcessing (SMP) Multiprocessing in which any CPU can perform a variety of different tasks. In SMP systems, CPUs share memory. Generally, one CPU acts as a scheduler which distributes work to other CPUs.

Synchronous transmission Data transmission in which both stations are synchronized. Synchronization is established by transmitting codes from the sending station to the receiving station. Data is then transmitted in continuous streams.

SYSTEM.INI Windows startup file that contains data about the hardware environment in which it will execute.

Systems integration The interoperability of diverse components.

Systems integrator Individual or service/consulting organization that builds integrated systems from disparate components.

Terabit (Tb or Tbit) One trillion bits.

Terabyte (TB or Tbyte) One trillion bytes.

Terminal emulation A personal computer that simulates a mainframe or minicomputer terminal.

Terminate and stay resident (TSR) Refers to programs that remain in memory at all times (most often in DOS systems) so they can be activated with a single keystroke even if another program is in memory at the same time. TSRs can crash a DOS system by invading the memory space of another program since DOS does not operate in protected mode. TSRs should not be used when working with production systems or important data.

Third-generation language Traditional high-level programming language such as Cobol, Fortran, Basic, etc.

Thread A process that is part of a larger process or program. Sometimes "thread" is used to refer to one transaction or message in a multithreaded system.

Token passing Communications network access method that uses a token to determine when a device can start transmitting data. The token, which is a frame, moves continually from device to device. When a device receives the token, it can start transmitting.

Token ring network A network architecturally formed as a ring that uses the token passing technology.

Toolkit A set of predefined routines or programs that a programmer can use to facilitate development of a program or system. The routines can be called by an application program to perform specific functions.

TOP Technical Office Protocol. A subset of the OSI communications protocols for office systems. It was spearheaded by Boeing who often worked in conjunction with General Motors who was spearheading the Manufacturing Automation Protocol (MAP).

Transmission Control Protocol/Internet Protocol (TCP/IP) Protocols developed for the federal government's Advanced Research Projects Agency (ARPA), formerly DARPA, for communications between different computer systems on a network an different networks. It is becoming one of the most widely-used communications protocols.

Transport layer The fourth layer of the OSI Reference Model. It is concerned with providing data transfer between two machines at an agreed-upon level of quality. It is a true end-to-end layer.

Transparent process A process that exists, but does not appear so to the user.

Transport protocol Communications protocol responsible for establishing a connection and ensuring that all data arrives safely.

Transport services The combined functions of the four lower layers (1–4) of the OSI Reference Model.

Twisted pair A pair of insulated wires that are twisted around each other to minimize interference from other twisted wire pairs in the same cable. They are commonly used in telephone wiring, but can be used for data transmission as well. They have less bandwidth than coaxial cable or optical fiber.

Two-phase commit In a distributed database, a two-step method used to ensure that transactions update all appropriate files. After each affected DBMS confirms that the transaction has been received and is recoverable (stored on disk), the two-phase commit instructs each DBMS to commit the transaction. *All* DBMS must be able to commit or *none* will be permitted to do so.

T1 A 1.544 Mbps multichannel wide areas transmission system.

T2 The equivalent of four T1s.

T3 The equivalent of 28 T1s.

UNIX A multiuser, multitasking operating system originated at AT&T's Bell Labs, and extended by various vendors and organizations. It is considered an open system because it is portable to many platforms. However, there are differences among the various implementations of UNIX.

UNIX-to-UNIX Copy (UUCP) A set of communication and networking programs that are generally provided as part of UNIX systems.

Usenet A public network of linked UNIX and non-UNIX machines used to send information to companies, the government, research laboratories, schools, universities, and individuals.

User interface The way a user interacts with a computer. It can include such things as a command language, menus, screen design, keyboard commands, command language, and help screens.

Value Added Network (VAN) A data communications network that adds features to the basic transmission services provided by a local telephone company.

Vector graphics The representation of a picture as points, lines, and other geometric entities.

Vendor Independent Messaging (VIM) An application program interface for cross-platform, mail-enabled applications. Initiated by Lotus, other vendors such as Apple, Borland, IBM, MCI, Novell, Oracle, and WordPerfect were also part of its origin. Microsoft's competitive offering is MAPI.

Video Graphics Array (VGA) IBM video display standard that provides medium resolution text and graphics. It is now considered as the minimum standard for PCs.

Virtual memory Technique that extends the size of a computer's memory beyond what actually exists by using part of the hard disk. It allows the computer to run several programs concurrently regardless of size.

Virtual Networking System (VINES) A network operating system from Banyan Systems, Inc., based on the UNIX System V operating system.

Virtual Telecommunications Access Method (VTAM) A set of IBM programs responsible for controlling communication between terminals and application programs running under various IBM operating systems.

What-You-See-Is-What-You-Get (WYSIWIG) Refers to software that shows text and graphics on the screen in the same manner that they will print. The screen and print version are not 100% identical since screen and printer resolutions rarely match.

Wide area network (WAN) A data communications network that covers large geographic areas, such as across states or countries.

WIN.INI WINdows INItialization. File accessed by Microsoft Windows when it is first activated. The file contains data about individual applications. While it contains information about the current environment such as desktop, fonts, sounds, etc., data about the hardware is provided by SYSTEM.INI, another Windows startup file.

Win32 Programming specification (API) for Windows' 32-bit mode.

Window   A rectangular area on screen that contains a document or message. A screen may contain multiple windows.

Windows   Microsoft Corp.'s graphics-based, multitasking operating environment for the desktop, with similarities to the Apple Macintosh. Applications are displayed in a resizable, movable window. Windows integrates with DOS, so Windows users can also launch and run DOS applications.

Windows environment   An operating system (or extension) or application that provides multiple onscreen windows.

Windows NT   Windows New Technology, from Microsoft Corp. (See New Technology.)

WinWord   Abbreviation for Microsoft Word for Windows.

Workflow automation   The automatic routing of data and documents over a network to the appropriate users.

Workgroup   Usually a LAN-based group of users, such as the users in a department, who share files and databases.

Workstation   A desktop computer that is generally faster than personal computers and better equipped for high-requirement graphics programs. Workstations (which are usually more expensive than PCs) are frequently found on the desks of engineers, scientists, and manufacturing designers.

XAPIA   The X.400 API Association which is concerned with developing APIs for the X.400 standard.

X/Open   A user and vendor consortium that selects standards to constitute its Common Application Environment. It uses international de jure standards where practical but also includes de facto industry standards. A primary activity of X/Open is to gather requirements from users and then provide these requirements to vendors.

X/Open Portability Guide (XPG)   Standards that specify compliance with X/Open's Common Application Environment.

X Protocol   The X Window system's message format.

X Terminal   A terminal with a built-in X Window Server (X Window display software).

XT   Extended Technology. IBM's first PC with a hard disk, based on Intel's 8088 processor.

XVT   eXtensible Virtual Toolkit. Developers kit for creating user interfaces across XVT Software's multiple operating environments.

X Window   Windowing environment developed by MIT, with help from IBM and Digital for graphics workstations. It allows graphics generated in one computer system to be displayed on another workstation.

X.12   An ANSI standard protocol for Electronic Data Interchange that is widely used in the U.S.

X.25   CCITT standard that defines an interface between a terminal and a packet switching network.

X.400 CCITT   Standard for electronic mail. Complies with OSI.

X.400 API Association   See XAPIA.

X.500 CCITT   Directory standard for electronic mail. It provides naming facilities for networks and improvement of addressing in large, distributed networks.

BIBLIOGRAPHY

Ambron, S., Hooper, K. (editors), *Interactive Multimedia, Visions of Multimedia for Developers, Educators, and Information Providers*, Redmond, Wash., Microsoft Press, 1988.

Arnold, N.D., *UNIX Security, A Practical Tutorial*, New York, N.Y., McGraw-Hill, Inc., 1993.

Atre, S., *Distributed Databases, Cooperative Processing, & Networking*, New York, N.Y., McGraw-Hill, 1992.

Baker, R.H., *EDI, What Managers Need to Know about the Revolution in Business Communications*, Blue Ridge Summit, Penn., TAB Professional and Reference Books, 1991.

Berson, A., *Client/Server Architecture*, New York, McGraw-Hill, Inc., 1992.

Bielawski, L., Lewand, R., *Intelligent Systems Design, Integrating, Expert Systems, Hypermedia, and Database Technologies*, New York, N.Y., John Wiley & Sons, Inc., 1991.

Black, U.D., *Data Communications and Distributed Networks, Second Edition*, Englewood Cliffs, N.J. Yourdon Press, Prentice-Hall, 1987.

Boar, B.H., *Implementing Client/Server Computing, A Strategic Approach*, New York, N.Y., McGraw-Hill, 1993.

Bucken, Mike, "PowerSoft Gearing Up Development to Defend Early Lead" in *Client/ Server Computing*, a supplement to *Software Magazine*, May, 1993, Vol. 13, No. 8, pp. 23–26.

Budd, T., *A Little Smalltalk*, Reading, Mass., Addison-Wesley Publishing Co., 1987.

Chaiken, C., *Blueprint of a LAN*, Redwood City, Calif., M&T Publishing, Inc., 1989.

Chorafas, D.N., *Handbook of Database Management and Distributed Relational Databases*, Blue Ridge Summit, Penn., TAB Professional and Reference Books, 1989.

Chorafas, D.N., Steinmann, H., *Intelligent Networks, Telecommunications Solutions for the 1990s*, Boca Raton, Fla., CRC Press, Inc. 1990.

Chorafas, D.N., *Systems Architecture & Systems Design*, New York, N.Y., McGraw-Hill, 1989.

Claybrook, B., *OLTP, Online Transaction Processing Systems*, New York, N.Y., John Wiley & Sons, Inc., 1992.

Cobb, Stephen, *The Stephen Cobb Complete Book of PC and LAN Security*, Blue Ridge Summit, Penn., Windcrest Books, (TAB Division of McGraw-Hill, Inc.), 1992.

Cole, G.D., *Implementing OSI Networks*, New York, N.Y., John Wiley & Sons, Inc., 1990.

Conklin, D., OS/2, *A Business Perspective*, New York, N.Y., John Wiley & Sons, Inc., 1988.

Coulouris, G. F., Dollimore, J., *Distributed Systems, Concepts and Designs*, Workingham, England, Addison-Wesley Publishing Company, 1988.

Currie, S.W., *LANs Explained, A Guide to Local Area Networks*, Chichester, England, Ellis Horwood Limited (Distributed by John Wiley & Sons).

Cypser, R.J., *Communications for Cooperating Systems, OSI, SNA, and TCP/IP*, Reading, Mass., Addison-Wesley Publishing Company, 1992.

Date, C.J., White, C.J., *A Guide to DB2, Third Edition*, Reading, Mass., Addison-Wesley Publishing Company, 1989.

Date, C.J., *An Introduction to Database Systems, Volume I, Fourth Edition*, Reading, Mass., Addison-Wesley Publishing Company, 1987.

Date, C.J., *An Introduction to Database Systems, Volume II*, Reading, Mass., Addison-Wesley Publishing Company, 1985.

Denning, D., *Cryptography and Data Security*, Reading, Mass., Addison-Wesley Publishing Company, 1983.

Derfler, F. J., *PC Magazine Guide to Linking LANs*, Emeryville, Calif., Ziff-Davis Press, 1992.

Desmond, John., "Building Around Unknowns of Client/Server", *Software Magazine*, March, 1992, Vol. 12, No. 3, pp. 68–69.

Desmond, J., Gold, J., "Financial Client/Server Applications Empowering Non-Technies" in *Client/Server Computing*, March, 1993, Vol.13, No. 5, pp. 51–52.

Desmond, John., "Firm Opted for More Risky–But 'True'—Solution", *Software Magazine*, August, 1991, Vol. 11, no. 10.

Desmond, John., "Moses Leads the Washy to Open Requirements," *Software Magazine*, March, 1993, Vol. 13, No. 4, pp. 67–78.

Dewire, D.T., *Client/Server Computing (James Martin McGraw-Hill Productivity Series)*, New York, N.Y., McGraw-Hill, Inc., 1993.

Doll, D.R., *Data Communications, Facilities, Networks, and System Design*, New York, N.Y., John Wiley & Sons, Inc., 1978.

Dvorak, J.C., Anis, N., *Dvorak's Guide to DOS and PC Performance*, Berkely, Calif., Osborne McGraw-Hill, 1991.

Elmagarmid, A.K. (Editor), *Database Transaction Models for Advanced Applications*, San Mateo, Calif., Morgan Kaufmann Publishers, 1991.

Firesmith, D.G., *Object-Oriented Requirements Analysis and Logical Design, A Software Engineering Approach*, New York, N.Y., John Wiley & Sons, Inc., 1993.

Fortier, P.J., *Handbook of Local Area Network Software, Concepts and Technology*, Boca Raton, Fla., CRC Press, (Multiscience Press, Inc.), 1991.

Freedman, A., *The Computer Glossary, the Complete Illustrated Desk Reference, Sixth Edition*, New York, N. Y., AMACON, American Management Association, 1993.

Frye, Colleen, "General Mills Stays Fit With EDI Diet" in *Software Magazine*, June, 1993, Vol. 13, No. 9, pp. 95–101.

Glines, S.C., *Enterprise Series: Downsizing to UNIX*, Carmel, Ind., New Riders Publishing, 1992.

Gookin, D., Rathbone, A., *PCs for Dummies*, San Mateo, Calif., IDG Books, 1992.

Green, J.H., *Local Area Networks, A User's Guide for Business Professionals*, Glenview, Ill., Scott, Foresman and Company, 1985.

Gray, J., Reuter, A., *Transaction Processing: Concepts and Techniques*, San Mateo, Calif., Morgan Kaufmann Publishers, 1993.

Greif, I. (Editor), *Computer-Supported Cooperative Work: A Book of Readings*, San Mateo, Calif., Henry Kaufman Publishers, Inc., 1988.

Groff, J.R., Weinberg, P.N., *Understanding*

UNIX, A Conceptual Guide, 2nd Edition, Carmel, Ind., Que Corporation, 1988.

Grochow, J.M., *A Guide to Implementing IBM's System Application Architecture*, Englewood Cliffs, N.J. Yourdon Press, Prentice-Hall, 1991.

Guengerich, S., *Downsizing Information Systems*, Carmel, Ind., Sams Publishing (A Division of Prentice-Hall Computer Publishing), 1992.

Gupta, R., Horowitz, E. (editors), *Object-Oriented Databases with Applications to CASE, Networks, and VLSI CAD*, Englewood Cliffs, N.J., Prentice-Hall, 1991.

Hackathorn, R. D., *Enterprise Database Connectivity*, John Wiley & Sons, New York, N.Y., 1993.

Halsall, F., *Data Communications, Computer Networks, and OSI*, Reading, Mass., Addison-Wesley Publishing Company, 1988.

Henle, R.A., Kuvshinoff, B.W., *Desktop Computers*, New York, N.Y., Oxford University Press, 1992.

Henshall, J., Shaw, S., *OSI Explained, End-to-End Computer Communication Standards*, West Sussex, England, Ellis Horwood Limited, 1988 (Distributed by John Wiley & Sons, Inc.).

Hutchison, D., *Local Area Network Architectures*, Workingham, England and Reading, Mass., Addison-Wesley Publishing Company, 1988.

Hyman, M., *Microsoft Windows Program Development*, Portland, Ore., Management Information Source, Inc., 1988.

IBM, *Common Programming Interface Communications Reference*, SC26–4399–04, White Plains, N.Y., 1991.

IBM, *Dictionary of Computing, Information Processing, Personal Computing, Telecommunications, Office Systems, IBM-Specific Terms*, White Plains, N.Y., 1987.

Inmon, W.H., *Integrating Data Processing Systems in Theory and Practice*, Englewood Cliffs, N.J., Prentice-Hall, 1984.

Jones, V.C., *MAP/TOP Networking, Achieving Computer-Integrated Manufacturing*, New York, McGraw-Hill Book Company, 1988.

Jordan, L., Churchill, B., *Communications and Networking for the IBM PC and Compatibles, Third Edition*, New York, N.Y., Brady (Simon & Shuster), 1990.

Jordan, L., *System Integration for the IBM PS/2 and PC*, New York, N.Y., Brady (Simon & Shuster), 1990.

Kahn, D., *The Codebreakers*, New York, N.Y., Macmillan Company, 1972.

Kehoe, B.P., *Zen and the Art of the Internet: A Beginner's Guide*, Prentice-Hall, 1993.

Khoshafian, S., Chan, A., Wong, A., Wong, H.K.T., *A Guide to Developing Client/Server SQL Applications*, San Mateo, Calif., Morgan Kaufmann Publishers, Inc., 1991.

Khoshafian, S., Abnous, R., *Object Orientation, Concepts, Languages, Databases, User Interfaces*, New York, N.Y., John Wiley & Sons, Inc., 1990.

Killen, M., *SAA and UNIX, IBM's Open Systems Strategy*, New York, N.Y., McGraw-Hill, 1992.

Kobara, S., *Visual Design with OSF/Motif*, Reading, Mass., Addison-Wesley Publishing Company, Inc., 1991.

Kochan, S.G., Wood, P. (Consulting editors), *UNIX Networking*, Carmel, Ind., Hayden Books, 1989.

Korzeniowski, Paul, "No Consensus on Dividing Client, Server" in *Software Magazine*, June, 1993, Vol. 13, No. 9, pp. 87–91.

Kraynak, J., *Plain English Computer Dictionary*, Carmel, Ind., Alpha Books, 1992.

Krol, E., *The Whole Internet User's Guide and Catalog*, O'Reilly & Associates, Inc., 1992.

LaQuey, T., *The Internet Companion: A Beginners' Guide to Global Networking*, Reading, Mass., Addison-Wesley, 1993.

Letwin, G., *Inside OS/2*, Redmond, Washington, Microsoft Press, 1988.

Libes, D., Ressler, S., *Life With UNIX, A Guide for Everyone*, Englewood Cliffs, N.J., Prentice-Hall, 1989.

Lorie, R.A., Daudenarde, J.J., *SQL & Its Applications*, Englewood Cliffs, N.J., Prentice-Hall, 1991.

Madron, T. W., *Enterprise-Wide Computing: How to Implement and Manage LANs*, John Wiley & Sons, Inc., 1991.

Madron, T.W., *Local Area Networks, The Next Generation, 2nd Edition*, New York, N.Y., John Wiley & Sons, Inc., 1990

Manes, S., *The Complete MCI Mail Handbook*, New York, N.Y., Bantam Books, 1988.

Martin, J., *Telecommunications and the Computer*, Englewood Cliffs, N.J., Prentice-Hall, 1990.

Martin, J., Kavanagh-Chapman, K., Leben, J., *DB2 Concepts, Design, and Programming*, Englewood Cliffs, N.J., Prentice-Hall, 1989.

Martin, J., Kavanagh-Chapman, The Arben Group, *Local Area Networks, Architectures and Implementations*, Englewood Cliffs, N.J., Prentice-Hall, 1989.

Martin, J., Kavanagh-Chapman, The Arben Group, *SNA: IBM's Networking Solution*, Englewood Cliffs, N.J., Prentice-Hall, 1987.

Martin, J., Kavanagh-Chapman, K., Leben, J., *Systems Application Architecture, Common User Access*, Englewood Cliffs, N.J., Prentice-Hall, 1989.

McConnell, J. *Internetworking Computer Systems, Interconnecting Networks and Systems*, Englewood Cliffs, N.J., Prentice-Hall, 1988.

McGlynn, D.R., *Distributed Processing and Data Communications*, New York, N.Y., John Wiley & Sons, Inc., 1978.

McGovern, T., *Data Communications, Concepts and Applications*, Scarborough, Ontario, Prentice-Hall Canada Inc., 1988.

Microsoft, *Microsoft Press Computer Dictionary, The Comprehensive Standard for Business, School, Library, and Home*, Redmond, Wash., Microsoft Press, 1991.

Microsoft, *Microsoft Windows Guide to Programming, New for Version 3*, Redmond, Wash., Microsoft Press, 1990.

Microsoft, *Microsoft Windows Programmer's Reference, New for Version 3*, Redmond, Wash., Microsoft Press, 1990.

Nance, B., *Introduction to Networking*, Carmel, Ind., Que Corporation, 1992.

Nunemacher, G., *LAN Primer, An Introduction to Local Area Networks*, San Mateo, Calif., M&T Publishing, Inc., 1990.

Nutt, G.J., *Open Systems*, Englewood Cliffs, N.J., Prentice-Hall, 1992.

Odell, P., *The Computer Networking Book*, Chapel Hill, N.C., Ventana Press, 1989.

Orfali, R., Harkey, D., *Client-Server Programming with OS/2 Extended Edition*, New York, N.Y., Van Nostrand Reinhold, 1991.

Ozsu, M.T., Valduriez, P., *Principles of Distributed Database Systems*, Englewood Cliffs, N.J., Prentice-Hall, 1991.

Padlipsky, M.A., *The Elements of Networking Style, and Other Essays and Animadversions on the Art of Intercomputer Networking*, Englewood Cliffs, N.J., Prentice-Hall, 1985.

Parsaye, K., Chignell, M., Khoshafian, S., Wong, H., *Intelligent Databases, Object-Oriented, Deductive, and Hypermedia Approaches*, New York, John Wiley & Sons, 1989.

Petzold, C., *Programming the OS/2 Presentation Manager*, Redmond, Wash., Microsoft Press, 1989.

Pfaffenberger, B., *Que's Computer User's Dictionary*, Third Edition, Carmel, Ind., Que Corporation, 1992.

Raymond, E. (editor) Steele, G.L., Jr.(cartoonist), *The New Hacker's Dictionary*, Cambridge, Mass., The MIT Press, 1992.

Reichard, K., Johnson, E., *Teach Yourself... UNIX, Second Edition*, New York, N.Y., Henry Holt and Company, Inc., 1992.

Reinhardt, Andy, T. Halfhill, J. Udell, *Smarter E-Mail is Coming*, Byte Magazine, March 1993, pp. 90–108.

Renaud, P. E., *Introduction to Client/Server Systems*, John Wiley & Sons, New York, N.Y., 1993.

Rieken, W., Weiman, L., *Adventures in UNIX Applications Programming*, New York, John Wiley & Sons, Inc., 1992.

Rinaldi, Damian, "Foxboro Co. Transforms Standards Vision to Reality", Software Magazine's *Client/Server Computing*, January, 1993, vol. 13., no. 2, pp. 55–57.

Rinaldi, Damian, "Mining Business Nuggets", Software Magazine's *Client/Server Computing*, November, 1992, vol. 12., no. 16, pp. 14–24.

Rinaldi, Damian, "Motorola's Massive Internet Poses New Type of Security Challenge", Software Magazine's C*lient Server Computing*, May 1992, vol. 12, no. 7, pp. 32–33.

Rose, M., *The Open Book, A Practical Perspective on OSI*, Englewood Cliffs, N.J., Prentice-Hall, 1990.

Rumbaugh, J., Blaha, M., Premerlani, W., Eddy, F. Lorensen, W., *Object-Oriented Modeling and Design*, Englewood Cliffs, N.J., Prentice-Hall, 1991.

Russell, D., and Gangemi Sr., G.T., *Computer Security Basics*, Sebastopol. Calif., O'Reilly & Associates, Inc., 1991.

Ryan, Bob, "RISC Drives PowerPC" in *Byte Magazine*, August 1993, Vol. 18, No. 9, pp. 79–90.

Salemi, J., *PC Magazine Guide to Client/Server Databases*, Emeryville, Calif., Ziff-Davis Press, 1993.

Schnaidt, Patricia, *Enterprise-Wide Networking*, Carmel, Ind., Sams Publishing (A Division of Prentice-Hall Computer Publishing), 1992.

Seymour, J., *Jim Seymour's PC Productivity Bible*, New York, N.Y., Brady Publishing, 1991.

Shlaer, S., Mellor, S.J., *Object Lifecycles, Modeling the World in States*, Englewood Cliffs, N.J., Yourdon Press, Prentice-Hall, 1992.

Sloane, J.P., Drinan, A., (editors), *Handbook of Local Area Networks*, Boston, Mass., Auerbach Publications, 1991.

Sloane, J.P., Drinan, A, (editors), *Handbook of Local Area Networks, 1992-93 Yearbook*, Boston, Mass., Auerbach Publications, 1992.

Smith, J.D., *Designing X Clients with Xt/Motif*, San Mateo, Calif., Morgan Kaufmann Publishers, 1992.

Smith, J.D., *Reusability & Software Construction: C and C++*, New York, N.Y., John Wiley & Sons, Inc., 1990.

Smith, P., *Client/Server Computing*, Carmel, In., Sams Publishing (A Division of Prentice-Hall Computer Publishing), 1992.

Sochats, K., Williams, J., *The Networking and Communications Desk Reference*, Carmel, Ind., Sams, 1992.

Stamper, D.A., Bus*iness Data Communications, Second Edition*, Redwood City, Calif., The Benjamin/Commings Publishing Company, Inc., 1989.

Stoll, C., *The Cuckoo's Egg: Tracing a Spy Through the Maze of Computer Espionage*, New York, N. Y., Doubleday, 1989.

Stoll, C., "Stalking the Wily Hacker," in *Communications of the ACM*, Vol. 31, No., May 1988.

Tanenbaum, A. S., *Computer Networks, Second Edition*, Englewood Cliffs, N.J., Prentice-Hall, 1988.

Tare, R. S., D*ata Processing in the UNIX Environment, with Informix-SQL, Embedded-SQL, C-ISAM, and Turbo*, New York, N. Y., McGraw-Hill, 1989.

Tello, E.R., *Object-Oriented Programming for*

Windows, New York, N.Y., John Wiley & Sons, Inc., 1991.

Tennant, R., et al, *Crossing the Internet Threshold: An Instructional Handbook*, Library Solutions Institute and Press, 1992.

Thyfault, M. E., Stahl, S., Panettieri, J. C., "Breaking Down the Washlls", *Information Week*, April 19, 1993, pp. 22–25.

Topham, D., *The First Book of UNIX*, Carmel, Ind., Howard W. Sams & Company, 1990.

Waite, M., Prata, S., Martin, D., C *Primer Plus, User-Friendly Guide to the C Programming Language, Revised Edition*, Indianapolis, Ind., Howard W. Sams & Company, 1987.

Waite, M., Prata, S., Martin, D., *The Waite Group's UNIX Primer Plus, Second Edition*, Carmel, Ind., Sams (A Division of Prentice-Hall, 1990), 1992.

Webster's New World, *Dictionary of Computer Terms*, New York, N.Y., Prentice-Hall, 1988.

Weiskamp, K., Aguiar, S., *Windows 3.0, A Self-Teaching Guide*, New York, N.Y., John Wiley & Sons, Inc., 1991.

Wilton, R., *Microsoft Windows 3 Developer's Workshop*, Redmond, Wash., Microsoft Press, 1991.

Yager, T., Smith, B., "Is UNIX Dead," *Byte Magazine*, Vol. 17, No. 9, September, 1992, pp. 134–146.

INDEX

Page numbers followed by "f" indicate figures; page numbers followed by "t" indicate tables. Terms in main headings are spelled out and followed by acronyms in parentheses; acronyms are listed alphabetically and defined on pp. 387–393.